Stalin: A New History

The figure of Joseph Stalin has always provoked heated and often polarised debate. The recent declassification of a substantial portion of Stalin's archive has made possible this fundamental new assessment of the Soviet leader. In this groundbreaking study, leading international experts challege many assumptions about Stalin from his early life in Georgia to the Cold War years with contributions ranging across the political, economic, social, cultural, ideological, and international history of the Stalin era. The volume provides a deeper understanding of the nature of Stalin's power and of the role of ideas in his politics, presenting a more complex and nuanced image of one of the most important leaders of the twentieth century. This study is without precedent in the field of Russian history and will prove invaluable reading for students of Stalin and Stalinism.

SARAH DAVIES is Senior Lecturer in History at the University of Durham. She is the author of *Popular Opinion in Stalin's Russia: Terror, Propaganda, and Dissent 1934–1941* (1997).

JAMES HARRIS is Senior Lecturer in History at the University of Leeds. He is the author of *The Great Urals: Regionalism and the Evolution of the Soviet System* (1999).

Stalin

A New History

Edited by

Sarah Davies and James Harris

CAMBRIDGE
UNIVERSITY PRESS

CAMBRIDGE UNIVERSITY PRESS
Cambridge, New York, Melbourne, Madrid, Cape Town, Singapore, São Paulo

CAMBRIDGE UNIVERSITY PRESS
The Edinburgh Building, Cambridge CB2 2RU, UK

Published in the United States of America by Cambridge University Press, New York

http://www.cambridge.org
Information on this title: http://www.cambridge.org/9780521616539

First published 2005
Reprinted 2006

Printed in the United Kingdom at the University Press, Cambridge

A catalogue record for this book is available from the British Library

ISBN-13 978-0-521-85104-6 hardback
ISBN-10 0-521-85104-1 hardback
ISBN-13 978-0-521-61653-9 paperback
ISBN-10 0-521-61653-0 paperback

Contents

Notes on contributors

DAVID BRANDENBERGER is Assistant Professor in the Department of History at the University of Richmond, Virginia. He is the author of *National Bolshevism: Stalinist Mass Culture and the Formation of Modern Russian National Identity, 1931–1956* (Cambridge, Mass.: Harvard University Press, 2002) and numerous articles on the culture and politics of the Stalin period.

WILLIAM CHASE is Professor in the History department at the University of Pittsburgh. His most recent book is *Enemies within the Gates? The Comintern and the Stalinist Repression, 1934–39* (New Haven: Yale University Press, 2001).

R. W. DAVIES is Professor (Emeritus) at the Centre for Russian and East European Studies, University of Birmingham. He has written extensively on Soviet history. His most recent book (written with Dr Stephen Wheatcroft) was the fifth volume of his history of Soviet industrialisation: *The Years of Hunger: Soviet Agriculture, 1931–1933* (Basingstoke: Palgrave Macmillan, 2004).

SARAH DAVIES is Senior Lecturer in the Department of History at the University of Durham and the author of *Popular Opinion in Stalin's Russia: Terror, Propaganda, and Dissent* (Cambridge: Cambridge University Press, 1997).

J. ARCH GETTY is Professor of History in the Department of History at UCLA. He is the author of numerous books and articles on Stalinist terror and the politics of the Stalin era, including (with V. Naumov) *The Road to Terror: Stalin and the Self-Destruction of the Bolsheviks, 1932–1939* (New Haven: Yale University Press, 1999). He is currently completing a biography of Nikolai Ezhov.

JAMES HARRIS is Senior Lecturer in the School of History at the University of Leeds. He is the author of *The Great Urals: Regionalism and the Evolution of the Soviet System* (Ithaca: Cornell University Press, 1999).

OLEG KHLEVNIUK is Senior Researcher at the State Archive of the Russian Federation, Moscow. His most recent book is *The History of the Gulag: From Collectivization to the Great Terror* (New Haven: Yale University Press, 2004).

ETHAN POLLOCK is Assistant Professor of History at the Maxwell School of Syracuse University. He is currently completing a monograph under the title *Stalin and the Soviet Science Wars*.

DAVID PRIESTLAND is Lecturer in Modern History at the University of Oxford and Fellow of St Edmund Hall. He is the author of *Stalin and the Politics of Mobilization: Ideas, Power, and Terror in Inter-war Russia* (Oxford: Oxford University Press, 2005).

ERIK VAN REE is Lecturer at the Institute for East European Studies of the University of Amsterdam. His most recent book is *The Political Thought of Joseph Stalin: A Study in Twentieth-Century Revolutionary Patriotism* (London: RoutledgeCurzon, 2002).

ALFRED RIEBER is Professor of History at the Central European University in Budapest and also Professor (Emeritus) at the University of Pennsylvania. His many publications include *Stalin and the French Communist Party, 1941–1947* (New York: Columbia University Press, 1962) and *Merchants and Entrepreneurs in Imperial Russia* (Chapel Hill: University of North Carolina Press, 1981).

JEREMY SMITH is Lecturer in Twentieth-Century Russian History at the Centre for Russian and East European Studies, University of Birmingham. He is the author of *The Bolsheviks and the National Question, 1917–1923* (Basingstoke: Macmillan, 1999).

Preface

Most of the chapters in this volume were presented to the twenty-ninth annual conference of the Study Group on the Russian Revolution held at Hatfield College, University of Durham, in January 2003. We are grateful that on the fiftieth anniversary of Stalin's death, the Study Group was willing to stretch its definition of the Revolution as far as 1953. The high standard of the papers and of the discussion among the participants made it a memorable event. While it has not been possible to publish all the papers presented to the conference, all of the participants contributed to the success of the event, and the quality of this volume. Neither the conference nor this book would have been possible without the generous financial support of the British Academy and the British Association of Slavonic and East European Studies. We are particularly grateful to those who have contributed chapters to the collection for their patience and rapid replies to our queries. Finally, we thank Michael Watson of Cambridge University Press for his unflagging interest in this project.

JAMES HARRIS
SARAH DAVIES

A note on transliteration

The Library of Congress system has been adopted except in the case of certain words which are commonly transliterated otherwise (Trotsky, Gorky, for example). Chapter 12 uses the transliteration system of the published trial transcripts on which it is based.

Glossary

Agitprop Department of Agitation and Propaganda
Artel' form of collective farm in which peasants retain some livestock and a plot
ASSR Autonomous Soviet Socialist Republic
Central Committee decision-making body of the Party
Central Control Commission department of Central Committee which investigated complaints
Cominform Communist Information Bureau
Comintern Communist International
Commissar Head of Commissariat
Commissariat equivalent of ministry (till 1946)
Council of Ministers, Sovmin formal government of USSR (from 1946)
Council of People's Commissars, Sovnarkom formal government of USSR (till 1946)
Dzhugashvili Stalin's surname
ECCI Executive Committee of Comintern
GKO Committee for State Defence
Glavrepertkom Main Directorate for the Oversight of Spectacles and Repertoire
Gorkom city Party committee
Gosplan State Planning Commission
Great Reforms reforms initiated by Alexander II
Great Retreat term used by N. Timasheff to describe turn towards conservative policies in 1930s
Great Terror period of mass arrests and executions, 1936–8
Guberniia province
GUKF/GUK Main Directorate of the Cinematic and Photographic Industry/Main Directorate of Cinematography
IMEL Marx-Engels-Lenin Institute
Kinogorod 'Cinema-city'; Soviet Hollywood
Kolkhoz collective farm

Komsomol Communist Youth League
Komzag Agricultural Collections Committee
Korenizatsiia indigenisation; a policy of promoting elites from within ethnic groups
KPG German Communist Party
KPK Party Control Commission, department of Central Committee responsible for checking the fulfilment of decisions
Kresy Poland's pre-war eastern provinces
Kul'tprop Department of Culture and Propaganda
KVZhD Chinese Far Eastern Railway
Leningrad Affair purges of Leningrad Party organisation in 1949
mesame-dasi Georgian Marxist Organisation
MVD Ministry of Internal Affairs
Narkomnats Peoples' Commissariat of Nationality Affairs
Narkompros Peoples' Commissariat of Enlightenment
Narkomzem Peoples' Commissariat of Agriculture
Narod, narody people, peoples
Narodnosti nationalities
Natsiia nation
Neo-NEP refers to policies introduced with overtones of NEP in 1932
NEP New Economic Policy, period of limited free market (1921–8)
Nomenklatura lists of leading posts, refers to Soviet political elite
NKVD Peoples' Commissariat of Internal Affairs
Oblast' province
OGIZ Unified State Publishing House
OGPU Unified State Political Administration – state security police
Okrug district
Opros/Oprosom poll/by a poll
Orgburo Organisation Bureau of the Central Committee of the Party
ORPO Department of the Leading Party Organs of Central Committee
Peoples' Will a terrorist, revolutionary organisation of populists
Politburo Political Bureau of the Central Committee
Politotdel Political department
POUM Workers' Party of Marxist Unification
Rabkrin Workers' and Peasants' Inspectorate
Raion district
RKP(b) Russian Communist Party (bolsheviks)
RSDWP Russian Social Democratic Workers' Party
RSFSR Russian Soviet Federal Socialist Republic
Samizdat 'self-published' (underground) literature
Secretariat of the Central Committee of the Party

Short Course *History of the All-Union Communist Party (Bolsheviks): Short Course*

Soiuzkino All-Union Amalgamation of the Cinematic and Photographic Industry

Soso a pet name for Stalin used by some of his close friends

Sovkhoz state farm

Sovmin see Council of Ministers

Sovnarkom see Council of People's Commissars

Stakhanovite a member of the movement in the 1930s, following the example of miner Aleksei Stakhanov, intended to increase production

Stanitsa village

STO Council of Labour and Defence

Supreme Soviet highest legislative body in the USSR (from 1937)

Vedomstva departments/institutions

Vedomstvennost' departmentalism

VKP(b) All-Union Communist Party (bolsheviks)

Vospitanie education

Vozhd' leader

VSNKh Supreme Economic Council

VTsIK All-Union Central Executive Committee, till 1937 highest legislative body in the USSR

1 Joseph Stalin: power and ideas

Sarah Davies and James Harris

Stalin, like the other 'evil dictators' of the twentieth century, remains the subject of enduring public fascination.[1] Academic attention, however, has shifted away from the study of 'Great Men', including Stalin, towards the little men and women, such as the now celebrated Stepan Podlubnyi, and towards Stalinist political culture more generally.[2] Ironically this is at a time when we have unprecedented access to hitherto classified material on Stalin, the individual.[3] The object of this volume is to reinvigorate scholarly interest in Stalin, his ideas, and the nature of his power. Although Stalin certainly did not single-handedly determine everything about the set of policies, practices, and ideas we have come to call Stalinism, it is now indisputable that in many respects his influence was decisive. A clearer understanding of his significance will allow more precise analysis of the origins and nature of Stalinism itself.

[1] Note the interest in several recent publications aimed primarily at a popular readership: Martin Amis, *Koba the Dread: Laughter and the Twenty Million* (London: Jonathan Cape, 2002); Simon Sebag Montefiore, *Stalin: The Court of the Red Tsar* (London: Weidenfeld and Nicolson, 2003); Donald Rayfield, *Stalin and his Hangmen* (London: Viking, 2004).

[2] Podlubnyi has been made famous by Jochen Hellbeck in a number of publications, including 'Fashioning the Stalinist Soul: The Diary of Stepan Podlubnyi, 1931–1939', *Jahrbucher für Geschichte Osteuropas* 44 (1996), 344–73. On the 'cultural turn' in Soviet history, see the introduction by Sheila Fitzpatrick in *Stalinism: New Directions* (London: Routledge, 2000).

[3] Much of this is in the 'Stalin *fond*' in the Russian State Archive of Socio-Political History (Rossiiskii gosudarstvennyi arkhiv sotsial'no-politicheskoi istorii, henceforth RGASPI fond 558, opis' 11), which includes correspondence received from and sent to everyone from the members of his inner circle to peasants and foreign journalists; documents relating to Stalin's activities in the organisations in which he worked; speeches, articles, biographical materials, and so on. Some documents from this collection have been published, including the two important volumes: Lars Lih, Oleg V. Naumov, and Oleg V. Khlevniuk (eds.), *Stalin's Letters to Molotov, 1925–1936* (New Haven: Yale University Press, 1995); R. W. Davies, O. Khlevniuk, E. A. Rees L. Kosheleva, and L. Rogovaia (eds.), *The Stalin–Kaganovich Correspondence, 1931–1936* (New Haven: Yale University Press, 2003).

The contributors to the volume do not subscribe to any single 'model'. Instead, they share a common agenda: to examine the new archival materials, as well as the old, with the aim of rethinking some of the stereotypes and assumptions about Stalin that have accumulated in the historiography. The vast literature on Stalin is of varying quality, including journalistic speculations, sensationalist potboilers, and political diatribes, as well as the important studies by Isaac Deutscher, Robert Tucker, and others.[4] Much of the work to date has been affected by both limited access to primary sources and the unusually intense politicisation of the field of Soviet studies.

The Soviet regime was obsessed with secrecy. Historians had to rely on a narrow group of useful sources, including published resolutions and decisions, stenographic reports of some major Party meetings, and published speeches of prominent officials. While these sorts of sources could be quite useful, they tended to reveal more about what was happening in the lower echelons of power. They divulged little or nothing about Stalin and his inner circle. Although the post-Stalin period saw limited selected archival access, as well as the increasing availability of memoirs, *samizdat*, and émigré sources, the thoughts and actions of the political elite remained largely a matter of speculation. In the polarised political climate of much of the twentieth century, it was not uncommon for scholars and other observers to see what confirmed their assumptions and prejudices.

The political context left a strong mark on both Soviet and western interpretations. Soviet historians were forced to conform to whatever happened to be the Party's current political line on Stalin, and produced what was essentially propaganda for the regime. Exceptions included the dissident Marxist Roy Medvedev, whose work, based primarily on Khrushchev-era reminiscences, went far beyond what was officially permissible in its criticism of Stalin for his distortion of Lenin's original project.[5] While Western analysts were not under such overt pressure, their interpretations were also heavily dependent on changing political circumstances. For example, the politically charged 1930s saw the publication in France of, on the one hand, the sycophantic biography of Stalin by the Communist Henri Barbusse, and on the other, the former

---

[4] Isaac Deutscher, *Stalin: A Political Biography*, rev. edn. (London: Penguin, 1984); Robert Tucker, *Stalin as Revolutionary, 1879–1929. A Study in History and Personality* (New York: W. W. Norton, 1973) and *Stalin in Power: The Revolution from Above, 1928–1941* (New York: W. W. Norton, 1990); Adam Ulam, *Stalin: The Man and His Era*, 2nd edn. (London: I. B. Tauris, 1989); R. McNeal, *Stalin: Man and Ruler* (London: Macmillan, 1988).

[5] R. Medvedev, *Let History Judge: The Origins and Consequences of Stalinism* (Oxford: Oxford University Press, 1989). This was first published in 1971.

Communist Boris Souvarine's vitriolic anti-Stalin study.[6] During the wartime alliance with Stalin, a spate of sympathetic evaluations appeared in the USA and Great Britain, which quickly evaporated as the Cold War began.[7] Academic Sovietology, a child of the early Cold War, was dominated by the 'totalitarian model' of Soviet politics. Until the 1960s it was almost impossible to advance any other interpretation, in the USA at least. It was the changing political climate from the 1960s, as well as the influence of new social science methodologies, which fostered the development of revisionist challenges to the totalitarian orthodoxy.

Over the course of these years, a number of influential studies of Stalin appeared, whose interpretations hinged on particular understandings of the relationship between the individual and his political, social, economic, ideological, and cultural context. One of the earliest was that of Trotsky, who advanced the notion of the 'impersonal Stalin' – a mediocrity who lacked any of his own ideas but who acted as the perfect representative of the collective interests of the new bureaucracy.[8] The Trotskyist sympathiser, Isaac Deutscher, writing after the war, was much more willing than Trotsky to credit Stalin's achievements, yet his Stalin was also to a great extent a product of circumstances. In Deutscher's view, the policy of collectivisation was dictated by the danger of famine conditions at the end of the 1920s. Stalin was a necessary agent of modernisation a man of 'almost impersonal personality.'[9] Likewise, E. H. Carr, while recognising Stalin's greatness, nevertheless stressed the historical logic of rapid modernisation: collectivisation and industrialisation 'were imposed by the objective situation which Soviet Russia in the later 1920s had to face'.[10]

While these analyses focused on the socio-economic circumstances which produced the Stalin phenomenon, totalitarian theories accentuated the functioning of the political and ideological system. In 1953, Carl Friedrich characterised totalitarian systems in terms of five points: an official ideology, control of weapons and of media, use of terror, and a single mass party

---

[6] H. Barbusse, *Stalin: A New World Seen Through One Man* (London: John Lane The Bodley Head, 1935); B. Souvarine, *Stalin: A Critical Study of Bolshevism* (London: Secker and Warburg, 1939).

[7] For example, J. T. Murphy, *Stalin 1879–1944* (London: John Lane The Bodley Head, 1945).

[8] L. Trotsky, *Stalin: An Appraisal of the Man and his Influence* (London: Harper and Bros. 1941).

[9] Deutscher, *Stalin*, p. 275.

[10] E. H. Carr, 'Stalin Victorious', *Times Literary Supplement*, 10 June 1949. In his introduction to a new edition of *The Russian Revolution from Lenin to Stalin*, R. W. Davies notes that Carr's understanding of Stalin's role shifted in later years. E. H. Carr, *The Russian Revolution from Lenin to Stalin, 1917–1929* (London: Palgrave Macmillan, 2004), pp. xxxiv–xxxv.

'usually under a single leader'.[11] There was of course an assumption that the leader was critical to the workings of totalitarianism: at the apex of a monolithic, centralised, and hierarchical system, it was he who issued the orders which were fulfilled unquestioningly by his subordinates. However, adherents of the model were not generally concerned with the leader except in his capacity as a function of the system and its ideology. There was certainly little empirical analysis of the significance of individual leaders: the personalities or ideas of a Lenin or a Stalin were not considered critical to an understanding of the inner workings of totalitarianism.[12]

It was partly dissatisfaction with this approach which lay behind Robert Tucker's attempt to reassess the significance of the leader. The first volume of his Stalin biography argued that the personality of the dictator was central to understanding the development of Stalinism. Tucker distinguished between the impact of Lenin and that of Stalin, suggesting that the Stalinist outcome was far from inevitable and was dependent in large measure on Stalin's own drive for power. Delving into the uncharted waters of psychohistory, he sought the roots of Stalinism in Stalin's experiences in childhood and beyond.[13] This was an important new departure, which coincided with other efforts to find alternatives to Stalinism, notably Stephen Cohen's study of Bukharin.[14] Yet the psychohistory on which it depended was always rather speculative.[15] The second volume of the biography was in many ways more rounded. *Stalin in Power* argued that Russia's authoritarian political culture and state-building traditions, as well as Stalin's personality, played a key role in shaping Stalinism.[16]

Tucker's work stressed the absolute nature of Stalin's power, an assumption which was increasingly challenged by later revisionist historians. In his *Origins of the Great Purges*, Arch Getty argued that the Soviet political system was chaotic, that institutions often escaped the control of the centre, and that Stalin's leadership consisted to a considerable extent in responding, on an *ad hoc* basis, to political crises as they arose.[17]

---

[11] C. J. Friedrich, *Totalitarianism* (Cambridge, Mass.: Harvard University Press, 1954), pp. 52–3.

[12] Robert Tucker, *The Soviet Political Mind* (London: George Allen and Unwin, 1972), p. 28.

[13] Tucker, *Stalin as Revolutionary*.

[14] S. Cohen, *Bukharin and the Bolshevik Revolution: A Political Biography, 1888–1938* (New York: A. A. Knopf, 1973).

[15] Although Tucker's approach was always much more historically grounded than the far less convincing psychoanalytical account offered by D. Rancour-Lafferiere in *The Mind of Stalin* (Ann Arbor: Ardis, 1988).

[16] Tucker, *Stalin in Power*.

[17] J. Arch Getty, *Origins of the Great Purges: The Soviet Communist Party Reconsidered, 1933–1938* (Cambridge: Cambridge University Press, 1985), pp. 4–9.

Getty's work was influenced by political science of the 1960s onwards, which, in a critique of the totalitarian model, began to consider the possibility that relatively autonomous bureaucratic institutions might have had some influence on policy-making at the highest level.[18] In the 1970s, historians took up the implicit challenge and explored a variety of influences and pressures on decision-making.[19] The 'discovery' of strong institutional interests and lively bureaucratic politics begged the question of whether Stalin did dominate the political system, or whether he was 'embattled', as one key study put it.[20]

During the 'new Cold War' of the 1980s, the work of the revisionists became the object of heated controversy, accused of minimising Stalin's role, of downplaying the terror, and so on.[21] With the the collapse of the Soviet Union, some of the heat has gone out of the debate. After the initial wave of self-justificatory 'findings', the opening up of the archives has stimulated serious work with sources. The politicisation of the field has become noticeably less pronounced, particularly amongst a younger generation of scholars in both Russia and the West for whom the legitimacy of socialism and the USSR are no longer such critical issues. Political history in general has attracted fewer students in favour of the more intellectually fashionable cultural history. However, there are signs of the emergence of a renewed interest in political history, of which this volume is one example.[22]

All the contributors to the volume represent the post-1991 wave of scholarship grounded in empirical work in the former Soviet archives. From North America and Europe, including Russia, they range from scholars who have been working on these problems for over half a century to those who have recently completed doctoral dissertations. Each

---

[18] For example, Gordon Skilling, 'Interest Groups in Communist Politics', *World Politics* 3 (1966), 435–51.

[19] See for example, Moshe Lewin, 'Taking Grain: Soviet Policies of Agricultural Procurements Before the War', in C. Abramsky (ed.), *Essays in Honour of E. H. Carr* (London: Macmillan, 1974); Jonathan Harris, 'The Origins of the Conflict Between Malenkov and Zhdanov, 1939–1941', *Slavic Review* 2 (1976), 287–303; Daniel Brower, 'Collectivized Agriculture in Smolensk: the Party, the Peasantry and the Crisis of 1932', *Russian Review* 2 (1977), 151–66; Sheila Fitzpatrick (ed.), *Cultural Revolution in Russia, 1928–1931* (Bloomington, Ind.: Indiana University Press, 1978); Peter Solomon, 'Soviet Penal Policy, 1917–1934: A Reinterpretation', *Slavic Review* 2 (1980), 195–217; Werner Hahn, *Postwar Soviet Politics: The Fall of Zhdanov and the Defeat of Moderation, 1946–1953* (Ithaca: Cornell University Press, 1982).

[20] William O. McCagg, Jr, *Stalin Embattled, 1943–1948* (Detroit: Wayne State University Press, 1978). See also Gabor Rittersporn, 'L'état en lutte contre lui-même: Tensions sociales et conflits politiques en URSS, 1936–1938', *Libre* 4 (1978).

[21] See, for example, the debates in *Russian Review* 4 (1986).

[22] For discussions on 'The New Political History' see *Kritika* (1), 2004.

considers a specific facet of Stalin as politician and thinker. In the discussion which follows, we focus on what light these analyses shed on two important questions. The first, the nature of Stalin's power, has long been a central issue in the historiography. The second, Stalin's Marxism, and the relationship between ideas and mobilisation, has received much less attention.

The majority of what we know about Stalin concerns his years in power. While this focus of the historian's attention is entirely logical, it is easy to forget that by the time he defeated Bukharin and became the uncontested leader of the Bolshevik Party, Stalin was fifty years old. He had lived two-thirds of his life. It would be surprising indeed if by this time Stalin was not fully developed as a personality, a thinker, and a politician. And yet somehow, few works on Stalin pay much attention to his 'formative years'.[23] Alfred Rieber's chapter on Stalin's Georgian background shows why this has been the case. He explains why sources on Stalin's early years were particularly subject to manipulation and censorship. He makes use of published and unpublished memoirs to cut through the myth-making and cast new light on Stalin's early life and the formation of his identity. He shows how Stalin adapted his political persona, shaped by his 'frontier perspective' to benefit his career as a revolutionary and politician. His early experiences left him with a preference for decision-making in small informal groups in place of large committees, a conspiratorial mentality, and an acceptance of violence.

In his study of Stalin as Commissar of Nationalities, Jeremy Smith picks up this story of Stalin's formative years in the period just after the Revolution. He shows Stalin already confident and consistent in his ideas on nationalities policy, willing and able to stand up to Lenin on questions of policy towards the national minorities and the relationship between Russia and the other Soviet republics. The chapter by David Priestland echoes this impression that Stalin was confident in his ideas and quite willing and able to engage other leading Bolsheviks on key issues. This is consonant with growing evidence that policy debates played a much stronger role in the Lenin succession than we had imagined.[24] Machine politics did, nevertheless, play a crucial role in Stalin's ability to defeat his opponents. In his chapter, Smith also discusses Stalin's early experiences of high politics within the Bolshevik Party in power, particularly as they developed his skills of factional

---

[23] One recent Russian study begins 'Let us not detain ourselves with Stalin's early years, for they do not contribute anything to an understanding of his later attitudes and worldview.' Iu. Zhukov, *Inoi Stalin* (Moscow: Vagrius, 2003), p. 8.

[24] See, for example, Lih et al. (eds.), *Stalin's Letters to Molotov*, pp. 25–6.

struggle and institutional empire-building. In observing the failure of the Commissariat of Nationalities to provide an adequate power base, he anticipates Harris' contribution on Stalin's next post, as General Secretary of the Party.

The idea that Stalin used his position as General Secretary to build a network of loyal political clients has long held a central place in our understanding of his rise to political supremacy. It has also shaped our sense of why the system evolved into a personal dictatorship, and how the system worked, suggesting that ideas did not matter as much as ruthless political manipulation behind closed doors. James Harris' study of Central Committee archives shows that the Secretariat played an important role in Stalin's rise, but not as we have commonly understood it. Harris argues that the Secretariat was barely able to cope with its tasks in the assignment and distribution of cadres. There is little evidence to suggest that Stalin was able to use it to build a personal following. The Secretariat was nevertheless invaluable to Stalin – as a source of information on the needs and wants of Party officialdom. In particular, he encouraged the common distaste for intra-Party democracy in order to harass and frustrate his rivals, to limit the dissemination of their ideas. In this way, the Secretariat played a critical role in Stalin's rise to power, though not as the source of the personalistic dictatorship which emerged in the 1930s. A substantial part of Party officialdom voted for him because they felt he served their interests. Harris observes that they were less sure that he did when he imposed the impossible targets of the First Five-Year Plan and the command-administrative system emerged. However, having themselves undermined intra-Party democracy and any prospect of questioning the 'Central Committee Line', there was little they could do.

While newly released archival materials on the 1920s have yet to attract much scholarly attention, there is already a considerable body of work on Soviet politics in the 1930s. We can now trace the steps by which Stalin achieved a steady concentration and personalisation of power. From the protocols of top Party organs and other materials, we can see in detail the steady decline in the consultative aspects of policy-making which characterised the 1920s. We knew that Party congresses and conferences were increasingly rare, as were meetings of the Central Committee. The meetings themselves ceased to involve any discussion of policy, but appear to have been orchestrated to publicise major policy shifts. We have learned that the Politburo stopped meeting formally by the middle of the 1930s as power shifted to an informal coterie around Stalin. The letters and other notes they exchanged has shown us that even with this group, relations were changing in the 1930s. The friendly informality that characterised their exchanges with Stalin in the early 1930s was replaced with a distinctly sycophantic tone a decade later. While there is evidence of debate and disagreements with Stalin in the early thirties, within a few years his word had become law. More sinister evidence of the entrenchment of personal dictatorship is his increasing reliance on the People's Commissariat of Internal Affairs (NKVD) as an instrument of rule.[25]

This picture of the concentration of personal power can be misleading, however, if taken in isolation. The contributions to this volume examine the nature of Stalin's power, but without losing sight of the context in which it was exercised. Even Khlevniuk, who most emphatically asserts the vastness of Stalin's dictatorial powers, observes that neither in the early 1930s nor later in the decade could Stalin act alone. His inner circle and others close to the centre of power retained some influence and autonomy (though Getty and Khlevniuk, for example, disagree on just how much influence and autonomy they had). Nor could Stalin decide every matter of policy. His interventions were decisive, but there were substantial areas of policy that he left to others. Though Stalin's power was great, he could not always translate his ideas into action. Political and social structures were not soft putty for him to mould to his will. Stalin may have been an extremely powerful dictator, but he may not have felt as though he was, for his personal dictatorship took shape against a backdrop of revolutionary change, economic crisis, bureaucratic chaos, and a fear of enemies.

In his contribution on Stalin as 'Prime Minister', Arch Getty criticises those who regard the 'decline' of formal decision-making structures as synonymous with the accretion of total power by Stalin. Rather, Getty sees the emergence of a decision-making process similar in key respects to a cabinet, which Stalin, as the 'Prime Minister', dominated. The reduction in regular, formal meetings constituted what he calls the 'normalisation of the Politburo' as it adjusted to the great increase in decision-making in a centrally planned economy in the midst of a crash program of rapid industrialisation and collectivisation. Meetings were streamlined and made more frequent. Most issues were decided without discussion by means of a vote (*oprosom*). Members of the Politburo were responsible for key commissariats and areas of policy, thus retaining substantial power bases and influence over decisions. Considerable influence over decision-making would also have been retained by those individuals and institutions that provided information on the basis of which decisions were made.[26]

[25] See Oleg Khlevniuk's contribution to this volume.
[26] Such as the Council of Peoples' Commissars, the Council of Labour and Defence, Commissariats and their commissars (including members of the Politburo, the Planning Commission, experts and advisors, temporary and permanent commissions

Rieber, Khlevniuk, and R. W. Davies share Getty's view that in areas where Stalin took an interest, he dominated policy-making absolutely. His views were rarely questioned. Particularly in the later 1930s, many of those around Stalin came to fear autonomous action, and merely tried to anticipate the leader's preferences. Where Stalin dominated policy, he could exhibit both flexibility and dogmatism. Rieber's second contribution to this volume provides a nuanced analysis of the apparent paradoxes of Stalin's security policy, showing where Stalin learned from his mistakes and where his ideas remained unchanged. In reference to intractable issues of economic policy, such as the function of money in a socialist economy, R. W. Davies observes Stalin's flexibility and ability to learn from experience, but he also points out occasions on which Stalin abjectly failed to anticipate the disastrous consequences of major decisions, such as the impact of swingeing grain collections in 1931 and 1932. Khlevniuk, in his contribution, refers to Stalin's propensity to shift his position in the face of such disasters as 'crisis pragmatism'.

Where Stalin did not actively intervene in policy, others filled the void. Working with Stalin's correspondence from his months on vacation in the mid-1930s, Getty observes the large number of decisions (89 per cent) taken by the Politburo without Stalin's participation. R. W. Davies' work on agricultural policy contrasts Stalin's detailed management of grain procurement campaigns with his relative lack of interest in livestock issues. Sarah Davies' contribution shows not only Stalin's extraordinary personal influence over film production, but also his desire to have a reliable lieutenant to realise his will, as well as the great difficulty of making individuals and institutions respond effectively to his will. Clearly, there existed coherent structures that allowed the system to function in his absence. Those structures served to implement the dictator's orders, but they could also act as a constraint on Stalin's freedom of action.

The idea that Stalin and the Soviet leadership had to contend with relatively autonomous institutions and groups is not new. In the 1950s, historians observed that technical specialists and managers did not always behave in ways the regime wanted.[27] In the 1970s and 80s, social historians observed that society was not a blank slate either, but only since the opening of the archives have we had the opportunity to study in depth the

established by the Politburo, and so on). G. M. Adibekov, K. M. Anderson, and L. A. Rogovaia (eds.), *Politbiuro TsK RKP(b)-VKP(b). Povestki dnia zasedanii, 1919–1952: Katalog*, 3 vols. (Moscow: Rosspen, 2000), I, pp. 18–19.

[27] David Granick, *Management of the Industrial Firm in the USSR* (New York: Columbia University Press, 1954); Joseph Berliner, *Factory and Manager in the USSR* (Cambridge, Mass.: Harvard University Press, 1957).

workings of institutions and officials higher up the administrative hierarchy. In this volume, Khlevniuk observes the strength of bureaucratic
self-interest, or, as Stalin would have known it, 'departmentalism'
(*vedomstvennost'*). Commissariats, planners, control organs, regional
Party organisations, and other institutions were constantly angling to
promote policies favourable to them and to limit their obligations, fighting amongst each other where their interests conflicted.[28] This can be
viewed as an important source of Stalin's power, given that he was
viewed, and acted, as supreme arbiter, but Stalin's persistent frustration
with 'departmentalism' suggests that he considered it anything but a
source of strength.

In spite of his uncontested position and immense political power, it
seems that Stalin never felt entirely secure. The failure to contain institutional self-interest has something to do with this, as did the constant fear
of war and of the infiltration of foreign enemies. Rieber's chapter on
Stalin as a foreign policy-maker makes a compelling argument that
beneath the surface of zigzags and contradictions in Soviet security policy
lay Stalin's enduring fear about the vulnerability of the Soviet borderlands
in the context of what he was convinced would be an inevitable war with
the capitalist world. Nor can the Great Terror (1936–8) be understood
except as a response to Stalin's insecurity. In his chapter on the changing
image of the enemy in the three Moscow show trials, Chase shows Stalin
at his most powerful and powerless, shaping and directing popular opinion in a massive and devastating campaign to unmask hidden enemies,
while lashing out at chimerical enemies who were largely the product of
his own conspiratorial mentality.

How much did Stalin's dictatorship change after the Terror? We still
know almost nothing about the period from the curtailing of the 'mass
operations' in late 1938 to the Nazi invasion in June 1941,[29] and only
somewhat more about the structure of the dictatorship in the Second
World War. The post-war period, often labelled 'High Stalinism' has
generated more work and debate. As the label indicates, many historians
argue that the period from 1945–53 marked the apogee of Stalin's personal
dictatorship, his power reinforced by terror and victory in war, imposed at
the expense of institutional coherence.[30] Others have questioned the image
of the disintegration of political structures in the post-war period,

---

[28] See also Paul Gregory (ed.), *Behind the Façade of Stalin's Command Economy: Evidence
from the Soviet State and Party Archives* (Stanford: Hoover Institution Press, 2001).
[29] One of the very few works on this period is Harris, 'The Origin of the Conflict'.
[30] See for example, Milovan Djilas, *Conversations with Stalin* (London: Hart-Davis,
1962), p. 73; Nikita Khrushchev, *Khrushchev Remembers* (London: Deutsch, 1971),

observing conflicts among powerful institutional interests and factions that shaped policy in the period.[31]

Recent archival research has tempered this debate somewhat. It has become clear that Stalin was feeling his age after the war and began to reduce his work schedule. The Council of Peoples' Commissars, renamed the Council of Ministers in 1946, was given almost exclusive control over economic issues, and some political issues, such as *nomenklatura* appointments, were passed to other organs within the Central Committee apparatus.[32] While Stalin's involvement in day-to-day decision-making declined, he continued to keep a close eye on things, intervening occasionally and often violently.[33] His interventions remained decisive, but his withdrawal from day-to-day decision-making only strengthened institutional coherence and intensified struggles for power and for his favour.[34] Khlevniuk argues that Stalin's personal dictatorship had never challenged institutional coherence. Though his power was limitless, the complexity of decision-making had 'consistently and inevitably reproduced elements of oligarchical rule'. Put simply, Stalin had always needed an inner circle with close ties to strong bureaucratic institutions. According to Khlevniuk, Stalin's power was at its height in his role as arbiter of conflicting institutional interests. His semi-retirement in the late 1940s made that role more difficult, and he was more inclined to resort to violence in his occasional interventions. In response, his inner circle adopted mechanisms of collective decision-making on the basis of which the system was able to work smoothly without him when he died.

While the nature of Stalin's power has been a constant preoccupation of scholars, until recently, few studies have paid serious attention to Stalin as a Marxist. Only in 2002 did a systematic study of his political thought appear.[35] He is typically viewed as the quintessential pragmatic politician, interested primarily in power for its own sake, and only superficially

pp. 298–301. Also Roger Pethybridge, *A History of Postwar Russia* (London: Allen and Unwin, 1966); Robert Conquest, *Power and Policy in the USSR* (London: Macmillan, 1961).

[31] In *Stalin Embattled*, William O. McCagg went so far as to argue that Stalin's power was challenged by these groups. See also Timothy Dunmore, *The Stalinist Command Economy: The Soviet State Apparatus and Economic Policy, 1945–1953* (London: Macmillan, 1980); Hahn, *Postwar Soviet Politics*.

[32] Yoram Gorlizki, 'Ordinary Stalinism: The Council of Ministers and the Soviet Neopatrimonial State, 1946–1953', *Journal of Modern History* 4 (2002), 705–9, 715.

[33] Yoram Gorlizki and Oleg Khlevniuk, *Cold Peace: Stalin and the Soviet Ruling Circle, 1945–1953* (Oxford: Oxford University Press, 2004).

[34] Iurii Zhukov, 'Bor'ba za vlast' v rukovodstve SSSR v 1945–1952 godakh', *Voprosy istorii* 1 (1995), 23–39; O. Khlevniuk, 'Sovetskaia ekonomicheskaia politika na rubezhe 1940–1950-x godov i "Delo Gosplana"', *Otechestvennaia istoriia* 3 (2001), 77–89.

[35] Erik van Ree, *The Political Thought of Joseph Stalin* (London: RoutledgeCurzon, 2002).

committed to Marxist ideology. In public he invoked Marxist principles cynically and represented himself as a theorist to legitimate his power. His dismissive attitude to these principles is evident in the many ways in which he apparently distorted and abandoned them when political exigency required. He is widely accused of having betrayed the original Marxist ideals in favour of inegalitarianism, social conservatism, and, especially, Russian nationalism, described by Carr as 'the only political creed which moved him at all deeply'.[36]

One of the advantages of the availability of new archival sources is the light they shed on this question of Stalin's relationship to ideology. If one accepts the argument above, one would have expected Stalin to invoke Marxist language in public, but not in private. Yet what is striking is that even in his most intimate correspondence with Molotov, Kaganovich, and others, Stalin did in fact continue to employ Marxist concepts and frameworks.[37] As Pollock points out in this volume, the USSR 'did not keep two sets of books, at least on ideological questions'.[38] It appears that adherence to Marxism was more than just a source of political legitimacy for Stalin. But what was the nature of his Marxism? Marxism itself is a diverse and in some respects inconsistent body of ideas. Which of these did Stalin draw on? How did his ideas evolve? And what was the relationship between the ideology and his political practice? Several of the contributors to this volume address these questions directly.

Erik van Ree is the author of the most comprehensive study to date of Stalin's political thought.[39] He has carried out extensive research in Stalin's unpublished papers, especially his library. What did Stalin read? How did this influence his thinking? Van Ree's research shows that his (non-fiction) library consisted of overwhelmingly Marxist works, which he continued to study and annotate until the end of his life.[40] Van Ree's conclusion is that these ideas mattered to Stalin, and that he remained a committed Marxist, if Marxism is defined in its broadest sense.

In his contribution to the present volume, van Ree grapples with the problem of the alleged Russification of Marxism under Stalin. He disagrees with a prevailing perception that Stalin fundamentally adapted and distorted Marxism to suit Russian conditions.[41] Instead he concurs with such scholars as Leszek Kolakowski and Andrzej Walicki that Stalin did not

[36] Carr, *The Russian Revolution from Lenin to Stalin*, p. 170.
[37] Lih et al. (eds.), *Stalin's Letters to Molotov*; R. W. Davies et al. (eds.), *The Stalin–Kaganovich Correspondence*.
[38] See also J. Arch Getty, *The Road to Terror: Stalin and the Self-Destruction of the Bolsheviks, 1932–1939* (New Haven: Yale University Press, 1999), p. 22.
[39] Van Ree, *Political Thought.*   [40] *Ibid.*, pp. 16, 258–61.   [41] Tucker, *Stalin in Power.*

substantially modify basic Marxist tenets.[42] Van Ree goes much further than his predecessors in tracing the influences upon and evolution of Stalin's thought. Ideas such as 'revolution from above', 'socialism in one country', or the continuing need for a strong state and for the flourishing of nations under socialism were far from Stalinist innovations. All had antecedents in the thinking of Marx or his interpreters (including Engels, Vollmar, Bauer, Kautsky, Lenin), or, in some cases, other Western revolutionary traditions (such as Jacobinism) which themselves influenced the followers of Marx. Only the extreme chauvinism and anti-cosmopolitanism of the post-war years are difficult to reconcile with Marxist thinking, yet even these had anti-capitalist overtones consistent with a Marxist approach. It was precisely because Marxism was so elastic, encompassing such a variety of sometimes contradictory tendencies that Stalin was able to reject the more democratic, liberal strands in favour of those which seemed most compatible with Russian/Soviet development. Van Ree concludes that the Western revolutionary tradition was itself 'more permeated with "Stalinist" elements than we would like to think'. Stalin simply elevated many of these elements to the status of dogma.

Several authors follow van Ree in taking Stalin's Marxism seriously. Alfred Rieber, however, reminds us that the young Stalin's journey to Marxism was not as straightforward as its description in the official cult biographies discussed in David Brandenberger's chapter. Rieber casts doubt on Stalin's claim to have become involved in underground Marxist groups at the age of fifteen. In the rich frontier situation of Georgia, the adolescent Stalin absorbed a variety of other intellectual influences: populism, nationalism, as well as a specifically Georgian nationalist-inclined strain of Marxism. He was also drawn to romantic literature with its vivid depictions of heroes defending the poor. All these influences may have contributed not only to the obvious nationalist currents in his thinking, but also to the less obvious romantic, populist interpretation of Marxism to which he was attracted.

It is this 'Bolshevik romanticism' which David Priestland emphasises. His chapter draws our attention to tensions within Marxism-Leninism and how these played out in Stalin's own thinking in the period 1917–39. He distinguishes between Marxism's 'scientistic and deterministic side' and its 'more voluntaristic and romantic side'. While the former accentuates the role of economic forces, technique (*tekhnika*) and so on, the latter focuses

---

[42] Leszek Kolakowski, 'Marxist Roots of Stalinism', in R. Tucker (ed.), *Stalinism: Essays in Historical Interpretation* (New York: W. W. Norton, 1977), pp. 283–98; Andrzej Walicki, *Marxism and the Leap to the Kingdom of Freedom* (Stanford: Stanford University Press, 1995), ch. 5.

on the active role of the proletariat, of politics and consciousness. Although, like many other Bolsheviks, he oscillated between these two approaches, Stalin seems to have been most consistently attracted to the 'quasi-romantic' view with its emphasis on heroism and will.

This voluntarism left a strong mark on Stalin's attitude to mass mobilisation, which is examined in several of the contributions. Priestland highlights how the leader's populist, anti-bourgeois outlook made him a strong advocate of unleashing worker activism, particularly during the Cultural Revolution. In the later 1930s, he continued to stress the importance of ideological mobilisation of what were now more often termed 'the people', for example, during the Stakhanovite campaign.

Stalin's conviction, highlighted by Priestland, that 'the production of souls is more important than the production of tanks' explains his constant attention to cultural matters, which Sarah Davies examines in her chapter on Stalin's role as patron of cinema in the mid-1930s. She shows how Stalin devoted an extraordinary amount of time to what he described as 'helping' to turn Soviet cinema into a truly mass art, capable of mobilising the people for the goals of socialism. Not only did he offer financial support and promote the prestige of cinema, but he also participated actively in the making of films, trying to ensure that they convey suitable ideological messages packaged in an entertaining way.

Mass mobilisation was one important dimension of the Great Terror. Debates about the Terror have tended to focus on matters of power and security (see above). While these must of course be paramount in any explanation, they should not overshadow the ideological issues. Van Ree has suggested that Stalin's Marxist convictions led him to believe in the continued existence of a class struggle, and that this belief shaped the form that the terror assumed.[43] The question of belief is a complex one, but what is abundantly clear is that Stalin recognised the potential of the terror to mobilise the population against real or imagined 'enemies of the people' and for Stalin and the Soviet state.[44]

Sarah Davies notes that Stalin was particularly concerned to shape the image of the internal and external enemy in films. Like films, the show trials served as powerful didactic tools. Bill Chase's chapter reveals the extent to which Stalin participated in the staging of the trials, both in Moscow and in the provinces. These performances provided an opportunity for the carefully orchestrated construction of threats to the public. Stalin was personally involved in the crafting of these threats, which changed markedly over the period 1936–8, as did the intended

---

[43] Van Ree, *Political Thought*, pp. 124–5.
[44] On the question of belief, see Getty's useful discussion in *Road to Terror* pp. 15–24.

audience. In 1936, the threat was defined as oppositionists turned enemy agents and terrorists, whose only aim was to seize power. The audience for this trial was primarily Party members. By 1937, the message had become more populist: the threat was now from Party officials who were engaging in terrorism, espionage, and wrecking in order to overturn the Soviet system and restore capitalism. This was designed to mobilise the 'little people', ordinary Soviet citizens, to unmask the 'enemies of the people' – scapegoats for economic failures. In 1938, the threat, and the audience, had turned truly global – a conspiracy of rightists and Trotskyists were allegedly intent on dismembering the USSR with the assistance of fascist and capitalist powers.

In Stalin's mind, the uncovering of such a vast conspiracy highlighted the need for a greater focus on the Marxist-Leninist education (*vospitanie*) of cadres. Priestland argues that Stalin attributed the ideological contamination of cadres to an excessive focus on *tekhnika* at the expense of *politika*. Henceforth ideas were to assume a much higher priority. The *Short Course* in Party history of 1938 was designed to be a primer in the theory and practice of Marxism-Leninism to inspire and instruct the intelligentsia, and to prevent them from going over to the enemy.

Stalin was sensitive to the limited appeal of the *Short Course* for the 'masses', however, appreciating that different approaches were required for different audiences. In his chapter, David Brandenberger argues that the Stalin cult – one of the most striking features of Stalinism – was part of a mobilisational strategy directed primarily towards 'the masses'. The cult appears to be a gross aberration from socialist ideals (although van Ree has argued that even this had antecedents within Marxist thought), and many historians have interpreted it as a symptom of Stalin's psychological need for self-aggrandisement.[45] While not denying that this may have played a role, Brandenberger maintains that Stalin himself was well aware of the problematic status of the cult of personality within Marxism. He justified the phenomenon as an effective way of appealing to ordinary workers and peasants for whom a heroic, biographical narrative was more inspiring than undiluted Marxism-Leninism. So while he deliberately removed from the draft of the *Short Course* sections which focused too closely on his own biography, he allowed the production of a separate Stalin biography for the 'simple people'. This finally appeared relatively late, at the end of 1939, partly because of the ideological and political turmoil of the 1930s. In Stalin's mind, the focus on personality was not incompatible with Marxist-Leninist

---

[45] Van Ree, *Political Thought*, ch. 12; Tucker, *Stalin as Revolutionary* and *Stalin in Power*.

teachings: 'the toiling masses and simple people cannot begin the study of Marxism-Leninism with Lenin's and Stalin's writings. They should start with the biography', he remarked in 1946.

Far from abandoning Marxism, Stalin remained committed to the ideology and to its dissemination amongst Soviet citizens. This was equally true of the post-war years which are often associated with Stalin's turn to extreme Russian nationalism. As van Ree has pointed out, the stress on nation in this period never replaced the emphasis on class. In his last years, Stalin spent much of his time intervening in academic disputes, from philosophy to genetics and linguistics. Ethan Pollock questions traditional assumptions that these interventions were simply 'the ultimate ravings of a dying megalomaniac', part of a campaign to intimidate the intelligentsia, an attempt to encourage conflict amongst his colleagues or to heat up the Cold War. Instead they represented Stalin's concern with the health of ideology and Soviet science.

Stalin recognised the existence of an ideological crisis in the post-war era. He sought to tackle this by reinvigorating a body of theory which he apparently recognised had become dogmatic. If Soviet science were to flourish, as it must with the development of the Cold War, then Marxist theory must be used creatively. Only then would scientific truths be uncovered. His forays into linguistics were apparently intended to curtail the Marrist monopoly over the discipline, and to encourage discussion of other approaches, with Stalin claiming that Marxism had to develop and change over time if it was to remain relevant. Likewise his meetings with political economists aimed to stimulate a genuinely fresh approach to the long-awaited textbook, rather than one which simply regurgitated Marxist-Leninist clichés. The problem, of course, was that Stalin's interventions tended to generate confusion rather than real debate, as everyone waited for an authoritative answer from on high. The crisis was thus deepened rather than resolved.

How is our image of Stalin changing following the opening up of the archives? We have only just begun to digest the extensive new materials already released, and more are likely to follow. Much work remains to be done on both the nature of Stalin's power, and the significance of his ideas. The related question of his political practices, touched on in some of the contributions to this volume, also requires more systematic study.[46] What is already clear is that the new materials do not paint a black-and-white picture of either an unbridled tyrant in the unprincipled

---

[46] Sheila Fitzpatrick offered some initial thoughts on the question of how to approach political practices in her paper 'Stalin, Molotov, and the Practice of Politics', presented

pursuit of power or an embattled leader reacting to uncontrollable forces. Stalin emerges as a far more contradictory and complex figure. As a leader, he ruthlessly destroyed his political rivals and built an unrivalled personal dictatorship, yet he was never secure in his power. He was obsessed with the division of the formal structures of power, but increasingly worked only in small informal groups. He wanted to delegate responsibilities, but never entirely trusted those who worked for him. He strove to be at the heart of every major political decision, and in the process directed some policy matters in great detail, while utterly ignoring others. He was a perceptive thinker, but also capable of failing to see what was right in front of him. He was genuinely driven by ideology, but flexible in his tactics. He was in some respects a conventional Marxist, but aggressively promoted the nation and the leader cult. He sought to disseminate Marxist ideas as a means of encouraging activism, but his methods often succeeded only in stifling initiative. Stalin's personal influence on the development of the Soviet Union was extraordinary, yet he did not operate in a vacuum and his ambitions were often thwarted. The studies that follow explore these complexities and contradictions.

to the conference 'Stalin: Power, Policy and Political Values', Durham, January 2003. See also her 'Politics as Practice. Thoughts on a New Soviet Political History', *Kritika* 1 (2004), 27–54.

2 Stalin as Georgian: the formative years

Alfred J. Rieber

'The devil knows what's in our heads.' A Georgian Proverb.

'The Persians are but women compared with the Afghans,
and the Afghans but women compared with the Georgians.'

A Persian Proverb

Stalin and his enemies appeared to agree about one source of his identity as a political man. 'I am not a European man', he told a Japanese journalist, 'but an Asian, a Russified Georgian.' Trotsky cited Kamenev as expressing the views of the Central Committee in 1925: 'You can expect anything from that Asiatic', while Bukharin more pointedly referred to Stalin as the new Ghenghis Khan.[1] Although they employed the term Asiatic to mean different things, their point of reference was the same. Stalin was born, raised, educated, and initiated as a revolutionary in a borderland of the Russian Empire that shared a common history and a long frontier with the Islamic Middle East. In this context, borderland refers to a territory on the periphery of the core Russian lands with its own distinctive history, strong regional traditions and variety of ethnocultural identities. In a previous article, I sought to demonstrate how Stalin as a man of the borderlands constructed a social identity combining Georgian, proletarian, and Russian components in order to promote

The research for this chapter was made possible by a grant from the Research Board of the Central European University. I am grateful to Barry McLoughlin for inviting me to deliver an earlier version at the Institut für Osteuropäische Geschichte der Universität Wien.
[1] Leon Trotsky, *Stalin: An Appraisal of the Man and His Influence*, 2nd edn. (London: Hollis and Carter, 1947), pp. 1, 2, 417, 420. After the Second World War Maxim Litvinov attributed Stalin's inability to work with the West to his Asiatic mentality. Vojtech Mastny, 'The Cassandra in the Foreign Commissariat: Maxim Litvinov and the Cold War', *Foreign Affairs* 54 (1975–6), 366–76. Even Beria, according to his son, claimed that Stalin had Persian blood and compared him to Shah Abbas. Sergo Beria, *Beria, My Father* (London: Duckworth, 2001), pp. 21, 284.

18

specific political ends including his vision of a centralised, multicultural Soviet state and society.[2]

One aim of the present essay is to refine this perspective by interpreting the south Caucasian borderland as a frontier society where during Stalin's early years boundary lines between cultural fields were crossed and blurred resulting in a dynamic, interactive process of change.[3] A second and related aim is to revisit the first twenty-two years of Stalin's life on the basis of fresh archival material in order to illustrate how the cultural milieu of the Georgian borderland influenced his evolution from seminary student to professional Marxist revolutionary. In the course of this analysis it will be necessary to expose his efforts to conceal or distort his rights of passage along this unusual trajectory.

There were four features of the South Caucasus frontier society that played a significant role in Stalin's construction of his persona and the evolution of his political perspectives. Elements of all four may be found in other borderlands of the Russian Empire but not in the same form or interactive combination. They are: 1) lengthy traditions of rebellion, conspiracies, and protest movements against foreign and domestic enemies exhibiting both social and ethno-religious, and later nationalist components; 2) kaleidoscopic patterns of population settlement and displacement that intermixed numerous ethno-religious groups within changing political boundaries; 3) multiple channels of external cultural and intellectual currents that permeated the region; 4) complex interactions among craftsmen, workers, peasants, and intelligentsia of different ethnic groups, some still rooted in highly traditional societies, that were entering revolutionary movements during a period of rapid industrial growth.

Throughout the South Caucasus a long history of the clash of empires, foreign conquest, and occupation gave rise to traditions of resistance and rebellion in which the Georgians featured prominently. They lived on an ancient and contested frontier between great empires. They had their own ancient state tradition, and periodically they were able by their own efforts to throw off foreign domination. In the process, they acquired the attributes of a warrior society and earned a reputation as

---

[2] Alfred J. Rieber, 'Stalin: Man of the Borderlands', *American Historical Review* 5 (2001), 1651–91.

[3] For a recent attempt to summarise and synthesise the large literature on frontiers are Alfred J. Rieber, 'Changing Concepts and Constructions of Frontiers: A Comparative Historical Approach', *Ab Imperio* 1 (2003), pp. 23–46. For a revisionist work on the American frontier that has comparative implications see Jeremy Adelman and Stephen Aron, 'From Borderlands to Borders: Empires, Nation-States, and the Peoples in between in North American History', *American Historical Review* 3 (1999), 814–41.

fierce fighters.[4] Most of the Georgian lands had been part of the Russian Empire for almost eighty years when Stalin was born, though some districts to the south and southwest had been annexed only after the Russo-Turkish War of 1878. Peaceful integration had not proceeded smoothly. Throughout the nineteenth century, periodic manifestations of anti-Russian sentiment broke to the surface in rebellions and con-spiracies.[5] The spirit of resistance was a major theme in Georgian folklore and the romantic revival in literature in the mid-nineteenth century that so deeply affected the young Soso Dzhugashvili. The cult of violence in the South Caucasus permeated the whole range of social relations from the traditional tribal societies to urban youth. At one extreme, the masculine code of warriorhood and the blood feud pre-vailed within the tribal regions to the north of Georgia.[6] At the other extreme, urban and rural violence during the revolution of 1905 and its aftermath reached higher levels in the Caucasus than elsewhere in the empire.[7]

Astride a strategic isthmus, the South Caucasus was exposed to fre-quent invasions, migrations, deportations, and colonisation that pro-duced the second major characteristic of this frontier society, its complex multicultural texture. No other borderland of the Russian Empire contained such a mix and variety of ethnic, religious, and tribal societies. It was no wonder that as political parties began to make their appearance in the region, the central question that preoccupied all of them was the national question. From early childhood, Soso Dzhugashvili was exposed to the cross-currents of ethnic interaction. A scant thirty kilo-metres to the north of Stalin's birthplace of Gori streched the tribal regions

---

[4] For general treatments see W. E. D. Allen, *A History of the Georgian People from the Beginning Down to the Russian Conquest in the Nineteenth Century* (New York: Barnes and Noble, 1971); David Marshall Lang, *The Georgians* (New York: Praeger, 1966); David Marshall Lang, *The Last Years of the Georgian Monarchy, 1658–1832* (New York: Columbia University Press, 1957); Cyril Toumanoff, *Studies in Christian Caucasian History* (Washington, D.C., Georgetown University Press, 1963), and M. M. Gaprindashvili and O. K. Zhordaniia (eds.), *Ocherki istorii Gruzii v vos'mi tomakh* (Tblisi: Metsniereba, 1988), III and IV.

[5] Ronald Grigor Suny, *The Making of the Georgian Nation*, 2nd edn. (Bloomington: Indiana University Press, 1994), pp. 71–2, 82–5, 119–20, 166–7, I. G. Antelava, 'Obostrenie klassovoi bor'by, razvitie i rasprostranenie antikrepostnicheskoi ideologii nakanune otmeni krepostnogo prava', in *Ocherki istorii Gruzii*, V, pp. 170–83, 217–24.

[6] M. O. Kosven et al. (eds.), *Narody Kavkaza* (Moscow: Akademiia Nauk, 1960), pp. 297–304; Sh. Inal-Ipa, *Abkhazy. Istoriko-etnograficheskie ocherki* (Sukhumi: Abgosizdat, 1960), pp. 276–8; I. L. Babich, *Pravovaia kultura Adygov (Istoriia i sovremen-nost')*, *avtoreferat* (Moscow State University, 2000), pp. 13–14, n.21. I am grateful to the author for bringing this source to my attention.

[7] Anna Geifman, *Thou Shalt Kill. Revolutionary Terrorism in Russia, 1894–1917* (Princeton: Princeton University Press: 1993), pp. 23–4.

of the Abkhazians, Svanetians, and Ossetians, traditional societies still deeply rooted in a feudal-patriarchal way of life.[8] Gori itself had a mixed population of Georgians, Armenians, and Russians. The town was poised, as it were, between two very different worlds of the patriarchal, tribal, and the urban, early industrial. According to contemporary accounts, the social structure, architecture, and urban grids of the three main cities – Tiflis, Batumi, and Baku – that formed the triangle of Stalin's early revolutionary activity were split along 'European' and 'Asian' lines.[9] Stalin bore the stigma of this discourse throughout his life although on at least one occasion he sought to turn the epithet of 'Asiatic' to his advantage.[10]

The third characteristic of the South Caucasus as a frontier society was the existence of multiple channels of communication that filtered external ideas into the region. In the second half of the nineteenth century, access to European thought produced a variety of cultural hybrids. The most powerful currents came from Russia channelled either through local ecclesiastical schools like those Stalin attended or else through small numbers of Georgian students who studied in Russian universities, mainly St. Petersburg. A second, narrower channel led to institutions of higher learning in Central Europe (including the Kingdom of Poland) and then on to the larger field of Europe as a whole. The importation of Russian literature, both in the original and in translation, and Russian translations of European works of literature, history, and politics fed these currents and left an indelible imprint on Stalin. Major Russian writers from Pushkin and Lermontov to Marlinskii and Tolstoy idealised aspects of Caucasian life although they displayed an ambiguous attitude toward Georgians.[11] Thus, the resentment felt by so many Georgian nobles and intellectuals toward the administrative and bureaucratic insensitivities of Russian officials and clerics, shared by the young Soso Dzhugashvili, was mitigated by appreciation and even admiration of Russian high culture.

---

[8] Many students from Ossetian schools came to study in Gori and Tiflis. M. D. Lordkipanidze and D. I. Muskhelishvili (eds.), *Ocherki istorii Gruzii v vos'mi tomakh* (Tbilisi: Metsniereba, 1988).

[9] K. N. Bagilev, *Putevoditel' po Tiflisu* (Tiflis, 1896), pp. 26–9 and especially Vasilii Sidorov, *Po Rossii. Kavkaz. Putevye zametki i vpechatleniia* (St. Petersburg: M. Akifiev i I. Leontiev, 1897), pp. 142–5, 163, 270, 274, 276, 595–6, 598, 605. There were similar descriptions of Stalin's home town of Gori. *Ibid.*, pp. 460–77 and A. Azhavakhov, 'Gorod Gori', in *Sbornik materialov dlia opisaniia mestnosti i plemen Kavkaza* (Tiflis, 1883), cited in Rossiiskii gosudarstvennyi arkhiv sotsial'no-politicheskoi istorii (henceforth RGASPI) f. 71, op. 10, d. 273, l. 14.

[10] See n. 47.

[11] Cf. Susan Layton, 'Russian Literature about Georgia', *Slavic Review* 2 (1992), 195–213. See also Katya Hokanson, 'Literary Imperialism, Narodnost' and Pushkin's Invention of the Caucasus', *Russian Review* 3 (1994), 336–52.

New political currents permeated the South Caucasus through the Russian connection. In mid-century it was populism (*narodnichestvo*) that strongly appealed to Georgian intellectuals disappointed by the liberation of the serfs under much worse terms in the Caucasus than in Central Russia.[12] Almost all the Georgian intellectuals who ultimately embraced Marxism in the early 1890s passed through a period of populism. Was Stalin an exception? Up to now there has been little discussion of his pre-Marxist views primarily because he chose to conceal them.

Modern forms of Georgian nationalism also owed much to Russian and European influences. Some local varieties favoured full independence; others combined political goals for autonomy and self-government with social reform.[13] It was the issue of Georgia's relations with Russia more than any other ideological dispute that set Stalin apart from the Georgian nationalists and the Georgian Mensheviks and put him on course for his own solution to the nationalities question.

Finally, Marxism found its way to the South Caucasus mainly along the Russian channel.[14] Yet the particular social and economic conditions in Georgia shaped the contours of Marxism in three fundamental ways. First, Caucasian Marxists boldly confronted the question of overcoming ethnic difference in forging a revolutionary movement.[15] Secondly, they adhered more closely than their Russian counterparts to a belief in the peasantry as a revolutionary force; the program of the Georgian Mensheviks in particular embraced this view compelling the Bolsheviks, Stalin among them, to compete with their rivals on this issue.[16] Thirdly, the early Georgian Marxists took a different view of the role of the worker in the revolutionary movement, stressing the importance of spontaneity and the equality of workers and intelligentsia in the movement, a position that created both problems and opportunities for Stalin.

---

[12] In contrast to the Georgians, Armenian revolutionaries were more concerned with national unification than the agrarian question. Suny, *The Making*, pp. 134–43; R. Suny, *Looking toward Ararat: Armenia in Modern History* (Bloomington: Indiana University Press, 1993), pp. 68–78.

[13] A. S. Bendianishvili, 'Gorodskoe samoupravlenie v poslednei tretii xix veka', in *Ocherki istorii Gruzii*, V, pp. 247–63.

[14] In addition to Suny, *The Making*, ch. 7, see S. T. Arkomed, *Rabochee dvizhenie i sotsial'-demokratiia na Kavkaze*, pt. 1, 2nd edn. (Moscow: Glavlit, 1923); F. Makharadze, *K tridtsatiletiiu sushchestvovaniia Tiflisskoi organizatsii. Podgotovitel'nyi period, 1870–1890, Materialy* (Tiflis: Sovetskii Kavkaz, 1925); V. S. Bakhtadze, *Ocherki po istorii gruzinskoi obshchestvenno-ekonomicheskoi mysli (60–90 gody XIX stoletiia)* (Tblisi: Izdatel'stvo Tblisskogo universiteta, 1960).

[15] Sh. Davitashvili, *Narodnicheskoe dvizhenie v Gruzii* (Tblisi: n. p., 1933), p. 23, translated from the Georgian and cited in RGASPI f. 71, op. 10, d. 273, l. 96.

[16] S. F. Jones, 'Marxism and the Peasant Revolt in the Russian Empire: The Case of the Gurian Republic', *Slavonic and East European Review* 3 (1989), 403–34.

Linked to the influx of external cultural influences was the fourth characteristic of the frontier society. Industrialisation in the South Caucasus occurred in a region of widely divergent social groups ranging from the tribal to the urbanised, and to an equally variegated number of ethnic groups rubbing shoulder-to-shoulder in the main cities. For Stalin, the most important social consequences arose from the multicultural profile of the working class and the peculiar relationship of the working class to the intellectuals. Social democracy in the Caucasus was from the outset a multicultural political movement unlike any of the others in the empire.[17] In the south Caucasus, relations between workers and intellectuals also exhibited regional nuances. In Georgia, and to varying degrees throughout the region, the working class had grown from two major sources – the old craft structure and modern industry such as oil, railroad construction, and mining. Many of the craftsmen were literate, having attended the special crafts schools, and were among the first workers to get in touch with students and intelligentsia of the populists and later the Marxists.[18] Modern industry attracted skilled Russian workers from the north and unskilled Azeri from Russian and Iranian Azerbaidzhan, creating a formidable obstacle to labour organisers but offering an opportunity to men like Stalin who saw personal advantages in organising the illiterate and politically unformed.

In Georgia and elsewhere in the South Caucasus, the combination of the traditional (mainly Georgian) crafts and newer (mainly Russian) worker solidarity led to a relatively early development of the strike movement in the Russian empire. Running in parallel with and independently of the strike movement in Petersburg, major strike activity in the South Caucasus began as early as 1878 and attracted national attention during the strike of Tiflis tobacco factories in 1894–5. That these strikes were all 'spontaneous', lacking an organisational centre or the guidance of a political party, did not mean that all workers lacked a political consciousness.[19]

---

[17] Noi Zhordaniia, *Moia zhizn'* (Stanford: Hoover Institution, 1968), pp. 38–9; *Vtoroi s"ezd RSDRP, iiul'- avgust 1903 goda. Protokoly* (Moscow: Gospolitizdat, 1959) p. 515; G. A. Galoian, *Rossiia i narody Zakavkaz'e* (Moscow: Mysl', 1976) pp. 357–64; Suny, *Looking toward Ararat*, pp. 90–2, 260.

[18] For the school of *remeslenniki* see Prince Masal'skii, 'Tiflis', in F. A. Brokgauz and I. F. Efron (eds.), *Entsiklopedicheskii Slovar'* (St. Petersburg: Izdatel'skoe Delo, 1901), XXX, p. 268; for populist contacts with them Davitashvili, *Narodnicheskoe dvizhenie*, pp. 60–5, 79; for revolutionary populist influence on the earliest strike movements, E. V. Khoshtaria, *Ocherki sotsial'no-ekonomicheskoi istorii Gruzii* (Tblisi: Metsniereba, 1974), pp. 204–8.

[19] F. Makharadze, *Ocherki revoliutsionnogo dvizheniia v Zakavkaz'e* (Tiflis: Gosizdat Gruzii, 1927), pp. 47–51.

In the seventies and eighties in the main cities of the South Caucasus, Tiflis in particular, a social stratum of 'worker-craftsmen' began to make contact with the young generation of populist intellectuals. Most of the craftsmen had attended the urban crafts schools (*remeslennoe uchilishche*), where they had an opportunity to meet students from other institutions and to encounter the floating population of exiles and immigrants from Russia. The populist students from rural Georgia found them a more receptive audience and more in keeping with the familiar image of 'the toiler' than the factory workers. The craftsmen produced their own writers such as the famous Iosif Davitashvili, the self-taught poet of the people. As early as the late seventies they formed their own mutual aid society in Tiflis, and in 1889 published an illegal handwritten journal.[20] According to a report of a police agent in 1900 'there does not exist a single factory, plant or workshop that does not have its secret circles, the leaders of which are in constant contact with one another, and which gather in general meetings [*skhodki*].' According to the same report the intelligentsia had not yet penetrated these circles but were taking 'the first steps' to draw closer to them.[21] This was the setting for Stalin's debut as a conspiratorial agitator within the working class.

The rapid spread of Marxist ideas among the workers in Georgia was attributed by Filipp Makharadze to the absence of any strong competition from other ideologies: 'among us the Marxist orientation did not have to struggle with any other kind of tendency for hegemony among the working class as took place in other countries' by which he meant trade unionism or economism inspired by a 'bourgeois world view'.[22] This was also true to a large extent in Russia as well. But in Georgia there was no 'naive monarchism' among the workers and no experiments with police socialism that had penetrated the working class in Russia. With the decline of populism, or rather its cooptation, Marxism had the field all to itself.

Stalin's political evolution as a revolutionary has not taken full account of his early life in this frontier society. The occasion for a reassessment of Stalin's Georgian background is the recent availability of unpublished sources. Important in themselves, they also offer opportunities to reevaluate the veracity of the published material, much of it hagiographic in tone. In 1949, the Marx-Engels-Lenin Institute received a bulky packet of documents, numbering 424 pages, entitled 'An Outline of the Years of

---

[20] *Ibid.*, pp. 62–3.
[21] G. A. Galoian, *Rabochee dvizhenie i natsional'nyi vopros v Zakavkaz'e, 1900–1922* (Erevan: Ayastan, 1969), p. 11.
[22] Makharadze, *K tridtsatiletiiu*, p. 29.

Childhood and Youth of Stalin'. The compiler, Vladimir Kaminskii, presented it as the work of ten years. He described the contents as similar to the material that he and I. Vereshchagin had edited and published in 1939 in the organ of the Central Committee of the Komsomol, *Molodaia Gvardiia*. But Kaminskii's second collection never saw the light of day. Buried in the archives of the Institute, it was only recently made available to researchers in the Russian Archive for Social and Political History.[23] A superficial reading does not elicit any startling revelations. But a closer analysis turns up valuable clues and even more suggestive contradictions in its various testimonies. These lead to a comparison with the *Molodaia Gvardiia* collection, and a re-examination of pre-Stalinist and post-Stalinist memoirs and monographs primarily published in Tblisi, Erevan, and Baku during the period of de-Stalinisation. This revised view of Stalin's Georgian background takes shape around three specific themes that reflect the frontier experience of the region: the towns of Gori, Tiflis, and Batumi as the cultural space in which Stalin passed his early years; the multiple cultural channels that shaped his political views from populism to Marxism; the pace and extent of his involvement with workers and intellectuals in the revolutionary activity.

When Stalin was born, in either 1878 or 1879, Gori was by no means an insignificant or obscure town.[24] Its history reproduced in miniature the characteristics of the frontier society of which it was a part. History lingered on in the shape of the dominant man-made feature of the town, the fortress (*Goris-tsikhe*), with its thick and high crenellated walls and the legends attached to it. The fortress image subsequently occupied a prominent place in the mature Stalin's imagery. In the centre of the court there was a large depression, possibly an ancient burial mound, and not far away a strangely shaped spherical yellow stone. Popular fantasy attributed to it a special meaning and linked it to the mythical figure of Amiran, the local Prometheus. It had been his sword that he hurled into the ground before he was chained to a cliff of the Caucasus. In a customary rite still practised at the end of the nineteenth century, the local

---

[23] RGASPI f. 71, op. 10, d. 273, l. 1. Kaminskii had taken as his model the technique of literary montage exemplified by V. V. Versaev, *Pushkin v zhizni* (Moscow: Sovetskii pisatel', 1936). The material got a mixed review from S. Pozner who noted that there was little of value on the early years although some useful material had been provided on how Stalin 'established ties with peasants, the penetration of revolutionary ideas among the peasants and how he acquired great influence over peasants.' These comments were dated 9 May, 1950. *Ibid.*, ll. 2–5.

[24] The exact date of Stalin's birth has long been disputed due to a confusion for which he is responsible. For the most recent analysis based on archival sources see Miklos Kun, *Stalin: An Unknown Portrait* (Budapest: Central European University Press, 2003), pp. 8–10.

blacksmiths went to their workshops at midnight on Maundy Thursday and simultaneously hammered their anvils as a sign that the chains binding Amiran still held him firmly. Otherwise the hero would break loose and avenge himself on those who had forged his bonds.[25] These and other tales of treachery, revenge, and embattlement were the stuff of Soso's childhood.[26]

Gori province had a reputation for being rebellious as well as a centre of conspiracies. Throughout almost the entire nineteenth century, the peasantry, especially in the region of Ossetia, repeatedly rose against their landlords. The liberation of the serfs in 1864 did nothing to improve their lot. On the contrary, it reduced most of them to landless labourers or smallholders eking out a living on wretched parcels of land burdened with heavy taxes and exposed to the arbitrary violence of local officials.[27] The peasants also suffered from the depredations of bandits, a persistent problem in the countryside. The bandits began to come down from the mountains in the northern part of Gori province in the post-liberation period and raided the big estates of Machabeli and Eristavi, as well as peasant villages. The rural police offered little assistance to the peasants, equating them with the bandits. Some bandit chiefs achieved brief notoriety, but their fame was overshadowed by popular avengers like Tarasei Andreevich Mgaloblishvili, a local noble with military training who organised his own small posse to hunt down bandits or protect villagers without extracting any payment from them.[28] The heroic and romantic tales that absorbed Georgian youth like Soso Dzhugashvili had their real equivalents in living memory. Subsequently, the role of the bandit became equivocal in Stalin's mind; as a revolutionary and 'expropriator' he identified with it, but once in power he used it to stigmatise popular resistance to his rule.[29]

By the time Stalin was born the population of Gori had exceeded ten thousand, but despite its rail link to Tiflis, the physical appearance of

---

[25] RGASPI f. 71, op. 10, d. 273, ll. 15, 44.

[26] For additional insights into the role of folkloric images in Stalin's writing see Mikhail Vaiskopf, *Pisatel' Stalin* (Moscow: Novoe Literaturnoe Obozrenie, 2001), and the discussion in Rieber, 'Stalin', pp. 1658–62.

[27] S. V. Machabeli, 'Ekonomicheskii byt krest'ian Goriiskogo uezda, Tifliskoi gubernii', in *Materialy dlia izuchenii ekonomicheskogo byta gosudarstvennikh krest'ian Zakavkazskogo kraia* (Tiflis: Merani, 1887), VI, p. 201, cited in RGASPI f. 71, op. 10, d. 273, l. 80.

[28] Sofron Mgaloblishvili, *Vospominaniia o moei zhizni. Nezabyvaemye vstrechi* (Tbilisi: Merani, 1974), pp. 35–6, 37–9.

[29] For the psychological significance of Koba see Robert Tucker, *Stalin as Revolutionary 1879–1929: A Study in History and Personality* (New York: W. W. Norton, 1973), pp. 79–82 and Philip Pomper, *Lenin, Trotsky and Stalin: The Intelligentsia in Power* (New York: Columbia University Press, 1990), pp. 158–63.

the town had changed little, with its narrow, crooked, and dirty streets, its great market, the ruins of its past glories. The social structure of Gori remained highly traditional, even feudal. The local merchants and landowners had made common cause with the Russian bureaucrats in order to retain their dominant position. The town craftsmen, of whom Stalin's father was one, conserved their hard-working but old-fashioned methods.[30]

Public life was limited to the celebration of holidays when historical and popular carnivals mingled with Christian ceremonies. On Holy Monday the Armenian and Georgian inhabitants commemorated the expulsion in 1634 of the Persians who had occupied the town for two decades and deported more than twenty-five thousand people to Iran. Replaying the event, the citizens of Gori divided into two groups who, following a ceremonial dinner, clashed in a mass fist fight. More than a thousand fighters were involved, with the children starting it and the adults then joining in. According to some stories, Soso Dzhugashvili was a partisan of the upper town boys and distinguished himself in the fighting.[31]

But there was another side to Gori as well. The introduction of the Great Reforms in the 1860s opened the way for a Georgian national revival and greater cultural interaction with Russia.[32] Gori soon became an important cultural centre and a hotbed of political activity. The key to its renaissance was the connection with Tiflis, about seventy-two miles away, and especially the relationship between the Gori parish school and the Tiflis seminary. A generation before Stalin was to follow the route to enlightenment, the top students from Gori went on to Tiflis, which served as a transmitter of fresh and bold ideas from Russia. They returned home as *kulturtragers*. In this way, Gori became in the late 1870s one of the main centres of populism in Georgia.

At the end of the Crimean War, the Gori parish school was still conducted along the harsh disciplinary principles of Nicholaevan Russia. After 1862 physical punishment declined and the following year the subsequently famous Georgian social activist and pedagogue Iakob Gogebashvili briefly taught at Gori before moving on to the Tiflis parish school. The graduates of Gori who entered the Tiflis seminary encountered an altogether different spirit. Gogebashvili had studied in Kiev with

---

[30] Mgaloblishvili, *Vospominaniia*, pp. 11, 14.

[31] V. Kaminskii and I. Vereshchagin, 'Detstvo i iunost' vozhdia', *Molodaia gvardiia* 12 (1939), 49–50 based on contemporary sources. The story of Soso's participation in the fist fight was omitted from the published account. See RGASPI f. 71, op. 10, d. 273, ll. 86–8.

[32] On the Georgian national revival see Suny, *The Making*, pp. 124–43.

Pirogov and introduced his methods in Tiflis. His students inspired and helped the boys from Gori. The library of the seminary was surprisingly good for the time and appeared to have made available more political literature than the young Soso Dzhugashvili would find twenty years later. Aside from spiritual, philosophical, and literary works (Shakespeare, Byron, Schiller in Russian translation) all the issues of Chernyshevskii's *Sovremennik* were available, as well as critical articles by Belinskii, Pisarev, the poems of Nekrasov, and even several issues of Herzen's *Kolokol*. There were no Georgian books, but the library subscribed to the few, often short-lived Georgian literary journals that were beginning to appear in the late sixties and early seventies. Informal student discussion groups appeared and met with leading Georgian intellectuals to debate forbidden topics in art and politics. Returning Georgian students from Russia were greeted with enthusiasm, especially those who had come into direct contact with Russian populists and participated in student demonstrations. Gogebashvili's rooms on the top floor of the Tiflis seminary were 'for the Georgian intelligentsia what Stankevich's home had been for Russian writers.'[33]

The provinces were still sunk in torpor when the young seminarist graduate, Sofron Mgaloblishvili, returned to Gori in the early seventies bringing with him as many Georgian books as he could. His personal library became a haven for young Georgian readers. By the mid-seventies the intellectual life of the town had quickened. The town became the first after Tiflis to create an amateur troupe of actors that by the end of the decade established a theatre that attracted performers and writers from Tiflis. A flow of ideas and people between Gori and Tiflis took on a marked political character.

In 1873, Mgaloblishvili and several friends formed a clandestine circle and founded an illegal press dedicated to awakening the political consciousness of the peasantry. They translated into Georgian, and read to peasants in the countryside around Gori, illegal Russian populist pamphlets. They kept in touch with similar circles in Tiflis, particularly with Anton Purtseladze, the irascible critic of Georgian liberals, who gained a great reputation among Tiflis workers and craftsmen for his simply written appealing stories and plays. According to Mgaloblishvili 'it was impossible to find a simple person who had not read *The Bandits*, a tale of men driven to banditry by material conditions'. But the Gori circle was infiltrated by police spies and broken up, Mgaloblishvili, Purtseladze, and others arrested.[34]

[33] Mgaloblishvili, *Vospominaniia*, pp. 44–7, 54, 55; Iakov Mansvetashvili, *Vospominaniia* (Tblisi: Literatura da khelovneba, 1967), pp. 7–9, 12–16, 20–58.
[34] Mgaloblishvili, *Vospominaniia*, pp. 109–21 (quotation p. 120).

The work of the populists in Gori did not end in 1878 with the police sweep. One of its activists, Sho Davitashvili, had been disappointed by the response of the peasants and left for Tiflis to work in a factory. But he soon returned to Gori and established the Transcaucasian Teachers' Seminary in order to spread populist ideas. He rapidly fell under suspicion and was dismissed. However, the seminary acquired a reputation among a later generation of revolutionaries. Among them was Nariman Narimanov, the Azeri Bolshevik who regarded it as a model for Azerbaidzhan; 'For twenty-seven years of its existence the seminary prepared students for our rural and town elementary schools. The majority of teachers teaching in Russian and Muslim schools in Baku and also in other elementary schools in the Caucasus in rural and urban areas had studied there.'[35] Davitashvili and Mgaloblishvili continued cautiously to conceal their propaganda activity under legal forms such as the organisation of a drama circle, a lecture series, a consumers' co-operative, and, in 1878, a village school where the students were almost all linked to Davitashvili and other populists.[36]

There were two conspiratorial groups operating in Gori at this time. The so-called 'military conspiratorial organisation' had ties to the People's Will in St. Petersburg. But it was soon rolled up by the police. The second group, 'the circle of seminarists', followed the more moderate path of the 'Land and Liberty' wing of the Russian populists and survived well into the 1890s. It was a mixed bag of individuals who once characterised themselves as 'democrat', 'revolutionary terrorist', 'atheist communist' without much ideological discrimination. The only non-noble member was Arsen Kalandadze, of peasant background, who printed the proclamations of the group and ran a little bookshop in Gori. Aside from the legal trade he made available books by 'anonymous authors' forbidden to students by the authorities. The town intelligentsia and mysterious visitors from the north could meet in a separate room with a convenient rear exit to a garden and escape route to another part of town. Among the *habitués* were 'schoolboys [from the Gori parish school] and then seminarists Lado Ketskhoveli and Soso Dzhugashvili'.[37] How significant was it that Stalin entered the conspiratorial world through the agency of populism? How deeply and for how long did he remain in that world?

In the Russia of the late 1880s and early 1890s it was not unusual for youthful rebels in the provinces to experience the rites of passage from

[35] Teimur Akhmedov, *Nariman Narimanov* (Baku: Iazychy, 1988), p. 118.
[36] RGASPI f. 71, op. 10. d. 273, ll. 97–8.
[37] Kaminskii and Vereshchagin, 'Detstvo i iunost'', p. 56; RGASPI f. 71, op. 10, d. 273, ll. 98–104.

populism to Marxism.[38] But Stalinist historiography expunged any evidence of this section of his path to revolution and Western scholars have ignored it as well. Stalin's claim in his official biography to have adopted Marxism at the age of fifteen has always been greeted with some scepticism in critical biographies, but the issue of how and when he became a Marxist has remained obscure. Clues from his life in Gori suggest a more complex process of finding his way to Marxism than has been generally accepted.

Stalin proceeded cautiously and by stages down the road to Marxism during his years in the Tiflis seminary. By the time he arrived at the seminary the relatively liberal atmosphere of the 1870s had given way to a harshly repressive regime. According to the anonymous memoirs of a former student published in 1907, the faculty were 'despots, capricious egotists who only had in mind their own prospects' which was to acquire a bishop's mitre. Mainly Russians, they openly displayed their contempt for Georgians and their language. By 1900, there were only fifty Georgians out of three hundred students. By 1905 there were no Georgians left.[39] In such an atmosphere it is hardly surprising that the long-established student circles for self-education turned more and more to politics. It is important here to make several corrections to the official picture of Stalin's participation in these clandestine activities. First, contemporary accounts and even some memoirs written after Stalin came to power demonstrate that the student circles had a history and were hardly the creation of a single individual, let alone the youthful Soso. Secondly, in the first two years of his study the literature that was actually discovered in his possession by the authorities was barely subversive, let alone Marxist. Thirdly, there had been a tradition of open confrontation with the authorities that was nourished by several of his fellow seminarians, but Soso avoided a direct clash and ended up resigning rather than being expelled from the seminary.

By the time Stalin enrolled, the Tiflis seminary already had the reputation of a centre of anti-governmental activity. Inspired by the spread of populist literature, the students repeatedly challenged the administration. Between 1874 and 1878, eighty-three of the recalcitrants were expelled. By the early eighties a new generation of Georgian populists coming from the lower strata of the population replaced the nobles and princes who

---

[38] These included F. Makharadze, N. Zhordaniia, S. Dzhibladze, M. Tskhakaia, and N. Chkheidze. L. E. Gorgiladze, 'Rasprostranenie marksizma v Gruzii', in *Ocherki istorii Gruzii*, V, p. 470. For the account of one participant see Zhordaniia, *Moia Zhizn'*, pp. 8–9, 13.

[39] RGASPI f. 71, op. 10, d. 73, ll. 153–4.

had founded the movement. Resistance to the government's repressive policies after the assassination of the tsar in 1881 accelerated their political shift from populism to Marxism and also took more violent forms. Closer to the People's Will in Russia, they were also turning their attention to students and worker-craftsmen rather than peasants. In 1882 a group of seminarists formed a populist revolutionary circle around Gola Chitadze that included several future leaders of Georgian social democracy such as Isidor Ramishvili and Noi Zhordania (subsequently Stalin's great rivals in the Menshevik wing of the Georgian party), Filipp Makharadze and M. Tskhakaia, the future Bolsheviks. In 1885 a student expelled for revolutionary activity, Silvester Dzhibladze, struck the rector in the face. A year later another expelled student assassinated the same rector. By this time a number of the expelled students had discovered Marx. Led by the young writer Egnate Ingoroqva (Ninoshvili), they met informally in Tiflis in order to enhance their self-education.

During the late 1880s a few seminary students began to read Marxist literature, in particular the early essays of Plekhanov. For some like Makharadze and Zhordania, the final stage in the transition to Marxism came only after they had left Tiflis in 1891 to continue their studies in Warsaw. They corresponded with their colleagues in Tiflis, Silvestr Dzhibladze and Ninoshvili, sending them illegal Marxist literature. When in 1894 Ninoshvili died prematurely, his friend, who had suffered expulsion with him, Silvester Dzhibladze, delivered a famous funeral oration at his grave-site that for the first time publicly invoked Marxism as the revolutionary wave of the future. The appeal for a new direction met an enthusiastic response among the mourners and inspired the radical intellectual Grigori Tsereteli to call them '*mesame-dasi*' (the third generation) which the Georgian Marxists then adopted as their name.[40] To be sure, there were disagreements among the early recorders of these events about how many of the group were 'real Marxists' and how many were 'under the strong influence of Marxist ideology'.[41] The differences that later emerged between Mensheviks and Bolsheviks were not clearly drawn at this time. Moreover, the youthful seminarians had very little direct contact with the emerging workers' movement. During these same years from the late 1870s to the early 1890s a parallel and independent movement of worker activism in the form of strikes and secret discussion groups spread rapidly throughout the South Caucasus.

---

[40] Zhordaniia, *Moia zhizn'*, pp. 11–15; Makharadze, *K tridtsatiletiiu*, pp. 4–5, 14–17, 40–2.
[41] The first position was held by Makharadze, a Bolshevik, *K tridtsatiletiiu*, p. 43 and the second by Arkomed, a Menshevik. *Rabochee dvizhenie*, pp. 145–51.

When Soso Dzhugashvili enrolled in the Tiflis seminary in autumn 1894 shortly before his fifteenth or sixteenth birthday (depending on which birth date is accepted), he was poised to cross the threshold of an established revolutionary movement. There was nothing unusual about the entry of the young Soso into this world except the subsequent attempts to make it appear so. His conversion to Marxism and active participation in the movement not only followed a conventional path but due to his cautious temperament and provincial origins required more time than several of his comrades, the process lasting until the very end of his five-year course of study at the seminary.

One part of the story of Stalin's Marxist epiphany that has remained almost completely obscure is his emergence from the cocoon of populism. The transition was, as we have seen, characteristic of the third generation and had an honorable pedigree in the example of Plekhanov, the father of Russian Marxism. But although there are even a few clues in the published materials on Stalin's early life that he too followed this path, the idea that he had not imbibed Marxism at the earliest possible opportunity did not fit the image of the *vozhd'* as it emerged in the elaboration of his cult in the late 1930s.[42] One of the main problems with the second compilation of biographical materials by Kaminskii was the contradictory evidence he gathered concerning this sensitive part of Stalin's biography.

In his official Party autobiography, Stalin asserted that he had entered the revolutionary movement at the age of fifteen when he made contact with a group of 'Russian Marxists then existing in the Transcaucasus. This group had a great influence on me and gave me a taste of underground Marxist literature.' He claimed that one of the first books that he read in 1894 was Marx's *Capital*. There are several problems with this 'recollection'. Who were these mysterious 'Russian Marxists'? Certainly, they were not in the seminary where no other source mentions such a group. Stalin's contact with Russian workers only came four years later even according to the account of his future father-in-law, Sergei Alliluev.[43] Other 'eye-witness' accounts written in the late 1930s under the watchful eye of L. P. Beria, recount that Stalin was seventeen when he created the first illegal Marxist study group and came forward as a propagator of Marxism.[44] This would put the awakening in 1897. But

---

[42]   In the documents published by Kaminskii and Vereshchagin in 'Detstvo i iunost'', there are two tantalising ellipses in the description of the Gori populists taken from 'Materials of the Gori Regional Museum, f. 20' that exemplify the judicious reticence of the editors on this issue.

[43]   S. Alliluev, 'Vstrechi s tovarishchem Stalina', *Proletarskaia revoliutsiia* 8 (1937), 154.

[44]   RGASPI f. 71, op. 10. d. 273, l. 178.

we already know that this circle, if it existed, was hardly 'the first Marxist study group' in the Tiflis seminary.

Stalin's account is also at odds with other records and reminiscences. According to a different informant of Kaminskii, there was only one copy of Marx's *Capital* in Tiflis. The story went that the students borrowed it for two weeks and pitched in enough money to have a copy made of the entire work (that is the first volume) and that Soso read it through and took copious notes.[45] Despite this and other laconic 'reminiscences' about Stalin's precocious interest in Marx, other sources reveal a more eclectic palette of reading. One of the memoirist-apologists mentions that the books available to the seminarians at that time in the so-called 'cheap' subscription library were mainly works of literature, with some books on history, geography, ethnography, natural science, and social questions. He mentions specifically the works by Max Weber and the historians D. I. Ilovaiskii and Boris Schlötzer.

Still a third account maintains that 'in the seminary Iosif read us the works of Ignatii Ninoshvili, explained the theory of Darwin on the origin of man' and 'at the end of the year we turned to reading political economy and excerpts from books by Marx and Engels.'[46] There is some confusion then about when and how much of Marx Soso read, but this is unsurprising given the dearth of Marxist literature and the eclectic disposition of most of the young seminarians. Moreover, the first volume of *Capital* had been legally published in Russia twenty years earlier. It was hardly a manual for revolutionaries.

It is instructive to compare Soso's meagre diet of reading mentioned by the memoirist-apologists with the materials that Makharadze had discovered in Warsaw and sent back to seminarist friends in Tiflis five years before Stalin began his studies. The books in Soso's possession that the authorities of the seminary confiscated were hardly the radical fare that his fellow seminarians recall him devouring. The items mentioned in the official records of the inspector of the Tiflis seminary in 1896 and 1897 were Victor Hugo's *Toilers of the Sea* and *The Year '93*, and a work by the French ethnographer and Darwinist, Charles Letourneau.[47] Perhaps Soso was particularly careful in concealing the Marxist literature he was allegedly carrying around. Still, it is surprising that the authorities with their network of spies among the students did not catch him with

---

[45] *Ibid.*, l. 181. Another account recalls that Stalin and his comrades read the first volume of *Capital* 'at the end of the nineties'. Kaminskii and Vereshchagin, 'Detstvo i iunost'', p. 71.

[46] RGASPI f. 71, op. 10, d. 273, l. 179. Ninoshvili's own writing was mainly fiction. G. Tsereteli, *Ignatii Ingorokva* (Tiflis: n.p., 1905), pp. 11–12.

[47] The work is *L'évolution littéraire dans les divers races humaines*, translated into Russian in 1895 by V. V. Sviatkovskii.

anything more inflammatory than Hugo and Letourneau. Even assuming that Stalin had read the first volume of *Capital*, did this turn him into a Marxist? Or was he like so many of the third generation who had read a bit of Marx and perhaps even Plekhanov, but remained attached to the populist ideals of their adolescent years?

Kaminskii's incautious collection of reminiscences once again provides a clue to Soso's state of mind in the summer of 1897 when he allegedly had a year of leading a Marxist study group under his belt. It turns out that he spent the idle months of vacation with 'his good friend' Misho Davitashvili in the village of Tsromu 'where he got to know [*znakomit'sia*] the life of the peasants'.[48] His preoccupation suggests that he was still in the state of transition from populism that was characteristic of many of his contemporaries in the seminary.

The following year at the seminary was crucial in Stalin's pilgrimage from populism to Marxism. The most revealing document tracing the evolution of his political thinking during 1897–8 is an unpublished memoir by his younger friend and comrade G. I. Elisabedashvili. Having returned to Gori in June 1898 during the summer holidays, as was his custom, Stalin volunteered to help prepare Elisabedashvili for his exams. When asked how he had arrived at his views on social injustice and the liberation of workers and peasants, Stalin replied that in his youth he had read many books. 'What had interested him were the works of A. [Aleksandr] Kazbek, the poetry of Rafail Eristavi, Pushkin, the works of Il'ia Chavchavadze, Lermontov and the knightly tales.' He acknowledged that he was attracted to heroes and individuals who defended the interests of the needy. He dreamed of growing up to participate in the struggle together with the poor. 'With this in mind Soso at first wished to become a village writer [*sel'skii pisar'*]'. Then he wanted to be a village elder (*starshina*). But his views 'changed fundamentally' when he came to understand the workers' question. 'Soso's aim was to draw closer to the working class, its way of living and dying, to set in motion all the rest of the masses who are close to the workers to struggle for victory with them'. Soso came to the conclusion 'with regard to the peasants' that their liberation was only possible with the help of and under the guidance of the working class. After that he began to defend the interests of the working class and poor peasants. 'That was the correct path', he said.[49] Unfortunately, Elisabedashvili provides no dates to mark Stalin's revealing account of his transition from populism to Marxism. But the absence of any mention of his specific involvement in practical, organisational activity suggests that

[48] RGASPI f. 71, op. 10, d. 273, l. 185.
[49] *Ibid.*, ll. 201–2.

Stalin was still in a preparatory phase. Indirect evidence from other sources confirms this assumption and at the same time provides a key to the process of Stalin's conversion to Marxism. During the crucial year preceding this confessional summer a new figure appeared on Soso's horizon that appears to have made a real difference in his political outlook and his involvement in revolutionary activity.

In autumn 1897, Lado Ketskhoveli returned to Tiflis illegally and renewed his contacts with seminarians some of whom still remembered him as the daring leader of a strike at the school four years earlier. As a result of that incident he had been expelled along with eighty-two other students. After a year he managed to enter the Kiev seminary but soon fell under suspicion and was arrested in 1896. He was still under police surveillance when he slipped away to Tiflis. According to the memoirs of G. Parkadze, Ketskhoveli and Soso became friends. 'Through Lado Ketskhoveli and Russian Marxists spending these years in the Transcaucasus comrade Stalin gained access to illegal Marxist literature.'[50] Even the most tendentious memoirist-apologists do not suppress all the evidence that Lado was the mentor and Stalin the student in this relationship.[51] The memoirist-apologists and Beria himself admitted that in 1897 Ketskhoveli immediately associated himself with the allegedly Marxist organisation *mesame-dasi* while Stalin only joined the group a year later.[52] This sequence was hardly surprising. Ketskhoveli was already a recognised force among the radical seminarists. A veteran of arrest and exile, he naturally assumed the role of a leader in the muted struggle among the emerging Marxists between those like himself committed to illegal activity and figures like Zhordania who had just returned from four and a half years in Europe to assume the editorship of *Kvali*, 'the first legal organ of the Georgian Marxists'.[53] The reappearance of Lado Ketskhoveli and his instruction of Soso in Marxist literature mark the beginning of a period when the historic memories of Soso's revolutionary activity become increasingly shot through with contradictions.

There are three problems in tracing Stalin's conspiratorial activity after his awakening to Marxism. The first is Soso's behavior in the seminary compared with assertions of his involvement in leading Marxist study circles; the second is his departure from the Tiflis seminary in 1899; and the third is the organisation and leadership of the Tiflis tram workers strike the following year. The scanty records of the seminary inspector in

[50] *Ibid.*, l. 85.   [51] Kaminski and Vereshchagin, 'Detstvo i iunost'', pp. 88, 92.
[52] Grigorii Uratadze, *Vospominaniia gruzinskogo sotsial-demokrata* (Stanford: Hoover Institution, 1968), p. 15.
[53] Zhordaniia, *Moia zhizn'*, p. 28.

1897 and 1898 portray Soso as a troublesome student but hardly a radical activist unlike, it might be added, Lado Ketskhoveli had been four years earlier. The most serious charges levelled by the authorities against Soso in these years (in addition to reading the forbidden books already mentioned) were having left church in the middle of a service while complaining about pains in his leg and arriving late for services.[54]

During the same period, according to the memoirist-apologists Stalin was meeting with groups of workers, although even they remain vague as to exactly what he was telling them. According to Stalin's future father-in-law, Sergei Alliluiev, the two men first met in 1898 when a group of railroad workers formed to listen to Stalin and were impressed with his 'direct and simple speech'. Similar phrases are repeated by others, but we are never told the content of these monologues. Several memoirist-apologists attribute to Stalin an active part in preparing the Tiflis railroad strike of 1898.[55] But the account of the Georgian Bolshevik, Filipp Makharadze, written before Stalin's rise to absolute power, makes it clear that the strike was organised and led by the workers themselves and that Stalin's role was marginal at best.[56] It takes some imagination to envisage Stalin organising eight workers' circles as featured in Beria's multiplication table and leading a major strike without raising a wisp of suspicion among the authorities of the seminary. There seems little doubt, however, that under Lado Ketskhoveli's guidance, Stalin first got in touch with workers. The most plausible accounts describe a group of five or six workers with whom Stalin discussed the 'mechanics of the capitalist system' and 'the need to engage in a political struggle to improve the workers' position'.[57]

The second problem with the official record of Stalin's revolutionary activity centres on his departure from the seminary. Once again there is a discrepancy between contemporary and later accounts. An entry for 29 May 1899 in the official organ of the Georgian exarchate notes laconically 'Dismissed [*uvol'niaetsia*] from the seminary for failure to appear at the examinations for unknown reason – Dzhugashvili, Iosip'.[58] Stalin later

---

[54] RGASPI f. 71, op. 10, d. 273, ll. 183–4, 222; Kaminskii and Vereshchagin, 'Detstvo i iunost'', p. 84.

[55] Kaminskii and Vereshchagin, 'Detstvo i iunost'', pp. 76–7. Other workers in the railroad workshops remember meeting Stalin in 1898 but make no mention of his role in organising the railroad strike. *Velikii vozhd' i uchitel'. Rasskazy starykh rabochikh o rabote tovarishcha Stalina v Zakavkaz'e*, 2nd edn. (Tiflis: ZKK VKP (b), Zaria Vostoka, 1936), pp. 13, 20.

[56] Makharadze, *Ocherki*, p. 53; see also Galoian, *Rabochee dvizhenie*, XI, based on police archives.

[57] RGASPI f. 71, op. 10, d. 273, ll. 195–7.

[58] Kaminskii and Vereshchagin, 'Detstvo i iunost'', p. 84.

gave a different version, claiming in 1931 that he had been 'kicked out for Marxist propaganda'.[59] But when he left, the seminary issued him a certificate (*udostoverenie*) that he had completed the fifth year of classes.[60] This was hardly the sort of testimony that would have been issued to one known as a conspiratorial Marxist organiser of workers' groups and strikes.

The third problem with Stalin's revolutionary record is the contrast between his alleged role and that of Lado Ketskhoveli in organising and leading the tram workers strike in Tiflis. This is another case in the Georgian period of Stalin's revolutionary career when historic memories, reassembled after the leader's rise to power, reveal more than was intended. Two out of the three available accounts of the strike mention Stalin either as a leader of the social democratic group in Tiflis or as directly involved in preparing the strike, but references to him are perfunctory. In contrast, Lado Ketskhoveli is not only identified as the organiser of the strike, repeatedly meeting with workers in their barracks or outside the city, but also as one of the fiery orators who, despite the presence of gendarmes and police, urged the workers once the strike had broken out to remain firm in their demands.[61] A third account of the strike by Vano Ketskhoveli presents two versions with a significant omission in the second one. In July 1939 he wrote, 'In this period Stalin and L. Ketskhoveli prepared a strike of the Tiflis tram workers.' A month later, when writing a tribute to his brother, he left Stalin out of the incident. 'At the end of 1899 on the Tiflis leadership of the social democratic group, Lado [Ketskhoveli] organised a strike of the workers of the horse drawn tram.'[62] Stalin continued to live in the shadow of Lado Ketskhoveli.

Eluding the police, Lado Ketskhoveli, on instructions from the Tiflis organisation, moved in 1900 to Baku, where he organised the largest illegal social democratic printing press then in existence, and printed the first illegal Georgian paper *brdzola*. The memoirist-apologists insist that Stalin headed the Tiflis committee at this time and continued to send Lado instructions and advice. This is a sheer fabrication. According to the gendarme report of the Tiflis section to the head of the Kutais section dated 1 July 1902, Dzhugashvili was elected to the Tiflis committee of the

---

[59] Tucker, *Stalin as Revolutionary*, p. 91.

[60] Vano Ketskhoveli, 'Na zare sozdaniia partii rabochego klassa', *Zaria Vostoka*, 17 July 1939, p. 3. In the autumn of 1899, forty to forty-five students of the seminary 'at their own request' resigned – a more pointed, collective protest than Stalin's solo flight.

[61] RGASPI f. 71, op. 10, d. 273, l. 240. Dzhugashvili's name was conspicuously absent from the list of worker-*intelligenty* who openly supported the strikers.

[62] Compare Ketskhoveli, 'Na zare sozdaniia partii', p. 3 and V. Ketskhoveli, 'Iz vospominaniia o Lado Ketskhoveli', *Zaria Vostoka*, 17 August 1939, p. 3.

RSDWP in the fall of 1901 and participated in two of its meetings on 11 and 18 November before being sent to Batumi.[63] From the outset, the Baku press was run by a group of future Bolsheviks – Vano Bolkvadze, Vaso Khudeshvili, Avel Enukidze, and Vano Sturua. With Lenin's encouragement, the press assumed the task of distributing *Iskra* in Georgia.[64] Lado and his brother were already contributing articles to the illegal press well before Stalin made his debut as a published single author.[65] In 1902 Lado and Enukidze were arrested and the following year Lado was killed by a guard in his prison cell.[66] The story that Stalin played a role in founding the press, let alone a leading role, became a *cause célèbre* in 1935 when Beria denounced Enukidze's memoirs and inserted the missing Stalin into the foreground of the printing press.[67] Stalin himself paid tribute to Lado by celebrating his life in ways that no other contemporary of these Georgian years enjoyed. The only rival in Stalin's memorialising memory was G. P. Teliia, another comrade of a slightly later period, but also one who died early.[68] It would seem that Stalin could only make room for equals in his presentation of self so long as they were no longer around to make claims on the basis of that equality. Although Lado died in 1902, Stalin never forgot his debt to his young friend. In 1938 an entire collection of articles devoted to Ketskhoveli was published including a paean from L. P. Beria.[69] Commemorative articles in the Soviet press from 1938 throughout the war years and a monograph in 1953 continued to celebrate Lado's exploits.[70]

---

[63] RGASPI f. 71, op. 10, d. 273, 292.

[64] Institut Marksa-Engelsa-Lenina, *Leninskii sbornik*, 20 vols. (Moscow: Gosizdat, 1924–53), VIII, pp. 188–9; Avel Enukidze, *Nashi podpol'naia tipografiia na Kavkaze* (Moscow: Novaia Moskva, 1925).

[65] For example, Lado's brother Vano published an article in *brdzola* in September 1901. RGASPI f. 71, op. 10, d. 273, 289–90; Galoian, *Rabochee dvizhenie*, p. 13. At this time Stalin had yet to publish anything except romantic poetry in the legal organs *Iveriia* and *Kvali*. Stalin's debut as an author came in September 1904. I. V. Stalin, *Sochineniia*, 13 vols. (Moscow: Gospolitizdat, 1946–52), I, pp. 37–52.

[66] 'Podpol'naia tipografiia "Iskra" v Baku (Materialy Vano Sturua)', in *Iz proshlogo. Stat'i i vospominaniia iz istorii Bakinskoi organizatsii i rabochego dvizheniia v Baku* (Baku: Bakinskii rabochii, 1923), pp. 137–8. Sturua records the subsequent history of the press but does not mention Stalin at all.

[67] Rieber, 'Stalin,' p. 1665.

[68] For Stalin's funeral oration at the gravesite of Teliia, see Stalin, *Sochineniia*, II, pp. 27–31. For later commemorative tributes, see Z. T. Gegeshidze, *Georgii Teliia* (Tblisi: Sabchota Sakartvelo, 1958).

[69] L. P. Beria, 'Lado Ketskhoveli', in *Lado Ketskhoveli* (Moscow, 1938), p. 9.

[70] RGASPI f. 71, op. 10. d. 275, ll. 55–60. Lado died on 17 August (old style) and the commemorative articles appeared on 30 August (new style). See also A. Guliev, *Muzhestvennyi borets za kommunizm. Lado Ketskhoveli* (Baku: Azernesir, 1953). Lado

In 1900, Stalin's initiation into Marxism proceeded more rapidly with the arrival of a group of Russian social-democratic exiles who injected fresh energy into the workers' movement in Tiflis and Baku. They arrived shortly after the workers had organised the first large-scale May Day demonstration with the participation of the Tiflis committee.[71] Among the newcomers was veteran social-democratic activist, M. I. Kalinin, the future Soviet leader. His later efforts to diminish his own contribution to the development of a Leninist spirit among the Tiflis workers in favour of Stalin ring hollow in light of the contemporary attention paid to him by the police.[72] Viktor Kurnatovskii, a former populist who had joined Plekhanov's Liberation Group in 1893 and got to know Lenin a few years later, appeared on the scene to bolster the local social democrats. The arrival of the Russian exiles coincided with a rapid growth of the strike movement that caused serious concern among the police. It was probably during this period, in the late summer or autumn of 1901, that the Tiflis committee was taken over by the more radical elements in *mesame-dasi* supported by the Russian exiles who advocated joining the Russian Social Democratic Workers' Party.[73] This was also the moment when Soso Dzhugashvili was co-opted to the committee, most likely in order to strengthen the radical group. For the first time, police reports mention the name Dzhugashvili as an agitator but note that 'he conducts himself in a highly cautious manner.'[74] Caution was still his watchword when, at the end of 1901, he arrived in Batumi on a mission from the reconstituted Tiflis committee.

For Stalin, Batumi was the first opportunity to step out of the shadows of better known and more active comrades and define himself more clearly against his enemies in the social democratic movement. Similar to Tiflis in many ways, Batumi bore even more clearly the stamp of a frontier town. An ancient urban site, it only passed under Russian sovereignty in 1878. Located twelve miles from the Turkish border but linked

Ketskhoveli's photograph hung on the wall of Stalin's former room in the Tiflis seminary along with two other old comrades, Peti Kapanadze and Misho Davitashvili. RGASPI f. 71, op. 10, d. 272, l. 67.

[71] Small gatherings in the previous two years were organised by the workers themselves. Makharadze, *Ocherki*, pp. 72–3. Stalin may have spoken but this is mentioned only by later memoir-apologists. Kaminskii and Vereschchagin, 'Detstvo i iunost'', p. 93.

[72] The gendarmes described Kalinin as one of the 'outstanding propagandists of anti-governmental ideas' who had a wide circle of acquaintances among like-minded thinkers and as an important revolutionary who maintained relations 'with the leading represent-atives of the revolutionary party in many cities of Russia' G. Glebov, 'M. I. Kalinin v 1900–1901 v Tiflise', *Zariia Vostoka*, 25 February 1940, p. 3. No such 'encomiums' for Stalin!

[73] Zhordaniia, *Moia zhizn'*, pp. 33–4.

[74] Arkomed, *Rabochee dvizhenie*, pp. 39–40, 47–51; Galoian, *Rabochee dvizhenie*, pp. 10–2; Glebov, 'M. I. Kalinin', p. 3

to Tiflis by rail, its population was ethnically highly mixed, as was the small working class concentrated in the late booming oil industry. The surrounding countryside was inhabited mainly by Georgians (Gurievtsy), Lazovs, and Kurds.

When Dzhugashvili arrived there was no social democratic organization in Batumi. But there was an active Sunday school propaganda programme run by two early adherents to *mesame-dasi*, Nikolai 'Karlo' Chkheidze and Isidor Ramishvili, both close associates of Zhordania and future Georgian Menshevik leaders. There were also small illegal circles of workers where social democratic propaganda circulated.[75]

At this point in Stalin's career all the sources, whether friendly or hostile, contemporary or retrospective, are marred by a lack of detail when they do not openly contradict one another. Those that are Bolshevik, or prefigure that orientation, portray Stalin as the driving force behind the increase of strike activity in Batumi in 1902. The local Mensheviks insisted that the workers' action was spontaneous, though directed toward political goals by social democratic propagandists who were on the ground before Stalin's arrival. The discrepancy, then, is not just over the role of one individual but reflects the deeper conflict over the importance of spontaneity versus consciousness within social democracy that defined the split between Bolshevism and Menshevism.[76]

In February 1902, a series of strikes in Batumi broke out in the big plants of Mantashev, Rothschild, and others. Arrests, dismissals, and counter-demonstrations followed, culminating on 9 March when police and soldiers fired upon a crowd of demonstrating workers killing more than a dozen and wounding many more. There is no dispute about these facts. Menshevik sources ignore the coincidence of Stalin's arrival and the intensification of strike activity, and emphasise another coincidence, i.e. the almost simultaneous outbreak of strikes in Baku and Batumi due to fundamental socio-economic causes. They also make clear, without mentioning Stalin, that the workers' movement in Batumi continued to expand in size and militancy after his arrest and exile.[77] Even more important to their argument, they relate how workers dismissed from their jobs flooded into the countryside where the future Georgian

---

[75] As early as 1897, the social democratic circles in Batumi had organised a partial translation of the *Communist Manifesto* into Georgian and hectographed 100 copies. Gorgiladze, 'Rasprostranenie marksizma', in *Ocherki istorii Gruzii*, V, p. 472.

[76] For the background to this ideological split see Leopold Haimson, *The Russian Marxists and the Origins of Bolshevism* (Cambridge, Mass.: Harvard University Press, 1955).

[77] Arkomed, *Rabochee dvizhenie*, pp. 112–13; Uratadze, *Vospominaniia*, p. 20.

Mensheviks organised them to conduct revolutionary activity among the peasants in Kutaisi province.[78]

Bolshevik accounts, written mainly after Stalin's rise to power, present him as the instigator and leader of the strike movement in the face of opposition from his future Georgian Menshevik rivals, Chkheidze and Ramishvili. Stalin's tactic was to ridicule them as legal Marxists.[79] The report of the Batumi Committee of the RSDWP to the second congress appears to steer a middle course, reflecting the views of the rapporteur, A. G. Zurabov, who shifted allegiance from Bolshevism to Menshevism and back to Bolshevism in the course of his turbulent career. In his analysis, the Sunday school movement had been a legal method in 1900–1 that had prepared the workers for illegal activity leading to the formation of social democratic circles in 1901. At that point 'one propagandist, a social-democrat, taking advantage of the advanced workers who had been in Tiflis founded an advanced circle which served as fermentation for the spread of social-democratic ideas among the workers.'[80] Was this Stalin? It would seem so.

Sifting through these sources a faint but discernible picture of Stalin's activity begins to emerge. It is clear that from the moment of his arrival Stalin attempted to distance himself from his putative rivals in the Sunday school movement by creating an alternative base of operations. He was not suited by education or temperament to lecture workers on 'natural science, sociology and culture'. In other words, he took his first bold step to distance himself, a man of the people (*praktik*) from intellectuals (*teoretiki*). In Tiflis his most effective work had been as a propagandist, speaking simply and directly to small circles of workers. In Batumi Stalin acted out the role of a conspiratorial revolutionary complete with disguises, clandestine meetings, and evasive action that was more characteristic of a populist than a social democrat.[81] He worked closely with the politically experienced workers streaming into Batumi from Tiflis. He printed his proclamations on a primitive hectograph. His hope of establishing a more sophisticated printing press sent him back to Tiflis for a meeting that once again revealed much about his methods and intentions. In Tiflis he made contact with friends in the apartment of S. A. Ter-Petrosian (Kamo). According to Stalin's old friend G. Elisabedashvili, 'Kamo was a specialist in such things ... Kamo was accustomed to collect parts of a printing press as only he could.'[82] The incident was significant because of the subsequent

[78] Uratadze, *Vospominaniia*, pp. 32–56.
[79] RGASPI f. 71, op. 10, d. 73, ll. 327–38. Ramishvili countered: 'We have not sanctioned his activities and he conducts these in a self-willed way [*samovol'no*].' *Ibid.*, l. 351.
[80] *Vtoroi s"ezd*, p. 681   [81] RGASPI f. 71, op. 10, d. 273, ll. 336–7.
[82] *Ibid.*, ll. 369–70.

scandal within the social democratic party over Stalin's alleged relations with Kamo as the notorious armed bank robber whose daring raids in Tiflis in 1907 helped to fill the coffers of the Bolshevik Party. Stalin's long relationship with Kamo, who had also been born in Gori, exemplified his attitude toward social banditry.[83]

What remains unclear is whether Stalin ever became a member of the Batumi Committee of the RSDWP. It appears unlikely. The Bolshevik sources make an implicit claim, but even Beria was reluctant to confirm this. His version asserts that on 31 December 1901 at a conference (*konferentsiia*) held in the room Stalin was renting from a peasant-worker, representatives of circles in the big factories 'founded the Batumi social-democratic organisation'. The conference, according to Beria was the guiding party group headed by Stalin that 'to all intents and purposes [*fakticheskii*] played the role of the Batumi Committee of the RSDWP of the Leninist-*Iskra* direction.' In April 1902 Stalin's arrest took place at a 'meeting of the Batumi ruling party group'.[84] A later memoir recalled that just before the police broke in, 'from the room where Soso was came the sounds of conversation in Georgian, Armenian, and Turkish languages. He was having talks with Armenian workers who had resettled from Turkey.'[85] No more symbolic representation, whether true or not, could be imagined of Stalin's revolutionary activity in a multicultural, frontier region. But this was his swan song in the city. When the Batumi Committee was formed that same year (the date is uncertain), its president was Nikolai Chkheidze, under whose leadership Stalin would no doubt have refused to serve.[86] After Stalin's arrest, imprisonment, and exile the Batumi committee remained a stronghold of the Georgian Mensheviks. Stalin returned to the city only once, briefly. Henceforth his main field of action in the South Caucasus would be Baku. His activities there open a new page in his revolutionary career.[87]

Stalin's exile at age twenty-two removed him for the first time from the frontier society of the South Caucasus. His formative years shaped his revolutionary career, and they provided the materials from which he constructed his revolutionary persona. He attempted to obliterate the

[83] On Stalin's subsequent connection with the expropriators including Kamo see Trotsky, *Stalin*, pp. 100–10 and Kun, *Stalin*, pp. 68–83.

[84] L. P. Beria, *K voprosu ob istorii bol'shevistskikh organizatsii v Zakavkaz'e. Doklad na sobranii tblisskogo partaktiva 21–22 iiulia 1935 g.* (1936) 9th edn. (Moscow: Ogiz, 1952), p. 30. Beria's choice of words suggests that Stalin's organisation was not the same as the Batumi Committee.

[85] RGASPI f. 71, op. 10, d. 73, l. 388.   [86] Uratadze, *Vospominaniia*, pp. 40, 48–51.

[87] Ronald Grigor Suny, 'A Journeyman for the Revolution: Stalin and the Labor Movement in Baku, June 1907–May 1908', *Soviet Studies* 3 (1971), 373–94.

difference between the two by adjusting the elements of reality to accommodate his own purposes. It is no easy matter to disentangle them one from one another in order to distinguish between what Erving Goffman has called 'untransformed reality' and the process by which Stalin sought to transform it.[88] He was raised in a society where rebellion was deeply rooted in folklore and popular rituals. Resistance to Russian rule and the reaction against the rapid development of capitalism in the countryside and cities expressed itself in peasant disorders, strikes, and intellectual protests that rapidly infiltrated schools and seminaries. Unlike most of the future leaders of Menshevism, Stalin did not come from the impoverished nobility of predominantly Georgian countryside in the western part of the country. He never became a Georgian nationalist, although he was Georgian by birth, language, and the formative culture of his childhood. For Stalin, the main channel of communication with the outside world was to the north with Russia, but this was through books and later personal contacts with exiles rather than direct experience. Russia was a source of ideas and power. But complete assimilation was just as impossible for him as complete identification with Georgian nationalism. Young Soso was embedded in a dominantly masculine culture that worshipped the warrior image. In its degenerate form, banditry, it still existed in the foothills of the Caucasus a short distance from his home. In the Georgian literature of the nineteenth century the romantic-heroic male figure acquired a patina of social justice, of revenge of the poor against the rich. Perhaps it was the discrepancy between his romantic-heroic ideals and his own cautious, if dangerous behaviour that impelled him to create a pantheon of dead hero-comrades of his youth – as if by posthumous association with them he could share their lustre – and to force a tendentious re-writing of his personal biography in order to place himself at the forefront if not at the head of the workers' movement in the south Caucasus.

Judging by what he read as a youth and what he came to demand from Soviet culture as the *vozhd'*, he remained captivated by heroic, romantic ideals of Georgian, Western, and Russian literature with which he identified himself. Standing on the frontiers of three cultures, he was free to assume the mask of each when it suited him. Are not the composite elements of socialist realism to be found in the fusion of the folkloristic-romantic tradition with the utopian dreams of a youthful revolutionary?

For Stalin, Marxism came down the same road as Russian literature but it was preceded by populism with its secret rendezvous, escape routes,

---

[88] Erving Goffman, *Frame Analysis: An Essay on the Organization of Experience* (Boston: Northeastern University Press, 1986).

concealment, and recourse to individual terror. Its appeal, however brief, was intense and left its mark in Stalin's conspiratorial mentality, his concept of the hero (already nourished by literature), his acceptance of violence and his readiness to accept Lenin's formula of the alliance between the working class and the poor peasantry. From the outset of his conspiratorial activities, Stalin found his metier in working with small numbers of workers, impressing them with his 'simple and direct' speech, avoiding established committees and creating his own groups, as in Batumi, a trait that remained central to his tactical maneuvering throughout his life. This, too, was a means of avoiding and undermining the authority of his rivals, the future Mensheviks, within Georgian social democracy. When it came to the split in Russian social democracy he allied himself to the Bolsheviks, not only because they represented the centralisers and a closer identification with Russians, but also because he could present himself as a representative of an all-Russian majority rather than being stigmatised as deviating from a regional Georgian majority.

There was always a strong element of opportunism in Stalin's self-presentation. His Georgian, proletarian, and Russian identities remained separate rather than integrated. Stalin's assemblage of a revolutionary persona that drew upon this three-part repertoire enabled him to find and enlarge a space within Bolshevism that assumed greater importance as the revolutionary events of 1905, 1917, and the Civil War unfolded. The Party was neither monolithic nor stable, and prone to shifting alliances and alignments. The Russian Empire was passing through tumultuous, violent, and ultimately fateful final years. The loose association of his multiple identities enabled him to shift opportunistically from one to the other in order to fit the changing circumstances both within the Party and in the country at large and make any one of them central to his aims. Therein lay his strength as a politician and statesman.

3 Stalin as Commissar for Nationality Affairs, 1918–1922

Jeremy Smith

Although Stalin had been an important member of the Bolshevik Party prior to 1917, nothing in his experience could have prepared him for the tasks thrust on him after the October Revolution. As a leading commissar in the Red Army, as a commissar, and as a Party secretary and eventually General Secretary, he had political and organisational responsibility for a large number of people. He had to learn not only how to exercise the authority that had been granted to him, but also how to deal with regular contact with a wide variety of people, how to juggle their demands, and how to defend himself politically in verbal conflict with subordinates and equals alike. His experience as Commissar of Nationality Affairs, a position he held from 1918 through to the winding-up of the position with the creation of the USSR at the end of 1923, provided Stalin with the opportunity to exercise leadership at both the theoretical and practical level. It can, therefore, be expected to have had a major influence on his later leadership both in the policies he pursued and in the ways in which he exercised power.

Nevertheless, Stalin's role as Commissar has often been overlooked in accounts of his early Soviet career. At first sight, there are good reasons for this neglect. First, the Commissariat for Nationality Affairs (Narkomnats), although theoretically responsible in many ways for some 22 per cent of the population of the RSFSR, was, and is, viewed as a minor commissariat dealing with a so-called 'soft' policy area which had little weight against the far more powerful institutions dealing with the economy, the army, and internal security, not to mention the Russian Communist Party (RKP(b)). The position's significance was greatly diminished by the fact that its portfolio did not cover the major non-Russian areas of Ukraine, Belorussia, and Transcaucasia, which were formally independent Soviet republics whose relations with the RSFSR were conducted, at the state level, through the Council of Peoples' Commissars (Sovnarkom) and the Commissariat for Foreign Affairs (NKID), but whose leaders were in practice subordinated to the authority of the Central Committee of the RKP(b). Compared with Stalin's other positions as a Politburo and Secretariat member, head of the Workers and Peasants' Inspectorate (Rabkrin), and a senior Commissar in the Red Army, and especially following his appointment as General Secretary of the RKP(b) in 1922, the post of Commissar held relatively less importance to him personally and to his leading colleagues. Secondly, Stalin played little direct role in the day-to-day affairs of Narkomnats for much of the time, rarely attending meetings of its Collegium and in effect leaving it in the hands of a series of deputies, most important among them Stanislav Pestkovskii and then Semen Dimanshtein. His role on the southern front in the Civil War and his other duties left him little time for his formal role in the Soviet government. Thirdly, Stalin's authority as an expert on nationality affairs was always going to be dwarfed by that of Lenin, author of 'The Right of Nations to Self-Determination' and chief rapporteur on nationality affairs at RKP(b) and Comintern conferences and congresses until his incapacitation towards the end of 1922. Consequently, most historians have viewed Stalin's role as Commissar from 1918–22 as either that of obedient servant to the master, Lenin, or as Lenin's secretive opponent on the national question who finally came out of the woodwork in the autumn of 1922.

However, there is every reason to suppose that Stalin's experience as Commissar profoundly affected his later attitude to non-Russian nationalities, and there are a number of reasons for reassessing Stalin's time in charge of Nationality Affairs.[1] Archival sources have highlighted the importance of Stalin's role in nationality affairs, not so much directly through Narkomnats, as through the Politburo and the Central Committee of the RKP(b). These sources show that, while Stalin may not have been a regular participant in the discussions of the Narkomnats Collegium, he did appear and intervene over key episodes, and was certainly in touch with its work. Moreover, his position as Commissar threw him into the spotlight on ceremonial occasions, be it the formation of an autonomous republic or the marking of an anniversary. On such occasions his published speeches and articles contained policy-making elements, which ultimately may have had more significance than Lenin's major speeches to Party and Comintern congresses. At these events

---

[1] Recent works which pay more attention to Stalin's position as Commissar for Nationality Affairs include Erik van Ree, 'Stalin and the National Question', *Revolutionary Russia* 2 (1994), 214–38; Terry Martin, *The Affirmative Action Empire: Nations and Nationalism in the Soviet Union, 1923–1939* (Ithaca: Cornell University Press, 2001); Jeremy Smith, *The Bolsheviks and the National Question, 1917–1923* (Basingstoke: Macmillan, 1999).

Lenin engaged in polemical debate on the principle of national self-determination rather than the concrete day-to-day tasks of introducing socialism to the non-Russians. Stalin's public utterances contained details and nuances that distanced him to some extent from Lenin, and it was these differences that came to the surface in disputes between the two over the Comintern, the creation of the USSR, and Georgia. The whole question of Stalin's relations with Lenin, and the role of nationality policy in them, remains largely unresolved.[2]

Finally, Stalin's tendency to delegate authority led to his placing a great deal of trust and responsibility in the hands of so-called 'national communists'. The revelation in the spring/summer of 1923 of conspiratorial activity on the part of one of his chief protégés, Mirsaid Sultangaliev, arguably presented a more severe challenge to Stalin's standing than Lenin's 'Notes on the National Question' and Last Testament of the previous winter, and must have permanently fuelled Stalin's suspicion of this group of people. The Sultangaliev affair followed close on the decision to form the USSR and consequently to abolish Narkomnats, at a time when there is some evidence to suggest that Stalin had been nurturing his Commissariat as a potentially influential power-base. These themes will be discussed in the remainder of this chapter.

As Commissar, Stalin was responsible on a number of formal occasions for delivering speeches or publishing articles on the national question. The impact of these public statements should not be underestimated. Throughout the early Soviet period, the pages of *Pravda* were scoured by Party officials at all levels for policy 'signals' which were to be followed in the regions and which may have carried more weight than official government decrees and even Politburo resolutions. Stalin's speeches and articles at this time were not noted for either the flamboyant rhetoric of which Lenin and Trotsky were capable of, or for the dramatic announcement of major new policy directions. But two more or less constant themes are worth drawing attention to. First, Stalin explicitly rejected the relevance of the principle of the Right of Nations to Self-Determination. As early as the first anniversary of the 1917 Bolshevik Revolution he proclaimed that

---

[2] An early, significant work on this question, Moshe Lewin, *Lenin's Last Struggle* (London: Pluto Press, 1975), undoubtedly exaggerated the extent of the differences between Lenin and Stalin, but nevertheless highlighted some important distinctions. Robert Service has uncovered major disputes between the two, over the conduct of the Civil War and the Polish Campaign in particular, but denies that there were any significant disagreements in principle over nationality policy. Robert Service, *Lenin: a Political Life, Vol. 3 – The Iron Ring* (London: Macmillan, 1995), p. 192. Terry Martin has taken this even further in arguing that the differences between the two were only differences of emphasis. Martin, *The Affirmative Action Empire*, p. 8.

the slogan was outmoded and 'should be subordinated to the principles of socialism'.[3] He went further in October 1920: 'the demand for the secession of the border regions from Russia ... must be rejected not only because it runs counter to the very formulation of the question of establishing a union between the centre and the border regions, but primarily because it runs fundamentally counter to the interests of the mass of the people in both the centre and border regions'.[4] While Stalin sidelined himself from the major Party debates on self-determination where Lenin locked horns with Piatakov and Bukharin, Stalin's comments could only have given encouragement to the latter in particular. It could even be surmised that Stalin's sentiments were heavily influenced by Bukharin. Although following the recognition of Finland's independence the principle of self-determination became in practical terms irrelevant, this did not render these debates meaningless. As E. H. Carr noted in the 1950s, 'from the moment of the triumph of the revolution the essence of the Bolshevik doctrine of national self-determination passed over almost insensibly from the concept of liberty to the concept of equality, which alone seemed to offer a radical solution'.[5] Debates about the largely abstract right of self-determination after 1917 were reflections of real arguments on the ground about the granting of preferential treatment to non-Russians, and also aimed at attracting the anti-colonial movements across the world. Inside the RSFSR, appeals to 'the spirit of self-determination' were frequently resorted to by non-Russian supporters of national rights against 'Great Russian' encroachments. Stalin's policies in this period consistently favoured the former against the latter, but whether he was aware of it or not, his public disowning of self-determination did much to encourage the 'National Left'.[6]

Secondly, a recurring theme in Stalin's works on the non-Russians is that of backwardness. A couple of many examples serve to illustrate the point. In an article published in *Pravda* on 9 April 1918, he wrote: 'Soviet power has not yet succeeded in becoming a people's power to quite the same extent in the border regions inhabited by culturally backward elements';[7] and in November 1920, in a speech declaring autonomy for Dagestan: 'The Soviet government has no other object than to raise Dagestan to a higher cultural level'.[8] Stalin's solution to the problem of backwardness was a range of policies which became collectively known as *korenizatsiia* (indigenisation): 'It is necessary to raise the cultural level of

[3] I. V. Stalin, *Sochineniia*, 13 vols. (Moscow: Gospolitizdat, 1946–52), IV, p. 158.
[4] *Ibid.*, p. 352.
[5] E. H. Carr, *The Bolshevik Revolution, 1917–1923* (London: Macmillan, 1950), p. 364.
[6] See below p. 58   [7] Stalin, *Sochineniia*, IV, p. 75.   [8] *Ibid.*, p. 396.

the labouring masses and to educate them in a socialist way, to promote a literature in the local languages, to appoint local people who are most closely connected with the proletariat to the Soviet organisations and draw them into the work of administering the territory.'[9] Backwardness was embedded in the policy of the RKP(b) in a resolution passed at its Tenth Congress in March 1921,[10] and was referred to on a number of occasions in Stalin's speech to the Congress.[11] References to backwardness necessarily imply the superiority of the Russian people, or at least their proletariat. Although Stalin was usually at pains to stress the equality and unity of peoples – 'The October Revolution only strengthened the alliance between the workers and peasants of the border regions and the workers and peasants of Russia'[12] – his belief in Russian superiority is never far from the surface. If we are to look for consistency in Stalin's thought, we can see here the roots of the 'rehabilitation of the Russians' and their elevation to the level of a leading role in the 1930s.[13]

A third important aspect of Stalin's thinking is revealed in a more recently published document. In a letter to Lenin in September 1922 Stalin claimed that 'for four years of civil war . . . in view of foreign intervention we were obliged to demonstrate Moscow's liberalism on the national question.'[14] Put differently, the national policies of the Civil War were temporary and liberal, implying that they could now be replaced with more genuinely socialist principles. Such a view was never advanced publicly by Stalin, although it was certainly shared by a number of leading Bolsheviks and possibly by a majority of the rank and file.

It is tempting to deduce a logical train of thought from these positions which can explain later developments: the main problem with Russia's minorities was one of backwardness which meant, above all, low levels of literacy and small numbers of proletarians. In such circumstances, it was impossible for these peoples to embrace socialism in the same way as Russian workers and peasants could. The policies of *korenizatsiia* therefore served the dual purpose of presenting socialism to the non-Russians in a form that would be more attractive to them in the short term on the one hand, and accelerating their level of cultural, political, and economic

---

[9] 'Message to the Soviets and Party organisations of Turkestan', 12 February 1919. *Ibid.*, p. 288.

[10] *Desiatyi s"ezd RKP(b), mart 1921 goda. Stenograficheskii otchet* (Moscow: IMEL, 1963), p. 252.

[11] Stalin, *Sochineniia*, V, pp. 39, 44.

[12] 'The October Revolution and the National Question', 17 November 1918. Stalin, *Sochineniia*, IV, p. 164.

[13] Martin, *The Affirmative Action Empire*, pp. 394–431.

[14] Rossiiskii gosudarstvennyi arkhiv sotsial'no-politicheskoi istorii (henceforth RGASPI) f. 5, op. 2, d. 28, ll. 23–4. Also published in *Izvestiia TsK KPSS* 9 (1989), 199.

development on the other. In this case, once a certain level of advancement had been achieved and forced industrialisation had taken over as the principal vehicle of accelerated development, it would be possible to revert to a more genuinely internationalist position and restore the Russians to their rightful place in the overall scheme. Such a schema would fit in with the reversal of the 'greatest danger principle' which Martin traces to November 1933, and which was accompanied by the slackening or partial reversal of affirmative action policies.[15] Attractive though such a line of reasoning may be, Terry Martin does not make this claim and there seems to be no direct evidence to support it in Martin's exhaustive work or elsewhere.[16] A multitude of other considerations lay behind the later development of national policies. But Stalin returned again and again to the theme of backwardness in general, most notoriously in a 1931 speech:

The Mongol Khans beat us. The Turkish Beks beat us. The Swedish Barons beat us. The Polish-Lithuanian landowners beat us. The Anglo-French capitalists beat us. The Japanese lords beat us. They all beat us – for our backwardness ... We are fifty or a hundred years behind the advanced countries. We must make good this distance in ten years. Either we do it, or we shall go under.[17]

By this time, Stalin had turned his attention from the backwardness of non-Russians *vis-à-vis* Russians to that of the Soviet Union *vis-à-vis* the industrialised West. This broader concern provides one of the explanations for the simultaneous tendency to give the Russian people a higher priority than had been the case before, at the expense of national minorities.

Furthermore, it is not clear whether Stalin was leading or being led in placing the emphasis in this manner. The obsession with backwardness was shared by numerous contributors to *Zhizn' natsional'nostei*, many of whom were senior officials in Narkomnats, while it has already been noted that Stalin's attitude to self-determination may have derived from (or, alternatively, encouraged) Bukharin. The temporary, transitional nature of nationality policy was also a widely shared idea among leading Bolsheviks and even national communists. Either way, these examples serve to illustrate two points of historiographical interest. First, they disprove the claim originated by Trotsky and backed up by historians of

---

[15] Martin, *The Affirmative Action Empire*, pp. 356–62.
[16] Although Yuri Slezkine comes close to such an interpretation in 'The Soviet Union as a Communal Apartment, or how a Socialist State promoted Ethnic Particularism', in Sheila Fitzpatrick (ed.), *Stalinism: New Directions* (London: Routledge, 2000), pp. 326–32.
[17] Stalin, *Sochineniia*, XIII, pp. 38–9.

all shades that Stalin never really engaged in nationalities questions before 1922, that 'in no sense was Stalin an independent figure in the development of Bolshevik national policy'.[18] Second, they show that Stalin's thinking on the national question was in crucial respects opposed to Lenin's. It is to this question that we should now turn.

The relationship between Lenin and Stalin over the national question was an odd one. Stalin had initially been promoted in the Bolshevik Party as a nationalities expert, largely at Lenin's behest. But this was also an area of Lenin's particular expertise, one which had probably engaged him in his early years.[19] It was to Lenin that the Party looked for guidance on this question, although he could rarely claim to have the support of a majority of members. The division between Stalin's role as Commissar and Lenin's role as theoretician-in-chief has contributed to the widespread characterisation of Stalin as an administrator who did not have two ideas to rub together. But it is clear that, even at an early stage, Stalin was responsible for significant policy developments and even contributions to theory. Yet he was also conscious of Lenin's authority in this matter, and left the stage to him in the key theoretical debates over self-determination. Where Stalin disagreed with Lenin, as in 1920 and 1922, his opposition was neither public nor lasting. But the unequal division of authority was always likely to lead to tension, and it is not surprising that the eventual deterioration of relations between the two had much to do with each man's perception of the other's failings on the nationality question.

The first clear disagreement between Lenin and Stalin on the national question concerned Lenin's theses to the Second Congress of the Comintern in June 1920. In these theses Lenin appeared (although he was not explicit) to be suggesting that the type of federal relationship that existed between the Soviet republics could be extended to other European countries following revolutions there.[20] Stalin's little-known reply is published in an end-note to the 1931 third Russian edition of Lenin's Works:

I am referring to the absence in your theses of any mention of confederation as one of the transitional forms of drawing together the workers of different nations. For the nations which came into the composition of old Russia, we can and ought to consider our (Soviet) type of federation as an appropriate path to international

---

[18] David Crouch, 'The Seeds of National Liberation', *International Socialism Journal* 94 (2002). Available at http://pubs.socialistreviewindex.org.uk/isj94/crouch.htm, p. 13.

[19] Isabelle Kreindler, 'A Neglected Source of Lenin's Nationality Policy', *Slavic Review* 1 (1977), 86–100.

[20] I. V. Lenin, *Polnoe sobranie sochinenii*, 5th edn. (Moscow: Gospolitizdat, 1958–65), [hereafter *PSS*] XLI, p. 164.

unity. The reasons are clear: these nationalities either have not enjoyed statehood previously, or lost it a long time ago, in view of which the Soviet (centralised) type of federation applies to them without particular friction.

It is impossible to say the same about those nationalities which did not come into the composition of old Russia, which have existed as independent formations, which developed their own statehood and which, if they become Soviet, will need by the force of things to stand in some sort or another of state relationship (bond) to Soviet Russia. For example, a future Soviet Germany, Poland, Hungary, Finland. These peoples, when they have their own statehood, their own armed forces, their own finances, on becoming Soviet, would hardly agree to enter straight into a federative bond with Soviet Russia on the Bashkir or Ukrainian model (in your theses you make a distinction between the Bashkir and Ukrainian model of federative bond, but in actual fact there is no difference, or it is so small as to be negligible): for they would look at a federation on the Soviet model as a form of diminishing their state independence, as an assault on their independence.

I have no doubt, that for those nationalities the most appropriate form of drawing together would be a confederation (a union of independent states). Here I am not even talking about other nationalities, like Persia and Turkey, in relation to whom the Soviet type of federation and federation in general would be even more inappropriate.

Starting from these considerations, I think that the given point of your theses on the transitional forms of bringing together the workers of different nations needs to include (along with federation) confederation. Such an amendment would provide your theses with more elasticity, and would enrich them with one more transitional form of drawing together the workers of different nations and would ease the state drawing together of those nationalities which were not previously part of Russia with Soviet Russia.[21]

Lenin's reply to Stalin on this point is lost, but according to Stalin three years later: 'comrade Lenin sent out a long letter – that is chauvinism, nationalism, we need a centralised world economy, run from a single organ'.[22] Stalin's insistence that 'in actual fact there is no difference' between the relationship enjoyed by Ukraine and Bashkiriia with the RSFSR has been noted by many historians (following the cue of the editors of later editions of Lenin's works, which quote only this line). What is equally interesting is that Stalin draws a clear distinction between nationalities which were part of 'old Russia' and those which were not, excluding Finland and Poland on the grounds that they had previously enjoyed more or less independent statehood. Implicit here is a clear downgrading of the status of those nationalities which had previously constituted part of the Russian Empire on the basis that they had no previous experience of statehood. Consequently, they would be in a

---

[21] I. V. Lenin, *Sochineniia*, 3rd edn. (Moscow: IMEL, 1931), XXV, p. 624.
[22] *Izvestiia TsK KPSS* 4 (1991), 171.

position of greater dependence on, not to say subordination to, Soviet Russia. The letter does make a number of valid points – Stalin's proposal seems more realistic compared to Lenin's utopian project for a Europe-wide federation even in the event of successful revolutions. We could, moreover, point to his consistency as this attitude was reflected in the policy he applied in Europe after 1945. But his disdainful attitude to the peoples of the Russian Empire were perhaps a sign of things to come, and would never have been countenanced by Lenin.

While the 1920 disagreement did not, as far as one can tell, go beyond a single private exchange of letters, the same could not be said for the dispute between Lenin and Stalin in 1922. The difference this time was that whereas the Comintern discussion concerned a future socialist Europe which could only be aspired to, the later dispute was central to the actual constitutional development of the USSR. In the first place, this dispute appeared to echo that of 1920. Stalin wanted to incorporate the Soviet Republics of Ukraine, Belorussia, Georgia, Azerbaidzhan, and Armenia directly into the RSFSR, while Lenin wanted to create a Union of Soviet Republics of Europe and Asia.[23] The resulting com-promise appeared to satisfy both Lenin's desire for a federation and Stalin's pragmatism in that Lenin's grand aspirational title for the federation was changed to 'Union of Soviet Socialist Republics'. While this compromise was quickly agreed, Stalin's resistance on a subordinate point shows that while he was ready to accept the wording of federalism he was not ready to embrace its practical implications. Lenin wanted to create an All-Union Central Executive Committee (VTsIK), while Stalin wanted its functions simply to be taken up by the TsIK of the RSFSR. What this indicated, again, was Stalin's readi-ness to subordinate the major non-Russian nationalities to an explicitly Russian centre, a position that was directly at odds with Lenin's policy of avoiding any suggestion that the Soviet state could be associated with the type of policies towards nationalities displayed by the former tsarist empire, and his insistence on the priority of making the Soviet Union a shining example to the rest of the world.

That Lenin was aware of these differences is clear from his 'Notes on the Question of Nationalities or "Autonomisation"' written in the wake of the political crisis in Georgia at the end of 1922. Here, he assigned Stalin political responsibility for the crisis and advised that 'Stalin's haste and his infatuation with pure administration, together with his spite against the notorious "nationalist-socialism", played a fatal role here'.[24] The reference

---

[23] Lenin, *PSS*, XLV, p. 211.   [24] Lenin, *PSS*, XLV, pp. 356–62.

to Stalin is significant given that Stalin had little direct link with the crisis other than his relationship with Ordzhonikidze (which may not have been as close as has often been supposed).[25] Lenin's suspicion of Stalin is highlighted by a supplementary question he sent to the group of his secretaries carrying out their own investigation of the Georgian crisis in February 1923: 'Did Stalin know (of the incident)? Why didn't he do something about it?'[26] In spite of this direct question, the secretaries had nothing to say about Stalin in their final report, either because there was nothing to implicate him, or because they themselves were too close to him.[27] Lenin's attitude to Stalin at this time was particularly strained by his fears over Stalin's power as General Secretary and by his rude behaviour towards his wife, but it is nevertheless noteworthy that he accused him of spite towards 'nationalist-socialism'. This 'spite' rarely showed itself on the surface, indeed we are about to see how Stalin may have over-indulged nationalist-socialism (or national communism as it is more commonly referred to) on occasion. But Lenin knew Stalin well, and his comments fit with the general picture of low regard for national minorities which is emerging.

Terry Martin notes that a different emphasis regarding the relative dangers of Russian nationalism and non-Russian nationalism was what divided Lenin from Stalin.[28] But this difference in emphasis becomes more significant if what lies behind it is the notion that the inferiority of other nationalities should influence policy. Lenin also acknowledged the superiority of Russian culture in his earlier correspondence with Stepan Shaumian, but drew the firm conclusion that Russian nationalism should in all cases be fought as the greater danger.

These observations also make more sense of Stalin's later policies towards nationalities in the 1930s, which appear to turn many of the governing principles of the 1920s upside-down. As already noted, the shift of attention to backwardness on an international scale meant a downgrading of the needs of non-Russians in favour of a more general drive to progress based on rapid industrialisation. Clearly, the population of the more industrialised and proletarian Russian regions of the country were to lead this drive, and Stalin's inclination to view other nations as inferior led easily to the new emphasis on promoting

[25] Oleg V. Khlevniuk, *In Stalin's Shadow: the Career of 'Sergo' Ordzhonikidze* (Armonk, N. Y.: M. E. Sharpe, 1995), pp. 17–20. For accounts of the 'Georgian Affair' see Lewin, *Lenin's Last Struggle*, and Jeremy Smith, 'The Georgian Affair of 1922 – Policy Failure, Personality Clash or Power Struggle?' *Europe-Asia Studies* 3 (1998), 519–44.

[26] Lewin, *Lenin's Last Struggle*, p. 96.

[27] RGASPI f. 5, op. 2, d. 32, ll. 69–73. For the relationships between Lenin's entourage and Stalin, see Service, *Lenin: a Political Life, Vol. 3*, pp. 290, 305.

[28] Martin, *The Affirmative Action Empire*, p. 8.

specifically Russian history and values.[29] But if all other nations were inferior, some were more inferior than others. Stalin seems to have been closely involved in various later exercises which, probably intentionally, ranked nationalities in a clear hierarchy – the drawing up of lists of national categories for censuses, the reorganisation of Union Republics, Autonomous Republics, and Autonomous Regions, and the opening and closing of nationality-based cultural institutions in Moscow and elsewhere. At its most dangerous, the policy branded some nationalities as so dangerous as to warrant political extermination: Chechens, Ingush, Balkars, Germans, Crimean Tatars, Karachai, Kalmyks, and Meshketian Turks – who were deported wholesale during the Second World War – and Jews who suffered from mounting persecution in the postwar years. On the other hand, it is notable that Stalin's home nation, Georgia, was subjected to less interference than anywhere else, especially while it was in the trusted hands of Lavrentii Beria. At the same time, Stalin did not abandon many of the key tenets of nationality policy which he had been instrumental in developing in the 1920s, or indeed the principles of federalism which he had accepted only reluctantly. For those nationalities which survived bureaucratic or physical destruction, the development of national culture continued apace, the system of national schools remained untouched, and non-Russians continued to enjoy promotion both within the republics and to the higher levels of the Party/state apparatus.[30]

As well as providing the background to Stalin's contributions to the development of nationality policy, the position of Commissar provided him with early experience of institutional problems and an opportunity for bureaucratic empire-building. Stalin appears to have set about the tasks of his new post with some relish, only to be shortly distracted by the demands of the Civil War. In 1918, he attended and presided over five or six of the first seven meetings of the Narkomnats Collegium, then failed to attend the remaining twenty-one of the year.[31] His only significant activity in this period was his approval of a list of Collegium members at a private meeting with his Narkomnats deputy, Pestkovskii.[32] In 1919 he

---

[29] David Brandenberger, 'Who Killed Pokrovskii? (the second time): The Prelude to the Denunciation of the Father of Soviet Marxist Historiography', *Revolutionary Russia* 1 (1998), 67–73.

[30] See Peter A. Blitstein, 'Nation-Building or Russification? Obligatory Russian Instruction in the Soviet Non-Russian School, 1938–1953', in Ronald Grigor Suny and Terry Martin (eds.), *A State of Nations: Empire and Nation-Making in the Age of Lenin and Stalin* (Oxford: Oxford University Press, 2001), pp. 253–74.

[31] Calculated from the minutes of the Narkomnats Collegium for 1918, Gosudarstvennyi arkhiv Rossiiskoi Federatsii (henceforth GARF) f. 1318, op. 1, d. 1.

[32] GARF f. 1318, op. 1, d. 1, l. 73.

does not appear to have attended once.[33] So impotent did Narkomnats feel at this time, that on 9 July the Collegium resolved to dissolve itself and did not meet again until 3 October (still with no Stalin).[34] In 1920, Stalin appeared once in forty-two meetings.[35] When he did chair the meeting, on 20 May, it was to oversee a reorganisation of the Commissariat and the creation of a five-man 'Small Collegium'.[36]

Stalin did attend the first two meetings of the full Collegium, and at least one later one, out of twenty-nine for 1921. But he seems to have been a regular participant in the fortnightly meetings of the Small Collegium.[37] For most of this period, however, he did not participate directly, although he was in regular contact with a succession of deputies, Pestkovskii and later Dimanshtein being the most important. He was consulted, or intervened, on a number of occasions, most notably in internal disputes which frequently pitted the Muslim Commissariat, headed by the Tatar Mirsaid Sultangaliev, against the rest of the Collegium.[38] He remained as the public face of Narkomnats, signing decrees and speaking on ceremonial occasions.

While Stalin's day-to-day involvement with Narkomnats may have been limited, he at least maintained enough contact to be aware of developments and to have the final say on any major issue. The most important policy development in 1918–22 in this sphere was the proliferation of autonomous republics and regions as part of the RSFSR. Stalin had advocated some form of territorial autonomy in his 1913 article 'Marxism and the National Question',[39] and the position was endorsed by Lenin and entered into official Bolshevik policy at their April 1917 conference.[40] It was subsequently included in both the Soviet government's 'Declaration of Rights' in November 1917[41] and the Soviet Constitution adopted in July 1918.[42] Although the first concrete proposal on national autonomy, for a Tatar–Bashkir Soviet Republic, originated from the Muslim Commissariat,[43] it is inconceivable that such a major policy development could have been initiated without at least Stalin's approval. The proposal itself was issued over the signatures of Stalin together with the Muslim leaders Vakhitov, Manatov, and Ibragimov. Stalin was also directly involved in at least the decisions behind the

---

[33] GARF f. 1318, op. 1, d. 1; d. 2.   [34] GARF f. 1318, op. 1, d. 2, l. 104.
[35] GARF f. 1318, op. 1, d. 4; d. 5.   [36] GARF f. 1318, op. 1, d. 4, l. 29.
[37] *Ibid.*, d. 5; d. 6; d. 7.   [38] E.g. GARF f. 1318, op. 1, d. 1, ll. 86, 94.
[39] Stalin, *Sochineniia*, II, p. 362.
[40] R. H. McNeal (ed.), *Resolutions of the CPSU*, (Toronto: University of Toronto Press, 1974), I, p. 226.
[41] *Velikii Oktiabr'* (Moscow: Nauka, 1987), p. 123.   [42] *Ibid.*, p. 138.
[43] *Zhizn' natsional'nostei*, 8 February 1920, p. 2.

formation of the Turkestan and Bashkir ASSRs, and the division of the Gori Republic into separate autonomous regions. Decisions concerning the implementation of autonomy were frequently referred to the Central Committee, or Politburo, of the RKP(b) for resolution, and in these deliberations it was invariably Stalin who acted as the main spokesman.[44] Frequently he appears to have acted in tandem with Lenin, as in the resolution of the conflict that affected the Bashkir Republic in 1919–20.[45] Stalin, and on occasion Lenin, were also known for throwing their weight behind a Narkomnats which frequently felt frustrated at being ignored by weightier commissariats and economic organs.[46]

There is also some evidence to suggest that Stalin was carefully and deliberately building up Narkomnats as a personal base for extending his own influence over the country in 1920 and especially 1921, which would tally with his more frequent attendance at Narkomnats meetings. Stephen Blank has suggested a number of strategies Stalin was pursuing towards this end: several reorganisations of Narkomnats, including the creation of the five-man Small Collegium, which aimed at concentrating authority inside the Commissariat itself; downgrading the status and functions of the sub-commissariats responsible for each nationality; increasing the authority of Narkomnats over the affairs of the autonomous republics; the proposed (though never fulfilled) creation of a series of Federal Committees, which would have allowed Narkomnats to bypass other central commissariats in the republics. The net result of all these moves, according to Blank, would have been a centralised commissariat tightly controlled by Stalin, which would have acted as a guiding organ over the republics rather than as their representative, and which would have had considerable authority over their internal affairs and been able to rival other commissariats.[47] In sum 'Stalin or other leaders could now deal directly with nationalities without encountering any intervening or mediating agencies, a lasting aim of Stalin's'.[48] While Blank's analysis owes much to an assumption of Stalin as a 'control freak', he does bring compelling evidence to bear, which is moreover supported by the archives, and it is consistent with Stalin's approach to institutions elsewhere.

[44] Smith, *The Bolsheviks and the National Question*, pp. 45–54.
[45] Daniel E. Schafer, 'Local Politics and the Birth of the Republic of Bashkortostan, 1919–1920', in Suny and Martin (eds.), *A State of Nations*, p. 181.
[46] Jeremy Smith, 'The Origins of Soviet National Autonomy', *Revolutionary Russia* 2 (1997), 75.
[47] Stephen Blank, *The Sorcerer as Apprentice: Stalin as Commissar of Nationalities, 1917–1924* (Westport, Conn.: Greenwood, 1994), pp. 68–81.
[48] *Ibid.*, p. 74.

An important consequence of Stalin's position as Commissar was that it brought him into regular contact with National Communists, far more so than any other Bolshevik leader. This resulted from the structure of inter-republican relations before the creation of the USSR. The leadership of Ukraine had direct access to the Party leadership in Moscow through their representatives in the Central Committee of the RKP(b) and Khristian Rakovsky's frequent attendance at Politburo meetings. Leaders in Georgia, Armenia, and Azerbaidzhan did not enjoy such direct access, operating instead through the Caucasian Bureau (*Kavbiuro*) of the RKP(b) whose head, Sergo Ordzhonikidze, was in turn a member of the Central Committee of the RKP(b) and an occasional participant in Politburo sessions. For the nationalities of the RSFSR and those without fixed territories, however, the only point of general contact with the centre was Narkomnats. And the only direct line between Narkomnats and the real centres of power was through Stalin. The importance of this channel was reinforced by Narkmonats' frequent frustrations in its attempts, without Stalin, to conduct business through official channels, i.e. through Sovnarkom or by direct contact with other commissariats and institutions.[49]

Narkomnats itself, while staffed at all levels almost exclusively by non-Russians, was divided on attitudes towards the national question between two tendencies, which since 1920 had become known as the National Rights and the National Lefts. Essentially, the Rights favoured an indulgent attitude to nationalist intelligentsias and a deepening of cultural and political *korenizatsiia*, while the Lefts favoured a more internationalist stance, although distancing themselves from the extreme positions of Piatakov and co. Not only was the Narkomnats collegium itself divided in this way, but many of the autonomous republics and regions were the scene of open conflict between representatives of the two tendencies. A result of this factionalism was that national leaders were even more inclined to seek direct contact with the one person who could intervene decisively on their behalf – Stalin. The arrangement also suited Stalin, who generally tended, as we have seen, to delegate most of his authority in nationality affairs but who needed a reliable mechanism for keeping on top of developments without depending exclusively on one or other channel of information. Hence contact with national leaders of all persuasions was regular and frequent in these years.[50]

---

[49] Smith, *The Bolsheviks and the National Question*, pp. 32–4.

[50] Admittedly this is a generalisation which is hard to substantiate precisely. It is a pity that in the early 1920s Stalin did not maintain an appointments diary of the type which is available for the 1930s and 1940s.

As already suggested, one result may have been that Stalin's own ideas were influenced by those of national communists. It is also true to say that Stalin retained to the end of his days an adherence to at least some aspects of *korenizatsiia*, and to the principle that a part of the visible leadership in the republics should be drawn from the local titular nationality. However, his faith in the reliability of such leaders in running the affairs of their republics must have been severely shaken by the general levels of factionalism which were evident in the republican leaderships, and by particular cases of severe disappointment and even personal betrayal. The most important such cases were those of the Bashkir leader, Zeki Validov, who was granted unprecedented support and privileges from the centre in return for bringing his troops over to the side of the Red Army in 1919, only to defect to the rebel Basmachi movement just over a year later;[51] and Mirsaid Sultangaliev who, after the death of Mulla Nur Vakhitov and the defection of Validov, was undoubtedly the most important Muslim national communist in the RSFSR. As such, he was also a leading spokesman of the National Rights and certainly the leading target of the Lefts.

In the spring/summer of 1923, documents were intercepted by the OGPU which indicated conclusively that Sultangaliev was engaged in conspiratorial activity among communists and non-communists both within the RSFSR and abroad, possibly with an aim of overthrowing Soviet power and realising the dream of a pan-Turanian republic. The development was particularly galling as Stalin had personally promoted and then stood by Sultangaliev in spite of his frequent clashes with other Narkomnats Collegium members and his known advocacy of an unorthodox interpretation of the legacy of colonialism leading to the existence of 'proletarian nations' in the East. The revelations of the OGPU investigation into Sultangaliev, which were disclosed at a special meeting of leading party activists from the republics in June 1923, turned the Stalin-Sultangaliev relationship from an embarrassment to a potential political disaster for Iosif. Apparently, earlier in the year, when the first pieces of evidence of Sultangaliev's conspiratorial activity emerged, Stalin warned him in writing to watch his back but prevented further action against him.[52] It was only with the discovery of subsequent letters that Sultangaliev was arrested.

Coming on top of the furore over the Georgian affair, Lenin's final notes on the national question and his Testament, and a series of climbdowns by Stalin at the Twelfth Party Congress in April 1923, this clear

[51] Schafer, 'Local Politics', pp. 165–90.
[52] *Tainy natsional' noi politiki TsK RKP – stenograficheskii otchet sekretnogo IV soveshchaniia TsK RKP, 1923 g.* (Moscow: INSAN, 1992), pp. 15–17.

case of serious misjudgement by Stalin must have led him to fear for his future, had anyone been willing to use it against him. As it turned out, on this occasion Stalin was saved by the dialectic. As the National Lefts literally bayed for Sultangaliev's blood and confidently expected a decisive resolution of the ongoing factional struggles in the Tatar and Crimean republics in their favour as a result of Sultangaliev's treachery, the Bolshevik leadership, represented at the June meeting by Stalin, Kuibyshev, Mikhail Frunze, and Trotsky, launched a frontal attack on – the National Left! The logic that Sultangaliev's actions (like Validov's earlier) could be seen as a response to the persistence of Great Russian attitudes under the guise of internationalism was not without merit, but the lenient treatment of Sultangaliev himself[53] and the indulgence shown to the Rights in general in this discussion must have been connected to the need to protect Stalin from any further humiliation.

These experiences had a lasting effect on Stalin. Most of the shifts in nationality policy of the 1930s can be related to broader political and economic developments. But his keen observation of affairs in the republics, including the appointment of some of his closest colleagues to the top positions there, frequent changes in personnel, show trials, and above all the levels of violence, extreme even by Stalin's standards, which were directed against particular national groups and their leaders before and during the Great Terror, and which included the extermination *without exception* of the early national communists, can in part at least be traced back to these early betrayals on the part of national communism.

In the shorter term, the Sultangaliev affair finally destroyed any notion Stalin may have had of using Narkomnats, the national republics, and the leaders he personally promoted there, as a basis for his own bid for power in the wake of Lenin's departure from active politics. But the main damage to any such plans had already been done by Lenin in 1922. Here, it is worth reflecting further on Stephen Blank's assertion that Stalin was engaged in institutional empire-building with Narkomnats, in the light of his later career. If Blank is right, and from 1921 Stalin was trying to both strengthen and centralise Narkmonats as a personal power base, then this suggests an intriguing interpretation of Stalin's 1922 spat with Lenin over the autonomisation project: the ethno-federal structure of the RSFSR meant that Stalin's Commissariat was largely responsible for the affairs of the autonomous republics and regions of the RSFSR, which between them contained about 30 per cent of the RSFSR's

---

[53] On this occasion Sultangaliev was released and returned to work in the Caucasus, without even losing his Party card, only to be rearrested five years later and eventually put to death.

population. The most important regions theoretically under Narkmonats influence were Turkestan, the North Caucasus, the Kirghiz (Kazakh), Tatar, and Bashkir Autonomous Republics, and Karelia. This is not bad as far as power bases go, but of the actual population of the autonomous republics about 36 per cent was Russian, while indifference on the part of the other central commissariats and local Russians considerably restricted Narkomnats' authority. If, however, Stalin had succeeded in incorporating the other republics into the RSFSR with Narkomnats extending its role to the larger republics, this would have given him a major say in Ukraine, Belorussia, and the much more ethnically homogenous and nationally developed republics of Transcaucasia. This would have been a mighty power base indeed. Stalin had every right to suppose that such a base was in his grasp – not only did he have the support or acquiescence of all the remaining members of the Politburo, he had also secured approval from the leaders of all the republics.

Lenin's opposition scuppered this project. Not only did the federal structure remove the larger republics from Stalin's possible authority, the creation of the Council of Nationalities, the point on which Stalin made his last stand, undermined any power he already had in the RSFSR: since the Council's members were to be chosen from the republics and it formed the less important part of a bicameral system it would wield authority only by negotiation with the federal Sovnarkom and not be subject to any single central authority. If Stalin's intention had been to develop Narkomnats as a power base, his defeat on this left him with only plan B – to focus exclusively on his alternative power base in the Secretariat of the Central Committee of the CPSU.

It is also conceivable, though even more speculative, in the light of Lenin's later remarks in his Testament and subsequently against Stalin, that as his health declined he was aware that his double-act with Stalin on nationality policy was also doomed to be replaced by a monopoly of policy in the hands of Stalin, and Lenin consequently moved to strengthen the independent position of the republics to counter such an eventuality.

This can be little more than speculation – the key discussions on the matter were held at a two-hour forty-minute private meeting between Lenin and Stalin on 26 September 1922, the precise nature of which we will never know (though we do know, from Fotieva, that Stalin left the meeting in a foul mood[54] – his carefully laid plans dashed?). It also depends on an unfashionable and always controversial intentionalist view of Stalin's own personal pursuit of power for its own sake. But it

---

[54] L. A. Fotieva, *Iz zhizni V. I. Lenina* (Moscow: Politizdat, 1967), p. 220.

would explain Stalin's behaviour at this time. Resentment at Lenin's frequent interference in Stalin's own acknowledged sphere of expertise, combined with the undermining of a carefully cultivated institutional power base and network of indebted clients, lay behind his unusually abrupt attitude towards Lenin and his wife.

Stalin retained a deep interest, and frequently intervened in, nationality affairs for the remainder of his life. But he never sought to reinstate a central body or individual with entire responsibility for nationalities affairs, and only ever tinkered with the federal structure. In spite of Lenin's role and their mutual opposition, Stalin could justifiably claim to have made a major contribution at both the theoretical and practical levels to the development of the main contours of this major area of policy, one in which the USSR could claim considerable success for many years to come. His experience as Commissar also provided Stalin with valuable lessons in institutional politics: while in his later career he surrounded himself not with people from Narkomnats, but rather with members of the Tsaritsyn group to whom he had become close in his military capacities, he understood both the importance of keeping people on his side and bred a mistrust towards even his clients. The failure of his institutional project with regard to Narkomnats and the RSFSR, coinciding as it did with Lenin's decline, arguably taught him a lesson which made him better prepared to launch his own bid for power. The final evaluation of this phase of Stalin's career is mixed: in policy terms, he could claim success; in institutional terms, he may have failed. But this failure itself made him more resolute, more wary, perhaps even more ruthless.

4   Stalin as General Secretary: the appointments process and the nature of Stalin's power

James Harris

The sources of Stalin's power is one of those subjects that are much described and little studied. The scores of political biographies and general histories covering the Stalin era suggest a variety of possibilities, from the use of terror and propaganda to the appeal of his policies, but almost without exception they mention Stalin's position as General Secretary. The common story suggests that, as General Secretary, Stalin used his control over appointments to build a personal following in the Party apparatus.[1] The mechanics of this process are sometimes referred to as 'a circular flow of power'.[2] Stalin appointed individual Party secretaries and gave them security of tenure. In return, they voted for him at Party Congresses. It is generally taken as given that Stalin used the power this afforded him to remove his political rivals in the course of his rise to power, and in later years, to remove those officials who had reservations

The Social Sciences and Humanities Research Council of Canada generously supported this work. I would also like to thank R. V. Daniels, Diane Koenker, and Sarah Davies for their comments on earlier drafts.

[1] Isaac Deutscher, *Stalin: A Political Biography* (Oxford: Oxford University Press, 1949); Adam B. Ulam, *Stalin: The Man and his Era* (New York: Viking, 1973); Robert C. Tucker, *Stalin as Revolutionary, 1879–1929: A Study in History and Personality* (London: Chatto and Windus, 1974); Dmitrii Volkogonov, *Triumf i tragediia: I. V. Stalin, politicheskii portret* (Moscow: Novosti, 1989); Robert Conquest, *Stalin, Breaker of Nations* (New York: Weidenfeld and Nicolson, 1991); Robert Service, *A History of Twentieth Century Russia* (Cambridge, Mass.: Harvard University Press, 1998); Ronald Grigor Suny, *The Soviet Experiment* (New York: Oxford University Press, 1998); Peter Kenez, *A History of the Soviet Union from the Beginning to the End* (Cambridge: Cambridge University Press, 1999); Christopher Read, *The Making and Breaking of the Soviet System* (Basingstoke: Macmillan, 2001).

[2] R. V. Daniels raised the idea in 'The Secretariat and the Local Organisations in the Russian Communist Party, 1921–1923', *American Slavic and East European Review* 1 (1957), 32–49. But he coined the phrase 'circular flow' in 'Stalin's Rise to Dictatorship' in Alexander Dallin and Alan Westin (eds.), *Politics in the Soviet Union* (New York: Harcourt Brace and World Inc., 1966). See also his *Conscience of the Revolution: Communist Opposition in Soviet Russia* (Cambridge, Mass.: Harvard University Press, 1960) and T. H. Rigby, 'Early Provincial Cliques and the Rise of Stalin', *Soviet Studies* 1 (1981), 3–28.

about his policies. In short, Stalin's power over appointment is commonly understood not only as a key factor in his rise to power, but also as the origin of his personalistic dictatorship.

In the late 1970s and the 1980s, 'revisionist' scholars began to cast doubt on the idea that Stalin could be sure of the personal loyalty of Party officials and that they would unquestioningly execute his will.[3] Since the opening of the archives, a substantial body of new evidence has reinforced their views. New studies have clearly shown that Party officials pursued agendas defined by their institutional interests and not solely by the will of Stalin or the directives of the central leadership.[4] Recent document collections portray a Stalin nagged by doubts that central directives were being fulfilled.[5] In this, his immediate subordinates were not the problem, but the greater mass of the Party and state bureaucracy, pursuing institutional interests and responding to impossible demands from the centre with foot-dragging and deception. Rather than being confident of his control of Party officials, Stalin appears to have been obsessed with the spectre of the '*dvurushnik*' (one who is two-faced, or a 'double-dealer') publicly professing his loyalty to the Party line while privately working to subvert it. The new evidence thus seems to contradict the way we have understood the emergence of Stalin's personal dictatorship.

The archives of the Central Committee, and those of the Secretariat among them, contain thousands of files from which it is possible to

---

[3] Their work has focused mostly on the 1930s and 1940s. W. O. McCagg, Jr, *Stalin Embattled, 1943–1948*, (Detroit: Wayne State University Press, 1978), pts. 2–3; Lynne Viola, 'The Campaign to Eliminate the Kulak as a Class, Winter 1929–1930: A Reevaluation of the Legislation', *Slavic Review* 3 (1986), 503–24; J. Arch Getty, *Origins of the Great Purges: The Soviet Communist Party Reconsidered, 1933–1938* (Cambridge: Cambridge University Press, 1985); Graeme Gill, *The Origins of the Stalinist Political System* (Cambridge: Cambridge University Press, 1990); Catherine Merridale, *Moscow Politics and the Rise of Stalin: The Communist Party in the Capital, 1925–1932* (Basingstoke: Macmillan, 1990); Gabor Rittersporn, *Stalinist Simplifications and Soviet Complications: Social Tensions and Political Conflicts in the USSR, 1933–1953* (Chur, Switzerland: Harwood, 1991).

[4] See for example, R. W. Davies, *Crisis and Progress in the Soviet Economy, 1931–1933* (Basingstoke: Macmillan, 1996); E. A. Rees, *Decision-Making in the Stalinist Command Economy* (Basingstoke: Macmillan, 1997); James R. Harris, *The Great Urals: Regionalism and the Evolution of the Soviet System* (Ithaca: Cornell University Press, 1999).

[5] A. V. Kvashonkin, A. V. Livshin, O. V. Khlevniuk (eds.), *Stalinskoe politburo v 30-e gody. Sbornik dokumentov* (Moscow: AIRO-XX, 1995); Lars T. Lih, Oleg V. Naumov, and Oleg V. Khlevniuk (eds.), *Stalin's Letters to Molotov, 1925–1936* (New Haven: Yale University Press, 1995), published in Russian as L. Kosheleva, V. Lel'chuk, V. Naumov, O. Naumov, L. Rogovaia, and O. Khlevniuk (eds.), *Pis'ma I. V. Stalina V. M. Molotovu, 1925–1936gg. Sbornik dokumentov* (Moscow: Rossiia Molodaia, 1995); A. V. Kvashonkin, A. V. Livshin, O. V. Khlevniuk (eds.), *Sovetskoe rukovodstvo. Perepiska, 1928–1941* (Moscow: Rosspen, 1999); J. Arch Getty and Oleg V. Naumov (eds.), *The Road to Terror: Stalin and the Self-Destruction of the Bolsheviks, 1932–1939* (New Haven: Yale University Press, 1999).

re-examine the relationship of the General Secretary and Party and state officials. The following analysis of these files concludes that, while the Secretariat played a crucial role in Stalin's rise to power, it never became a source of a personalistic control of the Party apparatus as is commonly assumed. The Secretariat was never able to cope with its task of assigning cadres to Party organisations. It assigned them in large numbers in an almost entirely impersonal process. Meanwhile, the Party organisations receiving cadres were profoundly involved in the appointments process. They could, and did, refuse candidates proposed by the centre. The fact of appointment was not sufficient to generate personal loyalty to the General Secretary. Stalin did, however, provide security of tenure to many Party secretaries. The gravest threat to their power in the first decade of Soviet power came from political infighting (*sklochnichestvo*) in local organisations. Stalin won the support of secretaries by attacking intra-Party democracy and reinforcing their power within their organisations. The political battles over the Lenin succession were exacerbating political infighting locally, and the secretaries were happy to see Stalin stop them. But only in this limited sense was there a 'circular flow of power'. Many Party secretaries voted for Stalin at Party Congresses. They helped him defeat his rivals in the Politburo because they had a common interest in it, not because they felt personally beholden to Stalin. In the early 1930s, their interests began to diverge with the crisis of the First Five-Year Plan, punishing grain collections, famine, and the emergence of the 'command-administrative system'. The secretaries had helped Stalin to power, but they may have begun to worry if they had made the right choice. There was nothing they could do about it though. In attacking intra-Party democracy, they contributed to a situation in which it was impossible to question the 'Central Committee line'. Where discussion and criticism of central policy was impossible, the footdragging and subversion we now see in the new sources was a logical response.

In order to understand how this apparently tense relationship between Stalin and Party officialdom emerged in the early 1930s, we must return to the very origins of the Central Committee Secretariat, in the October seizure of power.

The Central Committee Secretariat before Stalin

Following the October coup in Petrograd, the Bolsheviks faced the colossal task of taking control of, and governing the vast territories of the Russian Empire. They had to shut down, or take over, existing bureaucratic structures from the central ministries down to the local land councils. They had to do battle with other groups competing for power, including Mensheviks, Socialist Revolutionaries, and national minorities seeking to create independent states. By the spring of 1918, they also had to mobilise for civil war. They had long understood that they were undermanned. On the eve of the February Revolution, there were approximately twenty-four thousand members in the Bolshevik underground. By the end of the Civil War, over seven hundred thousand new members had joined the now ruling Party.[6]

Registering, assigning, and directing the inflow of new recruits were colossal tasks in themselves. Iakov Sverdlov, a close associate of Lenin, was the first 'secretary' of the Central Committee in charge of personnel questions. With a staff of only six, Sverdlov could only monitor the spontaneous growth of Party membership and issue general directives assigning cadres en masse. Though Lenin prized Sverdlov for his organisational skills, it would appear that his Secretariat kept few written records of its activities. Pressures to improve record-keeping came from state and Party organisations in the centre and regions that were frustrated by the inability of the Secretariat to meet their specific cadre needs.[7] After Sverdlov's death in March 1919, the responsibility for Party appointments was formally invested in the Secretariat and Sverdlov's successors[8] undertook to expand the staff in order to meet the ever-growing need for cadres throughout the Soviet Union. By 1921, the Secretariat employed over 600 officials, but it still could not meet the needs of organisations.

Of course, the Civil War had placed considerable extra burdens on the personnel apparatus. The Secretariat worked closely with the Political Administration of the Red Army leadership (*Politicheskoe upravlenie Revvoensoveta*, or PUR) to mobilise Party members to various fronts. While the Soviet state was under threat, the needs of civilian government had not been a top priority, but when victory seemed assured the Secretariat could demobilise and assign tens of thousands of Party cadres. Again, any more than the most rudimentary record keeping was impossible. Organisations from the top to the bottom of the new bureaucratic apparatus registered their demands for personnel with specific skills for work in specific organisations: factory administrations, banks, agricultural co-operatives, and so on.[9] With rare exceptions, all the

---

[6] T. H. Rigby, *Communist Party Membership in the U.S.S.R., 1917–1967* (Princeton: Princeton University Press, 1968), pp. 7–8, 52.

[7] Robert Service, *The Bolshevik Party in Revolution: A Study in Organisational Change, 1917–1923* (New York: Barnes and Noble Books, 1979), pp. 277–95.

[8] N. N. Krestinskii, L. P. Serebriakov, E. A. Preobrazhenskii, and V. M. Molotov.

[9] Rossiiskii gosudarstvennyi arkhiv sotsial'no-politicheskoi istorii (henceforth RGASPI) f. 17, op. 34, d. 7.

Secretariat could do was collect and collate these demands and attempt to meet them in purely quantitative terms.[10]

The low level of any accounting for personal qualities and administrative skills exacerbated existing weaknesses of Party and state structures in two fundamental ways. First, the general quality of officialdom was extremely low in terms of basic literacy, administrative skills, and even loyalty to the Party. In the process of the exponential growth of the Party, the standards for membership had fallen correspondingly. Particularly in the immediate aftermath of the October seizure of power, many had joined the Bolshevik Party in order to take advantage of the privileged access to food, housing, and jobs accorded to members.[11] At the very height of the Civil War, the Party leadership had felt compelled to initiate a purge of corrupt and 'morally dissolute' members.[12] The long struggle against the White Armies, combined with political training in the army, did reinforce loyalty to the Party, and literacy campaigns raised educational levels, but corruption and incompetence remained serious problems in administration.

Though competent and principled Party members were in short supply, that did not mean that there was any shortage of ambitious ones, and the conflict of ambitions presented another, and perhaps more troubling, problem for the Bolsheviks. Not everyone could be a provincial Party committee secretary, a department head in a commissariat, even a district Party committee secretary or village soviet chairman. Throughout the growing Party and state bureaucracy, officials wanted to give orders, not to take them. As the bureaucracy absorbed new cadres, struggles for power erupted at all levels in the drive to capture the 'responsible positions' within and among organisations. Local officials were locked in struggle with cadres sent in from Moscow. New recruits to the Party refused to accept the seniority of members with underground experience. Soviet executive committee chairmen refused to follow the directives of the Party committee secretaries, local economic councils (*sovnarkhozy*) fought with local trade unions.[13] No senior official could be sure that one of his colleagues was not conspiring to take his place. The struggles (*skloki*) pervaded the apparatus, paralysing entire organisations throughout the country.

---

[10] See RGASPI f. 17, op. 34, dd. 20–6 for statistical tables matching the supply and demand for cadres in 1921 and 1922.

[11] See for example, Rigby, 'Early Provincial Cliques', p. 8.

[12] This first Party purge was referred to as a re-registration of members. See T. H. Rigby, *Communist Party*, ch. 1.

[13] On the variety of conflicts in Party organisations, see RGASPI f. 17, op. 34, d. 110, ll. 7–35.

The task of dealing with these problems fell primarily to the Secretariat. In the fall of 1920, several new departments were created to deal with them. The establishment of the 'Record-Assignment' department was intended to make possible a shift from mass assignments to planned assignments on the basis of the specific needs of organisations. The 'Agitation-Propaganda' department was supposed to raise their ideological awareness. The 'Organisation-Instruction' department was directed to bring a measure of consistency to the structure of the apparatus and, by means of a staff of travelling (*vyezdnye*) instructors, to fight corruption and raise the efficiency of administration. It was given an 'Information' sub-department to process the great mass of information received from local organisations, and particularly, to summarise their monthly reports on their activities, and a 'Conflicts' sub-department to bring an end to power struggles that pervaded the apparatus.[14]

None of these departments was able to cope with its new responsibilities. Even after demobilisation, mass assignments continued to be the order of the day, making any sort of accounting of cadres impossible. In the process of demobilisation, the Record-Assignment department was assigning 5,000 cadres a month,[15] but even after that process had been largely completed, the numbers remained high. In 1923, the department assigned 14,000 cadres, including 4,000 leading workers.[16] Despite the sheer numbers of those assigned, organisations continued to complain about shortages of skilled officials.[17] Meanwhile, the Organisation-Instruction department could not possibly meet its responsibility of instructing weak organisations. Rather, its network of instructors contributed to the work of the sub-departments, investigating and reporting on general trends in the activities of organisations, particularly on the ongoing power struggles.[18] They worked with the Conflict department and the organisations themselves to resolve the worst of the struggles, but they had little success. In 1921, the department was receiving over 150 reports of conflicts a month, many from the Party officials involved. Hundreds of files were left for months without any response and the backlog was increasing.[19]

---

[14] 'Konstruktsiia rabochego apparata TsK RKP(b)', *Izvestiia TsK*, 23 September 1920, pp. 1–5.

[15] 'Otchet uchetno-raspredelitel'nogo otdela' *Izvestiia TsK*, 28 March 1921, p. 11.

[16] *Trinadtsatyi s"ezd RKP(b), mai 1924 goda. Stenograficheskii otchet* (Moscow, Gospolitizdat, 1963), p. 120.

[17] RGASPI f. 17, op. 34, d. 15, ll. 12–74.

[18] See RGASPI f. 17, op. 67. For a general discussion of the work of the instructor apparatus in the early 1920s see RGASPI f. 17, op. 68, d. 17, ll. 112–33.

[19] 'Otchet org-instruktorskogo otdela TsK za period vremeni s maia 1920 goda po 15 fevralia 1921 goda', *Izvestiia TsK*, 5 March 1921, pp. 7–9.

The work of the Secretariat was regularly criticised at Central Committee plena and Party congresses and conferences. The creation of new departments and the expansion of its staff had done little to improve matters and something had to be done. In his speech on 'intra-Party matters' to the Eleventh Party Congress in April 1922, Grigorii Zinoviev emphasised the 'paralysis' of Party work caused by the power struggles. He claimed that they had 'become the scourge and calamity [*bich i bedstvie*] of the whole Party'.[20] Immediately after the Congress had concluded its work, the Central Committee approved Lenin's draft resolution that assigned Stalin to head the Secretariat and created the position of 'General Secretary'. In assigning a Politburo member to the post, Lenin hoped to lend the Secretariat new authority, though he knew that was not enough. His resolution warned Stalin and the department heads not to get lost in the vastness of the Secretariat's responsibilities, but to stick to questions of a 'genuinely principal importance'.[21] Was this a fateful decision, one that fundamentally changed the course of Soviet history, as so many scholars have contended? Was Stalin able to use his position as General Secretary to build a personal following in the apparatus, to stifle Party democracy and defeat his political rivals? Did the members of the Politburo unwittingly place a powerful weapon in Stalin's hands with this decision, or were they burdening him with a bureaucratic millstone?

The Secretariat under Stalin

When Stalin took over the Secretariat in 1922, he introduced several changes to improve its efficiency. The changes he introduced were in keeping with Lenin's instructions not to get lost in the details. One of his first moves was to reduce the responsibilities of the Secretariat in the assignment of cadres. His predecessors had taken responsibility for assignments from the top to the bottom of the apparatus. Stalin encouraged Party and state organisations to promote their own cadres, and mapped a limited hierarchy of positions to be staffed under the direction of the Central Committee. The resulting list, known as 'Nomenklatura no. 1', included 4,000 senior positions from the Presidiums of the Peoples' Commissariats down to the department and section heads, and from the 'bureaus' of regional Party committees down to the secretaries of *okrug* Party organisations.[22] The total number of cadres

---

[20] *Pravda*, 2 April 1922.

[21] ' ... *priniat' za pravilo, chto nikakoi raboty, krome deistvitel'no printsipial'no rukovodiash-chei sekretari ne dolzhny vozlagat' na sebia lichno* ...' RGASPI f. 17, op. 2, d. 78, l. 2.

[22] RGASPI f. 17, op. 69, d. 259, l. 101; an example of the list can be found in f. 17, op. 69, d. 141.

assigned from Moscow was reduced from approximately 22,500 in the period between the Tenth and the Eleventh Party Congresses to barely over 6,000 between the Twelfth and the Thirteenth.[23]

In theory, this allowed the Record-Assignment department to keep more detailed personnel records and to improve its ability to match cadres' skills to the needs of organisations. In practice, the department continued to be swamped with demands for new officials and had little knowledge of the cadres it was passing to the Secretariat for approval. At a meeting of the leading officials of the Organisation-Assignment department[24] in early 1927, the poor state of Party records was a central topic of discussion. Department officials admitted that in the vast majority of cases, they were assigning Party members blindly (*sovershenno sluchaino*).[25] The consensus of the meeting was that the Organisation-Assignment departments of Party and state bodies had to be strengthened and accounting improved. As it was, unemployed Party members tended to head to Moscow to get 'Party' jobs and the department was being turned into an employment agency.[26]

One might assume that these concerns related largely to the great mass of lesser posts, but even in the case of appointments to the key positions in the Party and state bureaucracies similar issues arose. By 1926, the number of *nomenklatura* posts had expanded again by 50 per cent. As that number expanded and the burdens of the assignments process increased, the consideration given to each appointment decreased. The Organisation-Assignment department took no part in appointments at or below the *guberniia* level. It only kept records of decisions that were taken by the local organisations.[27] In the case of more senior positions, the organisations that were to receive the appointees were aggressively drawn into the appointments process.[28] Seven standing commissions, specialised according to branches of the state and Party apparatus, were created within the Organisation-Assignment department in order to parcel responsibilities for the appointments.[29] When these commissions

[23] RGASPI f. 17, op. 68, d. 429, l. 24.

[24] The sub-departments of the Secretariat were reorganised in 1924. The Record-Assignment department was renamed the Organisation-Assignment department. The responsibility for appointments remained unchanged.

[25] RGASPI f. 17, op. 69, d. 140, l. 30.

[26] ('*Po sie vremia mnogie kommunisty smotriat na Orgraspred kak na birzhu truda*') *Ibid.*, l. 85.

[27] See D. I. Kurskii's report of the Central Revision Commission to the Thirteenth Party Congress. *Trinadtsatyi s"ezd*, p. 132.

[28] RGASPI f. 17, op. 68, d. 60, l. 44.

[29] These included the Industry Commission, the Trade Commission, the Soviet Commission, the Co-operative Commission, and the Party Commission.; RGASPI f. 17, op. 69, d. 259, l. 96.

discussed specific appointments, they consulted members of the organisation to which the appointee would be assigned.[30] In this way, it was
ensured that those assigned to key posts were not unknown quantities.

The Organisation-Assignment department was concerned that
appointees had the appropriate training, experience, and skills necessary to perform effectively. Appointees who were incompetent could be,
and were, rejected and sent back to the Organisation-Assignment
department. Almost a third of appointees were fired within a year.[31]
The high rate of turnover was a consequence not only of the low skill
levels of appointees. The experience of the group struggles in the early
1920s had shown leading officials the importance of surrounding themselves with people whom they could trust. New appointees who 'did not
fit in' (ne srabotali) to an organisation were also rejected. In order to
ensure such a 'fit', some organisations preferred to assign officials on the
nomenklatura lists without the 'interference' of the centre.[32] The practice
did not last long. On the request of the Organisation-Assignment department, the Orgburo clarified and reissued the directives on the procedure
for appointments.[33] The Organisation-Assignment department objected
to being totally bypassed, though it did strongly encourage the leaders of
state and Party organisations to promote candidates from below for its
approval. The rapid expansion of the bureaucracy in the 1920s had
created terrible shortages of cadres with appropriate administrative skills,
such that when faced with a position to fill, the department often had no
one to recommend. A leading Organisation-Assignment department official observed in early 1927 that 'the system [khoziaistvo nashe] is growing,
and we don't have new people [to staff it]'.[34] Promotion from within
(vydvyzhenie) was the preferred method for staffing leading positions, and
in encouraging it, the department further strengthened the influence of
Party and state organisations over the appointments process. If appointees had personal loyalties, they were more likely to be to the organisation
to which he or she was assigned, rather than to Stalin.

This sense of local loyalties was further reinforced as the Secretariat
dealt with local power struggles. Rather than continue to investigate each
case and risk letting the backlog of unresolved struggles increase as his

---

[30] RGASPI f. 17, op. 69, d. 136, l. 131. See also Kurskii's speech to the Fifteenth Congress.
Piatnadtsatyi s''ezd Vsesoiuznoi kommunisticheskoi partii (b). Stenograficheskii otchet
(Moscow: Gosizdat, 1928), p. 164.

[31] RGASPI f. 17, op. 69, d. 136, ll. 10–11, 30–1, 136.

[32] This was particularly true of the Peoples' Commissars and other central state institutions.
RGASPI f. 17, op. 68, d. 149, ll.141–54. For a description of the unilateral actions of the
Commissar of Agriculture, Smirnov, see RGASPI f. 17, op. 69, d. 136, l. 131.

[33] RGASPI f. 17, op. 69, d. 136, ll. 167–8.   [34] RGASPI f. 17, op. 69, d. 140, l. 30.

predecessors had done, Stalin encouraged the resolution of conflicts locally. The simplest way to do so was to strengthen the hierarchy of existing Party and state organisations, and reinforce the powers of the current 'bosses', most notably, the network of local Party secretaries. Following Stalin's speech on organisational matters, the resolutions of the Twelfth Party Congress (April 1923) strengthened the role of Party secretaries in selecting 'responsible workers of the soviet, economic, co-operative and professional organisations' in their regions.[35] In effect, the Party secretaries became the main arbiters of the struggles, with the power to remove officials who refused to submit to their decisions.[36]

Not all struggles could be resolved so easily though. Many organisations were unable to settle conflicts on their own, and they continued to appeal to the Secretariat for intervention.[37] In such cases, the Secretariat despatched one of its instructors, who would call an extraordinary conference of the local Party committee and attempt to win the censure or expulsion of the weaker of the groups.[38] In cases of truly intractable conflicts, the Secretariat reassigned all parties to the conflict and replaced them. For most leading officials unable to work in the face of constant challenges to their leadership, the risk was worth taking. Generally, the worst outcome they could expect was to be assigned to a different institution or region. Most of them accepted the decisions of the Secretariat, though there were exceptions. On several occasions, those who were reassigned complained bitterly and took their cases on appeal to the Central Control Commission, the Politburo, or to Lenin himself. The best-known case is the so-called 'Georgian Affair'.[39] Stalin had sent Sergo Ordzhonikidze (then an instructor of the Secretariat) to remove two members of the Georgian Party organisation accused of 'local nationalism' in the hotly contested issue of Georgia's participation in the recently established Transcaucasus federation. They were removed in the autumn of 1922 by a decision of the Georgian Party, but not without controversy. Stalin's tactics and Ordzhonikidze's actions – including a physical assault on one of the participants – provoked a great deal of animosity in the

---

[35] *KPSS v rezoliutsiiakh i resheniiakh s"ezdov, konferentsii i plenumov TsK* (Moscow: Politizdat, 1984), pp. 74, 99.

[36] The research of the Information department suggests that the regional secretaries were not shy about asserting those powers. RGASPI f. 81, op. 3, d. 69, ll. 189–91. Kaganovich was the chairman of the Organisation-Assignment department at the time.

[37] See, for example, RGASPI f. 17, op. 34, d. 112, ll.79, 176; d. 114, ll. 12, 121. Many more such requests can be found in f. 17, op. 67, and f. 17, op. 112, 113.

[38] Anastas Mikoian describes his participation in such a case in his memoir *V nachale dvatsatykh* (Moscow: Politizdat, 1975), ch. 2.

[39] For more on this, see the chapter by Jeremy Smith in this volume.

process of settling the larger conflict.[40] The case is often cited not because it was typical, but because it incensed Lenin. Less than a year after he had recommended him to the post, Lenin expressed profound reservations about Stalin's 'hastiness and bureaucratic impulsiveness'. Privately, he considered recommending that he be replaced by someone 'more patient, more loyal, more polite and more attentive to comrades'.[41]

'Bureaucratic impulsiveness' was not the only charge levelled against Stalin in his role as General Secretary. Some Party leaders were also concerned that the Secretariat was stifling 'intra-Party democracy'.[42] Intra-Party democracy, meaning not only the election of officials, but also the open discussion of policy issues, had been a subject of considerable debate and controversy since the civil war had come to a close. Lenin had promoted the ban on factionalism specifically to deal with groups such as the 'Democratic Centralists' and the 'Workers' Opposition' which demanded a more participatory political system. Those 'factions' were crushed, but as the immediate threats to the survival of the Soviet state receded, the question of intra-Party democracy returned to the political agenda.

At the time Stalin was named General Secretary, the main subject of correspondence between the Secretariat and Party organisations was the struggles for power (*skloki*), rather than conflicts over political principles or policy platforms. Letter after letter referred to the conflicts among individuals and institutions as rooted in 'personal antagonisms', and 'lacking any ideological content'.[43] While there is no evidence to suggest that the Secretariat was enforcing conformity to any set of policies or 'political line', the decision to reinforce the power of Party secretaries was hardly conducive to political diversity or open discussion. Party secretaries were always on the lookout for conspiracies against their leadership, and there was no more dangerous time for them than the regular local Party conferences, at which key posts were filled by election. It was at these meetings that such 'oppositions' often came out into the open and challenged the authority of existing leaders. For example, a Secretariat instructor's report on the Bashkir *Oblast'* Party Conference in September

---

[40] In this case, Stalin was using his position in the Secretariat to pursue a vendetta from his work in the Commissariat of Nationalities. Tucker, *Stalin as Revolutionary*, pp. 224–38; Moshe Lewin, *Lenin's Last Struggle* (London: Faber, 1969), ch. 4.

[41] Lenin made these comments in his so-called political 'testament' the contents of which were not revealed until after his death.

[42] See particularly the comments of Kosior, Rakovsky, and Krasin to the Twelfth Party Congress. *Dvenadtsatyi s''ezd Rossiiskoi kommunisticheskoi partii (bol'shevikov), 17–25 aprelia 1923 g. Stenograficheskii otchet* (Moscow: Gospolitizdat, 1923).

[43] See, for example, RGASPI f. 17, op. 67, d. 6, l. 16; d. 109, ll. 168–9; d. 249, l. 68.

1922 observed that 'the group struggle began only with the discussion of the new composition of the *Obkom* ... All other issues were met with unanimity'.[44] Most often, local Party secretaries dealt with the threat by presenting pre-prepared slates of candidates to subordinate Party organisations in the run-up to the Party conferences. Then, at the Party conference itself, the slates were voted on as a whole, and without a discussion.[45] Those officials who challenged the slates were often accused of 'undermining the authority of the Party Committee', or some similar charge, and harassed or expelled from the organisation. Supplementing and reinforcing this tactic was the application of the secretary's own powers of appointment. Elected officials or others who were suspected of contemplating a challenge to the Party committee leadership could be replaced with someone more 'reliable'.[46]

The outlines of what Kamenev and Zinoviev referred to as the 'secretarial regime' were emerging in the first years of Stalin's tenure as General Secretary. The reference was not to any dictatorial powers accumulating in the Secretariat. Rather, they referred to the mass of Party secretaries who were stifling policy discussions on their own initiative.

The Secretariat and the Lenin succession

In the early 1920s, the situation in the Politburo was similar to that of Party committees in the provinces. The Lenin succession was yet another power struggle among ambitious Party leaders. Before his death, Lenin had identified the two top pretenders – Stalin and Trotsky – and worried about the consequences of the inevitable conflict between the two. Trotsky's arrogant certainty that he was uniquely suited to lead the Revolution after Lenin was well known, as was Stalin's ambitiousness. Stalin would not be restrained by concerns of political principle from using the Secretariat in any way that would further those ambitions. He would squeeze every political advantage he could from it. In his first year as General Secretary, it only seemed to be getting him into trouble. In the face of a direct attack at the Twelfth Congress on the question of intra-Party democracy, Stalin was on the defensive. While he argued that the goal of Party secretaries to 'build a unified and disciplined leadership group was healthy and necessary', he agreed that 'the means they have employed have frequently not been appropriate'. He also directly denied that the Secretariat was using the Record-Assignment department to

---

[44] RGASPI f. 17, op. 34, d. 112, l. 15. For other examples of group struggles at Party elections, see ll. 29–31; d. 114, l. 12, l. 70.
[45] RGASPI f. 17, op. 69, d. 269, ll. 54–5.   [46] RGASPI f. 17, op. 68, d. 105, l. 7.

exclude the members of political factions: the department was assigning honest and talented comrades, and that was all it did (*'Dal'she etogo Uchraspred, poprostu govoria, ne soval nosa'*).[47]

Lenin's criticisms of Stalin and the Secretariat only a few months before left him politically vulnerable, but Stalin quietly held to his position, understanding its popularity among Party secretaries. Through the summer and autumn of 1923, while Lenin's health was declining, divisions in the Party leadership were increasingly obvious. Trotsky and other prominent members of the Party attacked Stalin and the 'secretarial regime',[48] but only after it was clear that Lenin's condition was hopeless did Stalin drop his defensive tone in public. At the Thirteenth Party Conference in January, only days before Lenin's death, Trotsky's political ally Evgenii Preobrazhenskii railed at the dictatorial methods of Party secretaries:

> We must (encourage) a broad discussion of all crucial questions of intra-party life ... such that issues of concern to Party members can be posed not only by Party committees, but also on the initiative of Party cells and even individual comrades.

He recommended, among other things, that the 'elective principle be restored to executive Party organs (Party committee bureaus)'.[49] To any Party secretary, the implications of such a policy were immediately clear. They would be open to attack from any disgruntled Party member, to say nothing of groups of 'comrades' who might want to topple them from their leadership posts. With Lenin out of the way, unable to apply his overwhelming authority in the Party, Stalin could be sure of the support of the delegates. They were, after all, overwhelmingly made up of Party secretaries. Stalin told them what they wanted to hear:

> Democracy is not something appropriate to all times and places ... Democracy demands a certain minimum of culture [*kultur'nost'*] from the members of (Party) cells and organisations as a whole ... Of course we need to retreat from it.

Such a statement would have been unthinkable only a year before, but here, it was only the preface to a direct attack on Trotsky. He insisted that what Trotsky was promoting was not democracy, but a 'freedom of group struggle' (*svoboda gruppirovok*) that would be fatal in the 'current conditions' of the New Economic Policy:

---

[47] *Dvenadtsatyi s"ezd*, pp. 62, 66.

[48] The events of this period are best described in Isaac Deutscher, *The Prophet Unarmed, Trotsky: 1921–1929* (London: Oxford University Press, 1970), pp. 88–118.

[49] *Trinadtsataia konferentsiia rossiiskoi kommunisticheskoi partii (bol'shevikov)* (Moscow: Krasnaia nov', 1924), pp. 106–7.

It is not the (Secretarial) regime that is to blame (for the necessity of the retreat), but rather the conditions in which we live, the conditions of the country ... If we were to permit the existence of group struggle, we would destroy the Party, turn it from a monolithic, united organisation into an alliance of groups and factions. It would not be a Party, but rather the destruction of the Party ... Not for one minute did Bolsheviks ever imagine the Party as anything but a monolithic organisation, cut from one piece, of one will ... In the current conditions of capitalist encirclement, we need not only a united Party, but a Party of steel, capable of withstanding the onslaught of the enemies of the proletariat, capable of leading the workers into a decisive struggle.[50]

The 'retreat' from democracy proved to be very durable. Party secretaries were pleased to repeat Stalin's phrases about the importance of Party unity and use them to legitimise the repression of any challenge to their power.

Despite their expanded powers, challenges to the authority of local secretaries remained a fact of political life. In the early 1920s, the general confusion over administrative responsibilities had created a fertile soil for power struggles. Though the administrative hierarchy was gradually set and clarified, political ambitions could not be so easily satisfied and power struggles continued. In part, they were fuelled by policy differences among Politburo leaders. Certainly, some local officials were drawn by conviction to the ideas of the 'opposition', but probably fewer than the reports of the local secretaries would indicate. They often used the label of 'oppositionist' in order to create the impression that cases of local insubordination constituted opposition to the policies of the Central Committee, and not merely the local leadership. At times the labelling was transparent. In their reports to the Secretariat, some secretaries observed that the 'dissatisfied elements' and the 'persistent intriguers' (*neispravimye sklochniki*) in their organisations rallied behind the ideas of the so-called Left Opposition in Moscow.[51]

As a strategy for furthering one's career ambitions, joining an opposition was highly counterproductive. Groups that collectively objected to the so-called 'political line of the Central Committee', or that were labelled as 'oppositionist', were easy to identify and eliminate. Secretaries kept careful records of voting patterns at Party meetings and verified them for evidence of support for opposition groups. Suspected members were trailed by the local OGPU, and when evidence was found, their cases were presented to the local Control Commission for expulsion from the Party. The Secretariat was kept informed of the names and activities of

[50] *Ibid.*, pp. 93, 100–1.
[51] See, for example, RGASPI f. 17, op. 67, d. 249, l. 68; d. 285, l. 102; d. 378, l. 192; d. 193, l. 98.

oppositionists and of the actions taken against them by local authorities.[52] It quickly became apparent to Party members in the regions that to join an opposition was political suicide, and, as such, its leaders in Moscow had great difficulty generating support within local organisations.[53] Instead, they sent their members out from Moscow to organise demonstrations, speak at Party meetings, and distribute 'oppositionist literature'. These 'touring' oppositionists (*gastrolery*) could not be stifled so easily because they had no local status. When they appeared in a given region, the local Party committee would gather a team of leading officials to arrange a counter-demonstration.[54] The *gastrolery* never seem to have presented a threat to the local secretaries, but they were a constant source of irritation.

All this is not to say that the situation of the oppositions was hopeless from the start. Though Stalin sustained and deepened his relationship with Party secretaries in the course of the 1920s, the strength of that relationship alone was not sufficient to decide the succession struggle. Early explanations of Stalin's victory emphasised the victory of machine politics over political principle, but for the last forty years, historians have also focused on the role of ideas and policies.[55] New archival sources only serve to reinforce our sense of the succession struggle as a see-saw battle of thesis and counter-thesis, of alternative visions of the future of the Revolution, presented to the Party elite and the broader membership. In his letters to Molotov, for example, Stalin insisted on responding publicly to every speech and article of his rivals. For example, in the summer of 1926, Stalin told Molotov to make sure that Bukharin responded to Zinoviev's criticisms of the foreign policy of the Politburo majority. Zinoviev's views, he wrote, 'are in the air and find support among those in the Comintern with Rightist tendencies'.[56]

---

[52] These reports can be found in RGASPI f. 17, op. 67.

[53] A report of the Information department from December 1926 indicated that the overwhelming majority of oppositionist actions (*vystupleniia*) in that year took place in Moscow (222). Leningrad and Odessa were also important centres of oppositionist activity (169 and 139 incidents respectively), but for the rest of the country the numbers were insignificant (most under 10). RGASPI f. 17, op. 68, d. 105, l. 137.

[54] For a particularly vivid and detailed description of the response of a regional committee to the touring oppositionists, see RGASPI f. 17, op. 67, d. 378, ll. 192–5.

[55] Among the classic studies of the succession struggle are Leonard Schapiro, *The Origin of the Communist Autocracy* (London: London School of Economics and Political Science, 1955); Daniels, *Conscience of the Revolution*; Stephen F. Cohen, *Bukharin and the Bolshevik Revolution. A Political Biography, 1888–1938* (New York: A. A. Knopf, 1973). More recent works include Merridale, *Moscow Politics and the Rise of Stalin*; Gill, *The Origins of the Stalinist Political System*.

[56] Lih *et al.* (eds.), *Stalin's Letters*, p. 111.

Oppositionist ideas may have been 'in the air', but to what extent did they pose a threat to Stalin's ambition to take control of the Party? Stalin gave his own views on the subject in a conversation with his inner circle on the day of the twentieth anniversary of the October Revolution. Stalin observed that his victory over the oppositions, and Trotsky in particular, had been improbable. He had been an 'unknown', 'lacking talent as a theoretician' (*praktik*), a 'second-rater' (*zamukhryshka*). Trotsky was a great orator, and his closeness to Lenin was commonly acknowledged. How had he defeated him? Trotsky's mistake, according to Stalin, was to try to decide matters 'with a majority of votes in the Central Committee'. In contrast, Stalin attributed his victory to the mass of average Party members (*seredniatskaia massa partii*) who supported him for his concrete achievements. Stalin likened them to officers, who had shown loyalty not to the Generals who have the best training, but to those who bring victory in battle.[57]

Accepting that such utterances must be treated with caution,[58] Stalin's remarks make considerable sense in the context of what we know about the succession struggle. For Trotsky, seeking a majority in the Central Committee was a logical strategy. Central Committee members tended to have been in the Party longest. They had a higher level of education and stature in the Party.[59] They were likely to have been the most independent-thinking of Party members, the least beholden to Stalin, the most likely to have been open to Trotsky's views. Furthermore, as members of the Central Committee, Party statutes assigned them the right to elect the Politburo. They could, thus, have had a decisive influence in the struggle. And yet neither Trotsky nor any of Stalin's other rivals was able to obtain a majority.

Some have argued that Stalin tipped the weight of the Central Committee in his favour by excluding his opponents from it and appointing his supporters.[60] Yet there is little evidence to suggest that Stalin

---

[57] RGASPI f. 558, op. 11, d. 1122, ll. 161–5.

[58] For a fascinating and detailed discussion of Stalin's 'table talk' (an inadequate phrase for the untranslatable '*zastol'naia rech*''), see Vladimir Nevezhin, *Zastol'nye rechy Stalina: dokumenty i materialy* (Moscow: AIRO-XX, 2003).

[59] Evan Mawdsley and Stephen White, *The Soviet Elite from Lenin to Gorbachev: The Central Committee and its Members, 1917–1991* (Oxford: Oxford University Press, 2000), ch. 2.

[60] See for example, Deutscher, *Stalin*, p. 239; Schapiro, *The Communist Party of the Soviet Union*, 2nd edn. (New York: Random House, 1970), p. 262; Ulam, *Stalin: The Man and his Era* (London: I. B. Tauris, 1973), p. 236. R. V. Daniels, 'The Evolution of Leadership Selection in the Central Committee, 1917–1927', in Walter McKenzie Pintner and Don Karl Rowney (eds.), *Russian Officialdom: The Bureaucratization of Russian Society from the Seventeenth to the Twentieth Centuries* (Chapel Hill: University of North Carolina Press, 1980).

could control the slates of Central Committee members up for election at the Party congresses in the 1920s, or overtly manipulate its expansion in his favour. Rather, it appears as though Stalin largely carried the Central Committee on the basis of his policies and, in time, on the concrete results they brought. In this, Stalin appears to have had the upper hand from the beginning. From the earliest stages of the struggle in the early 1920s, those voting for the slates of candidates to the Central Committee struck members of the oppositions off their ballots more frequently than they struck off Stalin or the Politburo majority. By 1925, in the election of the Central Committee at the Fourteenth Party Congress, 217 voters struck Kamenev off their ballots; 224 struck off Zinoviev. By contrast, 87 struck off Stalin and 83 Bukharin.[61] Stalin had the clear advantage, though his failure to obtain those 87 votes suggests that if he did try to stack the Central Committee with his cronies, he was not doing a very good job.

In his own memory of the events, Stalin nevertheless placed greater emphasis on the support he had in the broader Party membership: 'In 1927,' he observed, '720,000 Party members voted for the Central Committee line. That is, the backbone of the Party voted for us "second-raters." Four to six thousand voted for Trotsky and a further 20,000 abstained.'[62] Stalin's control of the Central Committee may have been tenuous in the early stages of the struggle, but through his work in the Secretariat, his grip on broader Party officialdom effectively undermined the spread of ideas other than some abstractly understood 'Central Committee line'. Stalin's 'average' Party official saw concrete dangers in intra-Party democracy, that is, the unrestricted, open discussion of policy. They actively and aggressively helped Stalin to choke off debate, and to identify and eliminate signs of 'oppositional' activity. Stymied in the Central Committee, the oppositions could gain no purchase in the broader Party officialdom.

When Stalin led the purge of the Left Oppositionists in the Komsomol, when he directed the attack on Zinoviev's stronghold in the Leningrad Party, and when he initiated the campaign against the 'Right danger', he knew he had the support of the majority of Party officials. He did not demand the persecution of oppositionists. He needed only to defend that persecution in the name of 'Party unity'. It was not his position as General Secretary per se that won him this advantage. Rather, it was his ability to retain a majority in the Politburo. As long as he held the majority and could define the 'Central Committee Line', he could portray all

---

[61] Mawdsley and White, *The Soviet Elite*, pp. 36–9.
[62] RGASPI f. 558, op. 11, d. 1122, 1. 165.

challenges to it as 'opposition' and 'factionalism'. The secretaries willingly followed suit, and similarly defined challenges to their power. In this
sense, Stalin benefited from a confluence of interests with Party officialdom. The persecution of real and potential support for his Politburo
rivals should not be viewed as evidence of control over the Party apparatus. It was only natural that the leaders of the 'oppositions' should have
taken every opportunity to accuse Stalin of using the Secretariat to undermine intra-Party democracy, to exclude them from Party discussions and
take other measures that directly violated Party statutes. Their accusations were generally accurate and just, but they were largely ignored
because Stalin's actions were supported by the vast majority of state
and Party officials.

In December 1925, Lev Kamenev reviewed Stalin's abuses of power to
the delegates of the Fourteenth Party Congress and demanded that he
be removed from his post as General Secretary. The response of delegates
was overwhelming: 'No way!', 'Nonsense!', 'We will not give you the
commanding heights!' Stalin was then given a lengthy standing ovation.[63]
Their support for Stalin was rooted in their shared interests. Of course
they shared other interests apart from an opposition to intra-Party
democracy. Stalin remained attentive to the needs and desires of
Party officialdom. But in the early 1930s, Stalin's relations with senior
Party officials soured. The industrialisation drive descended into crisis.
Collectivisation and punishing grain collections targets resulted in
rural chaos and famine. Some historians speculate that Party officials
began to question their support for Stalin.[64] The Central Committee
rarely met after the early 1930s. It is possible that Stalin was concerned
to face an organisation that was, according to Party statutes, empowered
to replace him.

Conclusion

The Secretariat did play a key role in Stalin's victory over the Left and
Right Oppositions in the 1920s, but not in ways that we have traditionally
understood it. The Secretariat was an exceedingly blunt instrument of
political struggle. It was barely able to manage its bureaucratic functions,
including the assignment of cadres to key posts. There is no evidence to

---

[63] *Chetyrnadtsatyi s''ezd vsesoiuznoi kommunisticheskoi partii (bolshevikov): stenograficheskii
otchet* (Moscow: Gosizdat, 1926), pp. 274–5.

[64] See for, example, *Oni ne molchali* (Moscow: Politizdat, 1991), pp. 422, 427–8; Iu. Aksiutin
et al., *Vlast' i oppozitsiia: Rossiiskii politicheskii protsess XX stoletiia* (Moscow: Rossiiskaia
politicheskaia entsiklopediia, 1995), ch. 5; A. V. Gusev, 'Levokommunisticheskaia oppozitsiia v SSSR v kontse 20-x godov', *Otechestvennaia istoriia* 6 (1996), 85, 93.

suggest that the fact of appointment was the basis for a special relationship between senior officials and Stalin. Stalin could not automatically command the support of officials in leading Party and state organs. The Secretariat did, however, provide Stalin with an invaluable source of information on the needs and concerns of senior Party and state officials.[65]

In particular, the correspondence of the Secretariat shows that these officials were anxious to put an end to the factional conflicts of the 1920s. Factional conflict, in the sense of a struggle for power, had not been limited to the Politburo leadership. The creation and expansion of the new Soviet state had provoked struggles for power at all levels. Out of the relatively loose order of the Bolshevik underground, a new structure of power was created, and the conflicts among officials and new institutions were severe. Leading officials faced constant challenges from subordinates, and the conflicts among Party leaders in Moscow only exacerbated them. In the early 1920s, the Secretariat was charged with bringing order to the bureaucratic chaos and the General Secretary was in a unique position to take advantage. Stalin's measures to limit 'Party democracy' were welcomed by institutional leaders, who were thus freed from the challenges that almost inevitably arose when policy was openly discussed. His measures against the 'Oppositions' were similarly applauded — and aggressively implemented — because they opened the door to the repression of their own rivals. In this sense, Stalin's rise to power was made possible by the active collusion of leading Party and state officials.

Though Stalin provided security of tenure to Party secretaries, his actions did not guarantee him votes in Central Committee plena and Party Congresses. The secretaries did not passively submit to directives. They had their own agendas of which they were aggressive advocates. Of course, they could not speak out against the 'Central Committee line'. They had seen to that. But in the early 1930s, when central policy headed in directions disturbing to them, deception, footdragging, and other forms of passive resistance became a fact of political life. Stalin could no longer be confident of his control of a Party apparatus that was indeed populated with 'double-dealers'. This picture of Stalin's insecurity, reinforced by evidence from recent document collections,

---

[65] Though not as Niels Rosenfeldt describes it in his monograph *Knowledge and Power: The Role of Stalin's Secret Chancellery in the Soviet System of Government* (Copenhagen: Rosenkilde and Bagger, 1978). Since the archives have opened, no new evidence has come to light corroborating the idea of a 'network of exclusive communication structures' culminating in the Secret department of the Secretariat.

challenges fundamental assumptions about the nature of political power in the 1930s. In spite of over ten years of relatively free archival access, we have a long way to go before our assumptions are placed on more solid empirical ground.

5 Stalin as Prime Minister: power and the Politburo

J. Arch Getty

The 1930s was the time when Stalin achieved an extreme centralisation of decision-making functions in the top Party bodies and ultimately in his own hands. It was also the time when the formal supreme policy body fell into disarray and disuse. According to our literature, the ultimate institutional locus of power, the Politburo, became less and less a collective organ of decision-making. Its formal procedures and routines fell into disuse and its meetings became less and less frequent. In 1930, the Politburo met seven to eight times per month on average, but by 1936 it never met more than once per month and in three months of that year did not meet at all.[1]

Decision-making at the top, formerly the province of the Politburo, was now carried out by informal, *ad hoc* subgroups of top leaders (some of them Politburo members and some not) who gathered when necessary to make decisions that then emerged as Politburo resolutions, whether or not the Politburo actually met. As these 'small loose-knit kitchen cabinets' replaced the Politburo, 'procedural indeterminacy' and 'formlessness' replaced structure.[2]

Here we shall look at the changes in the Politburo in the context of the relationship between Stalin and his colleagues in order to raise questions of power at the top of the Stalinist system. We will look at the withering away of the Politburo in the 1930s in comparative perspective and in terms of 'who decided what' at the top, and then conclude with some reflections on power and institutions in the Stalinist context. We shall suggest that the Politburo was never an organ of collective decision-making but rather a façade masking the practices of persons and groupings (some of them operating without Stalin): a team of senior politicians

---

[1] O. V. Khlevniuk, *Politbiuro: mekhanizmy politicheskoi vlasti v 1930-e gody* (Moscow: Rosspen, 1996), p. 288. Although changes in reporting procedures make it difficult to determine exactly when the Politburo met in 1937 and after, it seems that in the two years before the outbreak of war in 1941, it did not meet at all.

[2] Y. Gorlizki, 'Stalin's Cabinet: the Politburo and Decision-Making in the Post-war Years', *Europe-Asia Studies* 2 (2001), 291–6.

with personal relationships to Stalin and to each other. Raising questions about the Politburo's very existence, we will suggest that it was always more a symbol than an institution, and will therefore question whether its organisation, structure, and frequency of meeting are as important as the practices it masked.

It seems that there is some relationship between Stalin's accretion of power and changes in the Politburo. In his masterful study of the Politburo, Oleg Khlevniuk has documented the two processes, suggesting a kind of inverse proportional relationship: as Stalin's power grew, those around him were reduced from independent politicians to slaves, and the Politburo's status as a 'collective organ of power' decreased.[3] Yet the relationship between the two processes remains unclear. In the 1920s, the Politburo had met in expanded venues that included not only Politburo members, but also a larger group of members of the Central Committee and Central Control Commission, Secretariat department heads, and other specialists and guests. In these larger meetings, Stalin was unchallenged. They offered him the opportunity to perform his power and, on the face of it, they would seem only to enhance that power. There are few better ways to dominate others than in face-to-face settings in front of others. It is not therefore immediately evident that eliminating Politburo meetings would necessarily be in Stalin's interest or that it would enhance or better demonstrate his power.

The official image of the Politburo, enshrined in the Party's rules and propaganda, was that the Central Committee elected the best comrades to the Politburo, which was an organ of collective decision-making. It reached unanimous decisions because they were the correct decisions. This 'collective leadership' myth really came into its own after 1956 when Stalin's heirs sought to link their rule with the supposedly halcyon, collective Lenin period, and it remains with us today.

In fact, the Politburo was never a collective or collegial organ of power. From the beginning, the Politburo was politicised around a dominant team and real decisions were made outside the meeting space of the committee. Well before Stalin took power, Lenin had packed the leading Party organs with Bolsheviks who followed his line. He personalised and factionalised the Party Congress, the Central Committee, and the Politburo, working against rather than for the institutionalisation of collective

---

[3] 'There is no doubt that with the strengthening of Stalin's personal power his need to discuss problems with his colleagues diminished.' R. W. Davies, O. Khlevniuk, E. A. Rees, L. Kosheleva, and L. Rogovaia (eds.), *The Stalin–Kaganovich Correspondence, 1931–1936* (New Haven: Yale University Press, 2003), pp. xii–xiii. See Khlevniuk, *Politbiuro*, ch. 2. Khlevniuk quotes Moshe Lewin's remark about Stalin converting his lieutenants into 'slaves' (p. 245).

decision-making. Pragmatist that he was, he had little respect for institutional boundaries or guidelines when his proposals were at stake.

In 1920, in a walk around the Kremlin, Lenin advised a young and naïve Central Committee Secretary named Molotov to politicise the Secretariat, leaving the 'technical work' of that body to underlings. In 1921, at the Tenth Party Congress, he sponsored a ban on factions, while using a faction (his 'platform of 10') to control the Congress and defeat any dissidence. In private, he was frank about what he was doing:

> Is the majority entitled to be a majority? If it wants to be, then how should it be done? ... if the majority does not come to an arrangement, then the minority can win. This does happen. We are not a faction. We came as a faction, but we do not constitute a faction here. We should use our right in elections. In elections of delegates we have fought to win at the Congress. And this we should do.[4]

In 1922, he sent Mikoian to Siberia to make sure no Trotsky supporters were elected to the Eleventh Congress.[5] Lenin found a room in the Kremlin to hold a secret preparatory meeting consisting of only his supporters and excluding others. Ironically, it was Stalin who worried about bypassing the Congress. Lenin replied, 'Comrade Stalin, you are an old experienced factionalist yourself. Do not worry. Right now, we cannot do this any other way. I want everyone to be well prepared for the vote'[6] Later, Lenin proposed holding Politburo meetings without Trotsky who was, of course, a member of that body.[7]

As Molotov remembered, important decisions and votes of the Politburo were always prepared in advance by a smaller group: 'There was always the leading team in the Politburo ... all issues of prime importance were first addressed by the Politburo's leading group. That tradition started under Lenin.'[8] After Lenin, the tradition of secret premeetings continued, both for the Politburo and the Central Committee, with positions formulated without the participation of the full membership. According to the Politburo's technical secretary Boris Bazhanov,

> On the eve of a Politburo meeting ... the Troika [Stalin, Zinoviev, Kamenev] decided how each question should be resolved at tomorrow's session, agreeing even on what roles each would play in the discussion ... In effect everything had already been decided in the Troika's tight little circle.[9]

---

[4] Quoted in Richard Pipes, *The Unknown Lenin* (New Haven: Yale University Press, 1996), p. 123.

[5] A. I. Mikoian, *Tak bylo: razmyshleniia o minuvshem* (Moscow: Vagrius, 1999), p. 199.

[6] F. Chuev, *Sto sorok besed s Molotovym: iz dnevnika F. Chueva* (Moscow: 'Terra', 1991), p. 181.

[7] Chuev, *Sto sorok besed*, p. 200.   [8] *Ibid.*, p. 424.

[9] Boris Bazhanov, *Vospominaniia byvshego sekretaria Stalina* (Saint-Petersburg: Vsemirnoe Slovo, 1992), p. 47.

Mikoian recalls party leaders sneaking into the Orgburo's meeting room for secret pre-meetings without Trotskyist members.[10] Trotsky was, of course, aware of these practices and made a kind of passive protest in Politburo meetings by refusing to speak or accept assignments and by obtrusively ignoring the proceedings while reading French novels.[11]

Stalin's letters to Politburo members show that later a 'leading group' continued to orchestrate and script Politburo meetings in special pre-paratory Monday sessions to prepare for the meeting.[12] In 1930, newly appointed Politburo member S. I. Syrtsov quickly discovered that the Politburo had become a myth: 'The Politburo is a fiction. Everything is really decided behind the Politburo's back by a small clique ... It seems to me an abnormal situation when a whole series of Politburo questions is pre-decided by a particular group.'[13] In fact, there was nothing abnormal about it. From the beginning, the Politburo was never an organ of collective leadership, never what it was represented to be. One could say that the Politburo-as-institution never existed. Like many committees in the real world, it was a mask for a team that made decisions outside of the space and time of Politburo meetings, which took place merely to perform and promulgate them.

Normalising the Politburo

We still have to explain the decline of the Politburo's meetings. They provided a stage for Stalin to perform his power before and over those present, and were hardly a threat to that power.[14] Actually, the attenuation of these meetings had causes other than Stalin's personal power. One way to investigate this is to look at the Politburo (and the upper Stalinist leadership in general) as a cabinet, in comparative terms. Changes in the Stalinist Politburo seem to have paralleled changes in other cabinets in contemporary industrial countries that did not suffer from Stalinist dictatorship or tyranny.

Convergence theorists in the 1970s pointed to a number of parallels between Soviet and Western political structures, and analysts of

---

[10] Chuev, *Sto sorok besed*, p. 224; Khlevniuk, *Politbiuro*, p. 48; Mikoian, *Tak bylo*, p. 266.

[11] Bazhanov, *Vospominaniia*, p. 73.

[12] O. V. Khlevniuk et al. (eds.), *Pis'ma I. V. Stalina V. M. Molotovu, 1925–1936: Sbornik dokumentov* (Moscow: Rossiia Molodaia, 1995). See especially the letters for 1926.

[13] Rossiiskii gosudarstvennyi arkhiv sotsial'no-politicheskoi istorii (hemefirth RGASPI) f. 589, op. 3, d. 9333 (2), ll. 120–36. For a full account of Syrtsov's travails, see Khlevniuk, *Politbiuro*, pp. 44–9.

[14] Whether one follows Durkheim (that ritual performance demonstrates power relationships) or Geertz and Foucault (that they inscribe and create social and power relationships), there is a consensus that power and performance are related.

Brezhnev's Politburo wondered if that body was not approaching the status of a collegial cabinet.[15] Nevertheless, there are obvious and important differences between Stalin's Politburo and Western cabinets. Stalin's Politburo was not elected nor was it composed or installed as the result of any meaningful elections. It had no parliamentary responsibility and manifestly dominated the body that it supposedly served, the Central Committee. Stalin, unlike other prime ministers, could and did capriciously kill or imprison any of his cabinet's members or their families. Yet it is precisely these differences that make similarities between Stalin's Politburo and other cabinets all the more suggestive.

The USSR shared many features with contemporaneous modern societies in the West, including the European democracies, Nazi Germany, and the USA. Although they had dramatically different political systems, they had much in common after the First World War. At varying stages of development, all were industrial societies where urban populations were outstripping (or soon to outstrip) peasantries in weight of numbers. All were being welded together more tightly by modern transportation and communication networks. All had large and modernising military establishments. All had state police forces that carried out surveillance over their populations. All were becoming mass societies with mass cultures, media, and entertainment. All were becoming economically deep and broad, intensive and extensive complex economies. Those economies were increasingly directed and planned by their governments, regardless of the forms those governments took. Everywhere, there was a bigger role for government.[16]

We take as our comparison the Stalinist Politburo and the British Cabinet, largely because both are well studied and documented.[17]

---

[15] See John W. Meyer et al., 'Covergence and Divergence in Development', *Annual Review of Sociology* 1 (1975), 223–46. For a recent example, see Thomas Baylis, *Governing By Committee: Collegial Leadership in Advanced Societies* (New York: State University of New York Press, 1989).

[16] For suggestive and challenging works that put modern Russia into a context of European modernity in the twentieth century, see: David L. Hoffmann and Yanni Kotsonis (eds.), *Russian Modernity: Politics, Knowledge, Practices* (Houndsmills, N. Y.: St. Martin's Press, 2000); Peter Holquist, 'Society Versus the State, Society Wielding the State: Educated Society and State Power in Russia, 1914–1921', *Mouvement Social* 196 (2001); Peter Holquist, '"Information is the alpha and omega of our work": Bolshevik Surveillance in its Pan-European Context', *Journal of Modern History* 3 (1997), 21–40; Stephen Kotkin, 'Modern Times: The Soviet Union and the Interwar Conjuncture', *Kritika* 1 (2001); Amir Weiner, *Making Sense of War: The Second World War and the Fate of the Bolshevik Revolution* (Princeton: Princeton University Press, 2001).

[17] E. A. Rees has engaged this cabinet comparison and the literature relating to it (without reference to the 2003 paper on which this chapter is based). See his 'Introduction', to E. A. Rees (ed.), *The Nature of Stalin's Dictatorship: The Politburo, 1924–1953* (Basingstoke: Palgrave Macmillan, 2004) pp. 10–11 and p. 17, n. 17.

In recent years, a number of students of British politics, inspired by the observations of cabinet veteran Richard Crossman, have argued that the British governmental system has evolved from a parliamentary-cabinet into a 'core executive' in which 'Cabinet is confined largely to rubber-stamping decisions rather than developing a strategic overview of government.'[18] As with the Politburo, meetings of the full cabinet become less frequent and tend to approve decisions reached earlier by the prime minister and smaller groups of associates.[19] When the cabinet does meet, the prime minister is in control.

Some parallels are quite striking. Politburo meetings were rarely minuted and transcribed, perhaps because as in the British case, 'they do not take down in shorthand what was actually said because they prefer to record what should have been said.'[20] Control of texts and meeting results is a crucial component of political power. Stalin's summaries of Central Committee plena exercised through his control over editing of the texts of the plena's minuted decisions, became sources of power for him as the final printed versions he produced sometimes bore little relation to what had actually been said. In this way, Stalin was able to represent his views as those of the Central Committee.[21] His habit of waiting until the end of the meeting to speak, to sum up the discussion, allowed him to characterise the decision of the meeting in any way he chose. In the British Cabinet, Cabinet decisions (minutes) are often formulated by the prime minister verbally and then recorded by the Cabinet; the prime minister has the right to 'interpret the consensus' and write up the decision. 'It is always understood in British Cabinet life that the Prime Minister can define the consensus as being what he thinks fit. Even though a majority of the opinions expressed were against him, that would not necessarily prevent him from deciding as he wishes.'

[18] Martin J. Smith, *The Core Executive in Britain* (London: Macmillan, 1999), p. 76. See also Richard Crossman, *Inside View* (London: Cape, 1972); Richard Crossman, *The Myths of Cabinet Government* (Cambridge, Mass.: Harvard University Press, 1972); Graham P. Thomas, *Prime Minister and Cabinet Today* (Manchester: Manchester University Press, 1998).

[19] 'we prefer not to use the word disintegration with its connotation of a process of movement away from an integrated cabinet, since we prefer to avoid the implication that in all countries there used to be "golden age" of cabinet government in which the cabinet members sitting collectively took the important decisions.' Thomas T. Mackie and Brian W. Hogwood, 'Decision Arenas in Executive Decision Making: Cabinet Committees in Comparative Perspective', *British Journal of Political Science* 3 (1984), 311.

[20] Crossman, *Myths*, pp. 41–2.

[21] See, for example, J. Arch Getty and Oleg V. Naumov, *The Road to Terror: Stalin and the Self-Destruction of the Bolsheviks, 1932–1939* (New Haven: Yale University Press, 1999), pp. 229–44; James Seaman, 'The Politics of Texts: Central Committee of the CPSU Plenum Stenograms, 1924–1941', unpublished Ph.D. diss., UCLA (2004).

'Sometimes, as a member of the cabinet [reading them], it was not your impression of what happened ... Once the Prime Minister has summed up, though, it may not represent the discussion at all, once he sums up, the Secretary of the Cabinet will record it.'[22]

As the Politburo met less and less often in the 1930s, decisions promulgated over its name were taken by smaller, *ad hoc* groups convened for specific purposes and often meeting in Stalin's office (the famous sextets, septets, etc.). At other times, standing or *ad hoc* commissions were charged with recommending decisions on various topics.[23] Stalin was not always a member of these groups, and it is unlikely that he ultimately approved each of their decisions.[24] Called 'segmented' or 'fragmented' decision-making, such arrangements are not at all uncommon in modern government arrangements (the American government being a prime example).[25] 'Real debates occur therefore in smaller groups, either formally constituted ... or informally called together – typically when two or three members see each other, one of them being, in many cases at least, the prime minister. Thus ... true debates of the full cabinet are relatively rare.'[26]

Given what we know of Stalin's practice, the following account by a British Cabinet participant would not be far wrong if 'Stalin' were substituted for 'Mrs. Thatcher':

> She would have an idea, or somebody would, and she would talk to them. She would bring two or three people in for the second meeting and we'd discuss it a bit further ... She ... would then identify those in the cabinet who had the most concerns about that policy and then they were talked to ... and by the time it came to the cabinet it was a *fait accompli*. (Lord Wakeham)[27]

---

[22] Crossman, *Myths*, pp. 33–7.

[23] On Politburo commissions see Jana Howlett et al., 'The CPSU's Top Bodies Under Stalin: Their Operational Records and Structure of Command', *University of Toronto Stalin-Era Research and Archives Project Working Paper No. 1* (1996), p. 7. O. V. Khlevniuk, *Stalinskoe Politbiuro v 30-e gody: sbornik dokumentov* (Moscow: AIRO-XX, 1995), pp. 44–73.

[24] Stalin was not a member of every Politburo standing commission. Gorlizki ('Stalin's Cabinet', p. 294) notes that the various –'tets' sometimes met without Stalin in the 1940s. For the matter of Stalin approving all such decisions, see below.

[25] Rudi Andeweg, 'A Model of the Cabinet System: the Dimensions of Cabinet Decision-Making Processes', in Jean Blondel and Ferdinand Muller-Rommel (eds.), *Governing Together: The Extent and Limits of Joint Decision-Making in Western European Cabinets* (London: St. Martin's Press, 1993), p. 29.

[26] Blondel and Muller-Rommel (eds.), *Governing Together*, p. 12.

[27] Smith, *Core Executive*, p. 89. Compare with Gorlizki's formulation: 'These narrow and informal Politburo meetings were freed from the schedules and procedures which hamstrung the official or de jure cabinet. In the company of a small circle of colleagues, all of whom were well known to Stalin and to each other, there was all the less reason to follow the inconvenient and time-consuming protocols of formal Politburo sessions.' Gorlizki, 'Stalin's Cabinet', p. 295.

Stalin never abolished the Politburo, even after it ceased to meet. Among the reasons for keeping it, in addition to the need for a formal, public institutional face for the leadership, was Stalin's desire to 'bind his co-leaders in a system of collective responsibility ... indispensable as a tool for controlling the leadership'.[28] Richard Crossman, during his years in the British Cabinet, seems also to have felt the pressure of democratic centralism: 'Collective responsibility ... means that everybody who is in the Government must accept and publicly support every "Cabinet decision", even if he was not present at the discussion or, frequently, was completely unaware the decision had been taken'.[29]

How can we account for the similarity in practices between the British Cabinet and Stalin's Politburo? One obvious answer would have to do with the leader's power. It is likely that Thatcher and Stalin shared a hunger for total power, if not an equal ability to realise it. In such segmented decision-making environments, the boss 'is at the centre of the networks that traverse the core executive and therefore he or she has access to all areas of government.'[30] It is therefore not obvious how the replacement of cabinet meetings (which he or she firmly controls) by segmented decision-making necessarily reflects changes in the leader's power.

Andeweg argues that although 'truly collective and collegial cabinets may have existed in the past in some countries ... It is highly improbable that this type will be found frequently in large and complex modern societies'.[31] In his study of cabinet practices, he found a positive correlation between size/complexity of government and economy on the one hand, and segmented, subcommittee decision-making on the other. Thus, segmented forms (with fewer meetings of the entire cabinet) were more common in Britain and France, while full cabinet meetings were held more often in Ireland, Norway, and other relatively small systems.[32] Other research produced similar results.[33] As Crossman put it, 'one

---

[28] Gorlizki, 'Stalin's Cabinet', p. 297.   [29] Crossman, *Myths*, p. 53.

[30] Smith, *Core Executive*, p. 77. Simon James argues that fragmented decision-making 'enhances the premier's position: he becomes one of the few who knows what is going on in all areas of government.' Simon James, *British Cabinet Government* (London: Routledge, 1992), p. 179.

[31] Andeweg, 'Model of the Cabinet System', p. 38.

[32] Andeweg, 'Model of the Cabinet System', pp. 29–30.

[33] 'The full meeting has also ceased to be regarded as crucial for decision-making, at least in a large number of cases and in most countries ... the ideal of a cabinet meeting truly taking the most important decisions does not correspond to reality.' Andre-Paul Frognier, 'The Single-Party/Coalition Distinction and Cabinet Decision-Making', in Blondel and Muller-Rommel (eds.), *Governing Together*, pp. 78–81. On Switzerland, see Baylis, *Governing by Committee*.

underlying cause of this change is quite simply the enormous growth in the powers of modern government'.[34]

There is no doubt that the complexity of Soviet government increased dramatically in the twenty years following 1917. The size of the apparatus grew tremendously after 1929 along with the economy, now a matter for state administration. The number of commissariats grew almost every year and, at the top, members of the Politburo came more and more to be economic administrators. With this expansion came an increasingly heavy workload for the Politburo. In 1930, 2,857 items came before the Politburo; by 1934 the annual number was 3,982.[35] The last Politburo meeting of 1930 (25 December) had 100 items on its agenda. The last meeting for 1936 (27 December) had 453.[36] The Politburo, like other cabinets, had 'a full agenda of issues for decision; it is to prevent over-crowding of the cabinet agenda that mechanisms for taking decisions elsewhere are established.' They needed 'a repertoire of formal and informal mechanisms for processing' the huge number of matters coming before it.[37]

The Politburo in the early 30s, like the Central Committee in the early 20s, was swamped and tried to cope with the crush of business in various ways, including trying to meet more often. In the 1920s, the Politburo typically met three times per month (on the 5th, 15th, and 25th) with extra sessions as needed.[38] At the end of 1930, six meetings per month were planned, but in 1931 the Politburo met more than six times in nine of the months for a total of ninety-four meetings instead of seventy-two.[39]

Members also tried to streamline their meetings. Mikoian remembers Lenin's vigorous chairing practices: each reporter got no more than three minutes to speak; seven for 'especially complex' matters. Items requiring any discussion at all were immediately referred to a working committee (*delovaia komissiia*) which was to report back and present a draft resolution. 'Only this can explain how Lenin could deal with so many varied questions in such a short time'.[40] It must have been in this spirit when, at the end of 1929, the Politburo ordered that no requests or reports from lower bodies to the Politburo could exceed five to ten pages and that they must reach the Secretariat no later than six days before the Politburo meeting, complete with a pre-drafted Politburo

---

[34] Crossman, *Myths*, p. ix.   [35] Khlevniuk, *Politbiuro*, p. 289.
[36] RGASPI f. 17, op. 3, d. 808 (Protocol No. 21) and d. 982 (Protocol No. 44).
[37] Mackie and Hogwood, 'Decision Arenas', p. 311.
[38] RGASPI f. 17, op. 3, d. 761, l. 11.
[39] RGASPI f. 17, op. 162, d. 9, l. 112; Khlevniuk, *Politbiuro*, p. 289.
[40] Mikoian, *Tak bylo*, p. 201.

resolution.[41] A year later, in November of 1931, the Politburo reduced the maximum size of submissions to four to five pages, but a few days later settled on a maximum of eight pages.[42] Stalin ordered in September 1932 that no more than fifteen items could appear on any Politburo meeting's agenda.[43] By the spring of 1931, all requests for Politburo decisions from localities were shunted to the Secretariat for decision, except for questions of 'exceptional importance' that could come to the Politburo.[44]

But the most important expedient the Politburo used to get through the mountain of paper was decision-making by polling the members (*oprosom*). Questions not requiring extended discussion were routed to Politburo members for their approval outside normal Politburo meeting times. By the beginning of 1931, the number of questions decided *oprosom* exceeded those on the agenda by a wide margin. By the end of 1934, at its final meeting of the year, the Politburo took up eight questions at its meeting but the protocols indicate that 260 questions had been decided *oprosom*.[45] It seemed less and less useful to call the entire Politburo together for a meeting and more often this happened only when some serious matter required the attention of all Politburo members, regardless of their current specialised activity.

As in other large and complex organisations, each member was busy with his own bailiwick. Khrushchev would later complain that decision-making by small groups shut the other Politburo members out of the process. He complained that even though he was a Politburo member, he knew nothing about the details of Soviet policy on naval affairs, Poland, Germany, and other topics: 'I was already a Politburo member, but we never discussed the problem [of West Berlin]. I do not know who discussed it with Stalin.'[46] But does the American Secretary of Agriculture participate in discussions about foreign policy? Does every British cabinet minister know or care much about the Navy? 'Ministers often do not have

---

[41] RGASPI f. 17, op. 3, d. 761, ll. 11–12. Fearing attempts to inflate the reports, the decree specified that a page could consist of no more than 1,500 characters: 30 lines of 50 characters!

[42] RGASPI f. 17, op. 3, d. 858, l. 2; d. 860, l. 2.

[43] RGASPI f. 17, op. 3, d. 898, l. 8.   [44] RGASPI f. 17, op. 3, d. 823, l. 9.

[45] RGASPI f. 17, op. 3, d. 771 (Protocol No. 112); d. 808 (Protocol No. 21); d. 955 (Protocol No. 17).

[46] Nikita Sergeevich Khrushchev et al., *Khrushchev Remembers: the Glasnost Tapes*, 1st edn. (Boston: Little Brown, 1990), pp. 18, 202. In Britain, 'it was usual, during and after the Second World War, for many other policy questions to be formulated and settled within cabinet committees and small groups of Ministers ... major decisions were not reported to the full cabinet but were, even at that level, shrouded in secrecy.' Mackie and Hogwood, 'Decision Arenas', p. 303.

the interest, time or ability to be involved in other areas of policy ... They do not read papers of other departments if they feel it has no implications for their own department'.[47] Did Khrushchev really want or have time to know about the Navy at the time? As Molotov recalls,

Had we convened to make a democratic decision on each question that came up, we should have inflicted harm on the state and on the Party, because this would have dragged out a solution to the question.[48]

With hundreds of *opros* cards flying about, with several commissions and *ad hoc* groups constantly meeting to draft decisions, with the steady traffic of groups of senior officials through Stalin's office, a continuous series of specialised meetings took the place of occasional assemblies of generalists. This is a quite logical development in any growing organisation. It is hard to imagine how they could have dealt with the mass of information and barrage of issues in any other way. Thus we can decouple the supposed decline of the Politburo as an institution from the process of Stalin's accretion of total power. That some of the evolution (or devolution) of the Stalinist Politburo seems to have been paralleled elsewhere where there was no dictatorship suggests that the withering away of the Politburo may have been the result of modernisation and complexity rather than dictatorship.[49]

---

[47] Smith, *Core Executive*, p. 76. 'In fact, your colleagues were a little apt to be cross with you if you bored them with a topic which was neither politically eye-catching, nor was something which any of the rest of them were involved with.' Maurice Kogan (ed.), *The Politics of Education: Edward Boyle and Anthony Crossland in Conversation with Maurice Kogan* (Harmondsworth: Penguin, 1971), p. 105.

[48] Chuev, *Sto sorok besed*, p. 468.

[49] However, it would be an exaggeration to use comparative modernity as the sole explanation here. Kenneth Jowitt called the Soviet Union a combination of modern and traditional political features: a historically distinct type of 'routinisation in a neo-traditional direction.' Modern features (science, empiricism, rational administration) were mixed with traditional ones (charisma, the heroic, personal, and voluntarist.) The traditional, pre-modern features that characterised Stalinist personal politics included patrons (the 'big men' of peasant-status societies), a public emphasis on 'notables', non-cash privileges, blat and reciprocity in social interactions, charismatic emphasis on secrecy, a precise array of titles, and a public (and private) understanding of power as patrimonial. See Kenneth Jowitt, *New World Disorder: the Leninist Extinction* (Berkeley: University of California Press, 1992). For an analysis of the popular understanding of patrimonial power under Stalin, see Jeffrey Brooks, *'Thank You, Comrade Stalin!': Soviet Public Culture from Revolution to Cold War* (Princeton: Princeton University Press, 2000). For similar approaches, see also T. Martin, 'Modernisation or Neo-Traditionalism? Ascribed Nationality and Soviet Primordialism', in S. Fitzpatrick (ed.), *Stalinism: New Directions* (New York: Routledge, 2000), and Andrew George Walder, *Communist Neo-traditionalism: Work and Authority in Chinese Society* (Berkeley: University of California Press, 1986).

Who decided what?

The Politburo protocols and other materials at our disposal still do not tell us much about the actual mechanics of decision-making in the narrow elite. The materials we do have make it clear that no major decision of national scope could have been taken without Stalin's initiative or explicit approval. Certainly, no Politburo member could advance fundamental criticism of the government's policy (the 'General Line') or argue for major changes of direction at odds with Stalin and the majority, even if he wanted to, and expect to keep his seat in the cabinet.[50]

Recognising this, however, does not exhaust the subjects of power or decision-making. The ability to decide the directions of national policy is only one form of power, and while it is important, it does not begin to encompass the myriad personal relationships and venues in which power was won, lost, and deployed. Thousands of decisions were taken at Politburo level that directly affected the real lives of real people no less than questions of global strategy, and Stalin did not take them all. Aside from the laconic Politburo protocols and the spotty memoir evidence, we now have a unique set of sources for the 1930s shedding light on decision-making in the inner circle: the correspondence between Stalin and L. M. Kaganovich while the former was on his lengthy annual holidays in the south.[51] During Stalin's absences, Kaganovich as tacit Second Secretary of the Central Committee, supervised decision-making in Moscow while in communication with Stalin.[52] For these annual periods, which in the 1930s ranged from two to three months, we have a continuous written record that provides an invaluable window on the policy process in the Politburo.

The editors of this correspondence stress the constant communication between Stalin and his Moscow lieutenants as evidence of Stalin's hands-on control of matters even when he was not present. But one can see this glass as half empty rather than half full. On the face of it, it seems quite remarkable that a micromanaging dictator would absent himself for three months per year to a faraway place with no telephone during what had

---

[50] Of course, the same might be said of the British or American cabinets.

[51] An excellent critical edition of this correspondence, with extensive notes and cross-references, has recently been published. O. V. Khlevniuk, R. U. Devis (R. W. Davies), L. P. Kosheleva, E. A. Ris (E. A. Rees), and L. A. Rogovaia (eds.), *Stalin i Kaganovich. Perepiska 1931–1936gg.* (Moscow: Rosspen, 2001).

[52] Formally, the position of Second Secretary of the Central Committee did not exist, but numerous documents show that Molotov filled this function until 1930. When Molotov was transferred to Sovnarkom, Kaganovich took over the job. Khlevniuk et al. (eds.), *Stalin i Kaganovich*, p. 26.

become the most crucial season of all for the Soviet economy: harvest time. One cannot imagine a British prime minister or American president so absenting her/himself, with or without a telephone.[53] It is really quite striking. Even though Stalin was in close contact with his lieutenants, that contact was not face to face nor even by voice; it was written and thereby without the nuance, body language, and voice inflection that are so important to any human communication. Those written communications took two to three days each way (telegrams were faster but rarer). Frequently questions and answers from both sides passed each other in transit.[54]

Looking closely at one of these periods can be quite revealing. 1934 was the last period of Stalin's absence without a telephone. It was also the busiest year of the 1930s for Politburo resolutions: there were 3,945 decisions listed on Politburo protocols for that year and the Politburo met forty-six times. During Stalin's holiday (August through October, 1934), more than a quarter of Politburo decisions (1,038 of the year's 3,945) were registered and sixteen of the Politburo's forty-six meetings took place without Stalin's presence.[55]

In general, communications Stalin received included protocols of Politburo meetings, notifications of decisions taken by polling or by Politburo commissions, communications received for information purposes (diplomatic and internal letters), and requests for his decision on various matters. The tone of the correspondence clearly shows the subordinate relationship. Kaganovich was often asking for guidance. 'I ask your opinion' or 'I request instructions' (effectively the same thing) were common ways for him to end a letter to Stalin, and Kaganovich flattered the boss by characterising the latter's decisions as 'wise' or 'absolutely correct'. All of Stalin's 'proposals' were of course quickly confirmed by Kaganovich and the others as Politburo decisions.

Yet Politburo members took a large number of decisions without Stalin's participation. Stalin intervened in only 119 (11 per cent) of the 1,038 recorded Politburo decisions taken during his vacation in 1934.[56] The great majority of his interventions (91 of 119, or 76 per cent) were

[53] We do not know when secure government (*VCh*) telephone service was established between Moscow and the south, but circumstantial evidence suggests 1935. Khlevniuk et al. (eds.), *Stalin i Kaganovich*, p. 8.

[54] Stalin and Kaganovich had to number each letter so the recipient could keep track.

[55] Khlevniuk, *Politbiuro*, pp. 288–9.

[56] These and the following calculations were made by comparing the decisions recorded in Politburo Prococols Nos. 11–15 (RGASPI f. 17, op. 3, dd. 949–53), August–October 1934, with matters answered or initiated by Stalin in the same period. Khlevniuk et al. (eds.), *Stalin i Kaganovich*, pp. 414–519.

Stalin and Politburo Decisions, August–October 1934	
Total Politburo decisions	1,038
Politburo decisions without Stalin's participation	919
Total Politburo decisions with Stalin's participation	119
Stalin replies to Politburo requests for ruling	91
Stalin agrees with Politburo proposal without modification	76
Stalin disagrees with or changes Politburo decision	15

responses to initiatives from Kaganovich. The remainder consists of points first raised by Stalin.[57] These numbers show that of all Politburo decisions taken in these three months, Stalin either did not respond to, or routinely confirmed, his lieutenants' decisions 96 per cent of the time. Of his replies to Kaganovich's requests for guidance, he confirmed his lieutenants' proposal or decision without modification 84 per cent of the time.

Clearly, some kinds of questions had to be referred to the boss. As in any cabinet system, foreign policy, military policy, security, major budgetary allocations, and government reorganisation were matters for the leader's personal attention and decision.[58] Virtually anything having to do with the NKVD or security matters came to Stalin.[59]

However, Stalin left many matters to Kaganovich and the other Politburo members for decision, and many of them were not trivial. Issues such as supply for the Far Eastern Red Army, most appointments at the RSFSR level (All-Russian Central Executive Committee (VTsIK), Gosplan RSFSR, and RSFSR Commissariats), specific matters of product import/export, agricultural seed loans to the regions, exceptions

---

[57] Stalin initiated very few new projects *in absentia*. His unsolicited communications often related to things he read in *Pravda* or *Bol'shevik*, objecting to particular journalistic formulations. (Khlevniuk et al. (eds.), *Stalin i Kaganovich*, pp. 419, 452.) On one occasion, he became excited over the accomplishments of aviator Gromov and suggested laudatory recognition. Other times, he sent general messages exhorting his Politburo colleagues in general to greater firmness on grain collection or in negotiations with foreign powers.

[58] Examples include treaties with foreign states, entry into the League of Nations, scheduling military manœuvres, appointments of Commissars and their deputies and of regional-level (*obkom, kraikom*) party posts, the reorganisation of trade unions and commissariats in industry and trade, and quarterly capital allocations.

[59] 'Security matters' were broadly defined under Stalin and included such things as proposed commercial flight routes by Lufthansa and PanAm (he was against them from fear of espionage). In another case, he dwelt at length on the case of a mentally unbalanced civil defence leader who made anti-Soviet statements to his young charges (Stalin wanted him to be shot).

from grain procurement targets, and allocations of housing funds and industrial materials were often left to the lieutenants' discretion.

On some very important questions, Stalin contented himself with providing general guidance or exhortation and then turning the matter over to Kaganovich and the team. The Japanese invasion of Manchuria had made the Soviet Far Eastern Railway (KVZhD) untenable, and negotiations were underway in 1934 to sell it to the Japanese. These negotiations were tense and difficult, with Japanese harassment and arrests of KVZhD personnel, border incursions on both sides, hard bargaining about price, and mutual strategic *démarches* in the press meant to embarrass the other side. The USSR had seen war scares on much less. The Politburo was continually formulating detailed instructions to its negotiators, statements to the Japanese, and oral messages to be sent unofficially. With Stalin gone, the Politburo took decisions nineteen times on the KVZhD. Of these, Kaganovich sent thirteen messages to Stalin, consisting of draft diplomatic statements and requests for advice. Of these thirteen messages, Stalin agreed six times without comment. He disagreed or suggested changes twice, and did not reply at all five times. Once, he sent an unsolicited message advising Kaganovich in general terms to be tough with the Japanese. Effectively, Stalin allowed his lieutenants to conduct these delicate and dangerous negotiations.

If, as Khlevniuk has argued, Stalin's growing political power reduced his colleagues from independent politicians to slaves, one would expect his micromanagement of all decision-making to increase. Instead, the opposite seems to have been the case: he often seems to have delegated more in the 1930s than previously. In September 1933, he wrote from his holiday location to Kaganovich and the Politburo in Moscow: 'I cannot and should not have to decide any and all questions that animate the Politburo ... you yourselves can consider things and work them out.'[60]

Stalin did not micromanage or even approve everything. Molotov remembers hundreds of Politburo resolutions sent to Stalin *after* going out over his signature. They remained piled up in bundles in the corner of his office, signed for him by his staff, but unread by him. Molotov recalls Stalin asking what was important for him to look at and decide; when *they* told *him* what needed attention, he would concentrate on it. 'You can't say, as Kirov did, that "Not one question is decided unless Stalin is the author of it." That's wrong. You can't even say that about Lenin.'[61]

[60] RGASPI f. 558, op. 11, d. 80, l. 87.
[61] Chuev, *Sto sorok besed*, pp. 258–9, 263. Similarly, 'the prime minister will rarely be directly involved in issues, though he or she will be able to select a very limited number of issues for personal intervention and that intervention will often be decisive. The prime

For example, N. I. Ezhov, as Orgburo member and Secretary of the Central Committee, in 1936 resolved major disputes between the First Secretary of Voronezh Regional Committee (*Obkom*) and the Commissariat of Heavy Industry over the right to appoint factory directors, and between party First Secretaries and the Council of Peoples' Commissars (Sovnarkom) over the appointment of State Harvest Plenipotentiaries.[62] Such issues involved high-ranking disputants and senior appointments.[63] Stalin frequently referred questions that had reached him down to his lieutenants for decision. His notation, '*kak byt'?*' ('What to do?') is frequently found on archival documents that Stalin directed to his associates for decision on such non-trivial matters as Evgenii Varga's resignation as Director of the Scientific Research Institute of World Economy, the appointment of senior political department (*politotdel*) workers on the railroads, and the staff of the newspaper *Izvestiia*.

Stalin's lieutenants also wielded considerable power as framers of questions. Matters coming to Stalin for his personal decision or approval, even on important personnel questions, arrived as recommended appointments. Sometimes, subordinates offered the dictator a choice of two or three candidates for a post, and sometimes Stalin refused the choices and appointed another candidate altogether. But most often a single proposed candidate came to Stalin and most often he approved the recommendation.

We have something like a picture of the process for 1935–6. Malenkov, as head of the personnel department of the Central Committee (ORPO), proposed candidates for high Party posts.[64] His recommendations went to Ezhov, a Secretary of the Central Committee, who negotiated with the parties concerned and put the matter on Stalin's desk for approval:

Comrade Stalin! I have summoned Pshenitsyn. He agrees to become Second Secretary in Sverdlovsk [replacing Strogonov]. I had a telephone conversation with Comrade Kabakov [Sverdlovsk First Secretary]. He is very satisfied at Strogonov being placed at the disposal of the Central Committee. He agrees with the candidacy of Pshenitsyn, and asks for a quick formulation.[65]

On other occasions, Ezhov was more forthright in his recommendations to Stalin: 'Comrade Stalin! To name Kalygin as Secretary of Voronezh

---

minister will often be unaware of decisions taken in the name of his or her government, even decisions taken in the name of cabinet committees.' Mackie and Hogwood, 'Decision Arenas', pp. 310–11.
[62] RGASPI f. 17, op. 120, d. 19, ll. 88–9; f. 671, op. 1, d. 18, l. 88.
[63] RGASPI f. 17, op. 120, d. 20, l. 24.   [64] RGASPI f. 671, op. 1, d. 18, l. 123.
[65] *Ibid.*, ll. 18–19.

City Committee [*gorkom*] Riabinin [First Secretary of Voronezh *Obkom*] agrees. Comrades Kaganovich and Molotov agree. I ask approval. Ezhov'.[66] On another occasion, Ezhov simply wrote to Stalin that 'we should approve Kogan's request to leave the Moscow-Volga project.'[67]

Stalin's lieutenants were powerful political actors. Each of them headed their own networks of patronage and were masters in their own bureaucratic houses.[68] They battled with each other over budgets and lines of turf authority. Among many notable fights, Zhdanov struggled with Malenkov; Ordzhonikidze with Kuibyshev; Kuibyshev with Andreev; Ordzhonikidze with Molotov.[69] These were more than just business-like squabbles; they were battles of titans whose resolution affected the livelihoods, powers, and fates of thousands of underlings, each of whom deployed their own powers in response. Although Kaganovich assures us that these fights were business, not personal,[70] we have evidence that sometimes they ran deeper. Aside from Mikoian's polite recollection that 'Sergo did not love Molotov very much',[71] we have correspondence between Stalin and Ordzhonikidze in which the latter calls Molotov an obscenity (*negodiai*) and complains that Molotov had opposed him from the beginning. Molotov and Ordzhonikidze began to ignore each other, and their mutual attempts to isolate the other threatened the government. In all these fights, Stalin was at pains to moderate and act as referee.[72]

Politburo members were not slaves, nor was their power reduced as Stalin's increased.[73] Sometimes Politburo members argued with Stalin; we know that Ordzhonikidze, Molotov, and Voroshilov did more than once, and occasionally they won the argument.[74] True, they were not able to challenge Stalin's control over global decisions, but what cabinet

[66] *Ibid.*, l. 97.   [67] *Ibid.*, ll. 59–61.

[68] Khlevniuk reminds us that each Politburo member had groups of followers in the provinces and in the *vedomstva* (institutions) he controlled (Khlevniuk, *Politbiuro*, pp. 262–3). Stalin frequently acted as referee among them and their empires.

[69] Sheila Fitzpatrick, 'Ordzhonikidze's Takeover of VSNKh: A Case Study in Soviet Bureaucratic Politics', *Soviet Studies* 2 (1985), 153–72; Jonathan Harris, 'The Origins of the Conflict between Malenkov and Zhdanov, 1939–1941', *Slavic Review* 2 (1976), 287–303; Khlevniuk et al. (eds.), *Stalin i Kaganovich*, pp. 20–1, 303; Khlevniuk, *Stalinskoe Politbiuro*, pp. 79, 85, 242–5, 59–60, 63–4; F. Chuev, *Tak govoril Kaganovich: Ispoved' stalinskogo apostola* (Moscow: Otechestvo, 1992), p. 130; Mikoian, *Tak bylo*, p. 324.

[70] Chuev, *Tak govoril Kaganovich*, p. 130.   [71] Mikoian, *Tak bylo*, p. 324.

[72] RGASPI f. 558, op. 11, d. 779, ll. 23, 29–31, 33. See also Khlevniuk et al. (eds.), *Stalin i Kaganovich*, p. 21; Khlevniuk, *Politbiuro*, p. 85.

[73] See Khlevniuk, *Politbiuro*, ch. 2. Khlevniuk quotes Moshe Lewin's remark about Stalin converting his lieutenants into 'slaves' (p. 245).

[74] Chuev, *Sto sorok besed*, pp. 70, 297, 453; Khlevniuk, *Politbiuro*, pp. 241–5; Khlevniuk et al. (eds.), *Stalin i Kaganovich*, pp. 33, 132.

minister can and why should he want to? Nevertheless, these were extremely powerful men whose authority grew along with Stalin's.

One source of Stalin's authority from the earliest days was his ability to work in committee: to listen, to moderate, to referee, to steer the discussion toward a consensus. This had earned him the respect, co-operation, and loyalty of senior Bolsheviks. Khrushchev tells us that Stalin did not like to be alone, that he always wanted people around him. Put another way, he functioned best in groups. His office logs do not suggest a lonely and solitary dictator who made decisions without discussion and consultation with others. During his working hours he was nearly always in the company of his team which often remained in his office for many hours at a stretch while lesser figures came and went.[75] As we have seen, team members were able to take decisions even when the boss was on holiday for months at a time. They were loyal to him and he to them. Although some recently appointed Politburo members were purged in the Great Terror of the 1930s, the core group (Molotov, Kaganovich, Ordzhonikidze, Mikoian, Andreev, Voroshilov) was untouched.[76] To a considerable extent, the top Stalinist leadership seems to have been a team effort in the 1920s, 30s, and 40s.[77] The supposition that the Politburo stopped meeting because Stalin's enhanced power obviated any need to discuss problems with his colleagues is not supported by any documentary evidence and contradicted by a good deal we now know. Whether or not the Politburo met in a given period, the group context of his decision-making seems to have remained largely the same throughout his reign.

Power and Stalin's government

What was the Politburo? Yoram Gorlizki has made a convincing case that the Politburo had two faces: a public one, a 'robust symbol' designed to project unity and wise leadership, and a hidden one. Behind the scenes, the hidden Politburo was actually many Politburos, a constantly shifting composition of senior members who came together for specific purposes

[75] The logs are published in *Istoricheskii arkhiv* 6 (1994); 2–6 (1995); 2–6 (1996); 1 (1997). Stalin defined this team as 'not accidentally ... having come together in the struggle with Trotskyist-Zinovievist and Bukharin-Rykov deviations.' Stalin letter to Ordzhonikidze, after 9 September 1931, RGASPI f. 558, op. 11, d. 779, ll. 21–3.

[76] T. H. Rigby, 'Was Stalin a Disloyal Patron?' *Soviet Studies* 3 (1986), 311–24.

[77] See Stephen G. Wheatcroft, 'From Team-Stalin to Degenerate Tyranny', in Rees (ed.), *The Nature of Stalin's Dictatorship*, pp. 79–107.

and decisions.[78] What Victor Thompson called the 'dramaturgy' myth of hierarchical formal organisations that concealed the real decision-making power applies here. The appearance of a stable and wise institution creates regime legitimacy and provides the public with a sense of stability and order. It is a far better and more respectable public image than the naked reality of changing groups of lieutenants and cliques.[79] But what lay behind the façade?

Was the Politburo, even the hidden one(s) ever an institution, either before or after it stopped meeting? Oleg Kharkhordin wrote that governments and institutions exist only because people believe they do. In reality, they are little more than collections of individuals banded together to deploy power behind an institutional façade. Foucault argued much the same thing; the state for him being 'nothing more than a composite reality and mythicised abstraction' of polyvalent and diverse relations of force.[80]

For Pierre Bourdieu, the notion of 'the state' makes sense only as a convenient stenographic label.[81] Going back to Max Weber, he notes that states (or in our case, the Politburo) are not really grounded in logical, linguistic, or empirical reality. Weber observed that the empirical reality of the state was united by idea and belief, hiding a plethora of human actions and reactions. We use words like 'state' or 'Politburo' to describe actions that are really performed by individuals.[82] The state (or the Politburo) belongs to the 'realm of symbolic production' and exists only at the level of belief. Those behind the façade are able to monopolise and manipulate what Bourdieu called 'symbolic capital.' The state is something that is naturally and subconsciously 'misrecognised' by the public as a real institution, a recognised authority, when in fact it is a set of contingencies and arrangements.[83] Further, part of the state's symbolic projection of itself involves structuring the very categories of thought that citizens (and we ourselves) use to understand it. Bourdieu wants

---

[78] Gorlizki, 'Stalin's Cabinet'. In other venues, 'cabinets perform a legitimating role, by their very existence as much as by what they actually discuss or decide.' Mackie and Hogwood, 'Decision Arenas', p. 306.

[79] Baylis, *Governing by Committee*, p. 16.

[80] Oleg Kharkhordin, 'What is the State? The Russian Concept of *Gosudarstvo* in the European Context', *History and Theory* 40 (2001), 234.

[81] Pierre Bourdieu and Loic Wacquant, *An Invitation to Reflexive Sociology* (Chicago: University of Chicago Press, 1992), p. 111.

[82] See Kharkhordin's discussion which follows Alf Ross and Bourdieu. Kharkhordin, 'What is the State?', pp. 206–9.

[83] Bourdieu defines 'symbolic violence' as the process in which elites impose meanings on symbols to produce 'misrecognition' of how they were produced. The result is 'illusio', in which people believe and are thus caught up in a system that seems naturally produced.

'to expose the danger of always being thought by a state that we believe we are thinking ... One of the major powers of the state is to produce and impose ... categories of thought that we spontaneously apply to ... the state itself.'[84]

The state (or Politburo) thus exists because we think it does and because it wants us to think so. The Politburo was particularly good at this: Soviet citizens and later scholars continue to believe it existed as an institution because it said it did. It issued decrees, was referred to in the controlled public discourse, and carried a roster of members even when it never met. Like Soviet citizens, we continue to fall for the trick; we imagine it as a real institution, study its procedures and organisation, worry about crises and changes in its work, and refer to it as a tangible, objective body.

The Stalinists instinctively grasped the unreality of institutions and the personal practices behind it. Their habit of creating a new institution for each new task, the chronic overlapping of functions between agencies, and the bewildering array of large and small agencies devoted to the same task were hallmarks of Bolshevik institutional nihilism. What counted was the personal power of the person leading an agency. That is why Stalin spent so much time on personnel questions. Of all the committees, temporary and permanent commissions, commissariats, and the like devoted to a given policy area, the one headed by an authoritative person was the one that called the tune.

Even at the top, the institutional indeterminacy would have horrified a management specialist but it did not bother the Stalinists at all. Although there were rough understandings of what issues were to come before the Politburo, the Secretariat, or the Orgburo, in practice the distinctions were vague. Lenin admitted as early as 1920 that the difference between the Orgburo (personnel) and the Politburo (policy) was artificial.[85] The boundaries between the Secretariat and the Orgburo were even vaguer. An examination of the protocols of these two bodies in the 1920s and 1930s shows that they handled precisely the same types of questions with only one difference: when several high-ranking members were available for a meeting, it was recorded as a meeting of the Orgburo. When only one or two was present, it was called a meeting of the Secretariat, but the agenda and the list of reporters were essentially the same.[86]

---

[84] Pierre Bourdieu, 'Rethinking the State: Genesis and Structure of the Bureaucratic Field', *Sociological Theory* 1 (1994), 1.

[85] Lenin quoted in Gorlizki, 'Stalin's Cabinet', p. 308.

[86] In the archives, protocols of these two bodies are kept together in the same folders, mixed together in one series: RGASPI f. 17, op. 112 and 113. According to interviews with archivists in the Central Committee Department of RGASPI the Orgburo and Secretariat were 'the same'.

Of course, if people believed that the Politburo existed, then it existed. If they believed it had authority, it had authority. But to say this is really to say that the elite's symbolic violence was successful enough that people accepted the proffered classifications and recognised the authority the symbols indicated. This allowed members of the elite to exert power behind the façade. But as Bourdieu warns us, we need not accept these classifications and misrecognitions. If our goal is the real locus of politics and power, we might profitably shift our focus from institutions, organisational charts, and meeting frequencies to the practices of personalised power behind them.[87] Looking for the real exercise of power, our agnosticism about the Politburo as institution can lead us to think of it not as a tangible entity with an objective life and death of its own, but as a symbol, a marker of power. Timothy Mitchell has argued that state structures are really 'effects' of practices that lay behind them. In his view, we should understand a state institution 'not as an actual structure, but as the powerful, metaphysical effect of practices that make such structures appear to exist ... an entity comes to seem something much more than the sum of the everyday activities that constitute it'.[88]

The essence of being a Politburo member was not institutional membership; this should be obvious for an institution that did not meet. When Stalin and the Politburo co-opted a new member, they were exercising the power of performative naming, an act of classification.[89] Politburo membership was an honorific, a symbolic credential that bestowed and reflected personal power, more than a job. It marked a person who held authority to do things, to go places, to settle disputes, and to exercise power. Politburo membership in the Stalinist system was not about the Politburo-as-institution; it was about personal power, about occupying a place in a personal table of ranks. The regularly meeting Politburo could disappear, insofar as it ever existed. But Politburo members continued to command more respect and obedience than others as a result of their closeness to Stalin, whether or not the Politburo actually existed. The same could be said of Orgburo or Secretariat membership, being First Secretary of a province, or a member of the State Defence Committee (GKO) during the war. These were men sitting in rooms (or travelling

---

[87] Graeme Gill described a personalised politics in which personal authority, connections, clientage, and connections were the operative mode of politics rather than institutions and bureaucracies. Graeme Gill, *The Origins of the Stalinist Political System* (Cambridge: Cambridge University Press, 1990).

[88] Timothy Mitchell, 'The Limits of the State: Beyond Statist Approaches and their Critics', *American Political Science Review* 1 (1991), 94.

[89] See the discussion of Bourdieu's idea of nomination as a form of symbolic capital in Kharkhordin, 'What is the State?', pp. 236–8.

around the country) exercising power. That power had little to do with the formal workings of the organisation or commissariat that defined the position on its personnel roster. The power was not about the meetings or rules of the institution (*vedomstvo*) that carried the job description. It was about the authority that accrued to the individual that held the power to judge disputes, enforce orders, and protect himself.

N. I. Ezhov was simultaneously Secretary of the Central Committee, candidate member of the Politburo, member of the Orgburo, head of the NKVD, the Commissariat of Water Transport, and the Party Control Commission (KPK), and Presidium Member of the Supreme Soviet and Executive Committee Member of the Comintern. Some of these bodies rarely met and when they did Ezhov did not attend. Each of these 'jobs' was really a symbolic badge on his imaginary official tunic. The combination of traditional honorifics (Supreme Soviet, Comintern), status-conferring ranks (Politburo, Secretariat), vestigial titles (KPK), and actual work (NKVD, Water Transport) demonstrated his power. His reputation as someone close to the main patrimonial personality gave him the authority he needed not only to arrest people, but to resolve disputes among those with lower rank, to satisfy petitions from supplicants, to exercise patronage, and in his own disputes to stand on equal footing with others having the same level on the table of ranks. His power and authority had absolutely nothing to do with the 'reality' of any of these agencies, their frequency of meeting, or the supposed collective nature of their deliberations.

Members of the high elite used symbolic emblems to enhance their own power: they carried 'authority' with them wherever they went because they were close to Stalin.[90] Precisely because institutions were so weak, high-ranking officials frequently went out on various *ad hoc* missions: to push forward the harvest, to change local leaderships, and so on. Their Politburo membership (even when the Politburo as a committee stopped meeting) was a sign of their personal connections in the complicated matrix of power in which they lived and travelled. When Kaganovich went to Smolensk, when Zhdanov went to Bashkiriia, when Molotov went to Ukraine, they exercised power not as institutional members but as power-laden individuals whose authority derived from their personal association with other powerful persons (Stalin). In these local venues, their presence was decisive and their personal power was as absolute as Stalin's.

---

[90] Of course, other personal attributes also provided symbolic authority, including one's revolutionary biography, friendship with Lenin, and Civil War accomplishments.

Authoritative persons also became members of higher bodies like the Politburo, Orgburo, Secretariat, and Central Committee as a reflection of personal power they had already accrued. Many of the younger politicians who frequented Stalin's office and functioned at the level of Politburo members became 'real' Politburo members only at the next Party congress, as symbolic confirmation of personal authority they already had.[91] Similarly, senior politicians could be excluded completely from Stalin's decision-making team while retaining their seats on the Politburo.[92] It was personal relationships, not institutions, that produced power.

Earlier we found that the declining frequency and changing structure of Politburo meetings were similar to those that characterised cabinets in European countries with large-scale and complex governmental tasks. Without overlooking some obvious differences, Stalin seems to have functioned rather like a prime minister, with the Politburo as his cabinet. Like strong British prime ministers, he controlled the agenda, led the decision-making process, and formulated the final decisions that were promulgated under the name of the Politburo regardless of the actual discussion and consensus of the meeting (if one were even held).

Some of the differences between Stalin's Politburo and, say, Margaret Thatcher's Cabinet are obvious. Others are less apparent but nevertheless intriguing. First, although Stalin was a dictator, his Politburo functioned much more as a team effort than Western cabinets generally do. When he was on the job in Moscow, he was constantly in contact or meeting with his senior lieutenants (whether or not such encounters were called Politburo meetings) to a much greater extent than typical prime ministers. Almost every day they spent hours together in his office. Secondly, while the membership of Western cabinets can change every few years with a new election, the membership of Stalin's cabinet/team was of much longer standing. The inner membership core was stable and of long duration, working with him from the early 1920s until his death in 1953. And thirdly, despite Stalin's life-and-death power over them, they seem to have exercised much more independent authority than British cabinet ministers. They not only had vast authority over bureaucratic

---

[91] Zhdanov, Ezhov, and Malenkov are examples from the 1930s; Malyshev, Patolichev, Pervukhin, Saburov, and Zverev from the 1940s. Ezhov was already functioning as an Orgburo member before 1934, when that status was made official for him. Acquiring the badge did not appreciably change his actual functions, but 'externally' it gave him the right to formally adjudicate disputes at higher levels without having to get Stalin's approval each time. See J. Arch Getty, *A Good Party Worker: the Rise of N. I. Ezhov* (New Haven: Yale University Press, forthcoming, 2006).

[92] This happened to Molotov, Voroshilov, and Kaganovich in the 1940s. My thanks to Sheila Fitzpatrick for stressing the importance of exclusion as well as inclusion.

empires, but also Stalin left them in charge while he absented himself for two or three months a year on holiday. It is difficult to imagine another European prime minister leaving his lieutenants so unsupervised, and not only because he knew that they feared him and would obey him. As members of the team, it did not occur to them to defy Stalin because that would mean defying the team, the consensus, the common understanding of the country's proper direction.

It is tempting to see these structural changes in the USSR and elsewhere simply as functions of modernity, of the changes in government that follow from the desire of modern states, whatever their ideology, to take upon themselves more and more control over and disciplining of the lives of their citizens. According to this view, the enhanced and growing mission and scope of modern governments might require new governmental arrangements including declining formal meeting frequency and segmented decision-making.

Yet we should beware of applying comparative modernity too rigidly. The fact that the Politburo and other cabinets were working even when they did not meet is a clue that something is at work here other than the comparative structural similarities inspired by growing complexity. The Politburo published decisions when it had stopped meeting altogether: it existed even when it did not exist. These decisions were received and obeyed just as if they had emanated from a formal meeting and vote. Common sense alone should suggest therefore that our focus should be less on the habits of organisations in their formal sense than on the practices and people behind them. When Mrs. Thatcher met with a few people, then consulted with a few more, then stamped the final decision as one of the Cabinet and personally phrased the text, she was doing exactly what Stalin did. The meeting of the actual organisation, its frequency, subcommittee structure, voting practices, and official membership composition were formalities, afterthoughts. In the case of the Politburo, it had always been so, even in Lenin's time.

Stalin's rise to absolute power is an established fact. It is also easily established that the decreasing frequency of Politburo meetings can be explained by increasing complexity of the system as happened elsewhere. But it is not clear that either of these mutually unrelated phenomena played the decisive role in the actual practices of decision-making, which seem to have been relatively unchanged before, during, and after Stalin's unchallenged reign. Those practices were personal and personalised, having to do with loyalty, team effort, patronage and clientage, and a behind-the-scenes fluidity and informality rather than with formal structures, which were used merely as symbolic devices to project a power whose origins were primordial and personalised. It would be interesting to investigate to what extent such ancient and traditional forms of power lay behind systems like those in the USA and Europe; systems that we are used to thinking of as modern, highly structured, and institutionalised. Although Bourdieu and others have drawn our attention to the importance of the personalised practices that lay behind apparent institutions, the general relationship between (or combination of) modernity and primordialism in the realm of political decision-making remains unexplored territory for future research.

6   Stalin as dictator: the personalisation of power

Oleg V. Khlevniuk

Though the 'personal factor' in Soviet history has been debated countless times, it should surprise no one that key events and even entire stages are associated with individuals, such as Lenin with NEP, Stalin with the Great Break, Khrushchev with the Thaw, Gorbachev with Perestroika. Though these are conventions and imprecise references, they reflect an obvious fact: Soviet leaders (like leaders of other countries) had a substantial influence on the course of events. What is at issue is just how strong that influence was, what were its mechanisms, what role was played by this or that leader to cause a period or event to be named after him.

Research on the role of Stalin in the Stalinist dictatorship has provoked widely divergent views. On the one hand, the totalitarian model proceeded from the assumption that Stalin was the lynchpin of the system, and that it would collapse without him. On the other hand, some historians for various reasons have expressed doubts about the strength of Stalin's power and have even written about a loss of real power in certain periods (a peculiar version of the theory of the 'weak dictator'). However, the majority of historians writing abut Stalin and Stalinism prefer to work with actual documents, thanks to which substantial material has been accumulated and important observations made. This tradition of careful work with sources has played the biggest role in the last ten years since the archives were opened.

Before reviewing the main results of that work, it is necessary to clarify its central subject. If one does not get lost in the fine details of different periods, one can identify two structures of power in the Soviet system: oligarchy and personal dictatorship. The latter existed only under Stalin. The fundamental difference between the two (from which most other differences follow) consists in the degree of the personal power of the leader over officialdom, and in particular its highest level. In the oligarchy, while the leader had significant power, he was surrounded by influential colleagues and a powerful elite (*nomenklatura*). He played the greatest role in decision-making, but decisions were implemented collect-ively. In the process of decision-making, the interests of various institu-tions and groups had to be negotiated. Members of the Politburo had networks of clients from among mid-level officials (the leaders of regions and ministries and so on) who formed the backbone of the Central Committee. These systems of collective decision-making worked in a regular fashion and served to limit the power of the leader and present the conditions for a relative political 'predictability'.

Stalin's personal dictatorship resulted from the destruction of the oligarchical system. At its root was the limitless power of the dictator over the fate of any Soviet official, including the members of the Politburo. The mechanisms of decision-making changed correspond-ingly. The dictator acquired exclusive right to initiate and confirm deci-sions, though this does not mean that in every case he chose to exercise that right. Stalin's dictatorship arose from the chaos of revolutionary change, and relied largely on violence. Society and politics functioned on the basis of a regime of 'extraordinary measures'. At times this was necessary, as in the war, but no less often it was imposed artificially.

In this way, to understand Stalin's role in the Soviet system and the extent of his power, one must address at a minimum two issues: to what extent Stalin controlled officialdom, and what role Stalin played in the process of decision-making and in the process of the day-to-day leader-ship of the country.

'The strong dictator': the consolidation of Stalin's dictatorship

The archives contain a rich supply of documents on the struggle for power following Stalin's death.[1] One can only regret that historians show so little interest in the subject. While there are not yet any specialised publications on the struggle at the highest echelons of power, one can already assert that the archives provide substantial new evidence that Stalin's victory was not inevitable. Stalin and his 'faction' worked very hard for their victory. Their opponents were by no means doomed to defeat.

Similarly, the transition to a personal dictatorship did not follow auto-matically from the victory over the oppositions. The documents allow one

---

[1] The most recent document collections on the subject include A. V. Kvashonkin et al. (eds.), *Sovetskoe rukovodstvo. Perepiska, 1928–1941gg.* (Moscow: Rosspen, 1999); V. P. Danilov et al. (eds.), *Kak lomali NEP. Stenogrammy plenumov TsK VKP(b), 1928–1929gg.*, 5 vols. (Moscow: Mezhdunarodnyi fond 'Demokratiia', 2000–1). The appendices are particularly interesting in this regard.

to characterise the beginning of the 1930s as a period of an unstable oligarchy in the Politburo. Politburo members derived their political influence from, on the one hand, the pre-revolutionary and post-revolutionary traditions in the Bolshevik Party, and on the other hand, the role which they played in the administration of the country. Each member of the Politburo led key institutions, as a result of which they controlled significant resources and played an important role making countless operational decisions. Each gathered round him a circle of dependent and personally loyal officials both in the centre and in the regions. Interventions by Stalin into the work of Politburo members were possible, but as a rule, they provoked conflict and tension. Stalin had to accept the existence of such 'patrimonies' and made great efforts to negotiate interests and pacify the 'institutional egoism' of his colleagues.[2]

It is obvious from archival sources that Stalin's power grew gradually in the course of the first half of the 1930s. His personal dictatorship only emerged as a result of the mass purges of the *nomenklatura* in 1936–8 which allowed him to destroy the oligarchical system. The thesis of the decisive role of the 'Great Terror' in the consolidation of Stalin's personal dictatorship has long been accepted in the historiography and new documents completely confirm it. Relying on the punitive organs, Stalin had several members of the Politburo executed and subordinated his remaining colleagues with threats of violence to them and their families. Younger leaders brought into the Politburo by Stalin were raised in the spirit a different political tradition, the essence of which was personal loyalty to the leader (*vozhd'*). In this new order, key political decisions were Stalin's exclusive prerogative. The Politburo as a collective organ ceased to function, and was replaced by meetings of Stalin and certain colleagues (commissions of the Politburo, the quintet (*piaterka*)).[3] In the middle ranks of the political hierarchy, many of the leaders of key central institutions had been removed, as had the majority of regional leaders. This meant that the Central Committee, made up of such officials, was transformed into a purely decorative appendage of the dictatorship. It also meant that members of the Politburo had lost the networks of political clients that had been an important source of their influence.

Stalin tried to maintain the structure of power emerging from the Great Terror into the post-war years. As yet, we still know very little about the

---

[2] The mechanism of collective leadership of the Politburo are well represented in O. V. Khlevniuk, R. U. Devis (R. W. Davies), L. P. Kosheleva, E. A. Ris (E. A. Rees), and L. A. Rogovaia (eds.), *Stalin i Kaganovich. Perepiska, 1931–1936gg.* (Moscow: Rosspen, 2001).

[3] See O. V. Khlevniuk, *Politbiuro: Mekhanizmy politicheskoi vlasti v 1930-e gody* (Moscow: Rosspen, 1996).

system of power during the war. However, from a raft of works on the post-war period, we know that the model of relations between Stalin and his inner circle which characterised the late 1930s was reproduced.[4] The only changes appear to have taken place in the relationship of the dictator and the nomenklatura, where purges were relatively less frequent and less harsh.

Obviously, to affirm and support his power, Stalin had to rely on some machinery of state (*apparat*). It would not be much of an exaggeration to argue that this machinery consisted of the entire Party-state system of the USSR. However, it is also obvious that Stalin needed some kind of organisation of his own, strong enough for everyday monitoring and repression. With this in mind, some historians have tried to find some kind of special 'chancellery' outside the formal structures of power (for example, in the system of special/secret departments).[5]

However, there is every reason to believe that Stalin's personal, punitive organisation was none other than the 'regular' organs of state security. The extensive use of the OGPU in the struggle for power in the Party dates back to the 1920s. From the 1930s to the 1950s, the OGPU-NKVD-MGB was under Stalin's direct supervision.[6] To ensure the unconditional subordination of the security organs, Stalin relied on the Party to purge them occasionally.

It has been conclusively established that the mass campaigns of repression, including campaigns directed against the *nomenklatura* and political leaders, were initiated and supervised by Stalin. His personal file contains many protocols of the interrogations of arrested officials. It is well known that Stalin personally sanctioned the execution of former *nomenklatura* officials who, as a rule, were tried by the military collegium of the Supreme Court. While we have lots of information on how Stalin conducted campaigns of repression through the OGPU-NKVD-MGB, the mechanisms by which the political police worked with other members of the Politburo is less well known. We only know that special sub-units acted as bodyguards and service personnel, which also constituted a constant, literally minute-to-minute surveillance of their every movement

---

[4] R. G. Pikhoia, *Sovetskii Soiuz: Istoriia vlasti, 1945–1991* (Moscow: RAGS, 1998); A. A. Danilov, A. V. Pyzhikov, *Rozhdenie sverkhderzhavy. SSSR v pervye poslevoennye gody* (Moscow: Rosspen, 2001); O. V. Khlevniuk et al. (eds.), *Politburo TsK VKP(b) i Sovet Ministrov SSSR v 1945–1953gg.* (Moscow: Rosspen, 2001); Y. Gorlizki, and O. Khlevniuk, *Cold Peace: Stalin and the Soviet Ruling Circle, 1945–1953* (Oxford: Oxford University Press, 2004).

[5] N. E. Rosenfeldt, Bent Jensen, and Erik Kulavig (eds.), *Mechanisms of Power in the Soviet Union* (Basingstoke: Macmillan, 2000), pp. 40–70.

[6] See *La police politique en Union sovietique, 1918–1953*, a special edition of *Cahiers du monde russe* 2–4 (2001).

and contact. Pavel Sudoplatov, a high-ranking official of the MGB, has confirmed that after the war Stalin had the phones of Voroshilov, Molotov, and Mikoian tapped.[7]

All that we know about Stalin and his relations with his inner circle and the wider ranks of the *nomenklatura* allows us to assert that Stalin used common, so to speak, traditional methods of surveillance and repression. Senior officials were the object of continuous oversight by the secret police, which kept Stalin informed about their lifestyle and contacts. On Stalin's orders, the organs of state security could, at any moment, arrest any Soviet leader, their deputies, or their relatives and fabricate any charges he wished. These methods were sufficient to ensure Stalin's dominance over the political system.

The dictator at work: Stalin in the system of decision-making

A characterisation of Stalin as a working dictator can be found in Adam Ulam's biography of Stalin,[8] though of course he did not originate the idea. Soviet propaganda, i.e., Stalin himself, made considerable efforts to create this very image of a 'leader (*vozhd'*) at work'. Official documents, even those not intended for the broader public, constantly underlined the leading role of Stalin in the formulation and implementation of the most important policies and programmes of government. The message was repeated in the speeches of Soviet leaders, the press, and propaganda literature. To what extent though did these clichés of propaganda correspond to reality? The opening of the archives has made it possible to examine this issue.

As mentioned, in reference to the first half of the 1930s, it has been commonly accepted that there were 'radical' and 'moderate' factions in the Politburo and that the zigzags of Soviet policy at the time were the product of Stalin's manoeuvring between these factions. The roots of this image come from the publications of *Sotsialisticheskii vestnik* in the 1930s and most famously the article of Boris Nikolaevskii, 'How the Moscow Trial was Prepared (From the Letter of an Old Bolshevik)'.[9]

The archives do not, however, confirm this theory of factions. Rather, a large number of documents support the position of those historians who focused their attention on the phenomenon of institutional self-interest in the Soviet system. The most interesting object for the study of this

---

[7] P. Sudoplatov, *Razvedka i Kreml'* (Moscow: GeiGag, 1996), p. 383.
[8] A. Ulam, *Stalin: the Man and his Era* (New York: Viking, 1973).
[9] *Sotsialisticheskii vestnik*, 23/24 (1936); 1/2 (1937), pp. 17–24.

phenomenon concerns the activity of the economic commissariats in the process of the composition and agreement of production plans and the distribution of capital investment.[10] One of the more influential members of the Politburo, G. K. Ordzhonikidze, was at the centre of this process, demonstrating contradicting patterns of behaviour as he shifted from one to another administrative position – at the end of the 1920s the chairman of the Central Control Commission, and from 1931 chairman of the Supreme Economic Council (VSNKh), and then Commissar of Heavy Industry. One may also observe that the conflict between Stalin and Ordzhonikidze, ending in the suicide of the latter, was the sole serious conflict between Stalin and his inner circle, as many studies have demonstrated.[11] The opening of the archives has revealed many other conflicts in the Politburo in the early 1930s. As a whole one can characterise these conflicts as 'departmentalist' (*vedomstvennye*). Various members of the Politburo took 'radical' and 'moderate' positions depending on their posts they held. In this period of 'collective leadership' in the first half of the 1930s, Stalin played two main roles. On the one hand, he acted as the supreme arbiter in inter-institutional conflicts, on the other, as the initiator of fundamental decisions of a general character. Of course such a division is artificial, for in a number of cases these functions coincided. As an arbiter of institutional conflicts, Stalin chose the position of the defender of the interests of the state as a whole, as any leader might. He frequently complained about 'departmental egoism' (*vedomstvennyi egoism*) and the damage it did to state interests. The example of conflicts between Stalin and his inner circle in 1931 over imports is revealing in this regard. Despite a serious financial crisis and the dangers of increasing foreign debt, central institutions continued to demand new imports. Stalin accused his lieutenants of undermining the state budget and of 'narrow departmental egoism'. The conflict became quite serious.[12]

Stalin's criticism of narrow institutional interests did not extend to the system that nurtured them. Indeed while he criticised 'departmental egoism', he encouraged it in his role as arbiter among conflicting

[10] H. Kuromiya, *Stalin's Industrial Revolution: Politics and Workers, 1928–1932* (Cambridge: Cambridge University Press, 1988); E. A. Rees (ed.), *Decision-Making in the Stalinist Command Economy* (Basingstoke: Macmillan, 1997) pp. 43–4.

[11] R. W. Davies, 'Some Soviet Economic Controllers – III. Ordzhonikidze', *Soviet Studies* 1 (1960); Sheila Fitzpatrick, 'Ordzhonikidze's Takeover of VSNKh: A Case Study in Soviet Bureaucratic Politics', *Soviet Studies* 2 (1985); F. Benvenuti, 'A Stalinist Victim of Stalinism: "Sergo" Ordzhonikidze' in Julian Cooper, Maureen Perrie, and E. A. Rees (eds.), *Soviet History, 1917–1953: Essays in Honour of R. W. Davies* (Basingstoke: Macmillan, 1995); O. Khlevniuk, *In Stalin's Shadow: The Career of 'Sergo' Ordzhonikidze* (Armonk, N. Y.: M. E. Sharpe, 1995).

[12] Khlevniuk et al. (eds.), *Stalin i Kaganovich*, pp. 54–7, 64–76, 79, 87–8, 90.

institutional interests. For example, in resisting the demands of economic (*khoziaistvennye*) commissariats for resources, Stalin was defending the positions of the Commissariat of Finance and Gosplan, which were responsible for balancing the budget and the harmonisation of plans. Stalin's position was not principled and unchanging. In general, he was more inclined to support the principle of forced industrial development, and thus defend the interests of the economic commissariats. We can, in this way, see Stalin as an essential part of a system of Soviet departmentalism. This was particularly the case during the period of the 'collective', oligarchic, leadership, but also, with a few modifications, in the period of his personal dictatorship. Indeed, departmentalism served to smooth the transition between these two forms of rule.

Not all decisions were arrived at in the process of negotiating institutional interests. There was a significant body of decisions that Stalin initiated directly. We can see this particularly in relation to administrative reorganisations, repression, foreign policy, and others. For example, we now know precisely that Stalin was the author of the infamous law of 7 August 1932 on the theft of 'socialist property'. Undoubtedly, Stalin was personally responsible for the pact with Hitler and so on.

Stalin's participation in decision-making on these two levels in the first half of the 1930s persisted beyond the emergence of his personal dictatorship, though from the late 1930s it took on a new quality. Within the highest echelons of power, there ceases to be any evidence, common in the early 1930s, of the inner circle contradicting Stalin. Stalin had come to monopolise the right to take decisions of a fundamental nature. The highest decision-making bodies became consultative organs for the dictator. Take, for example, the famous Special Committee governing the Soviet nuclear project. The Committee produced resolutions, which were then sent to Stalin for confirmation, after which they were published as decisions of the Council of Ministers.[13] Various decision-making groups centred on Stalin took the place of the Politburo completely.

The obvious impossibility of taking complete control of all spheres of government forced Stalin to limit his attention to certain priorities. These limits became particularly pronounced in the last years of his life. He increasingly focused on the oversight of the organs of state security, foreign policy, and military issues. Occasionally, he intervened in relatively less important spheres. This sort of unpredictable intervention was meant to create the effect of a 'continuous presence' and keep Stalin's lieutenants under constant pressure. No one knew at what moment, what

---

[13] L. D. Riabev (ed.), *Atomnyi proekt SSSR. Dokumenty i materialy, t. II, Atomnaia bomba, 1945–1954* (Moscow: Nauka, 1999), ch. 1.

issue might interest the dictator. This limited the independence of Stalin's lieutenants and forced them to work under the constant threat of intervention from above.

Though this system of surveillance was reasonably effective, its adoption was a sign of real changes in the role Stalin played in the system of decision-making. Stalin played an ever-decreasing role in the everyday administration of government. This followed from his decreasing involvement in the negotiation of institutional interests, that is, his retreat from decision-making of an operative nature. Particularly in the last years of his life, Stalin became a sort of superstructure above an entirely self-sufficient system of administration and decision-making. This was one of the key preconditions for a quick transition to a new oligarchy after his death.

The division of the systems of operative decision-making and of the dictatorship did not mean, however, that these two systems existed autonomously one of another. Decisions taken on Stalin's initiative and reflecting his own preferences had a profound (and in some cases decisive) impact on the development of state and society. One can identify certain of Stalin's priorities that became the priorities of the state as a whole. Among the first of these, one would have to name Stalin's inclination to use political violence as the resolution to any problem. This is not entirely unexpected if one considers the traditions of Bolshevism and the fact that the new state was born in revolution and civil war, but Stalin undoubtedly deepened this tradition and brought to it a particular cruelty and intolerance. Much of the evidence supports the view of Alec Nove that real Stalinism was excessively terroristic, and gave rise to extremes and excesses. These extremes, extraordinary even from the point of view of the Soviet legal and political order under Stalin, frequently went so far beyond what was needed that they had the effect of weakening the system, not strengthening it.[14] The most obvious example of this is the Great Terror of 1936–8, organised, as we now can confidently assert, by Stalin himself. The devastating consequences of mass repression were so obvious that, in the end, apparently even Stalin could not deny them. In any case, to the end of his life, he never again undertook a campaign of repression of similar scale and cruelty.

As other dictators, Stalin relied on what he perceived to be his gift of foresight and his own infallibility. He perceived these qualities almost in mystical terms, as, it would seem, did Hitler. In practice, they led to extreme obstinacy and a resistance to compromise. Historians of Soviet foreign policy often observe and underline Stalin's pragmatism, but

---

[14] Alec Nove, 'Stalin and Stalinism. Some Introductory Thoughts', in Alec Nove (ed.), *The Stalin Phenomenon* (New York: Weidenfeld and Nicholson, 1993) pp. 24–9.

archival sources also confirm the thesis that Stalin had very different approaches to domestic and foreign policy. Stalin's pragmatism in foreign policy was directed at preventing the deepening of crises. For example, his decision to support the North Koreans in war against the south was made after long hesitation, made under serious pressure from the Koreans and particularly from China.[15]

Stalin's pragmatism in domestic policy was so much more limited that it may be referred to as 'crisis pragmatism'. Stalin agreed to limited and inconsistent concessions only after things were at a dead end and the crisis situation had become dangerous. From recent research, we can see this in the limited measures of the so-called 'neo-NEP' of 1932. Strikingly, Stalin was opposed to some of the projects of economic reform promoted at that time.[16] One can say the same about those tendencies in social policy and shifts in ideology which are often referred to as the 'Great Retreat', the triumph of 'middle-class' values and so on. While there were such vacillations in the 'general line' under Stalin, there are no grounds for exaggerating their depth or significance.

Stalin's inflexible and extremely conservative position was particularly evident in the last years of his life. Despite extremely serious agricultural and social crises, Stalin blocked even minor correctives to the policy of forced pace investment in heavy industry and the military.[17] The need for such correctives became so serious that Stalin's successors introduced wide-ranging reforms almost immediately after his death. The events after the death of the dictator demonstrate the extent to which Stalin personally shaped many characteristics of the system which bore his name. In the few months after his death, Stalin's successors abandoned many of the extremes of Stalinism without any difficulty, particularly its extraordinary repressiveness. Together with other measures, this lent the system a new quality, in spite of the fact that many other fundamental characteristics remained the same.

The limits of the dictatorship

Superficially, Stalin's power always appeared to be so vast, that historians frequently questioned its real limits. Although no one, to my knowledge, has used the phrase 'weak dictator' to describe Stalin, some historians

---

[15] A. V. Torkunov, *Zagadochnaia voina: koreiskii konflikt 1950–1953 godov* (Moscow: Rosspen, 2000).

[16] R. W. Davies, *Crisis and Progress in the Soviet Economy, 1931–1933* (Basingstoke: Macmillan, 1996), pp. 142–228, 256–69.

[17] Gorlizki and Khlevniuk, *Cold Peace*.

have attempted to defend such a perspective on the Stalinist dictatorship. For example, there have been those who have argued that Stalin's power was weakened, and not strengthened by the Great Terror.[18] There is also A. Avtorkhanov's theory that Stalin had lost real power in his last years, and died at the hand of Beria.[19]

None of these theories are supported either by substantial document-ary evidence or even elementary logic. The issue of Stalin's 'weakness' should be addressed not in terms of 'conspiracies' or some 'loss of power', but rather in terms of the actual functioning of the dictatorship itself. One can formulate this approach as follows: at its core, the Stalinist dictator-ship generated processes deleterious a) to the Stalinist socio-economic model and policies, and b) to Stalin's power as a personal dictator.

Regarding the first part of this issue, most scholars who have studied the regime have uncovered one or other phenomenon on the basis of which they could negate the monolithic, 'totalitarian' nature of the Stalinist system. Literally in every sphere of social life and the economy (to one extent or another) there were forces contradicting the aims of the regime and challenging the direction of policy. In the system of forced labour it was necessary to provide incentives to labour. Traditional norms in private life survived the strict ideological demands of the regime. Even the onslaught of the regime's campaigns of repression could not guarantee results. In Stalin's last years there was a serious crisis of the Gulag system that set real limits to the further application of mass terror. One could list other examples. However, for the issue at hand, one must pay particular attention to the way the structures at the apex of the political system functioned. The limits of Stalin's dictatorship can be studied by looking at the extent to which the system of personal dictatorship depended on, and inevitably reproduced, oligarchic structures of power. There were several factors driving this tendency towards 'oligarchisation'.

Though they had lost their political autonomy, Stalin's inner circle retained a certain bureaucratic autonomy in so far as they were respon-sible for the functioning of the institutions they led. This became stronger as Stalin gradually withdrew from day-to-day decision-making. This 'bureaucratic autonomy' allowed members of the inner circle to develop networks of political clients. Evidence of these networks can be found in the cadre changes that took place after Stalin's death in which each

[18] J. Arch Getty and Roberta Manning (eds.), *Stalinist Terror: New Perspectives* (Cambridge: Cambridge University Press, 1993).

[19] A. Avtorkhanov, *Zagadka smerti Stalina (Zagovor Beriia)* (Frankfurt: Posev, 1976). A version of this theory has been presented more recently in Iurii Zhukov, *Tainy Kremlia: Stalin, Molotov, Beriia, Malenkov* (Moscow: Terra, 2000).

member of the leadership attempted to promote his clients. Every time a patron fell from power, so too did his clients.

To the extent that the personal dictatorship was, to a considerable extent, founded on rivalries within the Politburo which Stalin nurtured, a key precondition for overcoming the dictatorship was the ability of the members of the leadership group to act collectively. Archival documents have shown that while Stalin was alive, the inner circle made no conscious, deliberate effort to act collectively. However, we can observe that after the Leningrad Affair of 1949, there was a certain shift in the political behaviour of Stalin's inner circle. Fearing further political violence, they acted much more carefully, and tried to curb personal rivalries.

We can identify the formation of quasi-collective mechanisms of decision-making as evidence of the emerging oligarchisation of power in the last years of Stalin's life. From the original protocols of Politburo meetings, we can see that a leading group of Politburo members (Molotov, Mikoian, Kaganovich, Malenkov, Beria, Bulganin, and Khrushchev) met regularly during Stalin's long absences from Moscow between 1950 and 1952. It is obvious from the protocols that this group acted in the manner of the collective leadership of the 1920s and early 1930s, discussing issues, forming commissions for the further consideration of issues, preparing resolutions, and so on.[20] For those periods when Stalin was in Moscow, the evidence of collective decision-making is absent. Although the decisions of this group were sent to Stalin for approval, or were discussed with him over the phone,[21] the return to some of the procedures of collective leadership played an important role in the political transition after Stalin's death.

The regular and frequent meetings of the leading organs of the Council of Ministers played an even more important role in the spontaneous consolidation of collective leadership. The Bureau of the Presidium of the Council of Ministers, created in April 1950, was almost identical to the Politburo in its composition: Stalin, Bulganin, Beria, Kaganovich, Malenkov, Mikoian, Molotov, Khrushchev. However, in contrast to the meetings of the Politburo, which Stalin always led, the Bureau of the

---

[20] Rossiiskii gosudarstvennyi arkhiv sotsial'no-politicheskoi istorii (henceforth RGASPI) f. 17, op. 163, d. 1598, l. 60; d. 1604, l. 186; d. 1611, l. 140.

[21] O. V. Khlevniuk et al. (eds.), *Politburo TsK VKP(b) i Sovet Ministrov SSSR*, pp. 113–14, 116. According to M. A. Menshikov, the Minister of Foreign Trade, who frequently attended the meetings of the Politburo and the Bureau of the Presidium of the Council of Ministers, in the rooms where the meetings took place there was a telephone booth behind the chairman where communications with Stalin and his assistants would take place. He writes, 'The walls and door of the booth were well insulated, such that no one sitting in the adjacent hall could hear a sound.' M. A. Menshikov, *S vintovkoi i vo frake* (Moscow: Mezhdunarodnye otnosheniia, 1996) p. 148.

Presidium of the Council of Ministers always worked without Stalin.[22] It was to these top state organs that the fundamental weight of the operative leadership of the country fell.

Bureaucratic autonomy, patron–client relations, and the experience of collective leadership were all important preconditions for the oligarchisation of power. Fulfilling crucial functions of the Party-state system and holding in their hands the levers of, if not political than at least administrative, power, Stalin's inner circle were as important a part of the dictatorship as Stalin himself. Without exaggerating its importance, we can assume that Stalin was aware of this factor as a limit on his power. The relative stability of the membership of the Politburo can be explained in these terms (though perhaps not exclusively). The balance in the highest echelons of power was precarious, but it existed, and the necessity of sustaining the balance acted as a limit on Stalin's power.

From the archival materials we have available to us now, we can see that the basis of Stalin's dictatorship was a system of authoritarian oligarchy, or oligarchical departmentalism, functioning on a principle of competition and the negotiation of institutional interests. The dictator played the role of an 'active superstructure' in this system. On the one hand, he was one of the parties in inter-institutional conflicts (usually as arbiter). On the other hand, he acted as the initiator of many decisions, in many cases, fundamentally shaping the development of the country. In particular, the system of repression was formed, almost in its entirety, under Stalin's guidance. The politics of repression also serve as an excellent example of how Stalin's political ambition, obsessions, mistakes, and crimes shaped the character of the system and made it extraordinarily violent even for a dictatorship.

The organisation of supreme power on two levels, and the system of decision-making, was the basis of the continuous reproduction of oligarchy at the core of the dictatorship, the suppression of which took up much of Stalin's time. To a considerable extent, it defined the objective limits on Stalin's power. After Stalin's death, Soviet leaders were united in their determination to prevent the emergence of another personal dictatorship. In the absence of Stalin, their influence over operational matters naturally translated into political power. However, it is possible to see this process taking place even before Stalin's death.

Though both the levels of political power in Stalin's dictatorship were interwoven, the system of oligarchical departmentalism could exist without the dictatorial element. This helps to explain the smooth transition

---

[22] For a chronicle of the meetings of the organs of the Council of Ministers, see Khlevniuk et al. (eds.), *Politbiuro TsK VKP(b) i Sovet Ministrov SSSR*, pp. 438–564.

from collective leadership to personal dictatorship in the 1930s and back again to collective leadership after Stalin's death. In spite of the fact that many of the fundamental principles of the system remained 'untouchable' and that Stalin's successors retained a framework of authoritarian power, the rejection of the state terror of which Stalin had been the prime sponsor, already in 1953 changed the very nature of the system, making it less bloody, more predictable, and open to reform.

7   Stalin as economic policy-maker: Soviet agriculture, 1931–1936

R. W. Davies

This chapter examines Stalin's role in agriculture in 1931–6 in the context of the general development of Soviet agricultural policy. It is based primarily on the correspondence exchanged between Stalin and Kaganovich, Stalin's deputy in Moscow during his fifty-six weeks of vacation in these six years. The correspondence comprises some 850 letters and coded telegrams.[1] During his vacation Stalin also received a large packet of documents eight to twelve times a month via the courier service of the OGPU/NKVD; lists of these documents are also now available.[2] The correspondence and the lists of documents provide a unique opportunity to examine his behaviour as a political leader. This vacation material has been supplemented by the protocols (minutes) of the Politburo and Stalin's appointments diary for the much longer period when he was not on vacation, by the telegrams he sent while he was in Moscow (available far less systematically), and by his published writings and speeches.

Before examining the Stalin–Kaganovich correspondence, I sketch out the background up to 1930, and the main features of agricultural policy in 1931–6.

Background

The Bolsheviks took it for granted that, in the long term, the way forward for agriculture in peasant countries like Russia was to replace individual

I am grateful to O. Khlevniuk, M. Ilič, S. G. Wheatcroft, and the editors of this volume for helpful comments and suggestions, and to M. J. Berry for assistance in searching Stalin's publications.

[1] O. Khlevniuk, R. U. Devis (R. W. Davies), L. Kosheleva, E. A. Ris (Rees), and L. Rogovaia (eds.), *Stalin i Kaganovich. Perepiska, 1931–1936 gg.* (Moscow: Rosspen, 2001) (henceforth SKP). The English-language edition, containing the main letters and telegrams, is R. W. Davies, O. Khlevniuk, E. A. Rees, L. Kosheleva, and L. Rogovaia (eds.),*The Stalin–Kaganovich Correspondence, 1931–1936* (New Haven: Yale University Press, 2003) (henceforth SKC).

[2] For references, see note to Table 1.

household economies by large-scale mechanised farms. The victory of the working class in 1917 meant that the large-scale farms could be organised as socialist enterprises.

During the Civil War, many Bolshevik leaders and Party members became convinced that this transformation could take place rapidly, with the support of the victorious working class in other countries. But in 1921 the collapse of the Soviet economy and the failure of world revolution led to the introduction of the New Economic Policy. Many leading Bolsheviks (including Lenin) now concluded that the establishment of socialism in peasant Russia would involve a long period of patient re-education of the peasants, and the provision by the state of substantial resources to support mechanisation. For a long period state ownership of industry would be combined with a market on which the individual peasant households would willingly sell an increasing amount of their produce. In the Politburo, Bukharin and others were particularly ardent advocates of this view, which overwhelmingly predominated in the People's Commissariats for Agriculture and Finance.

Until 1926 Stalin unconditionally supported this approach, and together with Bukharin campaigned against Trotsky and the Left Opposition for their alleged underestimation of the peasantry.[3] But within this orthodox anti-Trotskyist framework, Stalin's view of the peasantry was quite different from Bukharin's. In a speech to a party audience in January 1925 he displayed a certain contempt for the peasantry:

It is at our side, we are living with it, we are building a new life together with it, whether that's bad or good, together with it. This ally, you know yourselves, is not a very strong one, the peasantry is not as reliable an ally as the proletariat of the developed capitalist countries. But all the same it is an ally, and of all the available allies, it is the only one that is providing and will provide us with direct assistance, receiving our assistance in exchange.[4]

In June of the same year, he firmly declared behind the scenes that Bukharin's slogan *'enrich yourselves'*, which he had addressed to 'all the peasants', was 'not our slogan' and 'incorrect' – 'our slogan is socialist accumulation'.[5] More boldly than the other Soviet leaders at the time,

---

[3] See, for example, his report to the Fifteenth Party Conference in October–November 1926. I. V. Stalin, *Sochineniia*, 13 vols. (Moscow: Gospolitizdat, 1946–52), VIII, pp. 286–8.

[4] *Ibid.*, VII, p. 28.

[5] See E. H. Carr, *Socialism in One Country, 1924–1926* (London: Macmillan, 1958), I, pp. 260, 284, and Stalin, *Sochineniia*, VII, p. 153.

Stalin declared in public that 'we need 15–20 million industrial proletarians' (instead of the present four million).[6]

At the end of 1927, the grain crisis turned the difference in emphasis between Bukharin and Stalin into a huge breach. Stalin launched the 'extraordinary measures' to coerce the peasants into handing over their grain, and, while publicly denying any such intention, abandoned the market relation with the peasants. In private, at the July 1928 Plenum of the Party Central Committee, he firmly rejected the idea that the free market in grain should be restored:

Try to open a free market (vol'nyi rynok), what would this mean? If the speculator pays 1 ruble 50 kopeks, we must pay 1r 60, if he pays 2r, you must pay 2r 10 ... this would mean to give up everything, because then wages would have to be trebled, prices of industrial consumer goods would have to increase, everything would turn upside down.[7]

Even to increase the price of grain by 40 per cent would cost at least three hundred million rubles a year, and 'in order to get this money, it would be necessary to take something from either industry or trade'.[8] Simultaneously with this rejection of the free market, Stalin was the prime mover in the campaign to established mechanised grain sovkhozy (state farms), which would supply grain to the state in the amounts so far supplied by the kulaks.[9] By the end of 1929, Stalin claimed that the new sovkhozy would be 'large grain factories of 50,000–100,000 hectares', which was larger than the largest farms in the USA.[10]

Against this background of rejection of the free market and strong emphasis on the advantages of large-scale mechanisation, Stalin led the campaign for the collectivisation of agriculture and the elimination of the kulaks as a class. Until the last months of 1929 the prevalent doctrine was that 'comprehensive collectivisation is unthinkable without the large machine'.[11] However, the amount of machinery available, even on the most optimistic estimates of the authorities, was wholly inadequate to enable the horses and ploughs of the twenty-five million individual

---

[6] *Pravda*, 13 May 1925. See Stalin, *Sochineniia*, VII, p. 132.

[7] *Kak lomali NEP* (Moscow: Mezhdunarodnyi fond 'Demokratiia', 2000), II, p. 649; this is the uncorrected typescript.

[8] *Ibid.*, p. 519; this is the version of the same speech as revised by Stalin.

[9] The Politburo protocols record that this scheme was proposed by Stalin personally, and, contrary to normal practice, immediately approved: Rossiiskii gosudarstvennyi arkhiv sotsial'no-politicheskoi istorii (henceforth RGASPI) f. 17, op. 3, d. 684, l. 7 (26 April 1928).

[10] *Pravda*, 7 November 1929; twenty years later, in republishing this speech in his *Sochineniia*, XII, p. 129, he prudently replaced '50,000 to 100,000' by '40–50,000'!

[11] *Pravda*, 7 August 1929 (editorial).

peasant households to be replaced by tractors and combine harvesters. Accordingly, on the eve of the all-out collectivisation drive of January–February 1930, Stalin, in his speech to the Marxist agrarians (reported in *Pravda* on 29 December 1929) announced a dramatic change in policy. This was based on the experience of the Khoper area in the Lower Volga region, where the 'simple putting together of peasant implements in the heart of the *kolkhozy* [collective farms] has given a result of which our practical workers have never dreamed'.[12]

In the 1930s, the development of large-scale mechanised *sovkhozy* was pressed ahead, while in the *kolkhozy* machinery was gradually introduced for the main agricultural operations. But even for the *sovkhozy* the machinery available was insufficient. By 1933 they supplied a couple of million of the twenty million tons of grain taken by the state; but their construction proved far more expensive than had been envisaged, and they had to employ an unexpectedly large number of unskilled workers to supplement the machinery.[13] In agriculture as a whole, the calamitous decline in the number of horses in the USSR from thirty-five million on 1 July 1929 to a mere sixteen million on 1 July 1934, meant that grain production, and agricultural production generally, fell instead of increasing. The state had to obtain food for the growing urban population, for the army, and for export from a reduced agricultural output.

Stalin's agricultural preoccupations, 1931–1936

One-third of the topics dealt with in Stalin's letters and telegrams to Kaganovich in 1931–6 were concerned with internal economic matters, and a further 9 per cent with foreign trade. Agriculture was by far the most prominent feature of the correspondence, accounting for half of Stalin's messages on the economy, over 100 items in all. During his vacations he paid far less attention to industry than to agriculture, largely leaving it to the redoubtable Ordzhonikidze: Stalin merely intervened from time to time when he thought Ordzhonikidze was overstepping his authority, and sometimes, it appears, just because some issue took his fancy.[14]

---

[12] This was the speech in which he also called for the 'elimination of the kulaks as a class'. For previous support for non-mechanised kolkhozy by Kalinin and Yakovlev see R. W. Davies, *The Socialist Offensive: the Collectivisation of Soviet Agriculture, 1929–1930* (London: Macmillan, 1980), pp. 115, 388–91.

[13] See R. W. Davies and S. G. Wheatcroft, *The Years of Hunger: Soviet Agriculture, 1931–1933* (Basingstoke: Palgrave Macmillan, 2004), ch. 11.

[14] See R. W. Davies, M. Ilič, and O. Khlevniuk, 'The Politburo and Economic Policy-making', in E. A. Rees (ed.), *The Nature of Stalin's Dictatorship: The Politburo, 1924–1953* (Basingstoke: Palgrave Macmillan, 2004).

Within the agricultural sector, the crucial problem for Stalin was the production of grain and its collection by the state. This approach had a rational justification. Bread and other grain products were by far the most important source of calories and proteins in the diet of the population, and fodder grain was a major component of horse and cattle feed. The failure of grain yields to improve led Stalin in 1929, 1930, and 1931 to support strongly the expansion of the area sown to grain. As a consequence of the excesses of this policy, rational crop rotation disappeared in many districts. At the same time, he compelled the agricultural experts and statisticians to adopt exaggerated estimates of grain production. On a famous occasion in June 1933, a telegram from Molotov and Stalin was published prominently on the front page of *Pravda*, insisting that 'the leaders of the Odessa Grain Trust have consciously reduced the harvest indicator for its *sovkhozy*', and that those responsible should be expelled from the Party and put on trial.[15] Throughout the 1930s and 1940s the grain collections by the state were conducted on the assumption that the harvest was considerably larger than any realistic estimate.

Throughout 1931–6 most of Stalin's letters and telegrams to Kaganovich about agriculture dealt with grain, and most of these with the procurement of grain. This emerges very clearly from Table 1, which shows that eighty-one of the 104 telegrams on agriculture sent by Stalin during his vacations were concerned with grain, and as many as fifty-nine of these with various aspects of grain procurement.[16] Of his eighteen telegrams on other crops, twelve dealt with cotton and sugar beet. Most remarkable was his failure to take a day-to-day interest in livestock. This was the second largest agricultural sector, and an essential provider of fats to the population. He sent only five telegrams on this topic. Only one, on a fairly minor matter, was the equivalent of the many telegrams he sent on grain procurement: on 27 August 1933, he confirmed that his signature could be added to the decree on the meat collections plan for 1934.[17] The three telegrams he sent in 1935 all dealt with the abolition of meat rationing, as part of the general campaign to abolish rationing in which he took a close interest. The telegram in 1936 agreed to delay the cattle census.

[15] *Pravda*, 20 June 1933; for this incident, see Davies and Wheatcroft, *Years of Hunger*, pp. 245–6.

[16] The concentration on grain procurement and loans in this correspondence was only to a small extent related to the months in which he took his vacation. Grain was a worry throughout the year. In July–December, and in the early months of the following year, grain was procured by the state; in the spring, the state had to cope with the grain shortages before the new harvest and to plan the procurements from the next harvest.

[17] SKP, p. 313 n. 2; the decree was published in *Pravda*, 29 August 1933.

Table 1   *Topics of telegrams about agriculture sent by Stalin on vacation to Kaganovich, 1931–1936*

	Grain	of which, grain collections	Livestock	Other topics	All agricultural topics
1931	5	4	0	3	8
1932	18	10	0	4	22
1933	13	11	1	2	16
1934	16	14	0	5	21
1935	19	11	3	3	25
1936	10	9	1	1	12
Total	81	59	5	18	104

Source: The telegrams analysed above are published in SKP. The lists of telegrams and other documents sent to Stalin and of telegrams sent by Stalin during his vacations, used in Tables 1, 2 and 3, are located in RGASPI f. 558, op. 11, in the following dela: 1931: d. 76, ll. 91–129; 1932: d. 79, ll. 61–138; 1933: d. 82, ll. 75–149; 1934: d. 87, ll. 67–146; 1935: d. 92, ll. 83–155; 1936: d. 96, ll. 1–53.

In all his correspondence about agriculture, Stalin never displayed the detailed interest which characterised his approach to armaments. In discussing the preparation of the Second Five-Year Plan, he sometimes attempted to take a wider view. But his observations on the prospects for cotton production, for example, did not get beyond generalities:

The main task: to guarantee fulfilment of the second five-year plan for cotton (I think it is 40 or 50 million puds [655,000–819,000 tons] of pure cotton) and to prepare this guarantee by years by getting to work without delay. The main ways to this goal: a) raising the yield year after year (improving cultivation, maximizing fertilisers, irrigation, etc.); b) expanding crop areas (preparing more and more new sown areas every year); c) bonuses for high yields, special benefits for expanding the sown area, medals for good workers; d) supervising the implementation of decisions.

Besides an overall guiding decision, specific planning-and-guiding decisions must be adopted for each cotton republic separately.

Without this the decision will drift towards a declaration with mere good intentions.[18]

Stalin did, however, take a close but intermittent interest in tractors and lorries, and in securing a fair share of them for agriculture.[19]

The most astonishing evidence of Stalin's preoccupation with grain procurement is provided by the record of the documents he received

[18] SKP, p. 460 (letter of 28 August 1934).

[19] See, for example, the correspondence with Kaganovich in September–October 1933 about the distribution plan for tractors and lorries in SKP, pp. 365, 367–9, 378–80. In the present chapter and the accompanying tables agricultural machinery has not been included in 'agriculture' but in 'industry'.

Table 2   *Statistical material on all topics sent to Stalin on vacation,*
1931–1936 (number of items by subject)

	Grain	of which, grain collections	Industry	Other topics	Total
1931	11	11	0	1	12
1932	9	8	5	0	14
1933	16	15	4	1	21
1934	17	17	2	1	20
1935	13	13	2	0	15
1936	13	13	0	0	13
Total	79	77	13	3	95

Source: see Table 1.

during his 1931–6 vacations. The 'lists [*opisi*] of materials sent to comrade Stalin' are classified in different ways in different years, but basically he received five kinds of documents:

1. TASS telegrams;
2. NKVD reports, etc.;
3. Other letters and memoranda, presumably selected by the head of his special sector, Poskrebyshev, as being of interest to Stalin; and materials for information, sometimes specifically associated with Politburo sittings;
4. Politburo protocols;
5. Statistical materials.

As Table 2 shows, the statistical materials sent to Stalin were overwhelmingly concerned with grain procurements and purchases by the state (*zagotovki, postavki, zakupki*). Each item listed in Table 2 usually consisted of several tables, presenting the grain collections on a five-daily and monthly basis, both for the USSR as a whole and for the separate regions. He received very few statistical materials on industry. In the course of his six annual vacations he was sent only two items concerned with aspects of grain other than procurements (on the spring sowing in 1932 and on the autumn sowing in 1933), and only one on crops other than grain (listed for 21 August 1931, as 'summary of collections of food crops for the first, second and third five-day period [of August]'). He was not apparently sent any statistical material about livestock and dairy products.

   Table 3 shows that the letters and other memoranda sent to Stalin (item 3) above) covered a wider range of topics, though even here by far the largest single item was grain procurements. Many of these memoranda were sent to Stalin because they were associated with items on the

Table 3   *Memoranda, etc., about agriculture sent to Stalin on vacation,*
1931–1936 (number of items by subject)

	Grain	of which, grain collections etc.[a]	Livestock[b]	Other crops	Other topics	Total
1931	19	19	6	13	0	38
1932	20	16	6	12	9	47
1933	28	23	5	6	11	50
1934	17	13	3	1	2	23
1935	7	3	0	6	2	15
1936	0	0	0	3	3	6
Total	91	74	20	41	27	179

Source: see Table 1.
Notes:
[a] Includes utilisation, loans, and thefts.
[b] Two items were concerned with livestock collections (both in 1932).

Politburo agenda; it will be seen from Table 1 that he rarely responded to those memoranda which dealt with topics other than grain.

The evidence about Stalin's concerns while he was in Moscow is less systematic. Stalin's appointments diary records his meetings with the senior officials responsible for agricultural procurements and with the Commissars (later Ministers) for agriculture and the *sovkhozy*. Table 4 shows that in the years 1933–7 he met the senior procurements' official 119 times, but met the People's Commissar of Agriculture only ninety-five times. This pattern was resumed after the Second World War, though his meetings were much less frequent. In 1946–52 he met the Minister of Agriculture fifteen times and the Minister of Agricultural Procurements twenty-nine times.

The Politburo protocols record items on its agenda which were introduced by Stalin, sometimes in association with other senior figures. This information is not very reliable. Topics in which he was known to take a close interest were often introduced in Politburo sessions by other Politburo members, or by senior officials. With this important proviso, the protocols for 1931 and 1932 again show the close interest he was taking in grain. In 1931, he introduced nineteen items on agricultural topics; seven of these were concerned with grain, seven with other crops, and three with livestock. In 1932, he introduced thirteen items; six were concerned with grain, and three with livestock.[20] From 1933 onwards, the Politburo met less frequently and its protocols rarely indicated who was responsible for introducing a particular item.

[20] Derived from the Politburo protocols: RGASPI f. 17, op. 3, d. 810–912, and from *Politbiuro TsK RKP(b)–VKP(b): povestki dnia zasedanii, 1919–1952: katalog*, 3 vols. (Moscow: Rosspen, 2001), II.

Table 4   *Stalin's meetings in his Kremlin office with the senior officials concerned with agriculture, 1933–1952 (number of occasions[a])*

	People's Commissar (Minister) of Agriculture	People's Commissar (Minister) of Sovkhozy	Senior official concerned with agricultural procurements
1933 from April 23[b]	19	10	29
1934	28	21	33
1935	13	7	19
1936	12	8	12
1937	13	5	16
1933–1937	**95**	**51**	**119**
1938	0	1	1
1939	1	0	0
1940	3	0	0
1941–1945	0	0	0
1946	4	0	6
1947	7	3	11
1948	0	0	3
1949	1	0	4
1950	0	0	0
1951	1	1	0
1952	2	0	5
1946–1952	**15**	**3**	**29**

Source: Obtained by combining data on Stalin's appointments in *Istoricheskii arkhiv* 4 (1998), and in the issues listing the dates and times of the appointments, with the names of senior officials listed in R. W. Davies, M. J. Ilič, H. P. Jenkins, C. Merridale, and S. G. Wheatcroft (eds.), *Soviet Government Officials, 1922–1941: A Handlist* (Birmingham: CREES, University of Birmingham, 1989); and in *Gosudarstvennaia vlast' SSSR: vysshie organy vlasti i upravleniia i ikh rukovoditeli, 1923–1991: statistiko-biograficheskii spravochnik* (Moscow: Rosspen, 1999).
Notes:
[a] These meetings frequently took place in the presence of a number of other Politburo members and officials apart from Stalin.
[b] Prior to 23 April 1933, Kuibyshev was in charge of agricultural procurements. As a member of the Politburo, and in other capacities, he frequently met Stalin on matters not connected with procurements, and his meetings about procurements cannot be separately distinguished.

Stalin's agricultural decisions

In the discussion which follows, I confine myself to those decisions for which Stalin was clearly personally responsible.[21] Two sectors of

---

[21] Many other decisions were probably taken with Stalin's active participation, but I deal here only with those decisions specifically attributed to Stalin's intervention in the records.

agriculture are compared and contrasted: grain, to which he paid very close attention; and livestock, to which he paid much less attention.

Decisions about grain. From the end of the 1920s, Stalin guided and controlled the successive grain procurement campaigns, beginning with his famous journey to Siberia in January–February 1928 in which he attempted to accelerate the grain collections. Then at the July 1928 plenum he theorised about the grain crisis by asserting that in the interests of capital accumulation to finance industrialisation it was essential in the absence of foreign loans to obtain 'tribute' *(dan')* from the peasants: a term which reached back to the days of the Mongol invasions.[22] Henceforth every harvest involved a public campaign to secure grain.

The senior official directly responsible for the grain collections until 1934, Chernov, answered to Mikoian in the People's Commissariat for Trade (later the People's Commissariat for Supply) until the beginning of 1932, and then to Kuibyshev as head of the new State Committee on Agricultural Collections (Komzag), before himself being appointed head of Komzag. But he reported not only to them but also to Stalin (and often also to Molotov as chair of Sovnarkom) about every important change proposed for the grain collection plans; and periodically prepared for their consideration budgets for the agricultural year or quarter showing the actual and proposed receipts and main expenditures of grain. The most important of these budgets were approved by the Politburo.

Stalin paid attention to the proposed changes, and usually but not always accepted them. All the changes and some of the grain budgets were formally endorsed by the Politburo (usually by poll). Full meetings of the Politburo considered important changes in grain collection policy.

The traditional depiction of Stalin as relentlessly pressing ahead with the grain collections without mercy or constraint is to a large extent confirmed by the archives. The grain collections from the 1932 harvest provide a striking example. He actively promoted the grain campaign, even when he was on vacation. At the beginning of the 1932 campaign, on 18 June 1932, he sent a letter to Kaganovich and Molotov which proposed that a conference should be convened of party secretaries and chairs of soviet executive committees in the fourteen grain regions or republics most important for the supply of grain. The conference should consider 'the organisation of the grain collections and the unconditional fulfilment of the plan'. His letter set out the main lines which the conference should take, and was read out by Molotov at the conference as in

---

[22] Stalin, *Sochineniia*, XI, pp. 159, 188–9; this text was published for the first time in 1949.

effect its main document. Thirteen subsequent letters and ciphered telegrams exchanged between Stalin and Kaganovich (or both Kaganovich and Molotov) between 20 June and 9 July dealt with the conference and the published Central Committee resolution on the grain collections which emerged from it.[23]

A few weeks later he personally instituted the notorious decree of 7 August which imposed the death penalty for the theft of grain from *kolkhoz* fields.[24] In the campaign which followed, Stalin publicly insisted on the view that most of the difficulties in collecting grain could be attributed to the attempts of the kulaks and other class enemies to sabotage the grain collections; this was his justification for the repression of those who opposed the grain collection policy. According to Stalin, these class enemies had infiltrated themselves into the *kolkhozy*, and were undermining the campaign by 'quiet sabotage (*tikhaia sapa*)'.[25] Stalin took the initiative in severe measures which forced the peasants to yield their grain. Thus on 8 November 1932, he personally insisted that villages which failed to deliver grain should be deprived of all consumer goods.[26] In the same month, he wrote on a document about the North Caucasus: 'Warn the population of the *stanitsy* (large villages) placed on the black list that they may be exiled.'[27]

As soon as the worst consequences of the famine were over, Stalin again pressed for additional grain. The archives show that in the autumn of 1934 Stalin insisted on large, more or less compulsory, additional collections of grain from the *kolkhozy* and the peasants in the form of so-called 'purchases [*zakupki*]', which were taken from the peasants at low prices in return for the supply of earmarked consumer goods. The purchases additional to the obligatory collections from the 1934 harvest made it possible to abolish bread-rationing.[28]

But this was not the whole story. On a number of occasions, Stalin reluctantly responded to evidence from his advisers that the grain collection plans were excessive, and paid serious attention to resistance by the peasants. At the plenum of the Party Central Committee in October 1931,

[23] SKP, pp. 179–80, 182, 186–8, 196, 201–3, 207–8, 211, 214, 218, 220. The document on p. 220 includes a very unusual correction of Stalin by Kaganovich and Molotov: Stalin so misunderstood a paragraph in the resolution about advance payments in kind to collective farmers that they asked him to withdraw his amendment, which assumed the paragraph referred to money payments – he promptly agreed.

[24] For details, see Davies and Wheatcroft, *Years of Hunger*, pp. 162–8.

[25] See *ibid.*, pp. 203–4.   [26] RGASPI f. 558, op. 11, d. 45, l. 32.

[27] See E. N. Oskol'kov, *Golod 1932/33: khlebozagotovki i golod 1932/33 v Severo-Kavkazskom krae* (Rostov-on-Don: Izdatel'stvo Rostovskogo universiteta, 1991), p. 93.

[28] See O. V. Khlevniuk and R. W. Davies, 'The End of Rationing in the Soviet Union, 1934–1935', *Europe-Asia Studies* 4 (1999), 557–609, especially pp. 571–2.

several regional Party secretaries insisted that in view of the bad harvest the grain plans for their regions were too high. Stalin unexpectedly called a meeting of the Party secretaries in the grain regions, as a result of which the annual grain plan was reduced from 25.8 to 24.3 million tons.[29] On 4 May 1932, Stalin introduced the Politburo discussion on the grain collection plan, which resulted in the adoption of a plan which was lower than in the previous year.[30] After the campaign began, he wrote to Kaganovich and Molotov proposing a substantial change in the grain plan for Ukraine in view of the poor harvest:

Our approach that the grain collection plan for the USSR must be unconditionally fulfilled is completely correct. But bear in mind that an exception must be made for the districts in Ukraine which have specially suffered.

He proposed that the plan for the peasant sector (*kolkhozy* plus individual peasants) in Ukraine should be reduced by 655,000 tons, from 5.8 to 5.2 million tons. He also suggested that the plan for the Transcaucasus would probably have to be reduced.[31] Many other cuts in the grain plan for Ukraine and elsewhere were also made in the course of the next six months, so that the total plan for the USSR was reduced from 23.5 to 19.6 million tons.[32] In the course of the campaign, the Politburo frequently announced that no grain loans would be made to the peasants for seed, food, or fodder. But the extreme shortage of grain in several major regions in the spring of 1933 led to a large number of decisions to issue small amounts of grain to the *kolkhozy* and the peasants, all of which had required Stalin's approval. For instance, as many as thirty-five decisions were made to issue small food loans in the spring of 1933. Eventually, the state issued seed assistance and loans amounting to 1,274,000 tons, and food assistance and loans amounting to 330,000 tons, 1,604,000 tons in all – none of which was originally scheduled.[33]

Stalin also revised other aspects of grain policy when he realised that previous measures had failed. The most remarkable change perhaps was in the plans for sown area. Following the drought in 1931, Iakovlev, Commissar for Agriculture, concluded that the over-expansion of sown area had disrupted crop rotation (see p. 125 above). Stalin did not accept this proposed change in policy until after the 1932 harvest. His correspondence with Kaganovich and Molotov in July and August 1932 reveals the confused and hesitant way in which he reached his change in policy. He received a number of reports about the poor state of the harvest,

[29] See Davies and Wheatcroft, *Years of Hunger*, pp. 90, 476.
[30] RGASPI f. 17, op. 3, d. 882, l. 3 (item 14).   [31] SKP, pp. 241–2.
[32] See Davies and Wheatcroft, *Years of Hunger*, p. 478.   [33] Ibid., p. 471.

including an alarming letter from Voroshilov describing the infestation of the sowings in the North Caucasus with weeds, and on 17 July launched a ferocious criticism of the Commissariat of Agriculture in a letter to Kaganovich. He accused it of failing to devote sufficient attention to raising yields, and contrary to previous practice insisted:

It is necessary:
1) To renounce the policy of wholesale extension of the sown area both of *kolkhozy* and (especially!) of *sovkhozy* (especially in relation to labour-intensive crops).[34]

Two weeks later, on 1 August, the Politburo adopted the plan for the autumn sowings in 1932 for the 1933 harvest. The total area to be sown was only slightly greater than in 1931, and less than the 1931 plan. On the following day Kaganovich wrote to Stalin somewhat complacently:

We have approved the figures for the autumn sowing and ploughing; our starting point was your completely correct approach that the amount of the expansion [*sic*] of the sown areas cannot be increased. Therefore we increased the expansion by one mill. for the *sovkhozy*, and left the whole of the remaining *kolkhoz* and peasant sector at last year's level. We think we acted correctly.[35]

However, Stalin soon made it clear that his conversion to the restriction of the sown area should not be taken too literally. On 5 August he sent a coded telegram about the plan for the autumn sowings, insisting that the sown area must continue to expand:

For the autumn sowing of the *sovkhozy* the increase of a million hectares may remain, though this is a tense figure. As for the *kolkhoz* sector, I consider it incorrect to keep to last year's areas: the autumn sowings of the *kolkhozy* must be obligatorily increased by a minimum of 500,000 hectares.

Kaganovich and Molotov replied on the same day with a telegram which makes it obvious that the decision rested entirely with Stalin:

The grain area of last year has been kept to for the *kolkhozy*, but they have an additional 672,000 hectares of industrial crops (sunflower, rice and coriander), transferred from spring to autumn on the basis of last year's experience.
    Is it necessary to add a further five hundred thousand hectares? Please inform us.

On the following day, 6 August Stalin replied: 'It would be good to add to the autumn plan for the *kolkhozy* five hundred thousand hectares of grain', and the Politburo immediately adopted this proposal.[36]

---

[34] SKP, p. 232.
[35] *Ibid.*, p. 257; for the Politburo decision, see RGASPI f. 17, op. 3, d. 894, ll. 16–17 (item 5).
[36] SKP, pp. 260–1, 268; RGASPI f. 17, op. 3, d. 895, l. 14 (dated 7 August).

However, ten days later, on 17 August, he wrote in a letter to Kaganovich:

I have thought over com(rade) Iakovlev's proposal about crop rotation in the USSR (he made it in a conversation with me in Sochi), and have come to the conclusion that the proposal should be adopted. Inform Yakovlev about this.[37]

The reintroduction of crop rotation necessarily required the restriction of the sown area. After Stalin returned from vacation, the Politburo embarked on a lengthy discussion about improving the yield, and, following the establishment of a Politburo commission which included Stalin, on 29 September a decree was published in the name of Sovnarkom and the Central Committee which declared that 'sown areas have expanded sufficiently'. In the spring of 1933 the total sown area should be only one million hectares more than in 1932, and a further expansion in the area sown to grain should be compensated by a reduction in the area sown to other crops.[38] In the outcome the total sown area for the 1933 harvest was 4.7 million hectares less than for 1932, and the area sown to grain increased by only 1.9 million hectares, less than in either 1930 or 1931.[39] This is a characteristic example of Stalin's reluctant adjustment of his policy in the face of stubborn facts and pressure from his advisers – exceptional in that the stages of his adjustment are recorded fairly precisely in the archives (alas, there is no record of his conversation with Iakovlev in Sochi, which might show us what arguments he found most convincing).

Decisions about livestock. As we have seen, nearly all the Politburo decisions about livestock in the years 1931–3 were not specifically associated with Stalin. Decisions about the livestock collections, and changes in them, were never introduced by Stalin at the Politburo, and, in contrast to the grain collections, there is little sign that he took much interest in them. He took the view that successful animal husbandry required enough grain to be available for fodder. Way back in August 1918, he recognised that fodder was a crucial problem, reporting to Lenin from the Volga region that 'there is more livestock here than needed, but there is extremely little hay here, and as it cannot be sent without hay, it has

---

[37] SKP, p. 285.

[38] *Sobranie zakonov i rasporiazhenii raboche-krestianskogo pravitel'stva SSSR* (Moscow: Iuridicheskoe izdatel'stvo NKIu SSSR, 1932), art. 434. For the Politburo sessions see Davies and Wheatcroft, *Years of Hunger*, pp. 233–4.

[39] *Sel'skoe khoziaistvo SSSR: ezhegodnik 1935* (Moscow: Selkhozgiz, 1936), p. 241. In 1932 the area sown to grain declined by 4.7 million hectares, contrary to the plans, as a result of the poor conditions in the autumn of 1931 and spring of 1932.

become impossible to send livestock in large numbers'.[40] At the Sixteenth
Party Congress in 1930 he insisted:

improving livestock breeding and solving the meat problem [must be brought
about] by securing for the areas concerned a sufficient quantity of cheap grain
products and fodder ... without solving the grain problem, without organising a
dense network of grain stores in livestock, cotton, sugar-beet, flax and tobacco
areas it is impossible to advance livestock farming and industrial crops.[41]

His relative lack of attention to livestock should not lead us to conclude
that he simply left the sector to be managed by the agricultural and
collection agencies. During the first collectivisation drive in January and
February 1930, when the Party and state machine was launched not only
on more rapid collectivisation but also on the socialisation of the animals
of the peasants, he failed to intervene. His lack of an explicit policy was a
green light to the collectivisers. But the ensuing chaos, and above all the
large-scale peasant unrest, led him to halt the collectivisation drive,
characteristically blaming its excesses on to his subordinates. His revised
policy was again based on the assumption that the crucial problem was
grain. In 'Dizzy from Success', published in *Pravda* on 2 March 1930, he
bluntly stated that 'the artel is *the main link of the kolkhoz movement*
because it is the most expedient form of solving the grain problem.'
This was because in the artel 'labour, land utilisation, machines and
other implements, working animals [i.e. horses and oxen] and farm
buildings are all socialised'. On Stalin's conception collective working
of the grain fields and collective utilisation of the capital needed to
cultivate grain would enable the distribution of grain to be kept firmly
in the hands of the state. At the same time, Stalin realised that the transfer
of peasant animals and vegetable gardens to the *kolkhoz* would be unpopular, and hoped that this would be a more or less voluntary process once the
grain problem was solved:

Who needs this rushing ahead, stupid and harmful to the cause? Torturing the
peasant collective-farmer with 'socialisation' of housing, all the dairy cattle, all the
small animals [i.e. sheep, goats, and pigs] and domestic poultry when the grain
problem is *not* yet *solved*, when the artel' form of the *kolkhoz* has *not* yet *been
consolidated* – surely it is obvious that such a 'policy' is useful and profitable only
for our cursed enemies?[42]

However, following the good harvest of 1930, Stalin supported the
campaign for the socialisation of livestock, believing that the grain problem had already been solved. He did not anticipate the very poor harvest

[40] Stalin, *Sochineniia*, IV, p. 125 (letter from Tsaritsyn dated 4 August).
[41] Stalin, *Sochineniia*, XII, pp. 278, 326 (report of 27 June).   [42] *Pravda*, 2 March 1930.

of 1931 and the troubles which resulted from the seizure from this harvest of the same amount of grain as in 1930. On 30 July 1931, a major decree on socialised livestock was introduced at a full session of the Politburo by Molotov and Stalin. It was published as a declaration of the Party Central Committee and Sovnarkom 'On the Development of Socialised Livestock Farming', on the following day.[43] According to the declaration, the establishment of livestock *sovkhozy* and of 'commodity units [*tovarnye fermy*]' in *kolkhozy* was a 'central task for the near future': '1931 and 1932 must be years of a breakthrough in the sphere of the development of livestock as decisive as 1929 and 1930 were in the organisation of grain farming'. A further Politburo decision on the same day was also introduced by Stalin. The decree 'On the Development of the Meat and Preserves Industry' planned to construct as many as eight large, fourteen medium, and thirty-five small meat combines in the course of 1931–3. Meat-canning shops associated with the combines would produce 2,400 million tins of preserved food in 1933, including 450 million tins of meat.[44]

These policies had calamitous results for the livestock, meat, and dairy industry, not merely because the grain harvest failed to provide adequate fodder, but also because hasty and clumsy socialisation of peasant animals led to disease and death, and to further peasant hostility. Within a year the policies were reversed. On 26 March 1932, a radical resolution was published in the name of the Party Central Committee. It condemned excessive socialisation and encouraged peasant ownership of livestock. It was presented to the Politburo by Iakovlev.[45] Stalin obviously knew about this decree and the associated measures. However, I have found no evidence that he initiated this reform. This lack of active interest was also characteristic of all other aspects of the 'neo-Nep' policies of the spring of 1932, which attempted to improve the situation in agriculture by incentives and concessions to the peasants.[46]

---

[43] RGASPI f. 17, op. 3, d. 839, l. 5 (decision no. 11/4), published as *Sobranie Zakonov* 1931, art. 312, and in the newspapers.

[44] RGASPI f. 17, op. 3, d. 839, 11. 26–35. The plan was submitted to the Politburo by the Commissariat of Supply on 20 May and accepted 'in the main' (RGASPI f. 17, op. 3, d. 826, l. 3 – no. 8/11). On July 10, the Politburo adopted a revised version of the plan which proposed that as many as 3,000 million tins of preserved food, including 750 million tins of meat, should be produced in 1933 (RGASPI f. 17, op. 3, d. 835, 11. 2. 9–24 –decision no. 6/10). By the end of 1933, four of the large combines had been built, but in 1933 only 108 million tins of meat, and 329 million tins of all kinds of food were produced. (For these figures see *Sotsialisticheskoe stroitel'stvo* (Moscow: Soiuzorguchet, 1935), p. 275; in addition, the industry produced 21 million jars of meat and 488 million of all kinds of food. Both the tins and the jars are measured in standard 400-gram units.)

[45] For details of the livestock crisis of the winter of 1931–2 and the subsequent reforms, see Davies and Wheatcroft, *Years of Hunger*, pp. 307–12.

[46] The grain collection plan of 4 May is an exception – see p. 132 above.

Nearly a year later, however, he personally and publicly identified himself with the reform. In February 1933, with the grain problem at its height, Stalin went even further in stressing the importance of the personal ownership of livestock than in 'Dizzy from Success'. In the section on 'women and women collective farmers' in his speech at the First Congress of *Kolkhoz* Shock Workers, after insisting that 'the question of women is a major question', and that 'women are a major force' and must be promoted, he continued:

The Soviet government did of course have a small misunderstanding with women collective farmers in the recent past. But the question of the cow is now sorted out, and the misunderstanding has vanished. (*Prolonged applause.*) We have achieved the situation that most collective farmers have a cow in each household. After a year – or a couple of years- you will not find a single collective farmer who does not have his own cow. We Bolsheviks will try to ensure that all our collective farmers have a cow (*prolonged applause*).[47]

The long-term aim of restricting and eventually eliminating the household plot and the personal ownership of animals was never abandoned. On 27 May 1939, a plenum of the Party Central Committee adopted a resolution 'Measures to Safeguard Socialised Lands from Being Squandered [*razbazarivanie*]'.[48] This resolution and subsequent legislation resulted in an immediate substantial decline in the number of personally owned animals, and played a major part in the general decline in livestock numbers on the eve of the war.[49] The squeeze on the household plot was resumed after the war by a further decree of the Central Committee and the Council of Ministers on 19 September 1946, and was maintained in Stalin's last years.[50] This policy was not, of course, a personal quirk of Stalin's. It was resumed by Khrushchev from 1956 onwards.

Conclusions

Stalin presented a public image to the peasants of a stern and implacable ruler, but one who nevertheless had their interests and needs at heart. Agriculture must satisfy the needs of the state in the long-term interests of the Soviet people (and the people of the world). Those

[47] Stalin, *Sochineniia*, XIII, pp. 251–2 (19 February 1933).
[48] *Direktivy KPSS i sovetskogo pravitel'stva po khoziaistvennym voprosam* (Moscow: Gospolitizdat, 1957), II, pp. 589–94.
[49] See R. W. Davies, Mark Harrison, and S. G. Wheatcroft, *The Economic Transformation of the Soviet Union, 1939–1945* (Cambridge: Cambridge University Press, 1994), pp. 128, 289.
[50] For the decree, see *Sobranie postanovlenii pravitel'stva SSSR* (Moscow: Upravlenie delami Soveta Ministrov SSSR, 1946), art. 254.

who opposed this policy would be treated as enemies and cast out of Soviet society. But the Soviet government under Stalin's leadership would provide good conditions for the peasants, enabling them to flourish and prosper.

In terms of policy-making, by the end of 1929, if not earlier, Stalin had become the predominant political leader, though until 1932 remnants of collective leadership remained. By 1933 he was already a personal dictator, whose proposals were apparently never challenged in the Politburo.[51] But, like all dictators, Stalin depended on colleagues and subordinates for advice and information; and had neither the time nor the ability to control all aspects of Soviet activity. This study has been concerned with what aspects of agriculture he sought to control; and how far he succeeded.

His handling of agriculture followed the general pattern of his political decision-making.[52] He concentrated on a small number of issues which he regarded as essential for the success of his policy as a whole. The state procurement of grain was central to the feeding of the growing urban population and the army, and he pursued the acquisition of grain relentlessly and ruthlessly. He paid little attention to many other aspects of agricultural policy: there is no evidence that he paid an active role, for example, in the decisions about the internal organisation of the *kolkhozy* or about the remuneration of the collective farmers.

This did not mean that he had no influence on aspects of the economy to which he paid much less attention. In this respect his influence varied, and in order to make a general assessment of the range of his influence, other aspects of his policy decisions will need to be examined in more detail. In the case of livestock, he was personally identified with the crucial decisions both to restrict the socialisation of livestock in March 1930 and to press ahead with it in July 1931. He does not seem, however, to have been explicitly associated with the decision to revise the socialisation policy in March 1932; but once he had become convinced that the new policy was viable and necessary, he strongly supported it in February 1933.

Stalin was more flexible in his policies than is generally believed.[53] For example, in the light of the poor results of the harvest, both in 1931 and 1932, he endorsed and sometimes initiated proposals to reduce the grain procurement plans. He also agreed to issue grain to the peasants for seed

---

[51] See SKC, pp. 1–20.

[52] See the discussion in SKP and SKC, *passim* for his decisions on other topics.

[53] See, for example, Robert Conquest's account of Soviet agricultural policy in *The Harvest of Sorrow* (London: Hutchinson, 1986), and the vast recent Ukrainian literature on the famine of 1933.

and food, although earlier he had insisted that such grain issues should not be permitted in any circumstances. In 1932 he was persuaded by his colleagues, including Iakovlev and Voroshilov, to support limitations on the sown area and to give strong encouragement to proper crop rotation.

Such modifications in policy were not always simply a matter of short-term tactics. At the end of the 1920s, the common view shared by nearly all the Bolsheviks was that 'socialism' would be a moneyless economy; already in the socialist stage of human development, the peasants would have been persuaded by the success of socialisation to relinquish their household plots and their personally owned livestock. By 1934, however, Stalin assumed that the money economy was an inherent part of social- ism;[54] and within a few years the household plot and the personally owned livestock of the peasants had been transferred in Soviet doctrine from the private to the socialist sector of the economy. The concept of the socialist economy was thus substantially modified. However, Stalin never abandoned the ultimate aim of eliminating the household plot, as was demonstrated in *Economic Problems of Socialism in the USSR*, which he wrote in 1952, the year before his death. But he had long recognised that this goal could not be achieved within the few years originally anticipated. The Soviet economic system which emerged under his leadership was significantly different from his original conception.

This 'flexibility' in Stalin's policies was limited in scope. He character- istically failed to envisage the consequences of his major decisions, and pressed ahead with them obstinately, and often brutally, until the damage to the economy and the suffering to the population had become obvious. After the 1930 harvest he assumed that the grain problem had already been solved, and this misjudgement magnified the damage inflicted on both the grain sector itself and on livestock. As in other spheres, he normally attributed such failures of policy to poor organisation by his subordinates and to the machinations of class enemies. He responded to crisis by administrative reorganisation and repressive measures.

---

[54] See his defence of Soviet trade in his report to the Seventeenth Party Congress in January 1934: *Sochineniia*, XIII, pp. 342–3.

8   Stalin as foreign policy-maker: avoiding war, 1927–1953

Alfred J. Rieber

Stalin's reputation as a wartime leader continues to be controversial at home and abroad because of the deep inconsistencies and paradoxes of his behaviour. He had anticipated war for at least a decade before it came, prepared for it, yet was taken by surprise when the Germans invaded in June 1941. As he mobilised the country for war in the 1930s, he weakened the institutions that might have served him best in fighting it: the army command, the diplomatic corps, the federal structure, the Comintern, even the armament industries. He failed to predict the breakdown of the wartime alliance with the USA and Great Britain, although he harboured deep suspicions over the behaviour of his allies during most of the conflict. A Marxist-Leninist who believed in the inevitability of war as long as capitalism survived, Stalin misconstrued the basic character of the Second World War, and the Soviet Union suffered terrible consequences as a result. He survived his mistakes, but his was a pyrrhic victory. The aim of this chapter is to explore the sources of these paradoxes as a way of shedding light on Stalin as a statesman and wartime leader who did his best to keep the Soviet Union out of both a hot and a cold war, but who failed on both accounts.

For Stalin, war rather than revolution was the major catalyst of social change. In 1917 he was conspicuously absent from the centre of the planning and execution of the October Revolution. During the Central Committee debates about a separate peace with Germany in the winter of 1917–18, he expressed his scepticism over an imminent European revolution: 'there is no revolutionary movement in the West, nothing existed, only a potential.'[1]

The research for this chapter was made possible by a grant from the Research Board of the Central European University.

[1] *The Bolsheviks and the October Revolution: Minutes of the Central Committee of the Russian Social-Democratic Labor Party (Bolsheviks), August 1917–February 1918* (London: Pluto, 1974), pp. 177–8; for Stalin's absence Robert Slusser, *Stalin in October: The Man Who Missed the Revolution* (Baltimore: The Johns Hopkins Press, 1987).

140

During the Civil War and intervention he regarded the Red Army as the main instrument of spreading the Bolshevik Revolution into the borderlands of the former tsarist empire. He pursued this policy with vigour in Ukraine, and most aggressively in Georgia where he not only convinced a reluctant Lenin to support an intervention by the Red Army, but ignored the local Bolsheviks in the campaign to overthrow the Menshevik government. He was, however, sceptical of the ability of the Red Army to carry the Revolution on its bayonets into Poland where 'class conflicts have not reached such a pitch as to undermine the sense of national unity'.[2] For Stalin, war was a necessary but not sufficient basis for radical change; domestic class relations also mattered. Instead of advancing on Warsaw he favoured defeating Wrangel in the Crimea, securing the rear of the Red Army, and then driving on to Lwow (L'viv) in order to complete the unification of Ukraine by incorporating East Galicia.[3]

Stalin favoured direct action by the centre over spontaneous fusion in reunifying the Great Russian core with the national borderlands of the old empire. As early as the Third Congress of Soviets in January 1918 he stated that 'the roots of all conflicts between the periphery and central Russia lie in the question of power'.[4] According to his analysis, the socio-economic backwardness of the periphery enabled local nationalists, especially his *bêtes noires* the Georgian Mensheviks, to promote separation from the centre, weakening Soviet power. This in turn created 'a zone of foreign intervention and occupation' that further threatened the proletarian heartland.[5] Stalin's obsession with the vulnerability of Soviet frontiers to foreign intervention in support of internal opposition shaped his interwar policies toward the republics of Belorussia, Ukraine, and the neighbouring states of Poland and Romania, the terms of the Nazi–Soviet Pact, his war aims, and his concept of post-war security.

The danger of external attack receded with the end of the Russian Civil War, intervention, and the Russo–Polish War. But these events were never far from Stalin's mind. He incorporated them, as he had done in the past and would do in the future, into his ongoing revision of Marxism-Leninism. Embedded in his concepts of the inevitability of war, socialism in one country, and capitalist encirclement was the implicit belief that the external world represented not so much an opportunity to launch further

---

[2] I. V. Stalin, *Sochineniia*, 13 vols. (Moscow: Gospolitizdat, 1946–52), IV, p. 336.

[3] I. V. Mikhutina, *Pol'sko-Sovetskaia voina, 1919–1920gg.* (Moscow: RAN Institut slavianovedeniia i balkanistiki, 1994), pp. 182–3. For a severe indictment of Stalin's behaviour during the campaign that does not mention the national question see Thomas C. Fiddick, *Russia's Retreat from Poland, 1920: From Permanent Revolution to Peaceful Coexistence* (New York: St. Martin's Press, 1990), ch. 12.

[4] Stalin, *Sochineniia*, IV, p. 31.   [5] *Ibid.*, pp. 162, 237, 372.

revolutionary offensives as a potential threat to the territorial integrity, indeed the survival of the Soviet state. He was prepared to exaggerate and manipulate the danger in order to confound his internal enemies and advance his own agenda. Yet it is no easy matter for the outside observer to draw a clear distinction, if one ever existed, among reality, fantasy, and invention in Stalin's perception of the external world.

A case in point is the war scare of the late 1920s. A series of international incidents during these years aroused fears within the Soviet leadership and the public that war was imminent. It is now clear that these fears were not only groundless but were manipulated by Stalin in his campaign to destroy the Right Opposition.[6] Stalin was, nonetheless, convinced that unreliable elements among the populations of the western periphery could prove troublesome in the event of a major conflict with Poland and Romania. OGPU reports strengthened his conviction. Peasant resistance to collectivisation in the borderlands confirmed it. Stalin's recurrent nightmare was the prospect of Polish intervention in Ukraine in support of domestic unrest. He responded by taking characteristically contradictory measures, deporting Polish villagers suspected of nationalist opposition, and at the same time creating a Polish national region along the Belorussia frontier in order to fight 'chauvinism'.[7]

Despite these 'alarms and excursions' Stalin only began in earnest to build a modern army and defence industry with the inauguration of the Second Five-Year Plan.[8] He reacted belatedly to the real danger signalled by the Japanese occupation of Manchuria and Hitler's coming to power in Germany. At the Seventeenth Party Congress in 1934, in his only major foreign policy address during the crucial decade of the thirties devoted to the nature of wars, he predicted 'an imperialist war', which he blamed on 'extreme nationalism' without naming the most likely aggressor. He sketched out four scenarios for war without indicating which was the more likely to occur. In every case war would promote revolution. But Stalin stopped short of describing the kind of regimes that might emerge from those revolutions, an omission which should be kept in mind when

---

[6] L. N. Nezhinskii, 'Byla li voennaia ugroza SSSR v kontse 20-x -nachale 30-x godov?', *Istoriia SSSR* 6 (1990), 14–30.

[7] O. N. Ken and A. I. Rupasov, *Politbiuro TsK VKP (b) i otnosheniia SSSR s zapadnymi sosednimi gosudarstvami (konets 20–30-kh gg.). Problemy. Dokumenty. Opyt kommenariia*, pt 1, 1928–1934 (St. Petersburg: Evropeiskii Dom, 2000), pp. 484–5, 491, 497. A special commission of the Politburo for studying the security of the frontier zone had been established as early as 1925. *Ibid.*, p. 486.

[8] The share of defence in the total budget expenditure rose in the following pattern: 1933–3.4%; 1934–9.1%; 1935–11.1%; 1936–16.1%; 1937–16.5%; 1938–18.7%; 1939–25.6%; 1940–32.6%. Alec Nove, *An Economic History of the USSR, 1917–1991* (Harmondsworth: Penguin, 1992), p. 230.

considering his policies in the borderlands during and after the Second World War.[9]

Thus, on the eve of the momentous shift in both Soviet foreign policy towards collective security and Comintern policy toward a popular front, Stalin's message fell short of a clarion call to resist fascism. The speech was vintage Stalinism. He met uncertainty with ambiguity. He staked out the middle ground without indicating the direction in which he might move. Events would dictate. Having exhausted all the possible combinations that might lead to war, he could never be proven wrong. The point was not to commit himself prematurely to a course of action that he might later regret, or that might be used against him by whichever internal enemies might emerge in a moment of political confusion and uncertainty. The one certainty remained his belief, rooted in Leninism, of the inevitability of war.

The ambiguity of Stalin's tactical moves from the Seventeenth Congress to the Nazi–Soviet Pact has given rise to conflicting views about his intentions. Did Stalin's genuine commitment to collective security and the Popular Front erode under the cumulative effect of Anglo-French actions during the Spanish Civil War, at Munich, and in their abortive negotiations in Moscow in the summer of 1939?[10] Or did Stalin plan all along to cut a deal with Hitler?[11] The problem of interpretation arises from the fact that Stalin prepared for war along two parallel lines, one internal, the other external. Internally he completed the process, begun for other reasons, of eliminating any potential opposition that in the event of a war might invoke what Trotsky had called the Clemenceau option of overturning a government in order to pursue the war effort more effectively. This explains in part the accusations of treason that Stalin levelled against suspected opponents among high-ranking party, army, defence, industrial, and Comintern personnel from 1936–9. The precise proportions of political calculation and psychological derangement that drove Stalin to these extreme measures will always be

---

[9] Stalin, *Sochineniia*, XIII, pp. 267–69.

[10] Jonathan Haslam, *The Soviet Union and the Struggle for Collective Security in Europe, 1933–39* (London: Macmillan, 1984) and Teddy Uldricks, 'Debating the Role of Russia in the Origins of the Second World War', in G. Martel (ed.), *The Origins of the Second World War Reconsidered* (London: Routledge, 1999). Both Haslam and Ulricks generally take this position.

[11] Jiri Hochman, *The Soviet Union and the Failure of Collective Security, 1934–1938* (Ithaca: Cornell University Press, 1984) and R. C Raack, *Stalin's Drive to the West, 1938–1945: The Origins of the Cold War* (Stanford: Stanford University Press, 1995) share this view. Haslam has recently reviewed one aspect of the debate in 'Soviet-German Relations and the Origins of the Second World War: The Jury Is Still Out', *Journal of Modern History* 4 (1997), 785–97.

a matter of speculation. But their effect cut two ways. When the Germans invaded there was no alternative to his leadership even though he had led the country to the brink of disaster. But in order to secure this position he destroyed what was arguably the most talented group of general staff officers in the world, and decimated the international communist movement including Party leaders in the front-line Soviet republics exposed to foreign invasion.

In his external relations, Stalin's attitude toward the Popular Front also displayed contradictions that were not, it must be admitted, entirely of his own making.[12] These showed up most dramatically in Spain and China, where the Soviet Union backed up its endorsement of a Popular Front with military aid and volunteers. Stalin even expanded on Dimitrov's definition with a public endorsement in the form of a letter to Largo Caballero that a Popular Front government could make the transition to socialism by parliamentary means.[13] Simultaneously, he pressed the Chinese Communists to enter a coalition government with the Kuomintang. He had adumbrated the idea of a transitional stage between bourgeois democracy and the dictatorship of the proletariat in 1928 during his first speech to the Comintern when he revived and revised the formula Lenin first mentioned in 1905 and then discarded of a 'democratic dictatorship of the proletariat and peasantry'.[14] Clearly, his policy was aimed at maintaining the broadest possible coalition of antifascist forces at both the international diplomatic level and at the local fighting fronts in wars far distant from the Soviet borders. Standing in the shadows of these pragmatic concerns was Stalin's fear of an autonomous, spontaneous revolutionary movement outside his control that could claim equal status with the Soviet Union by virtue of making its own October.

Local conditions in Spain and China proved far too complex for Stalin to manage by remote control. In China during the battle for Wuhan, Chiang Kai-shek rejected the advice of his Soviet advisors to commit his armoured forces consisting of Soviet tanks to a major offensive against the

---

[12] There was much uncertainty and disagreement within the Comintern over the Popular Front and little coordination between the new policy and the negotiation of the Franco-Soviet and Czech-Soviet treaties of mutual assistance. Julian Jackson, *The Popular Front in France. Defending Democracy* (Cambridge: Cambridge University Press, 1988), pp. 26–41.

[13] E. H. Carr, *The Comintern and the Spanish Civil War* (New York: Pantheon, 1984), pp. 86–7.

[14] Referring to such predominantly peasant societies such as Poland and Romania, Stalin had raised the possibility of intermediate stages such as the 'dictatorship of the proletariat and peasantry', dropping Lenin's modifier of 'democratic'. Stalin, *Sochineniia*, XI, pp. 155–6.

Japanese. At the same time Chiang resisted the urging of the Chinese Communists to arm the workers and conduct a revolutionary war against the Japanese.[15] Yet Stalin continued to urge the communists to cooperate with the Kuomintang. In Spain, disagreements among Comintern representatives, the activities of the NKVD, and the communist repression of the anarchists in the name of unity fatally weakened the republic. Yet Stalin permitted the defeated and exiled Spanish communists to defend their leftist policies.[16] It was becoming increasingly evident to him that each country presented a set of specific conditions that defied a uniform policy. As early as 1940, he had considered abolishing the Comintern and substituting bilateral relations with local communist parties. Yet despite the Spanish débâcle and the impotence of the Popular Front in China he continued to believe in the idea of a transitional stage; only henceforth it would have to conform to local circumstances as he interpreted them.

The Czech crisis of 1938 together with the crumbling of the Popular Front in Spain and China revealed to Stalin the weakness of the policy of collective security. The major stumbling-block to invoking the Franco–Soviet alliance in defence of Czechoslovakia proved to be the refusal of Poland and Romania to grant the Red Army transit rights in the event of war with Germany. Soviet military plans envisaged a campaign fought outside the western frontier of the Soviet Union. This would prevent a battleground in the borderlands, where strong resistance to collectivisation combined with nationalist ferment.[17]

Stalin reacted to the complexities of the international situation in the late thirties by permitting different voices within the Soviet elite to engage in a muted debate over an ideological question that masked real policy options. Was there a real distinction within the capitalist camp between 'peace-loving' and 'aggressive' powers that could be best exploited in the interests of security by a Soviet alignment with the former? This was the main assumption of Litvinov and his supporters. Or were all the imperialist powers, although antagonistic to one another, also equally hostile to the Soviet Union, in which case a policy of withdrawal or isolation would be in order, leaving the imperialists to fight it out until the propitious

[15] A. I. Cherepanov, *Zapiski voennogo sovetnika v Kitae*, 2nd edn. (Moscow: Nauka, 1976), pp. 323–32; A. Ia. Kaliagin, *Po neznakomym dorogam. Zapiski voennogo sovetnika v Kitae*, 2nd edn. (Moscow: Nauka, 1979), pp. 92n, 282.

[16] Rossiiskii gosudarstvennyi arkhiv sotsial'no-politicheskoi istorii (henceforth RGASPI) f. 495, op. 10a, d. 2521, ll. 17–50.

[17] Hugh Ragsdale, *The Soviets, the Munich Crisis and the Coming of World War II* (Cambridge: Cambridge University Press, 2004); R. Savushkin, 'K voprosu o zarozhdenii teorii posledovatel'nykh nastupatel'nykh operatsii', *Voenno-istoricheskii zhurnal* 5 (1983), 78–82.

moment arrived for a direct Soviet intervention? Such was the thinking of Zhdanov and Molotov.[18] In neither case was the idea abandoned that war was the harbinger of revolution, although Stalin had left open the nature of the regimes that would be established as a result.

In the parallel negotiations with the Anglo-French and the Germans during the summer of 1939, Stalin's dual aim was to avoid being drawn into a war that he believed inevitable, and to ensure that if and when he became involved it would be under the most favourable political and military circumstances. What he sought from the Anglo-French was an iron-clad mutual assistance pact embracing Poland and Romania as well as the three signatory powers, guarantees against 'indirect aggression' through a fascist coup in the Baltic states, and safe passage of Soviet troops through Polish and Romanian territory in case of a German attack on those two states or the Soviet Union.[19] If concluded, such a pact would have encircled Hitler with a powerful military alliance and confronted him with the certainty of fighting a three-front war in the event of his aggression. Would this deterrent guarantee the peace? If not, then at least the Red Army would be fighting on foreign soil; its presence as an ally on Polish and Romanian territory might well foster the kind of political changes in those countries that had not been possible in Spain or China. When the Anglo-French negotiators were unable to guarantee transit rights, Voroshilov suspended and effectively ended the talks.[20]

The Nazi–Soviet Pact did not, by contrast, involve a military alliance, and Stalin refused to conclude one with Germany over the following months. Its main advantages in Stalin's mind were to keep the Soviet Union out of the coming 'imperialist war' and to strengthen its strategic position by a division of Eastern Europe into spheres of influence. Given his assumption that the war in the West would be prolonged, the Soviet Union would also be in a position to advance its frontiers by annexing territories assigned to its sphere without German interference and to make additional demands on Hitler, especially in the Balkans, while German forces were tied up in a western campaign. Operating on the

---

[18] Silvio Pons, *Stalin and the Inevitable War, 1936–1941* (London: Frank Cass, 2002) presents the most sophisticated analysis of policy differences among the Soviet elite but concludes that 'Litvinov never managed to present a forceful alternative to this dogmatic view [combining a revival of 1914 and 1918] that dominated Stalinist thinking on foreign policy', p. 119.

[19] *Soviet Peace Efforts on the Eve of World War II (September 1938–August 1939)*, 2 vols. (Moscow: Novosti, 1973), II, pp. 202–10. The Soviet war plans were presented in detail by the Chief of Staff, Marshal B. M. Shaposhnikov. *Ibid.*, pp. 201–2.

[20] *Ibid.*, pp. 254–9.

same assumption, Stalin envisaged gaining a necessary breathing space because 'only by 1943 could we meet the Germans on an equal footing'.[21] His negotiation of a neutrality pact with Japan in April 1940 secured the Far Eastern front and further strengthened his position *vis-à-vis* Hitler.

In the wake of the Nazi–Soviet Pact, Stalin pursued a borderland policy based on strategic considerations but carried out in such a brutal fashion as to undermine the purpose for which it was designed. The massive deportations and repression that accompanied the incorporation of west Belorussia and West Ukraine into the Soviet Union left behind a residue of hostility that fed into anti-Soviet resistance during the Second World War.[22] The Winter War embittered the Finns who exacted revenge when the Germans launched their invasion by waging their own 'Continuation War'. The deportations of local elites and forced collectivisation that followed the annexation of the Baltic states created a deep antagonism that exploded in the rear of the Red Army when the Germans attacked in 1941 and then three years later sparked a prolonged guerilla resistance that lasted into the early 1950s. In part, these political disasters were the result of Stalin's hasty, not to say panic-stricken, reaction to the unexpectedly rapid German victories in the west. The fall of France shattered his illusions of a stalemate, upset his plans for the gradual sovietisation of the Baltic states, and exposed him to greater German diplomatic pressure.[23]

That Stalin was stupefied by the German attack in June 1941 can hardly be explained by his trust in Hitler's word – did Stalin ever trust anyone? Rather he was the victim of self-deception based on a set of perfectly rational, if faulty, calculations. He was convinced that Hitler would never risk repeating the error of the Germans in the First World War of fighting on two fronts.[24] He also discounted the mass of intelligence pointing to German's preparations for an eastern campaign as inspired either by the British who wanted to draw him into the war to save their skins or by the Germans who sought to check an active Soviet

[21] This is the way Molotov remembered it decades later: F. I. Chuev, *Sto sorok besed s Molotovym: iz dnevnika F. Chueva* (Moscow: Terra, 1991), p. 31.

[22] Jan T. Gross, *Revolution from Abroad: The Soviet Conquest of Poland's Western Ukraine and Western Belarus*, expanded edition (Princeton: Princeton University Press, 2002).

[23] A. O. Chubarian, 'Sovetskaia vneshniaia politika (1 sentiabria–konets oktiabria 1939 goda)', in A. O. Chubarian (ed.), *Voina i politika, 1939–1941* (Moscow: Nauka, 1999), pp. 11–13 and A. S. Orlov, 'SSSR i Pribaltiki', in *ibid.*, pp. 174–91.

[24] On the eve of the German attack he told Generals Zhukov and Timoshenko 'Germany is busy up to its neck with the war in the West, and I am certain that Hitler will not risk creating a second front by attacking the Soviet Union.' G. K. Zhukov, *Vospominaniia i razmyshleniia*, 2nd edn. (Moscow: Novosti, 1995), II, pp. 383–4.

policy in the Balkans. His relations with Germany oscillated between appeasement and provocation. Economic appeasement took the form of deliveries of raw materials right up to June 1941, although even in this Moscow proved to be a tough negotiator. Political appeasement took the form of Stalin's refusal to keep the lines open to London, ignoring Litvinov's advice.[25] The provocation came over Stalin's rigid negotiating stand on Soviet interests in Bulgaria and the Straits.[26] His balancing act only convinced Hitler that Stalin was both weak and dangerous, and he set Barbarossa in motion. The German invasion of the Soviet Union led to a reversal of alliances, but it did not change Stalin's long-term goals in any fundamental way. It did, however, open the way for him to expand the horizons of his borderland policy.[27]

From this perspective, it is possible to shed new light on Stalin's war aims. Reacting opportunistically to changing political and military circumstances, he gradually constructed a belt of concentric security zones, each possessing a different character and function, sloping outward like a defensive glacis from the inner, Great Russian core of the USSR. At the same time, he revised the official ideology once again in response to changing circumstances by blending elements of Soviet patriotism, Russian nationalism, Panslavism, and a 'united' rather than 'popular' front of 'all freedom-loving people against fascism' in order to avoid any hint of revolutionary aims. Mutually reinforcing one another, his real-politik and ideological stance represented Stalin's answer to the persistent geo-cultural factors that had confronted all previous rulers of the Eurasian land mass that had become the USSR: the need to stabilise a multicultural state; seal its porous frontiers, overcome relative economic backwardness, and end cultural marginality.[28]

His first aim, essential to all the others, was to restore Soviet power within the 1940 state boundaries; the second was to readjust those

---

[25] Kh. P. fon Strandman, 'Obostriaiushchiesia paradoksy: Gitler, Stalin i germano-sovetskie ekonomicheskie sviazi, 1939–1941', in Chubarian (ed.), *Voina*, pp. 366–83; Gabriel Gorodetsky, *Sir Stafford Cripps' Mission to Moscow* (Cambridge: Cambridge University Press, 1984).

[26] Gabriel Gorodetsky, *Grand Illusion: Stalin and the German Invasion of Russia* (New Haven: Yale University Press, 1999), pp. 67–75.

[27] From his first contact with the British during Anthony Eden's visit to Moscow in November 1941, he attempted to confirm his territorial gains from the Nazi–Soviet Pact and redefine the division of Europe into spheres of influence, this time with Great Britain. This foreshadowed the Churchill–Stalin percentages agreement of October 1944. *Dokumenty vneshnei politiki. 22 iiunia 1941–1 ianvaria 1942* (Moscow: Mezhdunarodnye otnosheniia, 2000), pp. 502–10.

[28] For a further analysis see Alfred J. Rieber, 'Persistent Factors in Russian Foreign Policy: An Interpretive Essay', in Hugh Ragsdale (ed.), *Imperial Russian Foreign Policy* (Cambridge: Cambridge University Press, 1993), pp. 315–59.

boundaries in order to acquire strategic strong points and eliminate potential irredenta. The third was to form a belt of 'friendly' governments (popular democracies) or autonomous regions under Soviet political and economic influence in the borderland states along the periphery of the USSR. The fourth was to encourage and support the participation of local communist parties in coalition governments outside the territories liberated by the Soviet Union as a guarantee against the formation of an anti-communist bloc. Underpinning this system of defence in depth was his interest in maintaining a working relationship with the USA and Great Britain that would acknowledge the legitimacy of his other four aims, assist in the post-war reconstruction of the Soviet Union, and delay for at least a decade the resurgence of Germany and Japan as great powers that could once again challenge Soviet control over the borderlands.

This analysis does not assume either that Stalin had formed a pre-established plan or that he conceived of this 'system' in the terms outlined above. The outcome was rather the result of a series of *ad hoc* decisions that reflected his conceptual thinking about the borderlands and his estimate of the 'balance of forces' as he sought to resolve the problems arising from the persistent factors. His policies reflected then both his experience as a revolutionary from a highly volatile ethnic region on the imperial periphery, his praxis, if you will, and his ideologically based understanding of class conflict and imperialist rivalries. He was not always able to combine these elements into an integrated world view. This helps to explain the contradictions, paradoxes, and abrupt shifts in his pre-war, wartime, and post-war pattern of behaviour.

Stalin faced serious internal and external problems in restoring the 1940 frontiers. For a period of up to three years the western periphery of the Soviet Union had been occupied by the armies of Germany and its allies and had been to a greater or lesser degree de-sovietised. German occupation policies were inconsistent and often brutal, failing to win large-scale support from the local population. Nevertheless, Soviet institutions virtually disappeared. The authority of the party evaporated. The collective farm system collapsed even though the Germans tried to keep it intact as a useful means of grain collection. Churches were re-established. In the first two years of war, Soviet efforts to create a partisan movement failed disastrously. By contrast, anti-Soviet resistance broke out in the first days of the war, especially in the newly acquired territories. By 1943 the occupied territories had become a twilight zone in which nationalist bands, pro-German auxiliaries, Soviet partisans (re-organised and centrally directed), and bandits fought one another. Some of these groups participated in the killing of Jews. The majority of the population remained passive, seeking merely to survive. In Stalin's view, these territories had to be reintegrated into the Soviet Union by a combination of repression, deportation, and vigorous Party work.[29]

With Beria's connivance, Stalin's security policy in the borderlands underwent a radical shift in 1944 when he began to authorise deportations based on ethnic rather than class criteria.[30] He uprooted the entire population of the Chechen-Ingush autonomous republic and Karachaev and Cherkesy autonomous *okrugs*, where armed bands had resisted collectivisation right up to the eve of the war and reappeared during the German advance into the North Caucasus. He also ordered a virtual ethnic cleansing along the shores of the Black Sea aimed particularly at the Crimean Tatars but including small pockets of national minorities such as the Greeks and Bulgarians, who had displayed no signs of anti-Soviet activity. In the frontier zones of the South Caucasus a similar fate befell Turks, Kurds, Meskhetian Turks (Islamicised Georgians), and Khemshily (Islamicised Armenians), deported presumably in order to forestall Pan-Turkish sentiment from spreading into the borderlands.[31]

For Stalin, the restoration of the 1940 frontier with Poland was undoubtedly a political imperative with the most sensitive international implications. At Teheran he had won verbal assurances from Churchill and Roosevelt recognising the incorporation of Poland's pre-war eastern provinces (*kresy*) into the Soviet Union. When the Red Army crossed the 1939 frontier it immediately encountered elements of the Polish Home Army who were committed to a plan of insurrection code-named Tempest (*Burza*) that would liberate major towns and cities from the Germans before the arrival of the Soviet forces. Stalin interpreted the refusal of the Polish forces to give up their operational independence and join the First Polish Army under Soviet command as an attempt to challenge Soviet control over the *kresy*. The Red Army was ordered to disarm the Home Army units and arrest the officers establishing a pattern that culminated in the tragedy of the Warsaw Uprising.[32]

---

[29] Alfred J. Rieber, 'Civil Wars in the Soviet Union', *Kritika* 1 (2003), 129–62.

[30] There had been a precedent before the war when Stalin ordered the mass deportation of Koreans from the Far Eastern borderlands fearing they were a potential source of Japanese espionage. Terry Martin, 'The Origins of Soviet Ethnic Cleansing', *Journal of Modern History* 4 (1998), 833–5; P. M. Polian, *Ne po svoei vole: Istoriia i geografiia prinuditel'nykh migratsii v SSSR* (Moscow: OGI and Memorial, 2001), pp. 91–3.

[31] N. F. Bugai, *L. Beriia – I. Stalinu: 'Soglasno vashemu ukazaniiu'* (Moscow: AIRO-XX, 1995); N. F. Bugai, *Kavkaz: Narody v eshelonakh (20–60 gody)* (Moscow: Insan, 1998).

[32] Stanislaw Okecki (ed.), *Polish Resistance Movement in Poland and Abroad, 1939–1945* (Warsaw: Polish Scientific Publishers, 1987) stands out in a highly controversial literature.

A second zone was to be constituted by a series of 'physical points', as Stalin called them at the Teheran Conference, that would reinforce Soviet frontiers in both Europe and, after the Yalta agreements, in the Far East as well.[33] In negotiations with the Finns, he gained the northern port of Petsamo with its valuable nickel mines, adjustments in Karelia for the defence of Leningrad, and a military base at Porkkala-Ud that served both to control the entrance to the Gulf of Finland and dominate the approaches to Helsinki. At Yalta and Potsdam he secured the northern half of East Prussia with the port of Koenigsburg, renamed Kaliningrad, as a forepost of the Russian Republic in Central Europe. His incorporation of the Sub-Carpatho Ukraine and Northern Bukovina brought almost all the Ukrainians into the USSR, and, together with the annexation of the *kresy*, gave the Soviet Union a common border with Czechoslovakia and Hungary.

In the Far East, Stalin's negotiations at Yalta confirmed by the Sino–Soviet Treaty of 1945 restored much of the Russian strategic position of 1905. The annexation of the Kurile Islands and the southern half of Sakhalin opened the Pacific to the Russian fleet at Vladivostok. The long-term lease of Port Arthur and the internationalisation of Dairen 'with the preeminent interest of the Soviet Union' plus joint Sino-Soviet management of the Chinese Eastern Railroad 'with the preeminent interest of the Soviet Union' erected scaffolding for Soviet economic penetration of Manchuria and a bridge to enlarging the second security zone in the Far East. In post-Yalta negotiations with Chiang Stalin secured the formal independence of Outer Mongolia, sometimes called the first Soviet satellite. He exploited a Muslim rebellion in Xinjiang in order to mediate the conflict and then win economic concessions from the provincial government so that by the time the Chinese Communists took power Stalin had deeply penetrated the entire northern rim of the Chinese borderlands, improving the position Russia had occupied in 1914.[34] Similarly, in the Middle East, Stalin encouraged local rebellions in Iranian Azerbaidzhan and Kurdistan in order to bring pressure on Teheran to grant oil concessions. He attempted to revive the claims he had advanced in his negotiations with Hitler over Soviet bases in the

---

[33] *Foreign Relations of the United States* (FRUS). *The Conferences at Cairo and Teheran* (Washington, D.C.: Government Printing Office, 1961), pp. 554, 604.

[34] *FRUS. The Conferences at Malta and Yalta 1945*, pp. 379, 984. George G. S. Murphy, *Soviet Mongolia: A Study of the Oldest Political Satellite* (Berkeley: Unversity of California Press, 1966); David D. Wang, *Under the Soviet Shadow. The Yining Incident. Ethnic Conflict and International Rivalry in Xinjiang, 1944–1949* (Hong Kong: The Chinese University Press, 1999), pp. 167–72.

Straits and recover the old tsarist provinces of Kars and Ardahan that had been lost to Turkey in 1920.[35]

Stalin faced two interconnected sets of problems in establishing a belt of 'friendly countries' and regional spheres of influence along the Soviet frontiers. First, how to manage relations with his wartime allies in order to legitimise Soviet territorial gains and confirm its political hegemony within the security belt thereby depriving any local opposition of the hope of external support. Secondly, how to devise instruments of influence or control in borderlands that varied enormously in culture, socio-economic structures, and historical experiences without precipitating civil war and/ or intervention by external powers, particularly the USA and Great Britain. Stalin responded to the complex circumstance in this zone with a policy of limited intervention.

The complications of the second set of problems arose from Stalin's relations with the local communists.[36] His murderous purges had decimated the Comintern apparatus and reached deep into the rank-and-file of individual parties; Hitler and his allies had smashed others; Moscow had lost contact with some, and those such as Yugoslavia, Albania, Greece, and China, which built strong underground movements, pursued their own agendas, to Stalin's annoyance, even as they professed loyalty to him and paid lip-service to the idea of the United Front.[37] Yet he would have to rely on them, up to a point, in representing Soviet interests in post-war coalition governments. He was opposed to any one of them taking power during the liberation or first few post-war years.[38] In

---

[35] For a suggestive comparison of Stalin's policies in Xinjiang and Iranian Azerbaidzhan see Alan S. Whiting and Sheng Shih-ts'ai, *Sinkiang: Pawn or Pivot?* (East Lansing: Michigan University Press, 1958), pp. 128–30 and Andrew D. W. Forbes, *Warlords and Muslims in Chinese Central Asia: A Political History of Republican Sinkiang, 1911–1949* (Cambridge: Cambridge University Press, 1986), pp. 261–3.

[36] For a different interpretation that emphasises Stalin's control over the local parties see Eduard Mark, 'Revolution by Degrees. Stalin's National Front Strategy for Europe, 1941–1947', Working Paper, No. 31 *Cold War International History Project* (2001).

[37] At the end of the war, the Foreign Department of the Central Committee acknowledged that contacts with foreign communist parties had 'an episodic character' and information about their activities was, 'with rare exceptions insufficient'. RGASPI f. 17, op. 128, d. 51, ll. 35–7.

[38] According to Stalin's instructions, Litvinov stated that the the post-war planning commission 'was to prepare its work ignoring the possibility of serious social upheavals (*perevoroty*) and taking its point of departure from the existing structure.' *Arkhiv vneshnei politiki Rossiiskoi federatsii* (henceforth AVP RF) f. 0512, op. 2, p. 8, d. 4, l. 31. Stalin was even more specific in April 1944 in the instructions of the State Defence Committee (GKO) to the General Staff of the Second Ukrainian Front that Soviet forces had no intention of changing the social structure of Romania but only to liberate it from fascism. T. V. Volokotina et al. (eds.), *Sovetskii faktor v vostochnoi evrope, 1944–1953, Dokumenty*, 2 vols. (Moscow: Rosspen, 1999–2000), I, pp. 53–6.

fact, he made it clear in his negotiations with wartime allies or enemies that he was perfectly willing to recognise the authority of any non-communist leader in the borderlands who was willing and capable of implementing Stalin's minimal demands for a friendly regime. This meant accepting his territorial demands as specified in his agreements with the USA and Great Britain, fulfilling the armistice agreements in the case of former enemies (Finland, Hungary, Romania, Bulgaria), including payment of reparations and purging fascists, signing treaties of mutual aid with allies (Czechoslovakia, Poland, Yugoslavia, China), forming a coalition government including all non-fascist parties, opposing the formation of an 'opposition' outside the government coalition, carrying out extensive land reform to destroy the old landowning class, and reorienting its commercial relations and establishing joint stock companies in order to aid Soviet economic reconstruction.[39]

Within the third security belt, the Soviet occupation zone in Germany represented something of a special case. Stalin's German policy was inconsistent and contradictory both during and after the war.[40] Initially, he called for a rising of the German people, then endorsed a campaign of unremitting hatred against Germany as a whole and reversed it in 1944 as the 'excesses' of the liberation threatened to destroy any future basis for Soviet influence. He favoured dismemberment and then rejected it, insisting on treating Germany as an economic whole in order to secure reparations. He tried working with captured German generals in order to subvert the Nazi war effort but then discarded them in favour of reviving the democratic parties of Weimar in a coalition government. He allowed different Soviet state agencies to act independently and at odds with one another without attempting to resolve the contradiction between stripping the country's industry and restoring its productive levels in order to pay reparations. After some hesitation, he assisted the German communists in taking over the zonal administration, but long delayed recognition of an East German sovereign state.[41]

A solution to the German problem eluded him because there was no way he could reconcile his conflicting aims, that is, to reach agreements

---

[39] These conclusions are drawn from evidence in G. P. Murashko et al. (eds.), *Vostochnaia Evropa v dokumentakh rossiiskikh arkhivov, 1944–1953gg* (henceforth VE), 2 vols. (Novosibirsk: Sibirskii khronograf, 1997–8), I.

[40] On Germany, Stalin got little help from his post-war planners. Litvinov lamented, 'it is difficult now [1944] to decide from which elements a new state power can be created', while old Comintern veteran Dmitri Manuilskii could only offer a vague suggestion to follow a 'humanistic line'. AVP RF, f. 0512, op. 2, p. 8, d. 4, l. 28.

[41] Kai P. Schoenhals, *The Free German Movement: A Case of Patriotism or Treason* (New York: Greenwood, 1989); Norman Naimark, *The Russians in Germany: A History of the Soviet Zone of Occupation, 1945–1949* (Cambridge, Mass.: Belknap, 1995); Wilfred

with the USA, Britain, and France over the treatment of Germany, exploit the German economy for Soviet needs, keep Germany politically weak, and promote the role of the German communists as a guarantee against the revival of fascism. Governed by a fear of a German revival he preferred a lesser evil in the form of a divided Germany in which one half was 'friendly' to a united Germany outside his control.

Stalin's policies in the third zone meant imposing a state of dependency that the majority of the population resented and resisted in most of the liberated countries, and that went far beyond what Stalin's Western allies considered a reasonable degree of friendliness within the Soviet sphere. But at least until 1948 it remained an open-ended question how long Stalin expected even this transitional phase of popular democracy to last. As Stalin reminded the Polish communists in May 1946, 'the democracy in Poland, Yugoslavia and partly in Czechoslovakia is a democracy that brings you close to socialism without the need to establish a dictatorship of the proletariat and a Soviet structure'.[42] Because of the victories of the Red Army, there would be no repetition in Eastern Europe of Russia's Civil War and foreign intervention and thus no need for a dictatorship. It would be up to the local communists to build a mass party, subvert, split or win over other parties, push for socio-economic changes short of nationalisation and collectivisation, and reorient the cultural life of their countries under the banner of fraternal relations with the Soviet Union. Stalin assumed the responsibility for shielding these regimes by diplomatic means against Western pressure and support for anti-communist forces, and only to intervene if and when there was a political stalemate or a perceived threat to the internal stability of the popular democracy.[43] The third security belt was, then, to be consolidated by applying the doctrine of limited intervention.

The fourth zone lying at the extreme edge of the Soviet defensive glacis was composed of states outside the reach of the Red Army but where communists had succeeded in building a mass party although under different circumstances. These included France, Italy, Greece, and China.

Loth, 'Stalin's Plans for Post-War Germany', in Francesca Gori and Silvio Pons (eds.), *The Soviet Union and Europe in the Cold War, 1943–53* (New York: St. Martin's Press, 1996), pp. 23–9.

[42] VE, I, pp. 456–8.

[43] Perhaps only in Poland did the local communists fear that Soviet intervention was excessive and undercut their credibility with the local population. Antony Polonsky and Boleslaw Drukier, *The Beginnings of Communist Rule in Poland* (London: Routledge, 1980), pp. 113, 119. More common was the reaction of local communists who sought to provoke crises with their political opponents and then call for Soviet intervention on their side. See, for example, Alfred Rieber, 'The Crack in the Plaster. Crisis in Romania and the Origins of the Cold War', *Journal of Modern History* 1 (2004), 62–106.

Stalin encouraged them to enter coalition governments, but discouraged them from expecting any Soviet direct assistance in advancing their political agenda. Stalin's control over these parties had diminished since the purges of Trotskyites in the Comintern, and their leaders had escaped his murderous scythe in the late thirties. When after the war they adopted two divergent tactics – the French and Italians opting for a parliamentary and the Greek and Chinese for an insurrectionary path – Stalin ultimately adopted a sceptical or critical attitude toward both. During the liberation of France and Italy the local communists generally subordinated their resistance forces to the Allied theatre commanders, although they came close to turning Paris into a battleground in order to liberate it before the arrival of the Allied armies.[44] Subsequently, they vigorously pursued a policy of taking power by parliamentary means. Nevertheless, at the first meeting of the Cominform, Stalin had them denounced for following what they had understood to be the Soviet leader's policy.[45]

He considered the Chinese 'margarine communists' overly reliant on the peasantry and the Nationalist Chiang Kai-shek the most effective anti-Japanese leader. Even after the defeat of Japan, Stalin was prepared to cut a deal with him that would have turned Manchuria into a Sino-Soviet condominium and would have placed the Soviet Union in a position to mediate a Nationalist–Communist rivalry in China. It was only when negotiations with Chiang over Manchuria broke down and American troops appeared in north China that he unleashed the Chinese Communists.[46] He continued to recognise the Nationalist government until its collapse, adhering to his legalist position and still leaving room for Chiang to meet Soviet demands in return for a share, however diminished, in a coalition with the communists.

Whatever his tactical adjustments, Stalin's policy in the fourth zone was to use the communists as a means either of bringing pressure to gain economic and strategic ends or of demonstrating how 'democratic' parties should behave in coalition governments by all-out support of the war effort and post-war reconstruction under the umbrella of the dominant regional power. Stalin's ultimate strategic aim was to delay for as long as possible what he regarded as the inevitable revival of German and Japanese flank powers while the Soviet Union reconstructed and strengthened its power behind the great defensive glacis.

---

[44] Adrien Dansette, *Histoire de la Liberation de Paris* (Paris: Fayard, 1958).
[45] Iu. S. Girenko, *Stalin-Tito* (Moscow: Politizdat, 1991), p. 398.
[46] Donald G. Gillin and Ramon H. Myers (eds.), *Last Chance in Manchuria. The Diary of Chang Kia-ngau* (Stanford: Hoover Institution Press, 1989); A. M. Dubinskii, *Osvoboditel'naia missiia Sovetskogo Soiuza na Dal'nem Vostoke* (Moscow: Mysl', 1966).

The key to Stalin's success or failure in achieving and consolidating his war aims rested ultimately upon his relations with his wartime allies. An unlikely alliance, it had survived a series of contradictions and crises: long-term ideological differences and suspicions, reinforced by Munich and the Nazi-Soviet Pact, the controversy over the Second Front, suspension of convoys and then Lend Lease, quarrels over implementing the Yalta agreements, the birth of atomic diplomacy. Yet Stalin was convinced that a new post-war relationship with the USA could be established on the basis of mutually beneficial economic relations.[47] Moreover, Stalin had good reasons to believe that Roosevelt and Churchill were sufficiently realistic to accept the emerging transformation of power relationships on the Eurasian continent in return for Stalin's tacit recognition of their basic geo-strategic interests and his willingness to join a new world organisation.[48] To what extent was Stalin responsible for tipping the balance toward ideological and political confrontation?

The main problem that Stalin faced in the borderlands at the end of the war was the resistance of local organised political groups and the population as a whole to the formal and informal arrangements agreed upon by the Big Three. During the Second World War all along the periphery of the Soviet Union (but in much of Western Europe as well) a series of civil wars had erupted in the occupied territories behind the lines of the conventional fighting. Of great complexity and variety, they were often multi-sided involving communist and nationalist resisters, collaborators, and hostile ethnic groups. Stalin, like his Western counterparts, sought to impose unity of action in the common struggle against the Axis. But neither he nor they were very successful because of the deep class and ethnic antagonisms released by the war and occupation. For Stalin, the continuation of these struggles or the prospect of new outbreaks in the rear of the Red Army after liberation could only have appeared as

---

[47] In conversations with an American Senate delegation in mid September 1945, Stalin restated the Soviet need for a low-interest, long-term, six-billion-dollar loan from the USA, dismissed his pre-war commitment to Soviet economic self-sufficiency, and concluded: 'the tie which has held us together no longer exists and we shall have to find a new basis for our close relations in the future. That will not always be easy ... [but] Christ said seek and ye shall find.' FRUS, *Europe 1945*, V, pp. 882–3.

[48] These included not only the agreements at Teheran, Yalta, and Potsdam and the October 1944 Stalin–Churchill accord on spheres of influence, but also a number of informal assurances and understandings among the Big Three over such matters as the Baltic and Polish frontiers. Sergei Kudryashov, 'Diplomatic Prelude. Stalin, The Allies and Poland', in A. Kemp-Welch (ed.), *Stalinism in Poland, 1944–1956* (New York: St. Martin's Press, 1999), pp. 27–34. In 1947, Stalin told the Finnish president that Roosevelt was an 'even-tempered, calm, far-sighted statesman', though by this time he was less enthusiastic about Churchill. RGASPI f. 77, op. 3, d. 82, ll. 9, 16.

extensions of the civil wars within Soviet territory that were in his eyes the major obstacle to re-sovietisation of the innermost security zone.

Local communists sought to gain Stalin's unconditional backing in their agitation for a greater share of power by denouncing their coalition partners for reactionary, anti-Soviet policies. But he was not impressed by their abilities, and Soviet leaders like Zhdanov, Voroshilov, and Vyshinsky reported from the field, in the spirit of limited intervention, that the local communists counted too much on the support of the Red Army.[49] But there were other times when Stalin berated the communists for moving too slowly as with agrarian reform in Poland.[50] How can this paradox be explained? Stalin perceived himself as the supreme arbiter, balancing the protection of Soviet interests within the security zones against the need to avoid antagonising the West or inviting their intervention. Stalin seems to have preferred to deal with a unified coalition that would guarantee stability and, in the case of Hitler's former satellites, rapid fulfillment of armistice terms, but he could not afford to stand idly by while the local communists were isolated or, as happened in Western Europe in 1947, excluded from the governments altogether. Just as the Western Allies assumed that Stalin was behind the communists' march to power, so he could not but conclude that the Western allies were supporting the anti-communist forces in order to subvert his sphere of influence. The internal struggle for power played out in a series of crises beginning in Poland in 1944 and continuing in Yugoslavia (and Albania), Romania, Bulgaria, Iran, and China. It was not by accident that relatively free elections in Eastern Europe took place in countries where, for different reasons, there was no real threat of internal breakdown and civil strife: Finland, Austria, East Germany, Hungary, and Czechoslovakia.

In relations with the western allies the denouement came for Stalin with the Marshall Plan. To him this represented two mortal dangers: a direct intervention by world capitalism through powerful economic weapons into his security zone, and the revival of Germany. After a brief hesitation, he brusquely forbade the popular democracies from participating.[51] For Stalin the time had passed for a policy of indirect intervention.

That Stalin used the war in order to expand or restore Soviet control over the Eurasian borderlands of Russia is clear enough, although

---

[49] RGASPI f. 77, op. 3, d. 48, l. 44; VE, I, pp. 274–5. Stalin warned the Yugoslavs not to take on the whole world and that if they clashed with the British over Albania or Greece the Red Army would not support them. VE, I, pp. 119–20.

[50] Polonsky and Drukier, *The Beginnings*, pp. 44–5.

[51] In his ultimatum to the Czechs delivered in person Stalin declared that what had changed his mind about accepting the proposals of the western powers was the information that it was 'a scheme to organise a Western bloc against the USSR'. VE, I, pp. 672–5.

questions remain over timing and scope. He manipulated the official ideology, but he was not entirely free from some of its basic assumptions. His methods were most hasty and brutal where his suspicion of opposition had been aroused by real signs or pathological imaginings of internal resistance. His policies were attuned to changing circumstances: the strength or weakness of local communist parties, the willingness of noncommunists to cut a deal, the advantages of prolonging the wartime alliance in order to rebuild the Soviet economy, and above all to prevent the revival of a German and Japanese power on his flanks under the auspices of the USA. These calculations helped shape his policy of indirect intervention which he believed he could fine-tune, but he discovered that both his clients and their enemies were not always willing to follow his irregular beat and shifting rhythms.

9 Stalin as Marxist: the Western roots of Stalin's russification of Marxism

Erik van Ree

Introduction

There exists an extensive scholarly literature highlighting the impact of Russia's national traditions on the Stalinist state and society. The present article focuses on ideology, understood as a body of interconnected ideas providing a comprehensive view of the actual and desirable state of society.[1] As a rule, scholarly literature is more interested in the Stalinist transformations of the real world than in the dictator's dogmatic pronouncements. Nevertheless, there exists a rough consensus that Stalin substantially russified Marxist ideology. Assuming that the Russian tradition powerfully influenced Stalinist realities, this is what we would expect. It goes against common sense for state ideology to have remained unaffected when state policies and everyday social realities have not. Not only in his day-to-day practice of power, but in his ideology, too, Stalin adapted himself to the authoritarianism, bureaucratic etatism, and patriotism that were important elements in the Russian political tradition.

However, on a closer look the consensus on Stalin's russification of Marxism is rather shallow. Some authors hold that the dictator did indeed impose a drastic shake-up of Marxist ideology. But others disagree, arguing that he did not change all that much in the existing ideology itself, and that to look in that direction would be to miss the point. The real change lay in his style of presentation and in the ideology's new function of legitimising his dictatorship. On a close examination of official dogma and formulas, one finds Stalin basically repeating

---

I want to thank Mark Tauger for suggesting the title of this paper, and David Brandenberger for making me think again about the problem of causality.

[1] The *Blackwell Dictionary of Political Science* discusses various usages of the term 'ideology', among which are a 'belief system'; a 'world-outlook [*Weltanschauung*]', consisting of 'characteristic ideas, systematised enough to have a semblance of universality'; and a 'bundle of ideas, "a family of concepts"'. Frank W. Bealey, *The Blackwell Dictionary of Political Science* (Oxford: Blackwell, 1999), pp. 157–99.

established Marxist ideas. This interpretation would imply that, strictly speaking, Stalin did not really russify Marxist ideology at all – a baffling and counter-intuitive conclusion. Nevertheless, in what follows I will argue (in line with the second 'school') that most of what appears shockingly 'heretical' in Stalin's work did indeed remain consistent with Marxism. Furthermore, even on those points where (as the authors of the first 'school' claim with justification) the dictator did reformulate Marxism, his innovations mostly remained consistent with other Western revolutionary traditions. Most of Stalin's apparently novel and truly Russian ideas were long ago foreshadowed among the mainstream of Western European revolutionary thought. My argument ends with a discussion of the real paradox we are, then, confronted with: how could Stalin have remained so close to Western revolutionary origins, and have nevertheless produced an obviously russified ideological system?

Stalinism and Marxism

Gustav Wetter is among the most prominent representatives of the first 'school'. In his *Der dialektische Materialismus*, he mainly discusses the contributions to 'historical materialism' allegedly made by Stalin.[2] In his discussion of Stalin's treatment of the 'national factor', Wetter mentioned the thesis that, provided they preserve a 'socialist content', nations are entitled to cultures with a 'national form' of their own: under Soviet socialism they may at first richly flourish, fusing later under global socialism. In accordance with the new patriotism under Stalin, Russia was treated as the central area of human history and figures from the tsarist past, such as Ivan the Terrible and General Kutuzov, were rehabilitated.[3]

Wolfgang Leonhard has argued that there is a 'vast schism' between original Marxism and Stalinism, listing Stalin's alleged innovations: 'socialism in one country'; the notion of 'building socialism'; the idea that the economic prerequisites of socialism may be established *after* forced industrialisation; the collectivisation of agriculture; the 'intensification of class struggle'; 'strengthening of the socialist state'; the sacrifice of world

---

[2] Focusing on political ideology, I will however not discuss purely philosophical questions. For Stalinist philosophy, see Robert C. Tucker, *The Soviet Political Mind: Stalinism and Post-Stalin Change*, rev. edn. (New York: George Allen and Unwin, 1972), ch. 7; Anton Donoso, 'Stalinism in Marxist philosophy', *Studies in Soviet Thought* 19 (1979), 113–41; Evert van der Zweerde, *Soviet Historiography of Philosophy: istoriko-filosofskaja nauka* (London: Kluwer, 1997); Erik van Ree, 'Stalin as a Marxist philosopher', *Studies in East European Thought* 52 (2000), 259–308.

[3] Gustav A. Wetter, *Der dialektische Materialismus. Seine Geschichte und sein System in der Sowjetunion. Vierte, bearbeitete und erweiterte Auflage* (Vienna: Herder, 1958), pp. 228ff, 233–4, 251–68.

revolution to Soviet patriotism; Great Russian chauvinism; and 'peaceful coexistence' with capitalism.[4]

Trotsky's critique presents Stalinism as a counter-revolutionary digression from Bolshevism. In his work he addresses the questions of Russian national isolation, codified in the formula of 'socialism in one country', and the preservation of the state bureaucracy, instead of its being smashed and absorbed by organs of direct democracy.[5]

Robert Tucker has discussed Stalin's 'Russian Red patriotism', expressed in his 1917 claim of 'creative Marxism' that Russia might lead the way to socialism, and in his acceptance of the formula of 'Russia One and Indivisible'. Lenin's idea of 'building socialism' modified the Marxist assumption that revolution could break out only in industrialised countries. But Lenin believed that a complete victory of socialism in backward Russia without support of the advanced countries was impossible. Stalin's 'socialism in one country' thus took a further step away from from Marx's conception of world revolution.[6] Stalin's 'Russian national Bolshevism' propagated a 'revolution from above', carried out by a terroristic state bureaucracy. This was at odds with the final, reformist Leninism in that Stalin reinterpreted the world revolution in the spirit of Russian nationalism as, mainly, a Red Army operation.[7]

Brandenberger and Dubrovsky discuss Stalin's 'state-oriented patriotic ideology'. The new 'national Bolshevism' accepted the progressive role of historical Russian state-building and celebrated the role of the individual

---

[4] Wolfgang Leonhard, *Three Faces of Marxism. The Political Concepts of Soviet Ideology, Maoism, and Humanist Marxism* (New York: Holt, Rinehart and Winston, 1974), pp. 95–125.

[5] See, for example, L. Trotsky, *The Revolution Betrayed*. (London: Faber and Faber, 1937).

[6] Robert C. Tucker, *Stalin as Revolutionary, 1879–1929: A Study in History and Personality* (New York: W. W. Norton, 1973), pp. 118, 156, 174–5, 245–8, 368ff. For a discussion of the doctrine of 'socialism in one country', see also Robert V. Daniels, *The Conscience of the Revolution: Communist Opposition in Soviet Russia* (Cambridge, Mass.: Harvard University Press, 1960), pp. 295–300.

[7] Robert C. Tucker, *Stalin in Power: The Revolution from Above, 1928–1941* (New York: W. W. Norton, 1990), pp. 28–32, 39–65. For others counterposing Stalin to the later Lenin, Trotsky, and/or Bukharin, see, for example, Stephen F. Cohen, *Rethinking the Soviet Experience: Politics and History since 1917* (New York: Oxford University Press, 1985), chs. 2–3; Moshe Lewin, *The Making of the Soviet System: The Social History of Interwar Russia* (New York: Pantheon Books, 1985), chs. 11–12. See also Roy Medvedev, *Let History Judge: The Origins and Consequences of Stalinism* (Oxford: Oxford University Press, 1989). The Leninist A. Zimin (*U istokov Stalinizma* (Paris: Izdatel'stvo Slovo, 1984)) researched the beginnings of Stalin's ideological digressions from Leninism in the years 1918–23. See also the multi-volume study of the Trotskyist opposition under Stalin by Vadim Rogovin (especially: *Byla li al'ternativa? 'Trotskizm': vzgliad cherez gody* (Moscow: Terra, 1992) and *Vlast' i oppozitsiia* (Moscow: Terra, 1993).

in history, including tsars and tsarist officials – a departure from materialist proletarian internationalism. The new Stalinist ideology became 'national in form, etatist in content'.[8] Recently, Terry Martin has argued that in abandoning the Marxist understanding of the nation as a modern construct, Stalin adopted the 'primordial' interpretation of the nation as an ethnic identity with deep historical roots. Russian centrality was the other pillar of the 'Friendship of the Peoples' around which the new Stalinist ideology was built.[9]

Authors in what I referred to as the second 'school' proceed from a different angle. Isaac Deutscher analysed the influence of the Orthodox tradition, which turned Stalin's Marxism into an 'atheistic creed', arguing that Stalin's formulations were dogmatic in style and presentation and not innovative in their substance.[10] Leszek Kolakowski noted that Stalinist Marxism 'cannot be defined by any collection of statements, ideas, or concepts'. His focus was not on matters of content but rather on the fact that there arose an all-powerful interpreter of Marxism: 'Marxism as codified by Stalin' was merely a 'bold, primitive version' of Leninism. Kolakowski saw two exceptions pre-1950, namely 'socialism in one country' and the 'intensification of class struggle'. But even 'socialism in one country' had little theoretical significance. Kolakowski believed that the debate between Stalin and Trotsky was largely a fake – both hoped for the construction of socialism in an isolated Russia and for world revolution. As to post-1949 ideological developments, according to Kolakowski, Stalin's 'linguistics' were mere 'sensible truisms' and his *Economic Problems of Socialism in the USSR* (1952) repeated 'traditional Marxist motives'.[11] Ewan Mawdsley takes the same position: 'Stalin added little to Marxism-Leninism'. Despite variations, Marx, Lenin, and Stalin shared a basic orientation on anti-capitalism, the urban working class, and violent class struggle. Even 'socialism in one country' was not incompatible with late Leninism.[12]

---

[8] D. L. Brandenberger, and A. M. Dubrovsky, '"The People Need a Tsar": the Emergence of National Bolshevism as Stalinist Ideology, 1931–1941', *Europe-Asia Studies* 5 (1998), 873–92.

[9] Terry Martin, *The Affirmative Action Empire: Nations and Nationalism in the Soviet Union, 1923–1939* (Ithaca: Cornell University Press, 2001), pp. 442ff.

[10] I. Deutscher, *Stalin: A Political Biography* (London: Oxford University Press, 1949), pp. 269–72. M. Vaiskopf, *Pisatel' Stalin* (Moscow: Novoe literaturnoe obozrenie, 2002) highlights Orthodox and epic influences on Stalin, his style of writing, his metaphors, and the structure of his thinking.

[11] Leszek Kolakowski, *Main Currents of Marxism: Its Origins, Growth and Dissolution*, III, *The Breakdown* (Oxford: Oxford University Press, 1981), pp. 4, 12, 21ff, 38, 97, 100–1, 104ff, 141–3.

[12] Evan Mawdsley, *The Stalin Years: The Soviet Union, 1929–1953* (Manchester: Manchester University Press, 1998), pp. 5–10.

Andrzej Walicki agreed that Stalin's contributions to Marxist theory were virtually nonexistent. The only thing that was new was its closed, didactic style and the use he made of it as a means of indoctrination. As far as ideas were concerned, Stalin was truly 'merely Lenin's faithful disciple'. 'Revolution from above' was no radical departure from Bolshevism, for Lenin had never abandoned the option of state violence. Discussing Stalin's patriotism, Walicki notes that the dictator continued to divide pre-revolutionary Russian culture into popular and reactionary sections. The relevance of Stalin's patriotism lies not in its perversion of Marxism, but in its function as an instrument of totalitarian control.[13] Other scholars, too, are not convinced that Stalinist patriotism amounted to serious doctrinal innovation. Discussing Stalin's nationalism, E. A. Rees observes mostly appeals to Russian national pride. Even under the anti-Semitic and xenophobic 'High Stalinism' the basic doctrines of Marxism-Leninism were not repudiated. Traditional symbols of Russian nationalism, monarchy, and church, were not as such rehabilitated.[14] The same position is taken by Mikhail Agursky. Though Stalinism was a form of National Bolshevism, an outright 'Russian etatist ideology', Stalin did not transform Marxism. He rather preserved it as a 'screen' to camouflage his nationalism.[15]

Summing up, if Marxism is treated strictly as an ideology, a body of interconnected ideas, there appears to be no clear consensus on Stalin's russifying it. Among those scholars who do perceive such a transformation, we find the expected focus on bureaucratic etatism and nationalism. The matter of the 'intensification of class struggle' may be linked to terrorist state activities. But not a few thoughtful scholars argue that, despite this bureaucratic etatism and nationalism, Stalinism cannot be

---

[13] Andrzej Walicki, *Marxism and the Leap to the Kingdom of Freedom: The Rise and Fall of the Communist Utopia* (Stanford: Stanford University Press, 1995), pp. 398, 403–9, 414, 424–54.

[14] E. A. Rees, 'Stalin and Russian Nationalism', in Geoffrey Hosking and Robert Service (eds.), *Russian Nationalism Past and Present*, (Basingstoke: Macmillan, 1998), pp. 77–106.

[15] Mikhail Agursky, *The Third Rome: National Bolshevism in the USSR* (Boulder, Colo.: Westview, 1987), pp. xii–iii, xv, 74, 80. In *Stalinshchina kak Dukhovnyi Fenomen (Ocherki Bol'shevizmovedeniia, kniga 1* (Frankfurt M.: Posev, 1971), Roman Redlikh treats Stalinist ideology as a pseudo-religion of 'myths and fictions' designed to enforce compliance with the dictatorship. Valerii Chalidze defends the thesis of Stalin's preservation of Marxist-Leninist 'phraseology'. See *Pobeditel' Kommunizma. Mysli o Staline, sotsializme i Rossii* (New York: Chalidze Publications, 1981), pp. 42ff. In his later years, the dictator introduced several 'heresies' of a patriotic and anti-cosmopolitan nature. Compare Vladimir Shlapentokh's thesis that Stalin preserved the ideology of 'world revolution' as a cover for Soviet state interests. 'The World Revolution as a Geopolitical Instrument of the Soviet Leadership', *Russian History/Histoire Russe* 3 (1999), 322–4.

significantly distinguished from Marxism or Leninism other than through its dogmatic, codified, and scholastic style and its strengthened function of legitimising dictatorship.

In discussing Stalin's russification of Marxism, we are faced with a daunting problem. Our conclusions depend not only upon an accurate reading of Stalinism but crucially also of the Marxist 'base line' against which it would be 'measured'. We will have to deal with the original Marxism; with Karl Kautsky's 'orthodox Marxism' of the Second International, among which Lenin initially counted himself; and with the mature Leninism, the school Stalin graduated from. To make matters worse, it would be wildly naïve to assume that pre-Stalinist Marxism is any less subject to interpretative debate than Stalinism itself. Through a critical discussion of existing accounts of Marxism and Stalinism, this study aims to produce a plausible reading of the Marxist status of the Stalinist ideology.

Proletarian revolution in a backward country and 'revolution from above'

According to Second International 'orthodox Marxism', socialist revolution was feasible only under conditions of developed capitalism. In much of the literature on Leninism this is taken as *the* Marxist orthodoxy.[16] However, most Marx specialists do not quite agree with this simple view. Alan Gilbert argues that Marx never made the triumph of proletarian revolution dependent on the proletariat comprising a majority of the population. Throughout his career Marx urged the workers of predominantly peasant countries to take power in a coalition with peasant parties.[17]

---

[16] See, for example: Leonhard, *Three Faces*, pp. 24ff, 67; Richard Pipes, *A Concise History of the Russian Revolution* (New York: Vintage Books, 1996), p. 395; Christopher Read, *The Making and Breaking of the Soviet System* (Basingstoke: Palgrave, 2001), pp. 4, 10.

[17] Alan Gilbert, *Marx's Politics. Communists and Citizens* (Oxford: Martin Robertson, 1981), p. 219; see also Richard N. Hunt, *The Political Ideas of Marx and Engels: Marxism and Totalitarian Democracy, 1818–1850* (Pittsburgh: University of Pittsburgh Press, 1974), chs. 5–7. In George Lichtheim's analysis, Marx and Engels adhered to a proletarian revolution in backward Germany until 1851. Thereupon Marx 'tacitly' abandoned the radical strategy. Engels broke consistently with it. See Lichtheim, *Marxism. An Historical and Critical Study* (London: Routledge and Kegan Paul, 1961), 51ff, 122ff. On the pre-1851 Marx, Kolakowski agrees with Lichtheim. After 1850, Marx could not make up his mind whether proletarian revolution was possible in predominantly peasant nations. *Main Currents*, I, *The Founders*, pp. 125ff, 227ff, 234ff, 309–10; II, *The Golden Age*, p. 409. For a stronger view of Marx's continued belief in proletarian revolutions in predominantly peasant countries: David McLellan, *The Thought of Karl Marx*, 2nd edn. (London: Macmillan, 1980), pp. 223–30.

In 1848–50, Marx and Engels advised the German communists to join up with the bourgeoisie against monarchy and feudalism. After the democratic revolution the workers should immediately turn to the proletarian revolution. There was no hint of postponing that until the workers formed a majority. In 1850 Marx did warn the German workers that they might perhaps be fit to rule only after decades of civil war. But in 1856 he was confident that a peasant war could help the German proletariat to victory. Marx's first use of the concept of the 'dictatorship of the working class' referred to the predominantly peasant France of 1850. Marx and Engels called the 1871 Commune a workers' government. Had Paris been triumphant, the peasant majority would naturally have recognised it. These well-known remarks are put in perspective in Marx's 1874–5 notebooks on Bakunin, in which he concluded that a 'radical social revolution' was possible only 'where, together with capitalist production, the industrial proletariat occupies at least an important place within the population'. It must do as much for the peasants as the French bourgeoisie did in 1789.[18] 'An important place within the population', no more. Even in the predominantly peasant countries of continental Western Europe Marx hoped for the establishment of proletarian governments supported by the peasantry.[19]

According to Marx and Engels, a breakthrough to communism in Russia might be possible provided a revolutionary government could stop the disintegration of the village commune. But without support from revolutionary regimes in Western Europe this would be unlikely. In an isolated revolutionary Russia capitalist development was inevitable.[20] But this prediction of the disintegrating village commune indicated no more than predicting the capitalist development of the Russian countryside. To my knowledge, Marx and Engels never claimed that a proletarian government could only take power in Russia once the

---

[18] Cited in Hunt, *Political Ideas*, p. 322.

[19] Shlomo Avineri argues against this interpretation. Marx did expect proletarian revolution to break out first in backward Germany, but mostly warned against premature proletarian revolutions, which, under conditions of economic unripeness, could only assist the bourgeoisie. *The Social and Political Thought of Karl Marx* (London: Cambridge University Press, 1968), pp. 151, 185–201, 219–20, 239ff. I do not find Avineri's argument convincing. His numerous quotations show that Marx found the Jacobin experiment misconceived and that he rejected wild insurrectionary tactics. At *that* time conditions for social radicalism were indeed absent. Avineri does not plausibly show that Marx rejected a strategy for proletarian takeover in Germany and France from 1848 onwards.

[20] See Karl Marx, Friedrich Engels, *Werke* (Berlin: Dietz Verlag, 1965–74), vol. XVIII, p. 565; XIX, pp. 107ff, 296; XXII, pp. 428–9, 435; Teodor Shanin (ed.), *Late Marx and the Russian Road. Marx and 'The Peripheries of Capitalism'* (London: Routledge and Kegan Paul, 1983), 99ff.

country had turned into a developed industrial state and the working class dominated numerically.

But what about the economic conditions of communism? In 1847 Engels called for the formation of democratic governments establishing proletarian rule in Great Britain as well as in France and Germany, where, as he mentioned explicitly, the working class was in the minority. These governments should start 'immediately' to attack private property and ever further concentrate all industry, agriculture, and trade in the hands of the state. This would only become realisable, though, 'in the measure in which the productive forces of the country are being multiplied by the labour of the proletariat'.[21] The *Communist Manifesto* urged the workers to nationalise all means of production and 'multiply [them] as quickly as they can'. The more advanced the country, the quicker preparations for uproooting private property could be taken, but in all countries it would come under immediate attack.[22] Hal Draper calls this a 'transitional programme'. The economic conditions for the abolition of private property were not yet available, but: 'One of the tasks of proletarian rule itself is to bring this about'.[23] The proletarian revolution created the conditions for communism through accelerated industrialisation. In 1874, Marx noted further that in continental Western Europe the peasants were still in the majority. Nevertheless, proletarian governments could win over the peasants and facilitate the transition from private to collective property in land.[24]

In 1895, Engels admitted that he and his friend had in 1848 and 1871 been too optimistic. *Only now* did he understand that 'the situation of the economic development on the continent had then been by far not ripe enough for the replacement of capitalist production'.[25] Engels' prudence highlights the shift towards a new moderation. According to Kolakowski, it was Kautsky who formulated the new view in a complete form that proletarian revolutions were only possible in developed capitalist countries.[26] Then again, even he at times wavered towards the old Marxism, as when he opted for a Russian revolution 'on the borders between bourgeois and socialist society'.[27] It appears that with proletarian revolution in

---

[21] Marx and Engels, *Werke*, IV, pp. 372–4.   [22] *Ibid.*, pp. 481, 493.

[23] Hal Draper, *Karl Marx's Theory of Revolution*, II, *The Politics of Social Classes* (New York: Monthly Review Press, 1978), pp. 187, 193.

[24] Marx and Engels, *Werke*, XVIII, pp. 630, 631; see also, XVII, pp. 551–2.

[25] *Ibid.*, XXII, pp. 512–17; quotation, p. 515.

[26] Kolakowski, *Main Currents*, II, pp. 44ff, 331ff.

[27] See Moira Donald, *Marxism and Revolution. Karl Kautsky and the Russian Marxists, 1900–1924* (New Haven: Yale University Press, 1993), pp. 70ff; Bruno Naarden, *Socialist Europe and Revolutionary Russia: Perception and Prejudice 1848–1923* (Cambridge: Cambridge University Press, 1992), pp. 220–30.

backward Russia and the notion of a 'revolution from above' in which the proletarian state organises collectivisation and industrialisation at an accelerated pace, the Bolsheviks were in effect backing away from the orthodoxy of the day to return to the original Marxist radicalism.

Socialism in one country

According to Marx and Engels, socialism in a single country was impossible. French and German revolutions could only be successful if the tsar, the bulwark of political reaction, and British capitalism, dominating the world market, were overthrown. Communism presupposed more or less simultaneous revolution in England, America, France, and Germany. Not all Marxists agreed, though. In *The Isolated Socialist State* (1878) the German social democrat Georg Vollmar argued, that '*the final victory of socialism in at first only one single state or several states*' was possible. A socialist economy could function in one state, and this state could defend itself against the bourgeois world.[28] In his book on the 1891 Erfurt programme, Kautsky argued that under socialism international trade would be strongly reduced. 'Economic independence' was the best model.[29] He foresaw nationally confined, more or less autarkic socialist states. Thus Marxism offered two 'orthodoxies' to the Bolsheviks.[30]

Without acknowledging his debt to Vollmar and Kautsky, Lenin wrote in 1915 that 'the victory of socialism initially in some or even in one given capitalist country is possible.' After 'having expropriated the capitalists and having organised socialist production at home', the victorious proletariat would face the capitalist world.[31] Defending Marx, Trotsky argued that even a socialist Germany could never survive on its own. Lenin did not refer to Russia, but there is no denying that he defended socialism in one country as a principle. In the following years he was often less sanguine, emphasising that even developed states needed assistance from abroad to bring a socialist project to completion. He did not believe that backward Russia could survive in revolutionary isolation at all. Then again, from 1918 onwards he did gradually begin to acknowledge that possibility. In his last writings he almost in so many

---

[28] Georg Vollmar, *Der isolierte sozialistische Staat. Eine sozialökonomische Studie* (Zurich: Verlag der Volksbuchhandlung, 1878), p. 4.

[29] Karl Kautsky, *Das Erfurter Programm in seinem grundsätzlichen Theil erläutert von Karl Kautsky. Sechste Auflage* (Stuttgart: Dietz, 1905), pp. 117ff.

[30] See also Walicki, *Marxism*, p. 220.

[31] V. I. Lenin, *Polnoe Sobranie Sochinenii* (henceforth *PSS*) (Moscow: Gospolitizdat, 1958–72), XXVI, pp. 353–5. See also XXX, p. 133.

words accepted the possibility of an isolated socialist Russia. But the question of Lenin is to a degree irrelevant for the present argument.[32] Whether Stalin and Bukharin were or were not faithful to him in 1924–5, the main thing is that the idea of socialism within national walls originated among the German 'orthodox Marxists'.

Proletarian dictatorship, class struggle, and the state

One only has to read *The Communist Manifesto* to see that Marx and Engels considered the communist party to be some sort of vanguard.[33] Kautsky followed them, and it is debatable whether Lenin's early formulations of *What is to be Done?* constituted a Blanquist position going beyond Kautsky.[34] However, there is no question that Lenin's doctrine of revolutionary minority dictatorship (in which the vanguard of the class embodies the proletarian dictatorship), was alien to Marx and Engels' political philosophy. But Kautsky's claim that the only point of their 'proletarian dictatorship' was that the proletarian majority would automatically dominate a democracy is dubious.[35] Marx and Engels envisioned the revolutionary state during the transitional period of expropriation of the bourgeoisie and leading up to communism as a radical direct democracy, with a legislative assembly elected by universal suffrage and which subjected and dismantled the executive bureaucracy. The 'dictatorship of the proletariat' represented the *Diktat* of the legislative power.[36] But this does not fully answer the question of the kind of measures Marx expected of the revolutionary state.

---

[32] See Erik van Ree, 'Socialism in one country: a reassessment', *Studies in East European Thought* 50 (1998), 77–117.

[33] Marx and Engels, *Werke*, IV, p. 474.

[34] For Lenin quoting Kautsky in good faith, see: Neil Harding, *Lenin's Political Thought*, I, *Theory and Practice in the Democratic Revolution* (London: Macmillan, 1977), chs. 2, 6, and 7 (especially pp. 167ff); Donald, *Marxism*, pp. 24ff. For the opposite position, see John Kautsky, *Karl Kautsky. Marxism, Revolution and Democracy* (New Brunswick: Transaction Publishers, 1994), 59ff. According to Hal Draper, Plekhanov took a Blanquist position before Lenin. *The 'Dictatorship of the Proletariat' from Marx to Lenin* (New York: Monthly Review Press, 1987), pp. 64ff. Robert Mayer disagrees. 'The Dictatorship of the Proletariat from Plekhanov to Lenin', *Studies in East European Thought* 4 (1993).

[35] Karl Kautsky, *De Dictatuur van het Proletariaat* (Amsterdam: J. Emmering, 1919), p. 25.

[36] See Hal Draper, *Karl Marx's Theory of Revolution*, III, *The 'Dictatorship of the Proletariat'* (New York: Monthly Review Press, 1986); Hunt, *Political Ideas*, pp. 284–336; J. Ehrenberg, *The Dictatorship of the Proletariat. Marxism's Theory of Socialist Democracy* (New York: Routledge, 1992); Kolakowski, *Main Currents*, I, pp. 124, 228, 234, 255–8, 310, 361; McLellan, *Thought*, pp. 210–18, 240–2; Avineri, *Social and Political*, pp. 31ff, 43–52, 202–14.

Marx and Engels condemned the Jacobin Terror. To establish a virtuous state on the basis of a private economy was impossible. The Terror was a product of despair provoked by fantastic and premature goals.[37] Nevertheless, Marx acknowledged that the Terror had been the '*plebeian way*' to deal with absolutism and feudalism.[38] In 1848–50 he himself called for '*revolutionary terrorism*'. Later, he and Engels remained convinced that the bourgeoisie would take up arms to resist the democratic state's policy of expropriation. Only violence could frighten them into submission. Even in democratic countries where the proletariat might come to power peacefully, 'slave-owners' rebellions' would put the sword into the hand of the revolution.[39] The question has been researched by David Lovell, who argues that, despite their democratic orientation, Marx and Engels expected the need for violent emergency measures against resisting defeated classes.[40]

This is the context in which to consider one of Stalin's alleged innovations of Marxism. The dictator insisted that, as socialism approaches, the class struggle will intensify because of the increased resistance of the defeated exploiters.[41] How original was this? Lenin, too, observed that after the establishment of the proletarian dictatorship, the class struggle often became more bitter instead of subsiding. Capitalism resists the more furiously the closer it comes to its death. It was precisely their defeat which enormously increased the exploiters' 'energy of ... resistance'.[42] Earlier, Plekhanov argued that defending a historically lost cause will often increase the reactionaries' 'energy of resistance' and 'turn it into an energy of *despair*'.[43] What is more, it was agreed among German social democrats of the late nineteenth century that 'the more successful the party was, the more its opponents would be forced into illegal actions'.[44] It was Stalin who formulated the intensification of class struggle as a principle, but the underlying idea of desperate resistance of the exploiters

---

[37] Avineri, *Social and Political*, ch. 7.   [38] Marx and Engels, *Werke*, VI, p. 107; IV, p. 339.

[39] See, for example, *Ibid.*, XVII, p. 546; XVIII, pp. 308, 630; Draper, *Dictatorship*, pp. 112, 369; Gilbert, *Marx's Politics*, p. 238.

[40] David W. Lovell, *From Marx to Lenin. An Evaluation of Marx's Responsbility for Soviet Authoritarianism* (Cambridge: Cambridge University Press, 1984). On Marx's proletarian dictatorship and the use of force, see also Kolakowski, *Main Currents*, I, pp. 310, 361.

[41] I. V. Stalin, *Sochineniia*, 13 vols. (Moscow: Gospolitizdat, 1946–52), XI, pp. 171–2; XII, pp. 34, 38; XIII, p. 211; I. V. Stalin, *Sochineniia*, 3 vols., ed. Robert McNeal (Stanford: Hoover Institution Press, 1967), I (XIV), pp. 213–14.

[42] Lenin, *PSS*, XXXVI, p. 382; XXXVIII, pp. 386–7; XXXIX, pp. 13, 280; XL, p. 302; XLI, pp. 6, 54–5.

[43] G. W. Plechanow, *Ueber die Rolle der Persönlichkeit in der Geschichte* (Berlin: SWA-Verlag, 1946), p. 21.

[44] Gary P. Steenson, *Karl Kautsky, 1854–1938: Marxism in the Classical Years* (Pittsburgh: University of Pittsburgh, 1978), p. 118.

in the face of defeat was only too familiar for Marxists. This had been the essence of why Marx and Engels considered proletarian dictatorship necessary at all.

Turning to the question of bureaucracy: Marx and Engels's abhorrence of it did not prevent them from adopting the Jacobin formula of the 'one and indivisible' republic. The Paris Commune led them to accept local self-government, but not federalism.[45] Eventually, Engels concluded that federalism did suit large states like the United States, but not Germany. And in *all* countries, centralism remained the end goal.[46] Moreover, Marx and Engels's negative assessment of bureaucracy did not remain unchallenged. As Massimo Salvadori analyses, Kautsky believed that the proletarian takeover would not diminish officialdom. Rather than be smashed, the state apparatus would be captured and set to work under strict parliamentary control.[47] In Marx and Engels' scheme, upon the completion of the expropriation process, the radical democratic state was expected to dissolve itself into a self-administering communist society. Kautsky did not, to my knowledge, explicitly reject the idea of an eventual withering away of the state, but his work implies this. Like Max Weber, he treated bureaucracy as the indispensable administrative machinery of any modern state. In his *Das Erfurter Programm*, he argued that the state should be transformed into a *'socialist community'*, but there is no indication of what this would imply apart from the working class taking control of it.[48]

Among Russian Marxists, Lenin rehabilitated Marx's smashing fantasies in *State and Revolution*, but even before October he acknowledged that the economic state apparatus should be captured intact.[49] What is more, the state could only wither away in the second, highest stage of communism. Under socialism, as Lenin called Marx's first stage of communism, it was still needed to enforce the norms of distribution.[50] Andrzej Walicki points out that it was Trotsky who, in his defence of terrorism against Kautsky, insisted that the road to socialism 'lies through a period of the highest possible intensification of the principle of the State.' He compared it to a lamp which, just before going out, shoots

[45] Marx and Engels, *Werke*, XVII, pp. 339–41; see also VII, pp. 252–3.
[46] *Ibid.*, XXII: pp. 235–6.
[47] Massimo Salvadori, *Karl Kautsky and the Socialist Revolution, 1880–1938* (London: NLB, 1979), pp. 11–14, 34–47, 155–64, 267–76; Karl Kautsky, *Die soziale Revolution*, II, *Am Tage nach der sozialen Revolution* (Berlin: Vorwärts, 1902), p. 16; Karl Kautsky, 'Die neue Taktik, IV. Die Eroberung des Staatsgewaltes (Schluss)', *Die Neue Zeit* 2, 46 (1912), 725, 727, 732.
[48] Kautsky, *Erfurter Programm*, pp. 119, 123–45, 229–32. See also Kolakowski, *Main Currents*, II, p. 49; Steenson, *Karl Kautsky*, p. 77.
[49] Lenin, *PSS*, XXXIV, pp. 306–7.   [50] *Ibid.*, XXXIII, pp. 94–5, 97, 99.

up in a brilliant flame. The proletarian dictatorship must be the most ruthless form of state.[51] In 1933, Stalin indicated that the dying of the proletarian state took place not through its weakening, but through its 'maximum strengthening'. As the state could only wither away after the demise of classes, it should first make a maximum effort 'to kill off the rudiments of the dying classes'. It was, furthermore, necessary for defence against capitalist encirclement.[52] In 1938–9, Stalin further proclaimed that, even though socialism was now in the main achieved, the military threat necessitated a further strengthening of the state. As long as capitalist encirclement endured, the state would be preserved, even under the second stage of full communism. Its withering away was postponed to the triumph of socialism on a world scale.[53] In the light of Lenin's and Trotsky's earlier pronouncements, Stalin's innovations look modest. More significantly, these Russian innovations were preceded by an acceptance of the bureaucratic state among German Marxists.

'Soviet patriotism'

One of Stalin's alleged innovations concerns his idea of 'socialist nations'. The fusion of nations could only be effected after the triumph of socialism on a world scale. In the absence of that, socialism would see a '*flourishing* of national cultures, *socialist* in content and national in form'.[54] It is a moot point whether Marx and Engels envisioned a complete fusion of nations or allowed the continued existence of some national particularities,[55] but the

---

[51] Walicki, *Marxism*, p. 344.   [52] Stalin, *Sochineniia*, XIII, pp. 211, 350

[53] N. N. Maslov, 'I. V. Stalin o "Kratkom kurse istorii VKP(b)"', *Istoricheskii arkhiv* 5 (1994), 18, 20–2; Stalin, *Sochineniia*, I (XIV), pp. 394–5. See also, *Ibid.*, III (XVI), pp. 165, 295. In 1946 the possibility of 'communism in one country' was proclaimed. *Ibid.*, p. 56.

[54] Stalin, *Sochineniia*, VII, pp. 137–9; X, pp. 150–1; XI, pp. 333–49; XII, pp. 362–8; XIII, pp. 3–7. See also Gerhard Simon, *Nationalismus und Nationalitätenpolitik in der Sowjetunion. Von der totalitären Diktatur zur nachstalinschen Gesellschaft* (Baden-Baden: Nomos, 1986), pp. 153–7; Martin, *The Affirmative Action Empire*, pp. 245–6, 447–8. For a discussion of 'national in form', *Ibid.*, pp. 13–14, 182–4.

[55] For various viewpoints on this matter, see: Solomon Bloom, *The World of Nations. A Study of the National Implications in the Work of Karl Marx* (New York: Columbia University Press, 1941), pp. 22–8, 70; Horace B. Davis, *Nationalism & Socialism: Marxist and Labor Theories of Nationalism to 1917* (New York: Monthly Review Press, 1967), pp. 10–18, 76–9; Walker Connor, *The National Question in Marxist-Leninist Theory and Strategy* (Princeton: Princeton University Press, 1984), pp. 7–8, 18–19; Roman Szporluk, *Communism and Nationalism. Karl Marx versus Friedrich List* (New York: Oxford University Press, 1988), pp. 52–4, 64–8. See also Erik van Ree, 'Nationalist elements in the work of Marx and Engels. A critical survey', *MEGA-Studien* 1 (2000), 42–5.

characterisation of socialism as an era of flourishing nations had been formulated earlier by the prominent Austro-Marxist Otto Bauer.[56]

In Stalin's 1944 definition, 'Soviet patriotism' meant dedication and loyalty to the motherland, conceived as a 'unified, brotherly family' of nations, each preserving its own tradition.[57] The USSR was represented as either a Brotherhood or a Family of the Peoples.[58] The leading role was for the Russian nation, though, on grounds of its size; its relatively developed industrialisation; its national homogeneity; its developed culture; its talent for state-building and loyalty to the state; and its revolutionary activism and socialist sympathies.[59] 'Soviet patriotism' referred, finally, to the Soviet state as the avant-garde of the international communist movement and the dynamic centre of world politics. The Russians were, as Stalin said in 1933, 'the most talented nation in the world'.[60]

Marx and Engels' alleged principled objections to patriotism are generally illustrated by their remark of the workers having 'no fatherland'. But this is followed by the announcement that, through its conquest of political power, the proletariat will 'raise itself to the status of a national class, constitute itself as the nation'. Then again, even under capitalism national differences were disappearing, and 'the rule of the proletariat will make them vanish even more'.[61] In interpreting this, lacking the vote and property, the proletariat of 1848 was practically excluded from the nation. But by taking power they acquired a fatherland. It is a widely held view among Marx scholars that the *Manifesto*, despite its expectation of the fusion of nations, contains this element of proletarian patriotism, of proletarian nation-states during the transitional period to communism.[62]

---

[56] Otto Bauer, *Die Nationalitätenfrage und die Sozialdemokratie* (Vienna: Ignaz Brand, 1907), pp. 105–18, 367–74. See also Kolakowski, *Main Currents*, II, pp. 286–7. Stalin took pains to quote Lenin's 1920 remark that 'national and state differences' would continue to exist for a long time even after the global triumph of proletarian dictatorship. *PSS*, XLI, p. 77. See also Martin, *The Affirmative Action Empire*, p. 5.

[57] Stalin, *Sochineniia*, II (XV), pp. 161–2.

[58] See: Martin, *The Affirmative Action Empire*, p. 270, chs. 9, 11. See also Simon, *Nationalismus*, pp. 171–9. For another interpretation: Frederick C. Barghoorn, *Soviet Russian Nationalism* (New York: Oxford University Press, 1956), ch. 1.

[59] See Jeremy Smith, *The Bolsheviks and the National Question, 1917–13* (Basingstoke: Macmillan, 1999), pp. 24–8, 144, 214; Tucker, *Stalin in Power*, pp. 50ff; Martin, *The Affirmative Action Empire*, pp. 399, 453. For Stalin's well-known pronouncements on the Russian nation, see also *Sochineniia*, II, p. 304; IV, p. 75–6, 285–7; V, pp. 34, 46, 265; VI, pp. 186; XIII, pp. 24–6; II (XV), pp. 203–4.

[60] Cited in Martin, *The Affirmative Action Empire*, p. 453.

[61] Marx and Engels, *Werke*, IV, p. 479.

[62] See, for example, Bloom, *World of Nations*, pp. 22–8, 70; Davis, *Nationalism*, pp. 10–18, 76–9; Connor, *National Question*, pp. 7–8, 18–19; Peter Zwick, *National Communism* (Boulder: Westview, 1983), pp. 20–1.

On several occasions, Marx and Engels did discuss the proletariat as a patriotic force, capable of revolutionary regeneration of the father-land.[63] The Bolshevik Civil War slogan of the 'socialist fatherland' was in line with this tradition. Lenin praised French 'revolutionary patriotism' as an example. The revolution served to regenerate Russia and make it capable of similar military feats by overtaking the advanced countries economically.[64] In his February 1931 speech, Stalin acknowl-edged that the workers did not have a fatherland before 1917, but *now* 'we have a fatherland and we'll defend its independence'. Whereas the tsars could not prevent Russia from being beaten, the Bolsheviks could.[65] The claim that the revolution created a fatherland for the workers and raised it into an object of dedication was not an unusual position for a Marxist to take.

Marx and Engels further supported the 'great' nations of Central Europe – Poles, Germans, Hungarians – as 'bearers of progress' deserving their own states. The small Slavic and Romanian peasant peoples, *'national refuse'* lacking the capacity for independent survival, should be assimilated. Engels even demanded a revolutionary *'war of annihilation and ruthless terrorism'* against the 'counter-revolutionary nations of Europe'.[66] A German declaration of war against Russia, the mainstay of bureaucratic absolutism, would serve as a contribution to the 'propa-ganda of civilisation'.[67] Then again, the Russian barbarians were advanced in relation to the Asians. As Engels noted, Russian colonial rule was a civilising force among Bashkirs and Tatars.[68]

Marx and Engels obviously adopted Hegel's distinction between 'his-toric' and 'non-historic' nations; those capable and incapable of indepen-dent state formation. Some scholars are of the opinion that this formed an alien element in their economic materialism.[69] Others argue that they recognised the progressive significance of the modern state, the frame-work for overcoming feudal fragmentation and for industrial capitalist development. History proceeds through 'progressive centralisation', *through* the national state to communism. It was only logical to support progressive nations capable of state formation and to block the path of

[63] See for example Marx and Engels, *Werke*, IV, p. 518; XVII, pp. 330, 341. See also Agursky, *Third Rome*.

[64] Lenin, *PSS*, XXXIV, pp. 195, 198; XXXVI, pp. 78–80.

[65] Stalin, *Sochineniia*, XIII, pp. 38–40.

[66] Cited in Roman Rosdolsky, 'Engels and the "Nonhistoric" Peoples: the National Question in the Revolution of 1848', *Critique* 18–19 (1986), 86, 125, 127.

[67] Marx and Engels, *Werke*, V, pp. 202, 395. [68] Cited in Davis, *Nationalism*, p. 61.

[69] For example: Rosdolsky, 'Engels', pp. 86, 104–18, 111, ch. 8; Ronaldo Munck, *The Difficult Dialogue. Marxism and Nationalism* (London: Zed Books, 1986), ch. 1; Connor, *National Question*, ch. 1.

retrograde others who were, for reasons of size or lack of character, incapable of that feat – as obstacles to capitalist modernity, i.e. precisely for reasons of economic materialism.[70] Whichever of these two interpretations is the most tenable, Marx and Engels had no problem with dividing nations into civilised, progressive and reactionary, barbaric ones.

Furthermore, early in their career Marx and Engels expected the world revolution to begin in France. Revolutionary France should declare war on England and sweep the English revolutionaries to power. Revolutionary France and Germany should also overthrow the tsarist state.[71] Impressed by the Jacobin and Napoleonic examples, Marx and Engels expected specific states to act as the vanguard of the world revolution. After the defeat of the Paris Commune, they observed a shift of the centre of gravity of the workers' movement. Theoretically, and organisationally more capable than the French, the German workers turned into the new international vanguard.[72] Then again, after the murder of Alexander II, Marx and Engels admitted that Russia formed the 'vanguard of the revolutionary action in Europe'.[73] In 1902 Kautsky noted that the Slavs entered the 'ranks of the revolutionary nations'. The 'centre of revolutionary thought and revolutionary action' shifted to them.[74] In sum, for all its real internationalism, Marxism contained patriotism and the idea of defining specific nations as progressive world leaders among its birthmarks.

When 'Soviet patriotism' began to be stressed after 1934, a new conception of Russian history – 'patriotic', 'russocentric', and 'statist'[75] – was worked out. The Christian conversion of Russia was a progressive event. Gathering and centralising the Russian state and expanding it into non-Russian areas, from early Kievan times to Peter the Great, were progressive. Ivan IV was a progressive tsar. Peter's reforms were progressive. However, from Catherine until the mid-nineteenth century Russia served as the reactionary gendarme of Europe. Nevertheless, Russian defensive wars were always progressive; battles to defend the homeland were

---

[70] Bloom, *World of Nations*, pp. 11–22, 33–6; Ephraim Nimni, *Marxism and Nationalism. Theoretical Origins of a Political Crisis* (London: Pluto Press, 1991), ch. 1; Ian Cummins, *Marx, Engels and National Movements* (London: Croom Helm, 1980), pp. 20, 29, 31–4. See also Walicki, *Marxism*, pp. 163–6.

[71] See for example: Marx and Engels, *Werke*, I, p. 391; VI, pp. 149–50; VII, pp. 19, 79. See also Agursky, *Third Rome*, pp. 19, 63.

[72] See, for example, Marx and Engels, *Werke*, XIX, pp. 4, 24, 544; XXII, p. 255; XXXIII, p. 5; XXXVI, p. 231.

[73] *Ibid.*, XIX, p. 296; see also XVIII, p. 567.

[74] Cited in Agursky, *Third Rome*, p. 71. See also Donald, *Marxism*, 70ff.

[75] Brandenberger and Dubrovsky, 'The People Need a Tsar', pp. 877, 879; Maureen Perrie, *The Cult of Ivan the Terrible in Stalin's Russia* (Basingstoke: Palgrave, 2001), p. 25.

praiseworthy even when part of the unjust Crimean and First World Wars. Finally, Russian expansion into Ukraine, the Caucasus, and Central Asia had been relatively beneficial to the peoples concerned. Asian historical leaders who had fought Russia were condemned as representative of backward socio-economic systems. Anti-colonial struggles were only approved of if part of a common struggle with the Russian people against the imperial government.[76]

This was 'history in the service of patriotism'.[77] But it does not follow logically that it strayed from Marxist historiography.[78] That tsarism represented classes exploiting the Russian and colonised peoples was never denied. Historians tending to a 'single stream' interpretation of Russian history were called to order.[79] The basic argument was that, *despite its reactionary class character*, the formation of the Russian state and important episodes of its expansion had been progressive *in its time*. The Russian people needed a centralised state to overcome feudalism and allow capitalist development; this state needed a certain geographical scope; and its expansion into 'backward' areas furthered progress. All this remained arguably within a Marxist paradigm.[80]

Furthermore, I do not find Martin's thesis of a Stalinist abandonment of the Marxist idea of the nation as a modern construct entirely convincing. The cultivation of national folklore and classical literature as phenomena with a continuous, ancient history is considered indicative of primordialism.[81] But although the pre-modern roots of the nation were emphasised, nations remained modern constructs. In the Stalinist scheme, 'nationalities' (*narodnosti*) or 'peoples' (*narody*) became modern nations by overcoming feudal fragmentation and the creation of national

---

[76] See Brandenberger and Dubrovsky, 'The People Need a Tsar'; David Brandenberger, " ... It is imperative to advance Russian nationalism as the first priority": Debates within the Stalinist Ideological Establishment, 1941–1945', in Ronald Grigor Suny and Terry Martin (eds.), *A State of Nations: Empire and Nation-Making in the Age of Lenin and Stalin* (Oxford: Oxford University Press, 2001), pp. 275–99; Perrie, *Cult*. See also Barghoorn, *Soviet Russian*, pp. 52–66.

[77] Perrie, *Cult*, 25ff; Brandenberger and Dubrovsky, 'The People Need a Tsar'; Brandenberger 'It is imperative'.

[78] Brandenberger and Dubrovsky call the new doctrine a 'significant departure from the materialist proletarian internationalism' ('The People Need a Tsar', pp. 873, 880). Brandenberger notes that the break was incomplete; in a balancing act, one attempted to popularise the 'central Marxist convictions' with the help of traditional vocabulary. ('It is imperative', p. 276).

[79] See, for example, the debates on Russian colonial rule over Kazakhstan in 1944. Brandenberger, 'It is imperative'; Perrie, *Cult*, pp. 99–102.

[80] Marx and Engels acclaimed the overthrowing of the Golden Horde and the gathering of the Russian lands by Ivan III. The early absolute monarchies represented the progressive phenomenon of 'national unity'. *Werke*, XXI, pp. 400–1; XVI, p. 160.

[81] Martin, *The Affirmative Action Empire*, pp. 442–51.

markets. Even in late Stalinism, the Russian nation (*natsiia*) arose only with modernity. The preceding ethnos represented the nation's prehistory. The interpretation of languages as phenomena with deep historicity paralleled this.[82] Stalinist attention to Russian struggles against foreign invaders in late medieval times, and to the character-building effect of these struggles, can be similarly interpreted as highlighting not the primordial character of the Russian nation but precisely the fact that this nation was a historical creation.[83]

Martin observes another transformation in Stalinist ideology after 1933, namely a 'shift from class to people and the popular'.[84] The concept of the *narod* referred to the common people, a conglomerate of popular classes and strata: workers, peasants, intellectuals. The exploiting classes, capitalist and landowning, were excluded. *Narodnost'*, 'popularity', had the dual meaning of conforming to national traditions and of being close to the common people. Popularity became the criterion to which Soviet life was supposed to conform. It should be acknowledged that this shift from class to people was not a complete one. Stalin announced that the lines between the Soviet classes were blurred.[85] The Soviet press treated cultural and scientific heroes such as Pushkin and Lomonosov as representatives of a 'Russian people' unspecified in class terms. But they did not represent tsarist Russia, whose ruling classes despised these heroes, selfishly putting their class interests above the people.[86] Likewise, one only has to leaf through the sixteenth volume of Stalin's *Works* to see that after the war he did observe a struggle between the 'peoples' and the outrageously rich and egotistic 'ruling circles' in the world at large, rather than a strict Marxist opposition of proletariat and bourgeoisie. But that capitalism remained the basis of the system he despised was never in doubt.

Thus, Marxist class analysis was only partially dissolved into the vague dichotomy of people and elite. Yet, this was enough to allow a further transformation of patriotism. Stalinist patriotism was rooted in the perspective of the world's development from feudalism through capitalism to communism. Pride was taken in the Russians and the Soviet state for their

---

[82] Stalin, *Sochineniia*, XI, p. 336; III (XVI), pp. 117–23. See I. Tsamerian, 'Natsiia i narodnost'', *Bol'shevik* 6 (1951), 57–62. Also, Klaus Mehnert, *Stalin versus Marx: The Stalinist Historical Doctrine* (London: George Allen and Unwin, 1952), pp. 29–30.

[83] Brandenberger and Dubrovsky, 'The People Need a Tsar', 878, 882; Brandenberger, 'It is imperative', 277; Perrie, *Cult*, pp. 29, 31–3, 98.

[84] Martin, *The Affirmative Action Empire*, pp. 449–50. See also Perrie, *Cult*, pp. 29–30.

[85] Stalin, *Sochineniia*, I (XIV), p. 146. See also Wetter, *Der dialektische Materialismus*, p. 260; Mehnert, *Stalin*, pp. 59–60.

[86] Compare Rees, 'Stalin and Russian', p. 100; Barghoorn, *Soviet Russian*, p. 246.

being the foremost agents of this socio-economic process. However, as the proletariat was de-emphasised in relation to the 'people', there was a shift from rivalry of socio-economic systems to rivalry of nations. The shift was never complete. Stalin never considered capitalist restoration, but it was real enough.

Late Stalinism has been analysed by Frederick Barghoorn and Klaus Mehnert as a mixture of Marxism and Russian nationalism.[87] For Mehnert, its basis is contained in Stalin's 1948 thesis that every people has a unique individuality which forms its particular contribution to world civilisation.[88] National authenticity is the central value. Self-reliant state development, rejecting 'borrowing' and 'kowtowing to things foreign', realises the unique potential of the people. World science and culture form no integrated wholes, but sums of separate national cultures and sciences. All nations must maximise their own uniqueness and contribution to world civilisation, that is, strive for the 'priority' of their own economy, culture, and science. The concepts of 'national pride' and 'national dignity', and the contrasting 'homeless cosmopolitanism', refer to the recognition or rejection of national authenticity.

The specific Russian and Soviet claim to world superiority was only an outrageous application of this general approach. It was claimed that, from earliest times, the Russian and Slav nations created their own states and cultures independently. Throughout their history the Russians were generally ahead of other peoples, in terms of inventions and discoveries, and in practically all fields: philosophically, culturally, politically, economically, and technologically. Theirs was the most vital language of all. That the Russians entered upon the socialist road first was only the latest example of their unique talent for pioneering activity.[89] Stalin's idea of 'Slav solidarity' against the Germans included the celebration of the deeply humane and progressive character of the Slavs, as well as negative characterisations of the Germans.[90] The campaign against cosmopolitanism, reaching high gear in early 1949, acquired an anti-Semitic focus. With his definition of nations including a common territory, Stalin suspected the Jews, with their tradition of diaspora, of

[87] Mehnert, *Stalin*, pp. 126–8; Barghoorn, *Soviet Russian*, pp. 246, 260. See also Roman Szporluk, 'History and Russian ethnocentrism', in Edward Allworth (ed.), *Ethnic Russia in the USSR: The Dilemma of Dominance* (New York: Pergamon Press, 1980), p. 42.

[88] Mehnert, *Stalin*, p. 29. Stalin, *Sochineniia*, III (XVI), pp. 100–1.

[89] Mehnert, *Stalin*; Barghoorn, *Soviet Russian*, pp. 199–262.

[90] Mehnert, *Stalin*, pp. 77–8; Erik van Ree, *The Political Thought of Joseph Stalin: A Study in Twentieth-Century Revolutionary Patriotism* (London: RoutledgeCurzon, 2002), pp. 181, 197, 237–9.

being unusually susceptible to cosmopolitanism and of lacking loyalty to the Soviet state.[91]

This anti-cosmopolitanism no longer fitted Marxist frameworks however generously interpreted. Attributing psychological profiles to nations, Marx and Engels did often not carefully reduce these to socio-economic roots either, but national authenticity never became their analytical point of departure. Then again, in a paradoxical twist, Stalinism's Marxist component was only slightly hollowed out. Stalin's upgrading of love of fatherland and national character to supreme values had little to do with Marxism, but anti-capitalism remained incorporated, when it was insisted that cosmopolitanism was produced by capitalism, which puts money and profit over fatherland.[92] Late Stalinism was an ideology that bluntly put *two* points of departure: nation and class, and *two* main goals: national development and world communism, next to each other and left the impossible job of reintegrating them into one whole to its baffled interpreters.

Discussion

It seems justifiable to conclude that most of Stalin's heretical innovations were in fact developed earlier within the broad mainstream of German Marxism: Marx, Engels, Vollmar, and Kautsky, or among the Austromarxists. We found this to be the case for proletarian revolution in backward countries; revolution from above; socialism in one country; the intensifying class struggle against the desperate, defeated classes; the unified and indivisible republic; preservation of the bureaucratic state under socialism; socialism as an era of national diversification; proletarian patriotism; the notion of vanguard and backward nations; and the idea of the relative progressiveness of early state centralisation and colonialism.

We found two elements without an obvious Marxist pedigree. First, Lenin's doctrine of revolutionary minority dictatorship. Second, the diffuse concepts of the 'people', the 'popular', and an 'anti-cosmopolitanism' that raised national authenticity into an independent, supreme concern. Then again, though, in embracing the idea of sectarian dictatorship, Lenin followed in the footsteps of Pestel', Zaichnevskii, and Tkachev, so this tradition was arguably the Russian branch of the Western ideology of

---

[91] Benjamin Pinkus, *The Jews of the Soviet Union: The History of a National Minority* (Cambridge: Cambridge University Press, 1988), pp. 145–61; also Arno Lustiger, *Rotbuch: Stalin und die Juden. Die tragische Geschichte des Jüdischen Antifaschistischen Komitees und der sowjetischen Juden* (Berlin: Aufbau Taschenbuch Verlag, 2000), pp. 225–30.

[92] See van Ree, *Political Thought*, pp. 204–5.

Jacobinism-Blanquism. The Russian originality of the complex of 'people', 'popularity', and 'anti-cosmopolitanism' is questionable too. Under Stalin it was claimed that such notions, especially in relation to cultural matters, were rooted in the Russian tradition of 'revolutionary democrats' such as Chernyshevskii and Belinskii. However, populist definitions of the national community as the people minus an aristocratic elite, and as a primarily political community nevertheless endowed with a unique cultural identity that needs to be nurtured, also repeat basic patterns from Rousseau and the Jacobins. This is not strange. The nineteenth-century Russian revolutionaries Stalin admired were influenced by early revolutionary thinking in the West.[93] Let me add that one observes further striking similarities between the ideology of High Stalinism and Hamburg's 'national bolshevism' of the early 1920s. Partly continuing Lassalle's work, Laufenberg and Wolffheim's communist patriotism recognised the non-class functions of the state and celebrated a national popular community from which the bourgeoisie was excluded.[94]

Looking at it from this angle, the Russian originality of Stalin's ideology seems almost to evaporate. It contains hardly anything specifically or originally Russian. Even where his tenets did diverge from Marxist frameworks, we can still find important precedents from among the West European revolutionary movement. This conclusion raises the question of causality. How organic was the development of Stalin's ideology in the Marxist context? The problem is that, with his wish to preserve his Marxist-Leninist credentials at all costs, Stalin locked himself in a tight straightjacket. He could not publicly refer to the German national Bolsheviks, once condemned by Lenin. He could never admit to in some respects preferring Jacobin revolutionary patriotism to the Marxist class approach. He could never refer to Kautsky, Vollmar, or Otto Bauer. Ironically, he could not even refer to Engels' work about historic and non-historic nations. The texts by Engels Stalin could have enlisted in support of his own theses contain anti-Russian outrages and terroristic, genocidal passages directed against the Slav peoples. Due to his own dogmatic presentation, Stalin could not speak freely about his sources and preferences. Instead, he had to cover his traces. To make matters worse, my own admittedly far from exhaustive research in some

---

[93] For discussions of Russian populism and Jacobinism, and Western influences, see Astrid von Borcke, *Die Ursprünge des Bolschewismus. Die jakobinische Tradition in Russland und die Theorie der revolutionären Diktatur* (Munich: Berchmans, 1977); Andrzej Walicki, *A History of Russian Thought from the Enlightenment to Marxism* (Stanford: Stanford University Press, 1979).

[94] L. Dupeux, *'Nationalbolschewismus' in Deutschland 1919–1933. Kommunistische Strategie und konservative Dynamik* (Munich: Beck, 1985), pp. 82ff.

of the Soviet archives concerning Stalin, the results of which I have presented in my recent book,[95] have convinced me that it will indeed be difficult to recover his traces. For example, a pretty thorough search through the leader's private library, though rewarding in many respects, does not clearly show Stalin's ideological indebtedness to non-Russian Marxists like Kautsky or to people like Belinskii and Chernyshevskii for that matter. His notes in the relevant books, even when rather extensive, often do not allow us to draw straightforward conclusions. Even in the private sphere Stalin was often a closed figure. In a way, the conclusion of the present paper leaves us, then, at the beginning rather than at the end of a line of research.

These caveats aside, we are left with the paradox that Stalinist ideology contained little that was not prefigured in the Western revolutionary movement; but was at the same time perfectly adapted to Russian traditions of authoritarianism, bureaucratic etatism, and patriotism. For all its lack of originality, it did at the same time represent a typically Russian Marxism. The explanation of the paradox is, perhaps, simple enough: the preceding Western revolutionary tradition was – formulated anachronistically – more permeated with 'Stalinist' elements than we would like to think. Stalinism did not have to be created from scratch, its elements were there for the picking. The real originality of the Stalinist ideology lay in its particular synthesis. When he rehashed Marxist and radical patriotic notions previously formulated in Western Europe, Stalin made a selection of what to adopt, discarding much of Western Marxism in the process – roughly all liberal and democratic elements. And his selection did produce a remarkable construct. I know of no other ideology preserving both Marxism and radical patriotism in almost unalloyed form and combining them boldly into a new, almost incoherent whole. This was a 'national bolshevism' in the fullest sense of the word.

[95] Van Ree, *Political Thought.*

10   Stalin as Bolshevik romantic: ideology and mobilisation, 1917–1939

David Priestland

Speaking at the Eighteenth Party Congress in 1939, Stalin argued that Marxist-Leninist ideology lay at the centre of Soviet politics:

> There is hardly any need to dwell on the serious importance of Party propaganda, of the Marxist-Leninist education [*vospitanie*] of our workers [*rabotnikov*] ... It must be accepted as an axiom that the higher the political level and the Marxist-Leninist consciousness of workers in any branch of state or Party work the better and more fruitful will be the work itself ... and, conversely, the lower the political level of the workers, and their Marxist-Leninist consciousness, the more probable will be disruption and failure in work, the more probable will it be that workers will become superficial and that they will degenerate into pragmatists and pedants [*deliagi-krokhobory*], the more likely their [complete] degeneration.[1]

The significance and meaning of statements such as this have been the subject of disagreement among historians of Stalinism. Why did Stalin, a leader so frequently denounced by his rivals as a mediocre theorist, pay so much attention to the role of ideas in politics? What was the relationship between ideas and Stalin's political behaviour? And what was the nature of the 'Marxist-Leninist' ideology he claimed to be so committed to?

It used to be common to assume that Stalin was indulging in empty rhetoric and that he had little interest in political ideas. For some, Stalin was best seen as a typical modernising state-builder, a pragmatist whose commitment to Marxism was 'skin-deep'.[2] For other commentators, the 'basic principle' of Soviet history was the creation of an all-powerful state and the oppression of the individual; ideology was merely something invented or manipulated by Stalin and his court intellectuals to justify this process.[3] Now it has become more common to take the political ideas of Stalin and the Bolsheviks seriously, and to relate them to the broader

---

[1] I. V. Stalin, *Sochineniia*, 3 vols., Robert McNeal (ed.), (Stanford: The Hoover Institution, 1967), I (XIV), pp. 380–1.

[2] E. H. Carr, *The Russian Revolution from Lenin to Stalin* (London: Macmillan, 1979), p. 163.

[3] See, for instance, Leszek Kolakowski, *Main Currents of Marxism. vol. 3. The Breakdown* (Oxford: Clarendon Press, 1978), pp. 7–8.

political culture of the Bolshevik Party, but there are disagreements over their nature. As Sheila Fitzpatrick has argued, many recent studies of Stalinist political culture and practice have tended to take either a 'modernity', 'Enlightenment' approach, or a 'neo-traditionalist' position.[4] For one group, Stalin and the Bolsheviks were trying to create an Enlightenment utopia, in the tradition of Condorcet and the French *philosophes*; working on the basis of 'scientific' principles, they used often brutal social engineering in order to create a rational harmonious society.[5] For the other, Stalinism was a system of thought and political practice that, whatever its intentions, led to the emergence of a 'neo-traditionalist' order in which a new society of ranks and estates was established. The ideology articulated by Stalinist leaders may have been a universalist and modernising one, but in practice it gave rise to a rigidly hierarchical and paternalistic political culture.[6]

Each of these approaches is useful in describing elements of Soviet political culture and practice in the 1920s and 1930s. They may also explain aspects of Stalin's own thought, although the neo-traditionalist paradigm is probably not as applicable as the Enlightenment approach. Yet neither are entirely successful in accounting for the less scientistic, rationalistic elements in Stalin's discourse. An analysis of Bolshevism as a religious or quasi-religious system of thought – whether as a Marxism influenced by Orthodoxy, or a form of 'political religion', a messianic ideology with ambitions to create a pure society, free of evil 'alien' groups – might contribute to an explanation of these ideas.[7] But I shall argue that it is more helpful to see Stalin's political ideas in the context of tensions both

---

[4] See Sheila Fitzpatrick, 'Introduction', in Sheila Fitzpatrick (ed.), *Stalinism. New Directions* (London: Routledge, 2000), p. 11.

[5] See in particular Stephen Kotkin, *Magnetic Mountain. Stalinism as a Civilisation* (Berkeley: University of California Press, 1995), pp. 6–8; David Hoffman, 'European Modernity and Soviet Socialism' in Yanni Kotsonis and David Hoffman, *Russian Modernity: Politics, Knowledge, Practices* (Basingstoke: Macmillan, 1999), pp. 245–60. Erik van Ree also places Stalin firmly in the Enlightenment tradition, although he does argue that there were romantic elements in his thinking. Erik van Ree, *The Political Thought of Joseph Stalin. A Study in Twentieth-Century Revolutionary Patriotism* (London: RoutledgeCurzon, 2002), pp. 283–7.

[6] See Terry Martin, 'Modernisation or Neo-traditionalism? Ascribed Nationality and Soviet Primordialism', in Fitzpatrick (ed.), *Stalinism*, pp. 348–67.

[7] For the argument that Stalin's thinking should be understood in a specifically Orthodox Christian context, see Mikhail Vaiskopf, *Pisatel' Stalin* (Moscow: Novoe literaturnoe obozrenie, 2002). For the view that Marxism and Bolshevism had an eschatological, fundamentally religious structure, see Igal Halfin, *From Darkness to Light: Class, Consciousness and Salvation in Soviet Russia* (Pittsburgh: University of Pittsburgh Press, 2000). See also Amir Weiner, *Making Sense of War: The Second World War and the Fate of the Bolshevik Revolution* (Princeton: University of Princeton Press, 2001), pp. 27, 32 for this emphasis on messianism and purification, although he also sees the Soviet

within Marxism and Bolshevik political strategy, rather than as a form of religious thinking. His ideas in the period 1917–39, like those of most Bolshevik leaders, changed over time and were often inconsistent. However, I shall argue that Stalin tended to adopt a voluntaristic and sometimes populist view of politics that had its roots in left Bolshevik thinking.[8] One might describe these ideas as a form of quasi-romantic (as opposed to 'Enlightenment') Bolshevism, characterised by an emphasis on heroism, socialist commitment, will, and struggle, and by a hostility towards a narrow 'petty-bourgeois', mechanistic, scientific view of the world.[9] Or one might use a Weberian typology, and define it as a variety of 'charismatic' (as opposed to 'rational-legal') Bolshevism, according to which the party, like Weber's charismatic agent, had the right to rule because it had extraordinary powers and access to a higher truth; members of the new socialist order were to be judged not primarily according to their technical knowledge or professional attainments, but according to their ability to transform the world through heroism and will.[10] This chapter will also argue that the appeal of this voluntaristic Bolshevism to Stalin was closely related to practical politics, and his interest in strategies of mobilisation.[11]

These aspects of Stalin's thinking have often been obscured by the common assumption that Stalin was a conservative figure, whose most significant contribution to Bolshevik ideology was his justification of political and economic inequality. In defining both a centralised state and the presence of economic inequalities within the planned system as

Union as a social engineering 'gardening state'. For older approaches of this type, see Jacob Talmon, *The Origins of Totalitarian Democracy* (Harmondsworth: Penguin, 1986), pp. 8–13. None of these works deals with Stalin's own thought in any detail.

[8] By 'populist' I mean a belief in the virtues of the 'proletariat' or the 'Soviet people'. I am not referring to the Russian 'Populists' and their commitment to the Russian peasantry.

[9] For a discussion of 'romanticism' in Bolshevik thought, see Katerina Clark, *Petersburg: Crucible of Cultural Revolution* (Cambridge, Mass.: Harvard University Press, 1995), pp. 15–23. Clark argues that 'romantic anti-capitalism' was a powerful strain within Bolshevik culture, a concept which unites hostility to the mundane and materialistic with antagonism to the 'bourgeois'. For another approach to the romantic elements in early Bolshevik thought, see Anna Krylova, 'Beyond the Spontaneity–Consciousness Paradigm: "Class Instinct" as a Promising Category of Historical Analysis', *Slavic Review* 1 (2003), 1–23; Igal Halfin, 'Between Instinct and Mind: the Bolshevik View of the Proletarian Self', *Slavic Review* 1 (2003), 34–40.

[10] Max Weber, *Economy and Society: An Outline of Interpretive Sociology*, Guenther Roth and Claus Wittich (eds.), (Berkeley: University of California Press, 1978), I, pp. 241–5. For the application of Weberian categories to Bolshevik politics, see Ken Jowitt, *New World Disorder: The Leninist Extinction* (Berkeley: University of California Press, 1992), ch. 1; Stephen Hanson, *Time and Revolution: Marxism and the Design of Soviet Institutions* (Chapel Hill: University of North Carolina Press, 1997).

[11] For the role of mobilisation in early Bolshevik politics, and the problems associated with it, see Thomas Remington, *Building Socialism in Bolshevik Russia: Ideology and Industrial Organisation, 1917–1921* (Pittsburgh: Pittsburgh University Press, 1984), pp. 14–17.

'socialist' in the early and mid-1930s, he did indeed develop Marxism-Leninism in this direction, but this did not affect his commitment to a voluntaristic version of Bolshevism; rather, he tried to divorce voluntarism from the egalitarianism with which it had been associated in the early years of the regime, and adapted it to a new political and ideological context. Stalin, like other Bolshevik leaders, changed his position frequently. But if we appreciate these tendencies in Stalin's thought, this chapter will argue, it becomes easier to understand Stalin's view of the relationship between ideology and political practice, and to explain why Stalin took commitment to Marxism-Leninism so seriously in the late 1930s.

Politika versus *tekhnika*

Marxism, as many have observed, is an ideological system which suffers from a fundamental contradiction between its scientistic and deterministic side and its more voluntaristic and romantic side.[12] At the root of the conflict is a tension within Marx's own thought: he argued that many elements of advanced capitalism – the division of labour, hierarchies based on technical expertise, material incentives – were vital for economic development and thus for building the foundations of a productive communism; this element of Marxism could be used to justify a technocratic society. Yet he also claimed that at some time in the future workers would be able to create an egalitarian and extraordinarily productive society in which work became 'self-activity', and there was no need for people to be compelled or 'bribed' to work, by means of material, wage incentives.[13] This utopia had something in common with a romantic ideal of a wholly unified society, governed not by material things but by human creativity and self-expression. Marx's views of the forces driving history could also be interpreted in different ways. He could be seen as a proponent of the scientistic view that economic forces, discoverable by scientific investigation, would drive society towards communism; the proletariat would bring about revolution and socialism because it was responding rationally to these forces. But some of his writings seemed to justify the more voluntaristic and potentially romantic view that the proletariat would

---

[12] For a classic treatment of these tensions within Marxism, see Alvin Gouldner, *The Two Marxisms: Contradictions and Anomalies in the Development of Theory* (London: Macmillan, 1980), ch. 3.

[13] For this tension see, for instance, Gareth Stedman Jones, 'Introduction', in Karl Marx and Friedrich Engels, *The Communist Manifesto* (London: Penguin, 2002), pp. 178–83.

establish socialism because its special qualities – its love of work and its innate collectivism – would drive it to do so.[14]

After 1917, the Bolsheviks had to address a specific set of practical issues: how to run a state and economy in a way that was both viable and non-capitalist. But they were divided, and they understood their conflicts within the context of the dualism within Marxism.[15] The 'left', made up of a number of disparate groups, tended to argue that the working class was in the process of being transformed into the ideal collectivist 'proletariat'. Workers, they insisted, were capable of running a polity and an economy in a highly egalitarian way, advancing rapidly from a capitalist towards a truly socialist order. Few called for the abolition of the state or of all authority relations, but they did claim that workers could participate to a limited degree in the administration of the economy and society, and that old 'capitalist' incentives (the carrot and the stick) could gradually give way to moral incentives founded on workers' collectivism. Their practical solutions included three main elements: first, the Party had to ensure that officials were to be committed to socialism, so that they could inspire the masses with socialist ideas. Secondly, officials were to be 'democratic' rather than 'bureaucratic': they were to avoid harsh 'administrative methods' (*administrirovanie*) in their treatment of workers, they were to establish 'links' (*sviazi*) with those they led and they were to 'educate' (*vospityvat'*) workers to become true 'proletarians' – disciplined, self-sacrificing, and committed. The left was divided over its attitude towards 'democracy'. Some seriously argued for a transition to some form of mass participation in administration, but many did not and were, in effect, advocating a form of centrally directed populist mobilisation. Thirdly, officials were to be proletarian by class origin, for only proletarians had the right approach to the masses. It was common among the left to argue that the proletariat had a special, collectivist, and fundamentally more

---

[14] For tensions within Marx's theory of history, see Helmut Fleischer, *Marxism and History*, Eric Mosbacher (trans.) (London: Allen Lane, 1973), ch. 1. Marx, from an early stage, claimed to be a rationalist, and while he argued that men's 'ideas' drove history forward, these ideas consisted of knowledge and science. For this view of Marx, see Allan Megill, *Karl Marx and the Burden of Reason. (Why Marx Rejected Politics and the Market)* (Oxford: Rowman and Littlefield, 2002), pp. 206–8. However, it is possible to identify romantic elements within Marx's thought; M. H. Abrams, *Natural Supernaturalism: Tradition and Revolution in Romantic Literature* (New York, W. W. Norton, 1973), pp. 313–16. For the political and economic thinking of the German romantics, and for comparisons with Marx's thought, see Liah Greenfeld, *Nationalism: Five Roads to Modernity* (Cambridge, Mass.: Harvard University Press, 1992), pp. 322–95.

[15] For a fuller discussion of these debates during the Civil War period, see David Priestland, 'Bolshevik Ideology and the Debate over Party–State Relations', *Revolutionary Russia* 10 (1997), 41–5; David Priestland, *Stalinism and the Politics of Mobilization: Ideas, Power and Terror in Inter-war Russia* (Oxford: Oxford University Press, forthcoming), ch. 1.

productive culture than the bourgeoisie.[16] The left, then, closely associated 'democracy' with the 'class struggle' against the bourgeoisie and its influence.

Lenin and his allies, however, took a more 'rightist' position, at least after the spring of 1918. While all Bolsheviks accepted that the old bourgeoisie was politically unreliable, Lenin argued that many of the achievements of capitalism and bourgeois culture had to be retained if the economy was to be rebuilt. As Lenin put it, 'we can only build communism out of the material created by capitalism, out of that cultured apparatus which has been cultivated under bourgeois conditions and which – so far as concerns the human material... – is therefore inevitably steeped in bourgeois psychology'.[17] Material incentives and coercion were to operate, and the 'bearers of science and technique' were to have some authority, even if they were of bourgeois class origin. Workers had a low 'cultural level', and therefore 'discipline' imposed from above was vital; plans for expanded 'democracy' and participation would have to be postponed to the distant future.

The conflict between the left and the leadership therefore revolved around a number of related issues: which social groups was the regime to rely on – proletarians or bourgeois specialists? Which incentives were to be used? And which 'style' of leadership should be encouraged? But it was also, more fundamentally, about the relationship between ideological and technical considerations in politics, or in the language of the time, between 'politics' (*politika*) or 'ideological principle' (*ideinost'*) and 'economics' or 'technique' (*tekhnika*). For Lenin, a socialist state and economy had to be run in a scientific way by expert leaders who had learnt from 'engineers and agronomists', just as organisations were managed under advanced capitalism.[18] For the left, however, this type of leader, however technically expert, might not only be disloyal but would also lack the psychology needed for the effective mobilisation of the masses. The regime would be much more successful if it adhered to its Marxist principles, and if it used socialist ideas to inspire the population. The left therefore accused Lenin of moving 'the central point from politics to industrial problems', neglecting *politika* by exclusively concentrating on *tekhnika*.[19] Bukharin described the essence of the conflict with his usual clarity in his contribution

---

[16] See, for instance, Alexandra Kollontai, *The Workers' Opposition* (London: n.p., 1923), p. 25.

[17] V.I. Lenin, *Polnoe Sobranie Sochinenii*, 5th edn. (Moscow: Gospolitizdat, 1958–65) (henceforth *PSS*), XXXVII, p. 409.

[18] Lenin, *PSS*, XLII, p. 157.

[19] Kollontai, *The Workers' Opposition*, p. 35; for the relationship between *tekhnika* and *politika*, see S.K. Minin, 'Voennoe stroitel'stvo', *Izvestiia TsK KPSS* 10 (1989), 187.

to the debate on the trade unions in 1921. He argued that there were two 'tendencies' in the discussion, 'one which assesses the situation exclusively from a political point of view, and the other which assigns primary importance to the economic point of view'. 'Political' tasks, for Bukharin, included 'the establishment of the complete unity of the proletariat' and the 'rallying of the party on the basis of the revival [ozhivlenie] of party thought and of the involvement of all members of the party in its active life', presupposing 'a system of inner-party workers' democracy'; 'economic' tasks, on the other hand, involved a more hierarchical, elitist approach to authority relations, and included the 'strengthening of a firm administrative framework' and the pursuit of 'planned work in economic life'.[20] Bukharin hoped to combine the two approaches, as did most Bolsheviks, but he was aware that he was describing two very different visions of the path to socialism, and of socialism itself: a technocratic and scientistic one, and a voluntaristic and populist one that valued ideological inspiration and mobilisation.

While Stalin generally followed Lenin on important ideological issues, he did have a history of adopting more voluntaristic and anti-bourgeois views than Lenin, particularly during and immediately after the revolution of 1905.[21] And this attitude to politics re-emerged after the October Revolution in his support for the leftist 'Military Opposition' during the debates between the left and the leadership on the Red Army in 1918 and 1919. The Military Opposition objected to Trotsky's employment of tsarist officers, both because they were potentially disloyal, and because, as Stalin's ally Voroshilov explained, the bourgeois officer was a 'dead commander', while effective commanders had to be the 'soul of their unit'.[22] Stalin had personal reasons for opposing the use of tsarist officers in the army: as plenipotentiary on the southern front he came into conflict with General Sytin, Trotsky's appointment as military commander and a former tsarist officer.[23] But he also joined the left in insisting that proletarian officers who had the 'confidence of their men' be appointed.[24] Similarly, Stalin echoed the left's rhetoric in his emphasis on the

[20] Desiatyi s"ezd RKP(b). Mart 1921 goda. Stenograficheskii otchet (Moscow: Gospolitizdat, 1961), p. 826 (Bukharin et al.).

[21] See Robert Williams, The Other Marxists. Lenin and his Critics 1904–1914 (Bloomington, Ind.: University of Indiana Press, 1996), pp. 119–23. See also Robert Himmer, 'On the Origin and Significance of the Name "Stalin"', Russian Review 3 (1986), 269–86; for the view that Stalin, while always to the left of Lenin, was closer to him than these authors suggest, see Erik van Ree, 'Stalin's Bolshevism, the First Decade', International Review of Social History 39 (1994), 361–81.

[22] Izvestiia TsK KPSS 11 (1989), 160.

[23] For the 'Tsaritsyn affair', see Francesco Benvenuti, The Bolsheviks and the Red Army (Cambridge: Cambridge University Press, 1988), pp. 42–52.

[24] I. V. Stalin, Sochineniia, 13 vols. (Moscow: Gospolitizdat, 1946–52), IV, p. 131.

importance of 'political education' (*vospitanie*) in the army, and in his criticisms of Trotsky's leadership for neglecting it.[25] He was also worried about the potential disloyalty of bourgeois officers, and indeed any 'propertied' recruits.[26] Yet Stalin's position was not identical to that of the Military Opposition, and he placed much more emphasis on strict discipline than they did. While all on the left accepted that compulsion, as well as *vospitanie*, was required in an effective army, Stalin criticised V. M. Smirnov's leftist theses for getting the balance wrong and underestimating the importance of hierarchy and discipline.[27]

Lenin generally supported Trotsky during the military debates, although ultimately he accepted a compromise.[28] During the subsequent trade union debates, he also opposed the left, but this time he moved more decisively against Trotsky, and now criticised him for being excessively disciplinarian and anti-'democratic'. Stalin followed Lenin's line but, as before, his language had a more voluntaristic and populist tone than Lenin's.[29] Stalin declared that he had argued for iron discipline during the military debates because the army included peasants and other unreliable non-proletarian social groups. But he argued that now that the party's attention was being redirected away from military questions towards economic issues, 'persuasion' was much more effective than 'force'.[30] He therefore strongly criticised Trotsky's proposal that 'military methods' be used by the regime in its dealings with the working class. Methods of 'democracy' and 'persuasion' were much more effective than those of 'coercion', because the struggle against economic ruin had to become a 'vital concern of the whole working class'. It was necessary to 'rouse the millions of the working class for the struggle against economic ruin', to 'heighten their initiative, consciousness and independent activity', so that they became 'vitally interested in the struggle' against economic ruin. If this were not done, 'victory on the economic front cannot be achieved'.[31] During the civil war, then, Stalin

---

[25] *Izvestiia TsK KPSS* 11 (1989), 164; Stalin, *Sochineniia*, IV, p. 209.

[26] Stalin, *Sochineniia*, IV, pp. 206–8; *Izvestiia TsK KPSS* 11 (1989), 164.

[27] *Izvestiia TsK KPSS* 11 (1989), 163–4 (Stalin); for Smirnov's theses, see *Izvestiia TsK KPSS* 9 (1989), 181–4.

[28] Benvenuti, *The Bolsheviks and the Red Army*, pp. 109–18.

[29] Lenin denied that he had any principled differences with Trotsky, and he strongly objected to the notion of 'industrial democracy'. Lenin, *PSS*, XLII, pp. 204, 210–11.

[30] Rossiiskii gosudarstvennyi arkhiv sotsial'no-politicheskoi istorii (henceforth RGASPI) f. 558, op. 11, d. 1101, ll. 108–10 (Speech to Moscow Party Committee, 1921). Lenin also appreciated the importance of popular enthusiasm, but in December 1920 he argued that the turn from the military to the 'economic front' required 'new forms associated with compulsion'. Lenin, *PSS*, XLII, p. 144.

[31] Stalin, *Sochineniia*, V, p. 9.

sympathised with the left's emphasis on class purity and 'democracy', but he seems to have seen its proposals in a pragmatic way – as a method of mobilising the masses. Unlike some on the left, he did not see them as part of a serious attempt to alter power relationships between the elites and the masses.

'Class struggle' and 'socialist construction'

After Lenin's death, the conflict between leftist and more technocratic notions of the proper relationship between officials and workers, proletarians and bourgeois, and *tekhnika* and *politika*, continued. But the focus of the discussion changed, as these questions of class and 'democracy' became associated with the industrialisation debate. During the Civil War period, the left had been on the defensive over economic policy because it appeared that workers' 'democracy' threatened economic order. But during the NEP the left's arguments appeared to be more compelling, as markets and the employment of bourgeois specialists all seemed to be inhibiting economic development and damaging the regime's legitimacy. For the leftist United Opposition towards the end of the NEP period, 'democratisation' was not only compatible with rapid industrial development, but was a necessary precondition for it. It declared that the country had to 'move forward as far as possible along the road of socialist construction by strengthening ourselves with a proper class policy'[32], and this 'class policy' included proletarianising the apparatus; strengthening 'links' between workers and officials; 'reviving the party' by sending officials to the factory floor so that they would retain their proletarian nature and spirit; and eliminating the 'steady stream of non-proletarian influences' which infected the apparatus 'through the specialists and upper strata of the office workers and intellectuals'.[33]

Stalin, as a defender of the NEP order, strongly argued against the left's 'democratic' critique of the regime. He objected to the left's populist denunciations of economic managers and he also refused to accept that there was a serious problem of 'bureaucratism' or class 'degeneration' in the apparatus.[34] Yet, on the whole, he did not challenge the left's fundamental assumptions: that proletarianisation, 'democratisation', and the 'revival' of Party life were desirable. He generally stated either that circumstances prevented the regime from pursuing them, or that the regime had already achieved a great deal in these areas and the left's

---

[32] 'The Platform of the Opposition', in Leon Trotsky, *The Challenge of the Left Opposition, 1926–7* (New York: Pathfinder Press, 1980), p. 336.
[33] *Ibid.*, pp. 360, 391.   [34] Stalin, *Sochineniia*, VI, pp. 223, 226.

criticisms were unreasonable.[35] His position was not unusual among Bolshevik leaders, but his tone contrasts with that of others. Bukharin, for instance, was much more forthright than Stalin in condemning the 'proletarian' arrogance of both the left and many Party officials. For Bukharin, the bourgeois specialists were only one source of 'bureaucratism'; equally dangerous were arrogant 'proletarian' bureaucrats who oppressed non-proletarian groups.[36]

Stalin and Bukharin also differed in their views of the ideal socialist culture. Both Bukharin and Stalin were sympathetic to the idea of a particular 'proletarian culture' which was superior to bourgeois culture, but Bukharin was more pessimistic than Stalin about the ability of workers to improve on existing bourgeois culture. For Bukharin, it would take a long time before the backward proletariat could surpass the bourgeoisie in its knowledge of the natural sciences, and even when proletarian culture had been created, it would have a highly technocratic character.[37] Stalin's language, however, was more populist, and he implied that science did have to be infused with some kind of non-bourgeois spirit. While, unlike some on the left, he did not believe that a new proletarian science existed, fundamentally different from the old bourgeois science, he did argue that 'new people' growing up in a society with its 'revolutionary habits and traditions' would be much better able to develop science than the 'old professors of the capitalist school' who were inhibited by 'philistine [*meshchanskaia*] narrowness and routine'[38] We can see a similar difference of emphasis and language if we compare Stalin's and Bukharin's discussion of the content of the ideal culture, 'psychology', or 'work style', in 1923 and 1924. Both used the cliché that it had to unite 'American' efficiency with 'Russian' revolutionary attitudes. But the main point of Bukharin's discussion was to criticise officials' lack of practicality and specialisation.[39] Stalin's condemnation of those who had 'Russian revolutionary sweep' without American business-like qualities (*delovitost'*), however, was combined with a denunciation of those who lacked broad 'perspectives'. These people,

---

[35] See, for instance, *ibid.*, pp. 7–11.

[36] N. I. Bukharin, *Proletarskaia revoliutsiia i kul'tura* (Petrograd: n. p., 1923), pp. 44–5.

[37] Bukharin, *Proletarskaia revoliutsiia i kul'tura*, pp. 23, 28; N. I. Bukharin, 'Problema kul'tury v epokhu rabochei revoliutsii', *Pravda*, 11 October 1922. Understandably, his notion of proletarian culture was appealing to Aleksei Gastev, the main proponent of Taylorism in the Soviet Union. See K. Bailes, 'Alexei Gastev and the Soviet Controversy over Taylorism, 1918–1924', *Soviet Studies* 19 (1977), 387. For differences between these views and leftist ideas, see Ilmari Susiluoto, *The Origins and Development of Systems Thinking in the Soviet Union: Political and Philosophical Controversies from Bogdanov to Bukharin and Present-day Re-evaluations*, (Helsinki: Suomalainen tiedeakatemia, 1984), pp. 106–7.

[38] Stalin, *Sochineniia*, VII, p. 88.

[39] Bukharin, *Proletarskaia revoliutsiia i kul'tura*, pp. 48–50.

guilty of 'narrow and unprincipled pragmatism [*deliachestvo*]' and 'empiricism', were likely to 'degenerate and abandon the cause of the revolution'.[40]

So, while Stalin was careful not to echo the left's call for a sharpening of the 'class struggle', he did echo the left's view of class psychology, arguing that there was a special proletarian revolutionary, ideologically informed spirit or attitude, which had to be encouraged, and a bourgeois 'philistinism' and lack of revolutionary perspective, which had to be rooted out. And when, in 1927–8, he became convinced that the Soviet Union needed to embark on rapid industrialisation, in large part so that it could defend itself against foreign threats, it is not surprising that he endorsed many of the left's assumptions: if the country was to be mobilised, both leaders and the population as a whole needed to be psychologically transformed so that they would be not only loyal, but also committed to the huge task ahead. This 'cultural revolution' was to involve the promotion of 'proletarian' values, and an assault on the 'pragmatic' bourgeois attitudes that were likely to undermine the mobilisation effort. There were, he claimed, 'colossal reserves latent in the depths of our system', 'deep down in the working classes and the peasantry', which the Bolsheviks could release; 'only the labour enthusiasm and labour zeal of the vast masses', he declared, 'can guarantee that progressive increase of labour productivity, without which the final victory of socialism over capitalism in our country is unthinkable'.[41] Like the leftist oppositions of the past, he argued that these energies could only be fully exploited if the relationship between leaders and masses were rendered less 'bureaucratic'. While workers might not yet be fully 'conscious', 'democracy' and 'criticism from below' would increase their 'activism' (*aktivnost'*), their 'culture' (*kul'turnost'*) and their conviction that they were masters of the country (*chuvstvo khoziaina*).[42]

But Stalin was not only demanding that leaders 'democratise' their style of leadership; he also insisted, as the left oppositions had demanded in the past, that they be ideologically committed to a 'socialist' course – of rapid 'advance' and 'class struggle' in all areas of policy. For Stalin, economic success was jeopardised by those who had an excessively 'rightist', technicist approach to politics – that is those who were sceptical of rapid industrialisation and class struggle on the grounds that it undermined an order based on science and economics. Bukharin, who argued against the possibility of sudden economic leaps forward on the grounds that they contravened economic laws, was regarded as particularly dangerous. He was accused of defending a 'bourgeois theory' and of exaggerating the importance of the

---

[40] Stalin, *Sochineniia*, VI, pp. 187–8 (April–May 1924).
[41] *Ibid.*, XII, pp. 110, 120.   [42] *Ibid.*, XI, p. 37.

'technical' at the expense of 'social-class' issues.[43] Only a correct, socialist theory could give 'practical people [*praktiki*] the power of orientation, clarity of perspective, confidence in their work, faith [*vera*] in the victory of our cause'.[44] Bukharin and his allies were accused of constituting a 'right deviation' in the party and were formally condemned. But Stalin also denounced those within the Party who were formally loyal but were not, deep down, committed to socialism and lacked a revolutionary personality. So, at the Fifteenth Party Congress in 1927, he described Party leaders who 'swim with the current [*po techeniiu*], smoothly and calmly, without perspective, without looking into the future'. The results of this attitude were 'obvious: first they become covered with mould, then they become drab, then the mire of philistinism [*tina obyvatel'shchiny*] sucks them in, and then they are transformed into commonplace philistines. And this is the path of real degeneration.'[45]

Stalin, then, used a mixture of biological, religious, and class language in his analysis of the dangers facing the party: if leaders were not active, because they did not have an ideological perspective that gave them faith in what the party was fighting for, they would both 'decay' and fall prey to petty-bourgeois philistinism. He also implied that they would succumb to 'rightism' which, for Stalin, did not only involve a coherent ideological opposition to his economic policies, but also constituted a character fault. Rightists, for Stalin, were 'people who fear difficulties, who want life to go along at a peaceful tempo', and he frequently expressed the view that Bolshevik leaders who did not implement ambitious economic plans did not have 'faith' in the prospects of socialism because they had been corrupted by rightist ideas.[46] He tended not to accuse Party leaders themselves of being ideological enemies, but he often argued, as the left had before him, that they were being influenced by bourgeois specialists, who were the real source of rightist ideas and scepticism. He also sometimes alleged that ultimately these ideas came from abroad.[47]

---

[43] *Ibid.*, XII, pp. 143–6; *Bol'shevik* 23–24 (1929), 70 (Kaganovich).

[44] Stalin, *Sochineniia*, XII, p. 142.   [45] *Ibid.*, X, pp. 332–3.

[46] RGASPI f. 558, op. 11, d. 112, ll. 3–4 (4 December 1928). See, for instance, the charge that M. L. Rukhimovich, the Commissar for Rail Transport, was sowing 'demoralising scepticism' 'in a Menshevik manner', Stalin to Kaganovich, 19 September 1931, RGASPI f. 81, op. 3, d. 99, l. 35. For these themes in Stalin's letters to Molotov, see Lars Lih, 'Introduction', in Lars Lih, O. V. Naumov, and O. V. Khlevniuk (eds.), *Stalin's Letters to Molotov, 1925–1936* (New Haven: Yale University Press, 1995), pp. 49–58.

[47] See, for instance, his discussion of Piatakov's sins. Stalin to Molotov, no earlier than 6 August 1930, in L. Kosheleva, V. Lel'chuk, V. Naumov, O. Naumov, L. Rogovaia, O. Khlevniuk (eds.), *Pis'ma I. V. Stalina V. M. Molotovu, 1925–1936gg. Sbornik dokumentov* (Moscow: Rossiia Molodaia, 1995) (henceforth *Pis'ma*), pp. 193–4; Stalin to Molotov, 13 September 1930, *Pis'ma*, p. 217.

'Class struggle' without the bourgeoisie

There was, however, a serious contradiction within Stalin's strategy of populist mobilisation: the 'class struggle' against bourgeois, 'bureaucratic' attitudes undermined the unity that was essential if the Party was to achieve economic and military successes. Populist campaigns also prevented the technically expert from running the economy effectively, and economic leaders, most notably G. K. Ordzhonikidze, protested at challenges to the authority of managers and specialists.[48] Stalin realised that the 'class struggle' and the 'struggle against bureaucratism' that he was waging were causing disruption, but for some time he was reluctant to stop them.[49] From 1931, however, he began to lead a slow move away from 'class struggle', and he now declared that the bourgeois specialists were no longer a serious threat to the regime.[50] By 1934–5, the leadership was prepared to state that there were no contradictions between classes in the Soviet Union, and that all Soviet citizens were part of a united 'people' (narod) or 'labouring people' (trudiashchiesia). The softening of the 'class struggle' against an officialdom previously alleged to have been infected with rightist ideas was, predictably, accompanied by a turn towards a more technocratic, scientistic view of socialism. Stalin now declared that 'tekhnika in the period of reconstruction decides everything' and it became increasingly uncommon to use the voluntaristic argument that leaders, inspired by 'politics' and 'ideological' commitment, would achieve miraculous economic successes.[51] The leadership began to restore material incentives, explicitly denouncing 'egalitarianism'; populist notions that a socialist economy had to be based on transformation in the relations between leaders and masses were replaced with a commitment to hierarchy and discipline.

Yet, there is some evidence that Stalin himself was not entirely happy with this turn from politika towards tekhnika, and he continued to stress the importance of 'ideas' and their role in mobilising people. For instance, at the Seventeenth Party Congress in 1934 he declared, in voluntaristic vein, that 'everything, or almost everything' depended on the work of Party and soviet leaders; 'the role of so-called objective conditions' had been 'reduced to a minimum'.[52] He also discussed the priority of ideas over the material and technical in a particularly striking way at two meetings with writers in Maksim Gorky's Moscow flat in October 1932. Addressing writers as 'engineers of human souls', he argued that 'the whole production

---

[48] RGASPI f. 85, op. 28, d. 7, ll. 135–6 (22 June 1931).
[49] See, for instance, Stalin to Molotov, 13 September 1929, Pis'ma, p. 164.
[50] Stalin, Sochineniia, XIII, pp. 56–7.   [51] Ibid., pp. 41.   [52] Ibid., pp. 366–7.

of the country is connected with your "production"'. 'The "production" of souls is more important than the production of tanks', he declared; 'your tanks will be worth nothing if the soul in them is rotten'.[53] A few days before, speaking to a more exclusive meeting of communist writers, he had justified his emphasis on the importance of ideas by defending romanticism in literature. While, he explained, there was a bad romanticism, represented by Schiller, whose work was 'saturated with gentry-bourgeois idealism', there was also a good romanticism, present in the work of Shakespeare and Gorky: 'Gorky's idealisation of man was the idealisation of the new man of the future, the idealisation of the new social system of the future', Stalin enthused. 'We need the sort of romanticism that would move us forward'.[54]

Just as he emphasised the power of socialist ideas to motivate people, so he continued to point to the real dangers presented by rightist ideas. While he triumphantly proclaimed the defeat of internal enemies at the Seventeenth Party Congress, he refused to declare the ideological 'class struggle' over. He insisted that the 'survivals of capitalism' had still not been overcome in the economy, and were particularly evident in the 'consciousness of people'. Changes in consciousness lagged behind developments in economic conditions, and as long as the capitalist encirclement existed, foreigners would conspire to 'revive and support the survivals of capitalism in the consciousness and people and in the economy'.[55] His private letters also show that he still blamed economic problems on officials' insufficient activism and their infection by rightist attitudes.[56] He did not accuse officials of rightism at the Seventeenth Congress, but he did warn them that there was a danger that the party would be 'demobilised' and its 'fighting preparedness' blunted. Only in the 'struggle against difficulties', he declared, could plans be fulfilled.[57]

From the end of 1934, Stalin went much further in stressing the importance of 'ideas' and 'politics', and again, as in 1927–8, he renewed his warnings of the threat from foreign-inspired 'rightism' – both among the politically disloyal and the insufficiently mobilised. This new voluntaristic rhetoric was accompanied by a renewed emphasis on moral incentives and more ambitious economic plans, and was probably driven by Stalin's fears of both internal conspiracy (following the murder of

---

[53] RGASPI f. 558, op. 11, d. 1116, l. 32 (26 October 1932).
[54] *Ibid.*, l. 27 (20 October 1932).   [55] Stalin, *Sochineniia*, XIII, p. 349.
[56] So, for instance, in July 1932 he threatened to charge Ordzhonikidze as a 'rotten slave to routine [*rutiner*] who supports the worst traditions of the right deviationists in Narkomtiazhprom'. Stalin to Kaganovich, 26 July 1932, RGASPI f. 81, op.3, d. 100, ll. 6–7.
[57] Stalin, *Sochineniia*, XIII, p. 376.

Sergei Kirov) and imminent war.[58] Even so, the turn to *politika* took place within a different ideological context to that of 1927–8. Stalin was never to go back on his endorsement of material incentives and economic inequality; indeed he sought to explain theoretically why economic inequality and the political inequalities implied by the strengthening of state power would survive well into the distant future.[59] He was also wary of reviving the old notion of 'class struggle' between proletarians and those of bourgeois class origin. Although Stalin continued to use populist language, he no longer promoted the proletarian 'cultural revolution', with its highly divisive implications. While Stalin still lauded the virtues of courage, revolutionary spirit, and activism, they were now seen as characteristics of 'simple people' from the '*narod*', rather than 'proletarians'.[60]

In May 1935, Stalin outlined his new turn to '*politika*' and 'ideas' in a speech to the Red Army academy that became the cardinal ideological speech of the time, and was endlessly discussed and quoted.[61] In the address, he famously declared that the 'old slogan, "*tekhnika* decides everything", which reflected the period which is already over, when we had insufficient *tekhnika*, must now be replaced by a new slogan, the slogan "cadres decide everything". This is the main thing now'.[62] The meaning of the slogan 'cadres decide everything' could be interpreted in different ways,[63] but the language used in the speech, and the way it was received, suggest that Stalin was making a voluntaristic point: too much emphasis had been placed on the technical and the economic in the past, and too little on transforming officials into special socialist, ideologically inspired people, who could both be mobilised and be effective mobilisers. As Stalin explained, using the vitalist language common among the leftists of the past, '*tekhnika* is dead without cadres, but with cadres it has the opportunity to produce miracles.'[64] These cadres, Stalin declared, had to be properly 'raised' and 'forged', so that they became 'good cadres, who do not fear and do not hide from difficulties, but

---

[58] This is strongly suggested by Stalin in his speech to the Orgburo in March 1935. RGASPI f. 558, op. 11, d. 1118, ll. 94–5, 97–9. For fears of war and the move towards more ambitious planning at the beginning of 1935, see R. W. Davies and O. V. Khlevniuk, 'Stakhanovism and the Soviet Economy', *Europe-Asia Studies* 54 (2002), 868–71.

[59] See, for instance, RGASPI f. 17, op. 165, d. 76, ll. 168–72 (October 1938).

[60] See, for instance, Stalin, *Sochineniia*, I (XIV), pp. 275–7 (May 1938).

[61] Stalin had already criticised the 'mechanical' understanding of the slogan '*tekhnika* decides everything' in a speech of 24 December 1934. RGASPI f. 558, op. 11, d. 1077, l. 13.

[62] Stalin, *Sochineniia*, I (XIV), pp. 61–2.

[63] For the interpretation of the slogan as a justification for paternalism, see Lewis Siegelbaum, '"Dear Comrade, You Ask What We Need". Socialist Paternalism and Soviet Rural "Notables" in the mid-1930s', in Fitzpatrick (ed.), *Stalinism*, pp. 235–6.

[64] RGASPI f. 558, op. 11, d. 1077, l. 48.

overcome them'.[65] Stalin also, as in the past, was calling for a 'democratic' style of leadership, declaring that 'the slogan "cadres decide everything" demands that our leaders should have the most attentive attitude towards our workers [*rabotniki*], both "little" and "big".' Officials, he claimed, were not operating in this way, and 'there are many cases of a heartless, bureaucratic and simply disgraceful attitude towards workers'.[66]

The combination of voluntaristic and populist 'democratic' sentiments is particularly evident in the Stakhanovite movement, initiated in the autumn of 1935. Stakhanovism, for Stalin, showed that the working class had now 'grown', and indeed that the gap between mental and manual labour was narrowing.[67] Therefore leaders had to treat workers in a more 'democratic' way, listening to them and taking account of their suggestions, giving 'scope to the new forces of the working class'.[68] They also had to accept that old, conservative science had to be abandoned; meanwhile 'revolutionary people' among Party and economic officials, had to strive to reform 'bureaucratic' officials.[69]

The allegation that engineers and managers, in particular, had fallen for conservative, 'rightist' ideas, and that some of them were even 'saboteurs', became increasingly common, particularly from the summer and autumn of 1936, and was central to the rhetoric of the unfolding 'Great Terror'. This is not the place to investigate the Terror of 1936–8, but the discourse used to justify at least its earlier stages was very similar to that of the late 1920s.[70] Officials, especially those in the economic apparatus, were yet again seen as the sources, or transmitters from abroad, of a whole range of 'rightist' (now frequently defined as 'Trotskyite') sins:[71] they were sceptical of high plan targets and were sabotaging the economy, they were irresolute in the face of difficulties, they were treating workers and other subordinates in a high-handed 'bureaucratic' way, and were therefore unable to mobilise their energies. These problems were the result of the infiltration of bourgeois ideas, in part as a result of the activity of foreign spies, and in part because all officials had neglected *politika* and exaggerated the importance of *tekhnika*. As Molotov said at the February–March 1937 Central Committee plenum, economic officials had been obsessed with plan fulfilment and

---

[65] *Ibid.*, l. 49.   [66] Stalin, *Sochineniia*, I (XIV), p. 62.

[67] RGASPI f. 558, op. 11, d. 1078, l. 65.   [68] Stalin, *Sochineniia*, I (XIV), l. 94.

[69] RGASPI f. 558, op. 11, d. 1078, l. 86 (uncorrected version).

[70] For a discussion of the relationship between this discourse and the Terror, see Priestland, *Stalinism and the Politics of Mobilization*, ch. 5.

[71] Although the term 'Trotskyite' was an extremely malleable one. See J. A. Getty and O. V. Naumov, *The Road to Terror: Stalin and the Self-Destruction of the Bolsheviks, 1932–1939* (New Haven: Yale University Press, 1999), p. 578.

were guilty of 'narrow *deliachestvo*'; 'among us it has frequently happened that the mastery of *tekhnika* has been accompanied by the weakening of the Bolshevik qualities of the worker [*rabotnika*]'.[72] Stalin was also determined to stress that economic under-performance was the result of neglect of *politika*, and in his amendments to Ordzhonikidze's undelivered speech to the plenum, he criticised his omission of this theme, instructing him to include a discussion of 'the causes of idling (the apolitical, pragmatic [*deliacheskii*] selection of cadres, the absence of the political *vospitanie* of cadres)'.[73]

Yet it was Party officials who were considered to be the most guilty of neglecting *politika*, as was to be expected, as the Party had special responsibility for maintaining the ideological integrity of the regime. In late 1936 and the first half of 1937, regional Party bosses were accused of failing to root out 'Trotskyism', largely in the economic apparatus, a failing that was blamed on their 'collusion' with economic officials.[74] They were also criticised for their neglect of the 'democratic' methods of leadership which alone could mobilise the masses. As Zhdanov argued at the February–March 1937 plenum, their breaches of the 'democratic' rules of the Party acted as 'a brake on the growth of the activism and independence of members of the Party' and undermined the masses' *chuvstvo khoziaina*'.[75]

The Terror was a complex phenomenon, and was not merely a repetition of the campaigns of the late 1920s. In large part it seems to have been driven by fears of internal and external threats.[76] Yet the leadership's discourse at the time suggests that it should be seen not only as an attempt to remove people considered to be conspirators and saboteurs, but also as a campaign to create a new apparatus full of mobilised and mobilising cadres – a course which Stalin probably believed was particularly necessary on the eve of war.

It is in this context that Stalin's statements on the importance of ideas and ideology in 1938 and 1939 need to be understood. In 1938 Stalin launched a campaign of ideological renewal, at the centre of which was the publication of the *History of the All-Union Communist Party (Bolsheviks): Short Course* of 1938 – a text that Stalin hoped would

---

[72] RGASPI f. 17, op. 2, d. 612 (vyp. 2), l. 11.
[73] RGASPI f. 85, op. 29, d. 158, ll. 6–7; *Kommunist* 13 (1991), 60.
[74] See, for instance, RGASPI f. 17, op. 120, d. 281, ll. 11–13, 22.
[75] A. A. Zhdanov, *Podgotovka partiinykh organisatsii k vyboram v verkhovnyi sovet SSSR po novoi izbiratel'noi sisteme i sootvetsvuiushchaia perestroika partiino-politicheskoi raboty* (Moscow, 1937), p. 24.
[76] For the leadership's fearful responses, see Getty and Naumov, *The Road to Terror*, particularly pp. 16–17.

prevent the intelligentsia from deviating again. Foreign spies, according to Stalin, had 'spoilt' the intelligentsia because the leadership had not engaged in enough 'political education [*vospitanie*]'.[77] Only if cadres understood that the Party was acting in accordance with the laws of history would they have the 'perspective' that would fire them with enthusiasm and prevent them from 'degenerating' into 'pragmatists without perspective [*besperspektivnye deliagi*]', people who 'blindly and mechanically [*mekhanicheski*]' followed orders from above.[78]

Stalin – the supreme vospitatel'

'Ideology', then, in the sense understood by Stalin, had a central role in Stalin's political strategy, and was closely connected with *vospitanie* and mobilisation. But how should we define his 'ideology' in the broader sense of the word – his political thought or worldview? His thinking was clearly not traditionalist: he was constantly calling for traditional forms of social organisation and ways of thinking to be 'smashed'.[79] Nor, in general, was it neo-traditionalist. His proclamation of class unity in the mid- to late 1930s might suggest that he was trying to create a static society without contradictions, in which a Party elite, a 'command staff', ruled over a stable order of class and ethnic estates. But while aspects of this system may have emerged in reality, he always insisted that there could be no immutable class and ethnic hierarchies. This is, perhaps, why Trotsky's criticism of his regime as a 'Bonapartist' neo-traditionalist one angered him so much, and why he was so desperate to present Trotsky himself as a 'rightist' who lacked revolutionary zeal.

It is, in certain respects, useful to compare Stalin's attitude to politics with religious ideas. Stalin's seminarian education doubtless affected his thinking, and Stalin's use of religious language, his demand that people have 'faith' in socialism, and his description of Marxism as the 'religion of the working class, its creed',[80] also indicates that we need to take account of the religious context of his thought. Yet his statements and behaviour suggest that it is less helpful to see him as a proponent of a messianic secularised religion who aimed to build a heaven on earth, than as a political leader interested in transforming the Soviet population into people who were willing to sacrifice themselves to the interests of the socialist

---

[77] RGASPI f. 17, op. 165, d. 76, l. 200.   [78] Stalin, *Sochineniia*, I (XIV), p. 381.
[79] See, for instance, Stalin, *Sochineniia*, I (XIV), pp. 275–7.
[80] Quoted in V. V. Maslov, 'Iz istorii rasprostraneniia stalinizma', *Voprosy istorii KPSS* 7 (1990), 100.

state.[81] It is most likely that Stalin saw Christianity and Marxism-Leninism as similar, in that both were movements which sought to change the population's outlook, 'converting' citizens into new, committed 'believing' people, even though the ultimate goals of each were different.[82] When questioned about his experience of the seminary by the German writer Emil Ludwig in 1933, it was the priests' methods of indoctrination Stalin dwelt on: he praised their 'systematic and persevering approach' in their attempt to achieve their 'bad ends', while decrying 'the basis of their methods – surveillance, spying, worming their way into people's souls, humiliation'.[83]

If the 'political religion' approach yields some insights, there is probably a stronger case for presenting Stalin as a politician with Enlightenment goals, in that he, like Lenin, claimed to be using reason and science to construct a rational order. He wanted to build a modern, powerful state founded on the latest science, modern planning, and the division of labour. He never denied the importance of *tekhnika*, and like all Bolsheviks he accepted that a balance had to be achieved between the *tekhnika* and *politika*, even though his view of that balance changed over time. Stalin always insisted that the new elite had to be as technically expert as the old bourgeois specialists. He also, at times, described the world in a technocratic way, most famously in his address to the victory parade in July 1945, when he proposed a toast to the 'simple, ordinary, modest people', 'to the "little screws"' who ensured that 'our great state machine' worked efficiently.[84]

But it has been argued here that if we are to understand Stalin's thinking, we need to see it in the context of continuing tensions within Bolshevism: between political strategies that emphasised mobilisation and those that stressed technocratic order, and between quasi-romantic and scientistic tendencies within Marxism-Leninism. In its extreme form, romantic Marxism could become the anti-materialist and irrationalist 'revolutionary syndicalism' of figures such as Georges Sorel, who denied that economic change would automatically create a new proletarian consciousness and argued that Marxists had to appeal to emotions, using 'revolutionary myths', to mobilise workers.[85] Before the revolution, Gorky and others were influenced by these ideas, but while Stalin

---

[81] Stalin seems to have had been less concerned with enforcing personal morality than many Bolsheviks. See, for instance, his speech at a meeting of military officials, 1937. RGASPI f. 558, op. 11, d. 1120, l. 103.

[82] For a similar point, see van Ree, *Political Thought*, pp. 167–8.

[83] Stalin, *Sochineniia*, XIII, p. 114.

[84] Stalin, *Sochineniia*, II (XV), pp. 206. See also RGASPI f. 17, op. 165, d. 76, l. 179 (1 October 1938).

[85] Zeev Sternhell, *The Birth of Fascist Ideology* (Princeton: Princeton University Press, 1994), ch. 1.

encountered them in his youth he was never convinced by them.[86] Stalin, like Lenin, subscribed to Marx's enlightened commitment to universalism, reason, and the ability of mankind to use science to master nature. Yet he was a less scientistic and rationalistic Marxist than many Bolsheviks, and his view of leadership is often best seen as a 'charismatic' one. He valued an ideologically inspired, quasi-military 'command staff' more than the 'agronomists and engineers' Lenin came to believe would be the Bolsheviks' ideal teachers. Like the left before him, he often implied that it was not enough for society to be run as if it were a machine, operated by experts; *tekhnika* and 'machines' were 'dead' unless they were infused with 'soul' and operated by cadres who 'believed'. His language was also full of romantic themes: Soviet people were to be self-sacrificing, 'active', 'energetic' fighters who swam 'against the current'. They were to reject narrow 'pragmatism', 'empiricism', petty-bourgeois philistinism (*obyvatel'shchina*), 'routine', and a 'dead', 'mechanical' approach to life.[87]

Stalin's statements also suggest that he believed that economic progress and the use of reason were not always sufficient for the construction of socialism. The *Short Course* was designed to convince people, through the study of history, that the Party was leading the Soviet Union along a course laid down by reason and science, and Stalin followed the orthodox Marxist view that economic conditions would ultimately produce a new 'proletarian' consciousness.[88] But Stalin's language was often less rationalistic: 'faith', 'heroism', and the transformation of men's 'souls' were all required if 'miracles' were to be achieved. Similarly, while he sometimes implied that the creation of the new revolutionary personality was a rational process by which cadres were carefully educated in their mistakes, he frequently suggested a very different method of *vospitanie*: cadres had to be 'forged' in 'struggle', and the masses had to be 'mobilised' if their 'energies' were to be released.[89] As has been seen, Stalin often

---

[86] For these trends within Russian Marxism, see Williams, *The Other Marxists*, ch. 5. For Stalin's rejection of 'idealist' tendencies within Marxism in this period, see Erik van Ree, 'Stalin as a Marxist Philosopher', *Studies in East European Thought* 52 (2000), 275–6.

[87] For some of these themes in avant-garde literature of the 1920s, see Clark, *Petersburg*, pp. 118–19.

[88] Although he did warn against 'vulgar materialism' and explain that 'consciousness' had to be a particular concern of the party because it was 'lagging' behind economic change. See Wetter for the view that Stalin was original in stressing the role of the superstructure at the expense of the base. Gustav Wetter, *Dialectical Materialism. A Historical and Systematic Survey of Philosophy in the Soviet Union*, trans. Peter Heath (London: Routledge and Kegan Paul, 1958), pp. 216–17.

[89] For the more rationalist view of *vospitanie*, see Stalin's speech at the February–March 1937 plenum, *Voprosy istorii* 10 (1995), 16–17. For the view that 'school' was not enough, and that 'forging' took place in the course of 'struggle', see RGASPI f. 558, op. 11, d. 1077, l. 49 (4 May 1935).

implied that an excessively scientistic worldview would inhibit the mobilisation he believed was so essential to the survival of the regime.

Stalin's view of his own role as leader also seems to have been closely
bound up with this conception of politics as mobilisation. The famous
poster image of Stalin as the locomotive driver of the revolution is a powerful one, but Stalin more often described himself as a 'teacher' (*vospitatel'*)
of cadres, who 'raised' them, protected them from corruption by alien ideas
and rooted out the 'enemies' spreading these ideas, rather than as a driver
at the controls of a machine, 'mechanically' issuing orders from above.[90]
He also saw himself as a mobiliser, who carefully assessed the moods of
officials and the population and decided how best to manipulate them. In
July 1932, for instance, he wrote to Kaganovich, explaining why he was
now willing to reduce grain procurement targets for the Ukraine, even
though he had previously refused to do so. To have set low targets at the
time when the harvest was being organised, he insisted, would have meant
the 'final demoralisation of (already demoralised) Ukrainians'; but it was
acceptable to do this when the harvest was already underway and 'Party
and soviet forces have already been mobilised'.[91]

As this episode suggests, Stalin's voluntarism was in part a pragmatic
response to the problems of managing a non-market economy. It may also
have been the result of an inherent propensity to political romanticism,
evident since his youth.[92] Or it could be that this view of politics would
have been appealing to most Soviet leaders during periods of crisis, when it
seemed that only 'miracles' could save the regime from imminent destruction. It is certainly possible to discern a 'zig-zag' pattern in the politics of the
1920s and 1930s: in 1927–8 and after 1935 Stalin seems to have moved
away from *tekhnika* towards *politika* when the threat from abroad appeared
to be particularly dangerous. But whatever the reasons for his behaviour,
Stalin's attempts to mobilise the Soviet Union undermined its ability to
defend itself; as the Red Army, devastated by the Terror, found to its cost,
Stalin's approach cannot be explained as a conventional 'rational' response
to external threats. His ambition to be the *vospitatel'* of the Soviet people
almost led to the ruin of the system he was so desperate to preserve.

---

[90] See, for instance, RGASPI f. 558, op. 11, d. 1077, l. 49 (4 May 1935); *Voprosy istorii*
10 (1995), 15–17. For a famous image of Stalin as a locomotive driver, see P. Sokolov-
Skalia, 'The Train Goes from "Socialism" Station to "Communism" Station', (1939).
[91] Stalin to Kaganovich, 25 July 1932, RGASPI f. 81, op. 3, d. 99, ll. 115–17.
[92] For Stalin's youthful political romanticism, see R. G. Suny, 'Stalin and the Making of the
Soviet Union', ch. 1 (unpublished manuscript). My thanks to Ron Suny for showing me
this draft.

11   Stalin as patron of cinema: creating Soviet mass culture, 1932–1936

Sarah Davies

At his two well-known meetings with writers at Gorky's home in October 1932, Stalin encouraged his audience to focus on writing plays, which he believed to be most accessible to workers: 'Poems are good. Novels are even better. But at the moment more than anything we need plays'.[1] His hierarchy did not include films and screen-writing, for, despite Lenin's sanctification of cinema as 'the most important of the arts', at this juncture it was less highly esteemed by Stalin, and many others in the Soviet Union. From January 1932 until February 1933 the status of the organisation responsible for the Soviet film industry, Soiuzkino, was merely that of part of the Commissariat of Light Industry.[2] The political leadership complained constantly that Soviet cinema was not fulfilling its potential. Audiences preferred imported films. Other artists tended to regard the young art of cinema as inferior to their own well-established fields.[3] By the mid-1930s, however, the situation had changed dramatically. In 1935, when informed that some cinemas in Moscow had been taken over for use as theatres, Stalin was appalled that as a consequence 'the art most popular amongst the masses' could not be exhibited so widely.[4] In the same year, film-workers were feted by the party and government at a lavish anniversary celebration which resembled to one contemporary 'an Academy Award evening, without the jokes'.[5]

---

[1] Rossiiskii gosudarstvennyi arkhiv sotsial'no-politicheskoi istorii (henceforth RGASPI) f. 558, op.11, d. 1116, l. 31.

[2] In February 1933 it was reorganised as GUKF (*Glavnoe upravlenie kinofotopromyshlennosti* – Main Administration of the Cinema and Photographic Industry), subordinate directly to Sovnarkom SSSR. In 1937 it became GUK (*Glavnoe upravlenie kinematografii*).

[3] V. Pudovkin commented in 1928: 'The respected representatives of our neighbouring arts, literature and theatre, condescendingly pat cinema on the shoulder, reproach it for its lack of culture and offer themselves as Varangians.' R. Taylor and I. Christie (eds.), *The Film Factory* (Cambridge, Mass.: Harvard University Press, 1988), p. 198. See also *Istoriia Sovetskogo Kino* (Moscow: Iskusstvo, 1973), II, p. 8.

[4] RGASPI f. 558, op. 11, d. 829, l. 61 (10 November 1935). Where sources are taken from the Shumiatskii notes (see below), dates are provided.

[5] J. Leyda, *Kino, a History of the Russian and Soviet Film* (Princeton: Princeton University Press, 1983), p. 319.

Meanwhile the public was flocking to the latest Soviet blockbusters: *Veselye rebiata, Chapaev, Iunost' Maksima, Krest'iane* ... Soviet cinema was no longer seen as second class, and this was causing envy in some quarters.

This study considers the part played by Stalin, in conjunction with his agent Boris Shumiatskii (from 1930 through 1937 head of Soiuzkino/ GUKF/GUK), in transforming Soviet cinema into what was considered the 'art most popular amongst the masses.' Stalin's passion for cinema is well known. The memoirs of Khrushchev, Djilas, Allilueva, Mar'iamov, and others have shed light on the important role played by the regular late-night film screenings for Stalin and his entourage.[6] These evenings, which seem to have become more frequent after the death of his wife,[7] served as both social occasions and opportunities to monitor forthcoming feature and documentary films.[8] Stalin's role as the ultimate film censor, particularly in the late 1930s and 1940s, has been well documented: his interventions in relation to films such as Eisenstein's *Bezhin lug* and *Ivan Groznyi* part 2 had catastrophic consequences.[9]

Less has been known until recently about Stalin's role in the mid-1930s. However, we now have full access to Shumiatskii's notes on the private screenings attended by Stalin, his colleagues, and relatives, which provide a detailed picture of Stalin's influence in this crucial period for the development of Soviet mass culture.[10] The notes, which read almost like verbatim reports, appear to be a relatively accurate record of the discussions at these occasions. They often reproduce the stylistic peculiarities of the various speakers.[11] In some cases, they are corroborated by other evidence, for example, the memoirs of directors, such as G. Aleksandrov and A. Dovzhenko, who were occasionally invited to the screenings of

---

[6] M. Djilas, *Conversations with Stalin* (London: Hart-Davis, 1962), p. 95; E. Crankshaw (ed.), *Khrushchev Remembers* (London: Book Club Associates, 1971), pp. 297–8; S. Allilueva, *Dvadtsat' pisem k drugu* (Moscow: Izvestiia, 1990), pp. 114–15; G. Mar'iamov, *Kremlevskii tsenzor. Stalin smotrit kino* (Moscow: Kinotsentr, 1992).

[7] E. Gromov, *Stalin: Vlast' i iskusstvo* (Moscow: Respublika, 1998), p. 63.

[8] Stalin also watched and commented on a variety of foreign films. This study will focus on Soviet feature films (excluding children's films).

[9] A recent publication which focuses on the period 1938–53 is N. Laurent, *L'oeil du Kremlin* (Toulouse: Privat, 2000).

[10] The notes, or at least a selection of them, made their way into the Stalin archives after Shumiatskii's arrest in January 1938. They begin in May 1934, and the final one is dated 3 March 1936. There is also an additional report for 26 January 1937. Shumiatskii's unpublished and unfinished manuscript of early 1935, *Stalin i kino*, accompanies the notes. Some of the notes have been published on the web at: *Rossiia. XX Vek. Dokumenty. 2003/3* http://www.idf.ru/15/word.shtml. Since this chapter was written, all the notes have been published in *Kinovedcheskie zapiski* 61 (2002) and 62 (2003).

[11] K. M. Anderson, 'Vstupitel'naia stat'ia', *Rossiia. XX Vek. Dokumenty. 2003/3* http://www.idf.ru/15/word.shtml.

their own films;[12] Politburo decrees which echo Stalin's decisions almost word for word; and newspaper reports which Shumiatskii records that Stalin ordered. In Shumiatskii's absence in the summer of 1935, his deputy Ia. Chuzhin made similar notes, while one of Shumiatskii's successors, I. Bol'shakov, also recorded all the comments in a notebook from which he was never parted.[13]

Of course, these notes are far from being a completely faithful record of the discussions. They were obviously written hastily, and doubtless omitted much. Presumably they are coloured by Shumiatskii's own preoccupations, for example Stalin's comments received more attention than those of others present. This may have been an accurate reflection of the nature of the discussions, but it may also indicate that Shumiatskii was simply more interested in recording Stalin's remarks. The notes do nevertheless present a relatively reliable and coherent impression of Stalin's ideas and influence, and this study draws extensively upon them.

It examines how and why Stalin emerged as supreme patron of cinema by the end of 1934 and the impact of his patronage upon the development of Soviet mass film. The term 'patron', in the sense of both political and cultural patron, is preferred to, for example, 'director' or 'censor', since it encompasses both Stalin's own self-definition as 'helper' of cinema, and the range of his activity.[14] This included securing funding for the industry, raising the public profile of Soviet cinema, and offering protection in the event of disputes. Like the Renaissance cultural patron 'who was the real initiator of the architecture, sculpture and painting of the period . . . [who] played a significant part in determining both form and content',[15] Stalin also participated actively in the film-making process itself.

Stalin's emergence as 'helper'

Apart from his well-known involvement in Eisenstein's *Oktiabr'* and *General'naia liniia*,[16] Stalin appears not to have taken great personal

[12] G. Aleksandrov, *Epokha i kino* (Moscow: Izdatel'stvo politicheskoi literatury, 1976), p. 184; A. Dovzhenko, 'The Artist's Teacher and Friend', in Taylor and Christie (eds.), *The Film Factory*, pp. 383–5.

[13] Mar'iamov, *Kremlevskii tsenzor*, p. 13.

[14] The two categories of 'political' and 'cultural' patronage are virtually indistinguishable in the Soviet case. Mar'iamov describes him as 'censor', as does P. Kenez in *Cinema and Soviet Society from the Revolution to the Death of Stalin* (London: I. B. Tauris, 2001), pp. 131–4. I. Christie refers to Stalin as 'director' in his 'Canons and careers: the director in Soviet Cinema' in R. Taylor and D. Spring (eds.), *Stalinism and Soviet Cinema* (London: Routledge, 1993), pp. 164–7.

[15] M. Hollingsworth, *Patronage in Renaissance Italy* (Baltimore: John Hopkins University Press, 1994), p. 1.

[16] These episodes are summarised in Mar'iamov, *Kremlevskii tsenzor*, pp. 14–15.

interest in cinema before the early 1930s. Until then, he was much more inclined to comment on literature and theatre. However, two parallel developments – the increasing potential of sound, and the emergence of the new socialist realist agenda – combined to ignite his enthusiasm for the medium as a tool for mobilising and entertaining the masses.

The production of sound films in the USSR from 1930 was a crucial factor. According to Shumiatskii, when Stalin saw the first of these in 1930–1, he insisted on the further development of the technology.[17] Sound films were politically more attractive to Stalin than silents. First, the director of a sound film had much less opportunity to indulge in artistic improvisation as he could now be tied to a controllable script.[18] The script, and scriptwriter, thus came to acquire increasing importance in this period, and the role of the director changed accordingly. Secondly, the use of sound opened up new possibilities for popular entertainment since the general public was more likely to be drawn to the spoken word and to the more realistic representations it allowed.

Mass appeal and 'realism' were, of course, central to the new approach to culture labelled socialist realism. At his meetings with writers in October 1932, Stalin outlined his vision of a culture based on 'the romanticism that would move us forward' as well as *revolutionary socialist realism*.[19] He maintained that in keeping with the emphasis on *narodnost'*, the current priority for writers should be plays, since these were most capable of exerting a powerful influence on workers:

After an eight-hour day not every worker is able to read a good short book. And yet we are concerned that a good work of art which helps construct socialism, which helps refashion the human psyche in the direction of socialism, should be available to millions of workers. A book cannot yet serve these millions. But a play, theatre, might.[20]

Cinema soon came to assume even more importance in Stalin's thinking. In 1932 he was already calling for a breakthrough towards more popular films.[21] As we know from Youngblood's work in particular, the taste of the average Soviet viewer was not always reflected in the masterpieces of

---

[17] RGASPI f. 558, op. 11, d. 892, l. 93 (Stalin i kino); B. Shumiatskii *Kinematografiia millionov* (Moscow: Kinofotoizdat, 1936), p. 121.

[18] Ian Christie, 'Making sense of early Soviet sound', in R. Taylor and I. Christie (eds.), *Inside the Film Factory* (London: Routledge, 1991), p. 186. Christie notes that local state censorship appeared in the USA after the arrival of sound films.

[19] RGASPI f. 558, op. 11, d. 1116, ll. 26–7; l. 33. Cf. the chapter by Priestland in this volume. Zhdanov expanded on Stalin's ideas at the First Writers' Congress in August 1934.

[20] RGASPI f. 558, op. 11, d. 1116, ll. 23–4; l. 31.

[21] RGASPI f. 558, op. 11, d. 828, l. 94 (Stalin i kino).

Eisenstein and Pudovkin. In the 1920s, Soviet viewers clearly preferred lighter entertainment, whether in the form of foreign imports or Soviet entertainment films, such as *Bear's Wedding* (K. Eggert).[22] The 'agitprop films' typical of the 'cultural revolution' period also had limited appeal. According to Shumiatskii, Stalin was insistent that Soviet films should henceforth focus on providing entertaining subject matter and good acting, as well as ideological correctness, as this was the only way of competing with foreign films.[23]

Between 1932 and early 1934, however, there was little progress in this direction. Part of the problem was the inevitable time lag between the conception of a film and its completion, which was not conducive to a sudden breakthrough. In addition, because the definition of socialist realism remained quite elastic, there were competing ideas about what was now required. Many continued to operate with very different notions from Stalin, including the various individuals and institutions who were jockeying for influence over the film industry in this period. While Soiuzkino/GUKF, headed by Shumiatskii, was responsible for day-to-day administration, other organs also played a role, notably Glavrepertkom and the Orgburo's cinema commission. The overlapping responsibilities of these bodies were a recipe for confusion and conflict.

Glavrepertkom, which was subordinate to Narkompros RSFSR, was officially responsible for deciding which films could be released.[24] Since 1929 it had been extremely active, but in this period its performance came under increasing scrutiny. In April 1933, after Stalin personally banned the film *Moia rodina* (A. Zarkhi, I. Kheifits), objecting to its portrayal of passive opposition to the enemy, Glavrepertkom ended up shouldering responsibility for having allowed the film to come out. In a note to Kaganovich, the head of Kul'tprop, A. Stetskii, accused Glavrepertkom's O. Litovskii and P. Bliakhin of 'liberalism' for having authorised the release of several films which had been or would be withdrawn, including *Gail'-Moskau* (V. Shmidtgof) and *Izmennik rodiny* (I. Mutanov), as well as *Moia rodina*.[25]

---

[22] D. Youngblood, *Movies for the Masses* (Cambridge: Cambridge University Press, 1992); R. Taylor, 'A "Cinema for the Millions": Soviet Socialist Realism and the Problem of Film Comedy', *Journal of Contemporary History* 3 (1983), 439–61.

[23] RGASPI f. 558, op. 11, d. 829, l. 94 (Stalin i kino); Shumiatskii, *Kinematografiia millionov*, p. 122. See also Aleksandrov, *Epokha i kino*, p. 159.

[24] On Glavrepertkom, see E. Margolit, 'Budem schitat', chto takogo fil'ma nikogda ne bylo', in L. Mamatova (ed.), *Kino: politika i liudi (30-e gody)* (Moscow: Materik, 1995), pp. 132–56.

[25] E. Margolit and V. Shmyrov, *Iz''iatoe kino* (Moscow: Dubl-D, 1995), pp. 34–5; Mar'iamov, *Kremlevskii tsenzor*, pp. 15–17; I. Kheifits 'Vzlet i padenie "Moei Rodiny"', *Iskusstvo kino* 12 (1990), 99–103; RGASPI f. 558, op. 11, d. 828, l. 95 (Stalin i kino); f. 17, op. 114, d. 344, l. 7; f. 17, op. 114, d. 345, ll. 79–80.

After the *Moia rodina* incident, the Orgburo set up a cinema commission which was designed to prevent further mistakes. Chaired by Stetskii, and including A. Bubnov, Shumiatskii, and others, it was assigned responsibility in June 1933 for scrutinising the plan for films to be released in 1933, ensuring that new themes had Central Committee sanction, and viewing all new films before their release.[26] It was not long before the commission came into conflict with Shumiatskii. Its attitude towards GUKF was often sharply critical, for example in October 1933 it accused GUKF of having failed to produce a single decent film that year.[27] The conflict came to a head in November when Stetskii informed Kaganovich and Stalin that the film *Odna radost'* (O. Preobrazhenskaia, I. Pravov) was completely unacceptable, and that 350,000 roubles had been squandered on it. He held Shumiatskii and others in GUKF responsible and said that they deserved a Party reprimand. Shumiatskii defended himself, insisting that the work of the commission was fundamentally flawed, and suggesting that Stalin and Kaganovich consider the film themselves. Stetskii naturally rejected this 'slander', calling on the Orgburo to resolve the matter. The Orgburo duly stepped in, backing Stetskii. It concluded that the commission's evaluation of *Odna radost'* had been correct and that the film should either be redone or scrapped; Shumiatskii was told not to waste any further resources, and to start work on ten major themes to be presented for consideration by the Orgburo.[28]

While the commission prevailed in this battle, in 1934 it began to lose ground to Shumiatskii. Certainly this is the impression left by latter's reports, which begin in May. These reveal Stalin's increasing personal involvement in cinema and his use of the head of GUKF as a direct conduit for his ideas about the creation of popular and useful films.

On various occasions over the course of 1934, Stalin emphasised to Shumiatskii that what mattered above all was the impact of a film on the public. In his view, the public needed a wide choice of films, and a variety of genres should be available.[29] He was particularly anxious to promote jolly films, rejecting as dull and gloomy those such as E. Piscator's *Vosstanie rybakov*, a story of the struggle of downtrodden German fishermen against a capitalist. When Shumiatskii tried to defend this, arguing that although it was not a film for the masses, in places it demonstrated

---

[26] RGASPI f. 17, op. 114, d. 351, l. 4; f. 17, op. 114, d. 352, l. 158. See also the subsequent decree of 9 September, RGASPI f. 17, op. 114, d. 362, l. 2. Protocols of the commission have been published: V. Listov, 'Nazvanie kazhdoi kartiny utverzhdaetsia komissiei orgbiuro...', *Kinovedcheskie zapiski* 31 (1996), 108–24.

[27] RGASPI f. 17, op. 114, d. 365, l. 1.   [28] RGASPI f. 17, op. 114, d. 375, ll. 41–9.

[29] RGASPI f. 558, op. 11, d. 828, l. 53 (30 October 1934); l. 99 (Stalin i kino).

great work with actors, Stalin retorted that this was beside the point: 'That's not what matters, but the influence on the viewer. The film is cheerlessly gloomy, deliberately cold. What's the point of such films, whom do they touch, who will watch them, whom are they made for?' Later, in response to Shumiatskii's assertion that some critics were very enthusiastic about the picture, Stalin was emphatic: 'Tell them, whoever they are, that their praise is not worth a brass farthing. The film is unnecessary, miserable'.[30]

He was also critical of the spate of films on old subjects which had been made over 1933–4, including adaptations of Ostrovskii's *Groza* and Saltykov-Shchedrin's *Golovlevs* (directed by V. Petrov and A. Ivanovskii respectively). Although Stalin recognised the merits of these – they were dramatically interesting, the acting was good – he considered the subject matter too gloomy and out-dated. 'The viewer needs joy, good spirits. He wants to see himself in films', maintained Stalin. But it was not sufficient for films to be popular, they had to be useful too, to deal with contemporary themes, and to do so in a way that was not too 'insipid, pompous and deliberately gloomy' as many films on contemporary topics tended to be.[31]

He was strongly in favour of comedies, which Soviet filmmakers had avoided, either because they considered them a frivolous distraction from serious, politically engaged films, or because they were afraid to make fun of aspects of Soviet reality. As Shumiatskii pointed out to Stalin in response to the latter's criticism that the silent comedy, *Liubov' Aleny* (B. Iurtsev), was not sufficiently funny: creative workers avoided satirical treatments of contemporary phenomena, while critics cultivated a 'puritanical' attitude to comedy. In the case of *Liubov' Aleny*, comic sections of the film had been cut out because of these concerns. One character, a director, was removed and replaced by a deputy director, because it was deemed inappropriate that the former should be the object of comedy. Details of the extremely run-down barracks were excluded even though these were necessary to show how in the second half of the film the barracks had been cleaned up. Stalin's view was that it had been a mistake to cut these sections as the film would have been funnier if they had been retained. In his opinion, it was important to expose the obstacles to be overcome, 'otherwise everything in the film appears too smooth, or rather not even smooth, but well-ordered, that is lacking emotion'.[32] Later, in

---

[30] *Kinovedcheskie zapiski* 59 (2002), 153–6; RGASPI f. 558, op. 11, d. 828, l. 32 (13/14 May 1934); l. 34 (31 May 1934). Shumiatskii's later evaluation of the film in *Kinematografiia millionov* (pp. 184–6) remained positive.

[31] RGASPI f. 558, op. 11, d. 828, ll. 32–3 (13/14 May 1934).

[32] *Ibid.*, ll. 27–9 (7/8 May 1934).

reference to two more silent comedies focusing on contemporary Soviet life and its problems, *Flag stadiona* (B. Kazachkov) and *Naslednii prints respubliki* (E. Ioganson), he reiterated that laughing at backwardness is always useful.[33] While some of his colleagues continued to take simplistic political correctness to extremes, Stalin's approach to comedies could be more relaxed. Kaganovich, for example, objected to the humourlessness of Ia. Protazanov's *Marionetki*, about a fascist state which chooses a prince to be its puppet king. When the prince flies in, he falls from the plane and his hairdresser is mistaken for him. Kaganovich was especially vexed that the object of humour was the hairdresser rather than the 'degenerate little aristocrat' (*dvorianchik*). Stalin, however, agreed with Shumiatskii that the point was to show that the ruling group could place anyone on the throne.[34]

As Stalin developed his own 'general line' on cinema which he transmitted directly to Shumiatskii, he exhibited increasing impatience with the judgements of the Orgburo cinema commission and Glavrepertkom. In May, he attacked *Vozvrashchenie* (*Nasten'ka Ustinova* – K. Eggert) on the grounds that it would not educate mass taste, describing it as 'a total imitation of an American film, but lacking intelligence, plot and action'. He rebuked Stetskii for saying it was interesting and asked how such films were allowed. When Stetskii told him it had been through the commission, Stalin retorted 'I'm against such a commission'. Stetskii replied that recently the commission had passed some good scenarios and that future films would be better, but Stalin remained sceptical.[35]

In the summer, Stalin backed Shumiatskii in a conflict with the commission and Glavrepertkom centring on *Veselye rebiata*, G. Aleksandrov's Hollywood-influenced musical comedy about a shepherd who becomes a conductor of a jazz orchestra. The film, which was apparently made in direct response to an appeal for comedy films in 1932, was throughout its making, and afterwards, the subject of public controversy.[36] Its many critics jumped on its apolitical, Hollywood-like features, accusing it of lacking 'social backbone'.[37] It is possible that the completed film would have been jettisoned had it not been for Stalin's personal intervention. Voroshilov asked Shumiatskii to show it to Stalin in July 1934, and the latter was delighted with it, responding to it with 'homeric laughter'. He remarked that Soviet filmmakers tried to be original with their gloomy

[33] *Ibid.*, l. 53 (30 October 1934). He was, however, mildly critical of the humour of *Naslednii prints respubliki* which he described as 'pleasant, but not very witty. They joke like elephants and hippopotami – rather coldly, moreover. It should be more witty and subtle.'
[34] *Ibid.*, ll. 41–2 (23/24 June 1934).   [35] *Ibid.*, ll. 34–5 (31 May 1934).
[36] Aleksandrov, *Epokha i kino*, p. 163.   [37] *Ibid.*, p. 175.

'rehabilitations' and 'reforgings' and that although he was not opposed to these themes on principle, they, too, should be joyful and funny. He had come away feeling as if he had had a day off – the first time he had felt this after watching a Soviet film. He was particularly complimentary about the acting of L. Orlova and L. Utesov, and the film's jazz music. He thought that the masses would like the song 'March of the Happy Guys', and that gramophone recordings should be produced to popularize it.[38]

This blessing from on high did not forestall criticism of the film. At the end of July, Shumiatskii complained to Stalin and other Politburo members that even though he had forewarned Stetskii that the film had been highly rated by 'several comrades', members of the commission were demanding the cutting of entire sections. According to Shumiatskii, Bubnov had called the film 'counter-revolutionary', while N. Antipov had described it as 'rubbish, hooligan, false through and through'. Shumiatskii emphasised that the commission had also been critical of other films endorsed by Stalin, such as *Liubov' Aleny*, while praising those he had criticised, including *Vosstanie rybakov, Vozvrashchenie, Dezertir* (V.Pudovkin), *Garmon'* (I. Savchenko).

Furthermore, Glavrepertkom had apparently refused permission for *Veselye rebiata* to be taken to the second Venice Film Festival (August 1934).[39] After long discussions, the first half had finally been allowed, while three parts were retained by Glavrepertkom at the station. Shumiatskii requested urgent Politburo intervention to release the rest of the film in time for the festival, and also to sort out the relationship between the commission and GUKF. In a further letter to Voroshilov, Shumiatskii reiterated these points, suggesting that Bubnov, resenting the relative independence of GUKF, was responsible for these difficulties.[40] Shumiatskii's appeal clearly succeeded, because the film was shown in its entirety in Venice, where it made a major contribution to Soviet success in achieving the award for best programme.[41]

Following this success, and that of *Chapaev* (S. and G. Vasiliev) in November (see below), Stalin evidently concluded that Glavrepertkom

---

[38] RGASPI f. 558, op. 11, d. 828, l. 48 (13/14 July 1934); ll. 51–2 (21 July 1934); Aleksandrov, *Epokha i kino*, p. 184.

[39] Stalin changed the composition of the delegation to the festival. The draft submitted by Shumiatskii and A. Arosev included Shumiatskii, Pudovkin, Iutkevich and two camera-men. This was altered to V. Petrov and G. Roshal' (directors of *Groza* and *Peterburgskaia noch'* respectively), Shumiatskii, and A. Shafran (cameraman of *Cheliuskin*). RGASPI f. 17, op. 163, d. 1032, l. 78. Stalin's selection of directors of adaptations of Russian classics may have been a deliberate signal to the international audience.

[40] *Istochnik* 3 (1995), 72–5.

[41] Shumiatskii complained to Voroshilov on 28 September that the press were failing to highlight their success. *Istochnik* 3 (1995), 76.

and the commission no longer served a useful purpose. When Shumiatskii informed Voroshilov on 7 November that Glavrepertkom was preventing the release of two recent comedies, *Flag stadiona* and *Zhenitba Iana Knukke* (A. Ivanov), Voroshilov suggested that Shumiatskii should be helped and not hindered. Stalin agreed 'If we can trust Shumiatskii to make films, then we should release him from petty guardianship [*opekunstva*]. We should tell Zhdanov'.[42] The commission was also deemed superfluous, and liquidated by Politburo decree on 25 December 1934. According to Stetskii, whose note accompanied the decree, the commission had achieved its aims of eliminating rubbish (*khaltura*) from cinema, and generating more scripts. Writers had been brought in, and cinema organisations directed to make great films. Now it was necessary to give GUKF more independence, with Kul'tprop to oversee plans, scenarios, and completed films, and to introduce writers.[43]

Meanwhile, Stalin's personal patronage of Shumiatskii and GUKF was becoming more explicit. He now increasingly defined himself as 'helper' of cinema.[44] In November 1934, when Shumiatskii complained to Stalin that cinema was often regarded as second class, Stalin replied, '*Nuzhno naoborot*' (the opposite should be the case). Advising Shumiatskii to continue to work persistently, he declared 'I will be taking a greater interest in this than before. Tell me about your problems'.[45] A few weeks later he remarked that he did not mind watching an unfinished feature film when there were no completed ones available 'it might even be better for us to approach this matter more closely and *help* you with our instructions *before* their completion (my emphases, SD).' He then proceeded to watch the as yet unfinished *Tri tovarishcha* (S. Timoshenko). He made some suggestions and was obviously pleased to hear that these coincided with those Stetskii had made previously: 'You see, our advice was along the same lines'.[46] From then on, Stalin frequently watched films prior to their completion.

Stalin's 'help' inevitably invited comparisons with that of the commission. Following a screening of *Iunost' Maksima* (G. Kozintsev, L. Trauberg)

[42] RGASPI f. 558, op. 11, d. 828, l. 60 (7 November 1934). Glavrepertkom's influence on cinema declined from the middle of the 1930s. According to Margolit, from the mid-1930s the protocols of Glavrepertkom are absent from the archives. See 'Budem schitat', chto takogo fil'ma nikogda ne bylo', p. 153.

[43] RGASPI f. 17, op. 163, d. 1048, l. 56.

[44] Fitzpatrick notes that 'help' was one of the common euphemisms used to denote patronage relations. S. Fitzpatrick, 'Intelligentsia and Power. Client–Patron Relations in Stalin's Russia', in M. Hildermeier (ed.), *Stalinismus vor dem Zweiten Weltkrieg* (Munich: R. Oldenbourg Verlag, 1998), p. 36.

[45] RGASPI f. 558, op. 11, d. 828, l. 63ob (9/10 November 1934).

[46] *Ibid.*, ll. 85–7 (23/4 November 1934).

just after the liquidation of the commission, Stalin offered some advice, and said 'That's how we're going to watch new things with you and help you'. When Shumiatskii then expressed his belief in the significance of direct leadership by the Politburo and Stalin personally, Kaganovich laughed that this was better than any commission. Shumiatskii responded rather too quickly that he had not been intending to compare them, especially because he was not a fan of the composition and methods of work of the commission.[47]

Stalin continued to refer to his special 'help' for cinema throughout this period. After watching Dovzhenko's *Aerograd* and *Lunnyi kamen'* (A. Minkin, I. Sorokhtin) in November 1935 he stated that they had learned to make films well 'they deserve our extra help'.[48] In March 1936 he maintained that showing films in the Kremlin was a necessity as well as a convenience:

because cinema has become a factor of great significance. It's a genuine art of the masses, and at the same time a very sharp instrument of influence, organisation, leadership. We are not simply watching films, but are helping to direct (*rukovodit'*) them with decrees.[49]

He encouraged other *vozhdi* to help too. Just before Kirov's death, he invited him to get involved in the Leningrad studio, which was currently in favour for producing films such as *Chapaev*, *Iunost' Maksima*, *Krest'iane* (F. Ermler). According to Shumiatskii, Kirov had never visited the studio or watched a film there even though he lived close by. Stalin joked that he had turned into a bureaucrat '*zabiurokratilsia*'.[50] A 'bureaucratic' approach was, of course, the antithesis of the personalised style he himself favoured. He later told Postyshev that film, as well as being a great weapon of agitprop in the hands of talented people, was also a very powerful art: 'All that's needed is for us, the leaders, to monitor directly the work of cinema, to help this most important of matters'.[51]

Championing cinema's interests

How significant was Stalin's patronage? It was certainly vital in helping to secure some of the vast funding for which Shumiatskii constantly pressed. Cinema was often viewed as less important than other branches of the economy with which it was competing for scarce resources. Stalin

---

[47] *Ibid.*, l. 105 (1 January 1935).
[48] RGASPI f. 558, op. 11, d. 829, l. 59 (8 November 1935).
[49] *Ibid.*, l. 91 (4 March 1936).
[50] RGASPI f. 558, op. 11, d. 828, ll. 64–64ob (10/11 November 1934).
[51] *Ibid.*, l. 74 (6/7 December 1934).

encouraged others to regard it as strategically important.[52] He recognised the need for high quality technology, if necessary imported, but preferably domestically produced, and on several occasions in 1934 gave his personal support to measures to invest in the domestic industry, or authorised costly imports.[53] This often entailed promoting the interests of cinema to less enthusiastic colleagues. On one occasion in November 1934, after watching *Chapaev*, he asked Shumiatskii and some colleagues to supper. He praised the work of cinema in front of the others, arguing that the industry needed support. When Shumiatskii complained that Gosplan was not offering as much funding as he had requested, Stalin asked Sovnarkom chairman Molotov to check up on this.[54] In December Shumiatskii complained again, so Stalin telephoned Molotov to arrange for extra resources. When it transpired that the Sovnarkom official responsible for GUKF, Chubar', was unwilling to be generous, Stalin accused him of underestimating the importance of cinema and urged them to help in a serious way.[55] He continued to offer support in later years, for example for the development of colour film technology, which he considered a high priority.[56]

He also supported investment in cinema construction. Echoing his speech to the Fifteenth Party Congress in 1927, he argued (like Trotsky) that revenue from cinema should replace income from vodka. When Shumiatskii explained that this could easily be achieved by increasing the number of cinemas, Stalin agreed that they should work towards this.[57] A few days later he argued again for the importance of immediately constructing more cinemas equipped for sound so that people could see films like *Chapaev*. Given that the USSR boasted only 400–500 sound projectors at this stage, this was an urgent priority.[58] However, when the

---

[52] See Stalin's comments in 1932 cited in Priestland's chapter that 'the production of souls is more important than the production of tanks.'

[53] RGASPI f. 558, op. 11, d. 828, l. 37 (3/4 June 1934); ll. 46–7 (13/14 July 1934); l. 51 (21 July 1934); l. 63 (9/10 November 1934); a Politburo decree of 23 November 1934 granted the film industry 100,000 roubles for the fourth quarter. This superseded an earlier decision of 5 November 1934 declining Kuibyshev's request for extra imports. f. 17, op. 162, d. 17, l. 85; f. 17, op. 162, d. 17, l. 79. On 21 May 1935, GUKF was granted 200,000 in hard currency to purchase the latest equipment in the USA, France, and Germany. f. 17, op. 162, d. 18, l. 42.

[54] RGASPI f. 558, op. 11, d. 828, l. 65 (10/11 November 1934).

[55] *Ibid.*, ll. 77–8 (11 December 1934).

[56] RGASPI f. 558, op. 11, d. 829, l. 76 (31 January 1936), l. 81 (7 February 1936); On 17 April 1936, the Politburo assigned $62,000 for the purchase of material for colour film. f. 17, op. 162, d. 19, l. 138.

[57] RGASPI f. 558, op. 11, d. 828, l. 63ob (9/10 November 1934).

[58] *Ibid.*, l. 67 (15 November 1934). A silent version of *Chapaev* was authorised to allow more viewers to enjoy the film.

demands of *kinofikatsiia* (expanding the cinema network) came into conflict with those of the film industry itself, as they did in 1935 when Gosplan was advocating investment in cinema construction, Stalin sided with Shumiatskii, who was pressing for the resources to go to the industry instead, saying 'What's the point of cinemas, when there's nothing to show?'[59]

One of the major projects associated with Shumiatskii was the development of a Soviet Hollywood (*kinogorod*) in the south of the USSR, which he saw as a way of increasing film production and cutting costs.[60] Stalin was also enthusiastic, and had thoughts about its possible location, agreeing that the Crimea would probably be better than the Transcaucasus which was too cloudy. But he also suggested investigating Krasnodar, Azov, Taganrog – areas in need of cultural development. He was dismissive of those who were lobbying against the idea, describing colleagues from Sovnarkom who opposed it as unable 'to see further than their nose'. When the writers Il'f and Petrov wrote to Stalin in February 1936 questioning the need for a special *kinogorod*, after learning in Hollywood that the Americans tended not to film in natural sunlight, Stalin was scornful, doubting that artificial light and decorations could adequately replace natural conditions. He was keen for the development to be undertaken quickly, evidently feeling a sense of competition with Mussolini's Cine-Citta project.[61] Given Stalin's initial enthusiasm, it is unclear why the project collapsed, but as Taylor suggests, it was probably related to its prohibitive cost and to Shumiatskii's fall from grace.[62]

As well as promoting the film industry's economic interests, Stalin was also responsible for disbursing the social honour which was so central to the Soviet system.[63] Various methods were employed to overturn cinema's 'second-class' reputation including publicity in the press, public celebrations, and the conferral of awards.

'The Bolsheviks were journalists long before they were state leaders',[64] and Stalin was no exception. He frequently used the press to promote film, telephoning *Pravda*'s editor, L. Mekhlis, to arrange for the necessary

---

[59] RGASPI f. 558, op. 11, d. 829, l. 66 (25 December 1935).

[60] R. Taylor, 'Ideology as mass entertainment', *Inside the Film Factory*, pp. 213–15.

[61] RGASPI f. 558, op. 11, d. 829, l. 55 (26 July 1935); l. 65 (25 December 1935); l. 94 (3 March 1936).

[62] Taylor 'Ideology as mass entertainment', p. 215. Certainly Shumiatskii's obsession with 'sunny cinema cities' was raised in Shcherbakov's critique of him in March 1936. See below, p. 224.

[63] See Jeffrey Brooks, *Thank You, Comrade Stalin! Soviet Public Culture from Revolution to Cold War* (Princeton: Princeton University Press, 1999), p. 126.

[64] J. von Geldern and R. Stites (eds.), *Mass Culture in Soviet Russia* (Bloomington: Indiana University Press, 1995), p. xi.

coverage.[65] The most notable example of this practice was the smash hit of 1934 – the Vasilievs' Civil War adventure *Chapaev*, which Maya Turovskaya has described as a classic example of the genre of 'Eastern' (a Soviet-bloc counterpart to the 'Western').[66] Although this received critical acclaim, and was undoubtedly genuinely popular, without Stalin's personal endorsement it would hardly have achieved the cult-like status it enjoyed as the first model socialist realist film. Stalin was obsessed with it, watching it on numerous occasions – every few days in November and December, on one occasion twice in one day! In March 1936 he informed Shumiatskii that he had seen it thirty-eight times.[67] He reacted positively from the first viewing: 'You should be congratulated. It's done very well, cleverly and tactfully. Chapaev, Furmanov and Pet'ka are good. The film will have great educational significance. It's a good gift for the holiday.' At a later screening he remarked that the film's fundamental qualities were its simplicity and sincerity.[68]

He was determined that the press should set the right tone. When he heard that *Pravda* had included a favourable if not energetic review, while *Izvestiia's* critic was positive but found the portrayal of the political commissar, Furmanov, weak and superficial, Stalin proceeded to accuse the critics of disorienting people, and immediately phoned Mekhlis to arrange for the paper to give the correct line. A rebuttal appeared in *Pravda* accusing the *Izvestiia* review of being cold, and of wrongly criticising the film's portrayal of Furmanov and the Party.[69] Stalin continued to take an interest in the press reaction to the film, and decided that *Pravda* should publish an article summing up the achievements of Soviet cinema. The next day the paper included a celebratory lead article 'The Whole Country is Watching *Chapaev*' which highlighted the numerous qualities of the film, particularly its patriotism.[70] It was a very public triumph for Soviet cinema.

Following the success of *Chapaev*, Stalin strongly endorsed the celebration of the fifteenth anniversary of the nationalisation of film studios, expressing irritation when the preparations were held up.[71] He publicly identified himself with cinema's achievements at the anniversary events

[65] On Stalin and the press, see Brooks, *Thank You, Comrade Stalin*, pp. 59–60, and, more generally, M. Lenoe, *Closer to the Masses: Stalinist Culture, Social Revolution, and Soviet Newspapers* (Cambridge, Mass.: Harvard University Press, 2004).

[66] M. Turovskaia, 'The Tastes of Soviet Moviegoers', in T. Lahusen (ed.), *Late Soviet Culture from Perestroika to Novostroika* (Durham: Duke University Press, 1993), p. 101.

[67] RGASPI f. 558, op. 11, d. 829, ll. 94–6 (9 March 1936).

[68] RGASPI f. 558, op. 11, d. 828, l. 56 (4 November 1934); l. 76 (9 December 1934).

[69] *Ibid.*, l. 65 (10/11 November 1934); *Pravda*, 12 November 1934.

[70] RGASPI f. 588, op. 11, d. 828, l. 69 (20 November 1934); *Pravda*, 21 November 1934.

[71] RGASPI f. 558, op. 11, d. 828, l. 59 (9/10 November 1934); l. 75 (6/7 December 1934).

which eventually took place in January 1935, publishing in *Pravda* a personal telegram of congratulation to Shumiatskii in which he exhorted him to produce new *Chapaevs*.[72] Stalin also bestowed awards on leading film workers at a ceremony in the Bol'shoi Theatre, taking care to prescribe the exact hierarchy of honour. He edited the draft decree on the awards, elevating some recipients and demoting others. Among those who received the highest Order of Lenin were the Lenfil'm studio, Shumiatskii, P. Tager (responsible for development of sound), and the directors – the Vasilievs, Pudovkin, Dovzhenko, Chiaureli, Ermler, Kozintsev, and Trauberg (but not Eisenstein, whose planned Order of the Red Banner of Labour was changed at a stroke of Stalin's pencil to a lesser Honoured Activist of the Arts).[73] Stalin also supported another high-profile event – the first Moscow film festival of February–March 1935, which brought international guests to the capital at great expense,[74] and the fortieth anniversary celebrations of Lumiere's invention later that year.[75]

In a culture in which competition for patronage was crucially important,[76] these highly visible expressions of support for Soviet cinema by Stalin inevitably aroused the jealousy of some other branches of the arts. As conflicts emerged, Stalin intervened to protect cinema and Shumiatskii. One of these conflicts focused on *Veselye rebiata*, which continued to serve as a magnet for attacks, particularly from writers,[77] and which Stalin continued to defend after it was released with great fanfare in the Soviet Union at the end of the year. When Kaganovich reported on 30 October that some writers were criticising the 'hooligan' aspects of the film, Stalin maintained that it was really jolly, even if the theme was not profound, and that it would be popular.[78] He was incensed by *Literaturnaia gazeta*'s treatment of the film on 18 November. The lead article praised *Chapaev* as 'Genuine Art of Socialism', contrasting it favourably with *Veselye rebiata*:

[72] Brooks notes that Stalin commonly used this practice as a way of making people personally responsible to him. *Thank You, Comrade Stalin!*, p. 66.

[73] *Pravda*, 11 January 1935. For the draft and changes, see RGASPI f. 17, op. 163, d. 1051, ll. 90–4.

[74] RGASPI f. 558, op. 11, d. 828, l. 63ob (9/10 November 1934). The Politburo assigned 35,000 gold roubles for this event. f. 17, op. 162, d. 17, l. 124.

[75] RGASPI f. 558, op. 11, d. 829, l. 22 (3 April 1935); f. 17, op. 163, d. 1059, l. 136.

[76] Fitzpatrick, 'Intelligentsia and Power. Client–Patron Relations in Stalin's Russia'; G. Peteri, 'Patronage, Personal Networks and the Party-State: Everyday Life in the Cultural Sphere in Communist Russia and East Central Europe', a special issue of *Contemporary European History* 1 (2002).

[77] It was criticised at the Writers' Congress in August, where A. Surkov noted its 'lemonade ideology'. *Pervyi Vsesoiuznyi S"ezd Sovetskikh Pisatelei, 1934: Stenograficheskii otchet* (Moscow: Khudozhestvennaia literatura, 1934), p. 515.

[78] RGASPI f. 558, op. 11, d. 828, l. 54 (30 October 1934).

Chapaev summons us to the world of great ideas and moving images. It throws from our path the cardboard barricades of the lovers of non-ideological (*bezideinogo*) art who do not regret the great talent wasted on, for example, *Veselye rebiata*.

An article by Eisenstein, 'At last', did not specifically mention *Veselye rebiata*, but implied that with *Chapaev* 'at last' a worthy film had appeared, heralding a new era in Soviet cinema which would involve a synthesis of previous 'poetic' and 'prosaic' phases.[79] Stalin complained that these articles would disorient the work of cinema, that it was irresponsible to compare *Veselye rebiata* with *Chapaev*, and that it was wrong to attack the cinema leadership at a time when it was encouraging cinema. He was very critical of Eisenstein's implication that prior to *Chapaev* nothing significant had been achieved: 'only windbags and good-for-nothings could give space to articles such as "At last" which aim to prove that until now nothing substantial has been created and that only now has something appeared,' and he instructed Zhdanov to launch a counter-attack.[80]

The swipes against the film continued nevertheless as part of a sustained onslaught on Shumiatskii during the first Moscow film festival. Several newspapers, including *Izvestiia*, criticised the allegedly poor organisation of the festival. The poet A. Bezymenskii also claimed in *Literaturnaia gazeta* that music from *Veselye rebiata* had been plagiarised from the Mexican film *Viva, Villa!* which was being screened at the festival. When Shumiatskii's attempts to defend himself against the allegations failed, his patron stepped in. Using characteristic military metaphors, Stalin applauded Shumiatskii for putting up a good fight, but suggested that he did not have enough support from his own cadres 'and since his army and general staff are not brave, and lurk in corners, hiding from the battle, we have to help'. It was now necessary to attack *Literaturnaia gazeta* and *Izvestiia*, and for Mekhlis to raise this to a political level.[81] The following day, *Pravda* responded, criticising the newspapers for their distorted coverage of the festival, and Bezymenskii's unfounded accusation of plagiarism. Bezymenskii was forced to apologise in *Pravda*. Stalin later asked whether the newspapers were still being unprincipled, to which Shumiatskii responded that they had not been since the *Pravda* article. In Stalin's view Shumiatskii had had a hard fight partly because of poor cadres, but also because he had not had the backing of the press – *Izvestiia* had a run of 1.5 million, while *Komsomol'skaia Pravda*, which served as a platform for Shumiatskii, only 100,000.[82]

---

[79] *Literaturnaia gazeta*, 18 November 1934.
[80] RGASPI f. 558, op. 11, d. 828, l. 69 (20 November 1934).
[81] RGASPI f. 558, op. 11, d. 829, ll. 9–10 (11 March 1935).
[82] *Ibid.*, ll. 13–14 (13 March 1935).

Stalin was clearly conscious of the effects his overt patronage could have. He attributed the attacks on cinema during the Moscow film festival to the envy of writers. 'They've become accustomed to their work being praised, they can't stand that others are being praised rather than them. But they themselves don't do the work, or produce anything sensible. But cinema has produced and is producing.' When Shumiatskii reported that during a discussion of dramaturgists' work, the theory of 'the unequal development of certain forms of art' had been proposed, Stalin commented 'but they themselves work unevenly. That's the thing'.[83] A week later he reiterated that it was not surprising that some 'esteemed colleagues' were envious. Cinema had produced masterpieces such as *Chapaev*, *Iunost' Maksima*, *Krest'iane*, *Novyi Gulliver* (A. Ptushko), *Letchiki* (Iu. Raizman), which other forms of art had not yet equalled.[84]

Stalin continued to show favour towards cinema when it appeared to be vulnerable to the ambitions of other arts towards the end of 1935. He chose to intervene to back GUKF when it transpired that Mossovet had given the cinema 'Forum' to the Realistic Theatre and the 'Kollizei' to the VTsSPS Theatre. He criticised the 'pilfering' of the cinemas, and accused theatre of lacking proper leadership and organisation. He immediately asked Khrushchev to return the former cinemas to GUKF, as well as transferring to GUKF the cinemas of the former Society of Political Prisoners and the House of Government, and he decreed that a model cinema be built in Moscow in 1936.[85]

Creative help

Stalin did not restrict himself to this type of practical support. His 'help' with the actual making of films became ever more detailed and specific and his instructions to Shumiatskii were incorporated into films and often paraphrased (usually without attribution) in Shumiatskii's many

---

[83] *Ibid.*, l. 14 (13 March 1935). In an earlier incident, the actress A. Tarasova, who had appeared in the film version of *Groza*, was apparently refused a role in MKhAT's stage production. Shumiatskii himself also attributed this to 'envy of cinema'. RGASPI f. 558, op. 11, d. 828, l. 62 (8/9 November 1934).

[84] RGASPI f. 558, op. 11, d. 829, l. 15 (19 March 1935).

[85] *Ibid.*, ll. 61–2 (10 November 1935). The Politburo formalised this in a decision of 14 November, RGASPI f. 17, op. 163, d. 1085, l. 32. When it later transpired that part of the building of the former Society of Political Prisoners was still being occupied by a canteen, Shumiatskii appealed to the Politburo, on the grounds that it was absolutely inadmissible that this space should continue to be occupied 'by a canteen, existing for corporate reasons'. For once, the Politburo was not united on this: while the majority followed Stalin's lead in siding with Shumiatskii, it is remarkable that Kalinin actually voted against the motion that the canteen be closed with those attached to it – presumably *politkatorzhane* – transferred to alternatives. RGASPI f. 17, op. 163, d. 1091, ll. 90–1.

publications. Stalin was preoccupied by the difficult question of how to make films entertaining as well as ideologically correct, and regularly offered his thoughts on stylistic matters such as the length and tempo of films and their musical accompaniment. He also influenced their content in various ways, particularly when this touched on matters of state security.

In Stalin's opinion, entertaining films should be short with plenty of action. According to Shumiatskii, at the end of 1933 Stalin raised the question of the *metrazh* (length in metres) of a film which, in jest, he called its '*kilometrazh*' (length in kilometres). He developed an idea about a 'limited time budget for each form of spectacle': a spectator would never devote as much time to a film as to a play, not because he preferred the theatre but because cinema is a different form – mobile and dynamic.[86] He was particularly intolerant of the slow tempo of film adaptations of dramas, such as *Groza*, calling on Shumiatskii to give directors clear instructions about this:

Evidently when people are redoing a work they can't cope with the conditions required by the dynamism of cinema [*kino-dinamichnost'*]. In general this is a task for you now. Directors need to be reeducated to understand that all lengthiness leads to failure. Even the very best films lose considerable appeal from one or two drawn out scenes. This requires strong leadership as well as education. The director will not listen to bits of good advice, he must be made to do this since it's for the sake of the cause, art.[87]

Later, in reference to *Iunost' Maksima* he maintained that:

Lengthy passages of a film are always bad. They reveal the expert's lack of confidence in the depiction of events and actions, in their link to the subject. The viewer always experiences them as annoying interruptions, as a distraction from the main thing.[88]

He also felt that the slow sections in films about contemporary reality inaccurately reflected the new fast pace of life in the USSR.[89] For example, he criticised the slow scenes in *Letchiki* of dancing and of legs going upstairs, stressing that directors should highlight the new tempo of life instead. This was particularly the case in films about the countryside, in which any slowness was automatically equated with backwardness.[90] One

---

[86] RGASPI f. 558, op. 11, d. 828, ll. 96–7 (Stalin i kino).
[87] *Ibid.*, l. 57 (7 November 1934); l. 62 (8/9 November 1934).
[88] *Ibid.*, l. 104 (1 January 1935).
[89] For similar observations by Shumiatskii, see his *Puti masterstva. Stat'i i doklady* (Moscow: Kinofotoizdat, 1935), pp. 62–5.
[90] Cf. Shumiatskii in *Kinematografiia millionov*, pp. 163–5.

of the reasons Stalin was opposed to I. Savchenko's *Garmon'*, a musical set in the countryside, was that it was drawn out and lacking the action 'in the name of which people go to the cinema'. He also disliked its artificial 'psychologism' and portrayal of the Soviet countryside as backward (the harvesting being done by hand and so on).[91] He reacted similarly to the slow scenes in *Krest'iane*. When Shumiatskii claimed that these represented the peasant rhythm of life, Stalin and Molotov criticised his 'Buninism', arguing that the countryside had changed, and that Shumiatskii should get out there more often.[92]

Stalin actively promoted film music in his quest for entertaining films, for he believed that music and film complement each other, and that music helps reception.[93] As well as supporting musical films such as *Veselye rebiata*, he frequently pointed out to Shumiatskii examples of the successful use of music in non-musical films such as *Iunost' Maksima* and *Chastnaia zhizn' Petra Vinogradova* (A. Macheret), and criticised music which he felt did not fit in with the overall tone of a film, including Shostakovich's 'lyrical' accompaniment to *Podrugi* (L. Arnshtam).[94] He argued that the role of film in promoting music should be emphasised more clearly, and, during the 1936 campaign against formalism, complimented cinema for setting a good example for realistic music in comparison with other media.[95]

While Stalin had an input into films on a variety of themes, he was especially anxious to be involved in the growing number which focused on the subject of mobilisation for the defence of the state and against the enemy in its various guises. He encouraged the development of defence themes – for example, after the success of *Chapaev*, he commissioned further civil war films, including Dovzhenko's *Shchors*,[96] and Dzigan's *Pervaia konnaia*.[97] He carefully considered the depiction of sensitive

---

[91] Shumiatskii and Voroshilov both tried to defend the film, but Stalin was not convinced – he later referred to it as rubbish (*drian'*) – although he did not prevent its release in June 1934. RGASPI f. 558, op. 11, d. 828, ll. 39–40 (9/10 June 1934); l. 46 (13/14 July 1934). In 1936 Molotov ordered that the film be withdrawn, describing it as 'stupid, vulgar and alien'. RGASPI f. 82, op. 2, d. 959, ll. 14–16.

[92] RGASPI f. 558, op. 11, d. 829, l. 3 (16 February 1935).

[93] RGASPI f. 558, op. 11, d. 828, l. 43 (28/9 June 1934). See also *ibid.*, l. 93 (Stalin i kino).

[94] *Ibid.*, l. 112 (29 January 1935); l. 64 (25 December 1935).

[95] RGASPI f. 558, op. 11, d. 829, l. 58 (8 November 1935); l. 69 (29 January 1936).

[96] On Stalin and *Shchors*, see G. Liber, *Alexander Dovzhenko. A Life in Soviet Film* (London: BFI Publishing, 2002); RGASPI f. 558, op. 11, d. 829, l. 12 (13 March 1935); l. 15 (19 March 1935); ll. 62–3 (10 November 1935); ll. 97–8; f. 558, op. 11, d. 164.

[97] In January 1935 Stalin suggested that a film, *Pervaia konnaia*, be made to celebrate the fifteenth anniversary of the cavalry. He was involved in its production from the earliest stages, suggesting possible scriptwriters, advising on the structure of the film and so on. He edited the scenario twice in 1939. However the film was ultimately shelved. RGASPI

defence-related issues, in some cases taking a more flexible position than his colleagues in the military. While Voroshilov accused a film about the relationship between a tank commander and a young student, *Goriachie denechki* (A. Zarkhi, I. Kheifits), of portraying idiots untypical of the Red Army and petty-bourgeois (*meshchanskie*) relationships, Stalin defended it on the grounds that it would be popular amongst soldiers because of its lively tone and characters.[98] When Voroshilov then objected to the portrayal in *Letchiki* of 'hooligan' behaviour by pilots and so on, Stalin countered that the film successfully captured the new relationships and inner world of young people, and argued that the features Voroshilov criticised were justified on aesthetic grounds.[99] He also intervened to help Dovzhenko when he learned that Gamarnik was preventing him from filming aviation scenes for *Aerograd* against the backdrop of the Far East for security reasons.[100]

At other times, particularly in 1936, as international tensions increased and the anti-formalism campaign took off, he was less inclined to be flexible. Ukrainfil'm's *Zastava u Chertova broda* (M. Bilinskii, K. Isaev), an adventure film set on the Soviet-Polish border, was shelved after Stalin and his colleagues deemed that the hero was an idiot who discredited the border guards and the prestige of Soviet defence.[101] Another Ukrainian production, I. Kavaleridze's *Prometei*, which depicted the struggle of Ukrainians and Georgians against the Russian imperial order, had apparently enjoyed some support not only from Ukrainian organisations, but also from the central press and certain Politburo members, including Kosior, who had advised that it should be corrected rather than banned. However others, including Shumiatskii, were opposed to the film and it was left to Stalin to decide its fate. Stalin disliked it, criticising its lack of plot, schematism, and absence of historical understanding (this was at the time of the anti-Pokrovskii campaign), and concluded that there was no point correcting it.[102] A week later, a *Pravda* editorial, 'A crude scheme

---

f. 17, op. 163, d. 1053, ll. 47–9; f. 558, op. 11, d. 829, l. 19 (2 April 1935); l. 72 (29 January 1936); f. 558, op. 11, dd. 165, 166; Margolit and Shmyrov, *Iz"iatoe kino*, pp. 74–6.

[98] RGASPI f. 558, op. 11, d. 829, ll. 7–8 (9 March 1935).

[99] *Ibid.*, l. 11 (13 March 1935); l. 16 (2 April 1935).

[100] RGASPI f. 558, op. 11, d. 828, l. 64ob (11 November 1934). In April 1934 Dovzhenko read the scenario of *Aerograd* to Stalin, Voroshilov, Molotov, and Kirov, who gave him various instructions. Liber, *Alexander Dovzhenko*, p. 167. When Stalin saw the completed film, he was enthusiastic, despite Dovzhenko's predilection for symbolism ('he cannot do it more simply'), praising its depiction of Soviet patriotism. RGASPI f. 558, op. 11, d. 829, l. 57 (8 November 1935).

[101] Margolit and Shmyrov, *Iz"iatoe kino*, p. 48; RGASPI f. 558, op. 11, d. 829, l. 75 (31 January 1936).

[102] RGASPI f. 558, op. 11, d. 829, ll. 79–80 (7 February 1936).

instead of historical truth,' denounced the film's vulgar historical conception and formalism.[103]

On several occasions he provided quite concrete instructions on how the state's enemies should be portrayed on film, in much the same way as he played an active part in constructing threats through theatrical show trials.[104] After watching *Tri tovarishcha*, a comedy about three different leaders at a construction site, he insisted that the film should be altered to emphasise how the corrupt practices of one of the leaders, Zaitsev, had brought much harm to the state.[105] He was particularly concerned to make the fate of the various enemies unambiguously clear. He was impressed by Ermler's *Krest'iane*, but stressed to Shumiatskii and the director that the scene of revenge against the kulak should be shown more explicitly, to highlight that he had been *shot* rather than simply disappearing: 'The people demand clarity in relation to him, demand punishment for his subversive work, terrorist activity. But you approached this symbolically. It won't do'.[106] He intervened similarly in relation to I. Pyr'ev's *Anka*, the story of a kulak who murdered a komsomol activist, took on his identity, came to Moscow, and gained the love of a young woman, Anna, whose party card he then stole to give to foreign agents. When Stalin saw the film in February 1936, he invented a new melodramatic finale in which Anna, learning about the villain's past, aims a revolver at him. The secretary of the party committee then explains that not only did he kill the activist, but that he is also a spy and traitor, and the film concludes with him being taken away by the NKVD. Stalin gave the reworked film a new title to reflect the new emphasis: *Partiinyi bilet*.[107]

Conclusion

It is clear that Stalin took greater personal interest in certain areas of policy than others. While matters such as foreign policy dominated his daily agenda, he left some areas to others, intervening only

---

[103] *Pravda*, 13 February 1936.

[104] See the chapter by Chase in this volume. One of the final documents in the Shumiatskii files is Stalin's infamous letter written at the end of the trial of the Anti-Soviet Trotsykite centre in January 1937. In this, Stalin's stage management of the show trial and his construction of the enemy on film dovetailed perfectly, as he issued detailed instructions on how to portray the opposition in Ermler's *Velikii grazhdanin* in the light of the latest trial. RGASPI f. 558, op. 11, d. 829, ll. 109–10. For more on this, see A. Latyshev 'Stalin i kino', in *Surovaia drama naroda* (Moscow: Politizdat, 1989), pp. 489–507.

[105] RGASPI f. 558, op. 11, d. 828, ll. 86–7 (23/4 December 1934).

[106] RGASPI f. 558, op. 11, d. 829, ll. 1–6 (16 February 1935).

[107] *Ibid.*, ll. 84–5 (28 February 1936).

sporadically.[108] Cultural matters clearly interested him enormously, and cinema most of all. As K. Simonov noted, of all the arts Stalin was most concerned to 'programme' cinema.[109] Shumiatskii's important record of the Kremlin screenings illuminate in remarkable detail just how significant cinema affairs became for Stalin from the mid-1930s. He devoted many hours a week to watching and talking about films with his Politburo colleagues. Although the distinction between informal and formal decision-making in Soviet politics is never clear-cut, these evenings represent a good example of Stalin exercising power through primarily informal structures.[110] Of course, watching films was partly an enjoyable leisure activity for Stalin. But his commitment to this activity also reflected his fundamental belief in the power of ideas and images to mobilise the Soviet people, and in his own responsibility to shape these.

Stalin's influence on the development of Soviet cinema was decisive in many respects – his support for the principle that films should be entertaining as well as ideologically sound, and his encouragement of the genre of comedy; his advocacy of material support for the film industry, and his efforts to raise the status of cinema; his active criticism and reworking of films at all stages of production. Although Stalin listened to his colleagues' opinions of films, there is little evidence of him deferring to them on the relatively rare occasions when they took a different view. He clearly considered his own judgements to be authoritative. When Voroshilov told him that he had already managed to see the whole of *Veselye rebiata* and had found it amusing and interesting, Stalin retorted 'He acted in military fashion, quickly. But as for the evaluation of the film – we'll discuss that when we watch it together'.[111]

Influential though he was, Stalin was not the only important factor shaping Soviet cinema. Mass taste, Soviet filmmaking traditions, technological changes, international influences (especially Hollywood), all played a role. So, too, did other individuals, not least (in this period), Shumiatskii. The question of Shumiatskii's role, and his relationship with Stalin, deserves a study in its own right.[112] Although he has often been criticised, particularly for his role in the *Bezhin lug* incident, it is clear that he acted capably in difficult (impossible?) political conditions to

---

[108] For discussions of the pattern of Stalin's interests, see the chapters by Getty, Khlevniuk, and Davies in this volume, and those by Rees, R. W. Davies, M. Ilic, and O. Khlevniuk in E. A. Rees (ed.), *The Nature of Stalin's Dictatorship* (London: Palgrave, 2004).

[109] K. Simonov, *Glazami cheloveka moego pokoleniia* (Moscow: Kniga, 1990), p. 164.

[110] See Getty's contribution to this volume; Rees (ed.), *The Nature of Stalin's Dictatorship*, ch. 1.

[111] RGASPI f. 558, op. 11, d. 828, l. 51 (21 July 1934).

[112] R. Taylor, 'Ideology as mass entertainment' is the best study to date.

represent to Stalin what he considered to be cinema's interests. For a couple of years he enjoyed stunning success. Invited to Stalin's box in the Bol'shoi Theatre after the screening of the new documentary film *Lenin* for the anniversary of the leader's death in January 1935, some 'comrades' jokingly called him 'the man with the most successes'.[113]

But success carried its own dangers. How could Shumiatskii live up to the great expectations which Stalin had outlined in his telegram of 11 January 1935? Continual failures to meet plan targets began to erode Stalin's support for his client. As early as December 1935, Stalin turned down a request by Shumiatskii to hold a second film festival in Moscow and Leningrad in 1936. The Orgburo had previously agreed to this, but Stalin concluded that it should be postponed for a year as the first festival had been poorly organised, and the hard currency would be better spent on more urgent tasks.[114] In January 1936, GUKF lost some of its independence, subordinated to the newly formed Committee for Artistic Affairs (*Komitet po delam iskusstv*) headed by P. Kerzhentsev.[115] By this stage, Shumiatskii himself was becoming a frequent target of high-level criticism. A. Shcherbakov of Kul'tpros wrote a damning report to Stalin, Andreev, and Ezhov in March 1936 which claimed that:

The work of the leadership of GUKF is characterised by a lack of Bolshevik self-criticism, self-satisfaction, over-estimation of its successes, getting carried away with 'sunny cinema-cities', along with a lack of everyday work to fulfil the 1936 plan, struggle with failings and hold-ups in production.[116]

He survived this, but the *Bezhin lug* debacle and sustained onslaughts in the press throughout 1937 were followed by his arrest in January 1938. He was sentenced and shot for an alleged attempt to commit a terrorist act against Stalin in the Kremlin cinema.[117]

The termination of Shumiatskii did not signify the end of Stalin's close relationship with cinema. After the reorganisation of the film industry under a Committee for Film Affairs (*Komitet po delam kinematografii*) in 1938,[118] the role of the Politburo (and Stalin) acquired greater formal

---

[113] RGASPI f. 558, op. 11, d. 828, l. 111 (21 January 1935).

[114] RGASPI f. 17, op. 114, d. 726, ll. 140–4.

[115] The KDI is discussed at length in L. Maksimenkov, *Sumbur vmesto muzyki. Stalinskaia kul'turnaia revoliutsiia 1936–1938* (Moscow: Iuridicheskaia kniga, 1997). Shumiatskii was its deputy head.

[116] RGASPI f. 17, op. 114, d. 949, ll. 109–17. The item was removed from the Orgburo agenda in favour of considering the 1936 plan. In May and June the Orgburo noted the drastic failure to fulfil the plans for 1935 and 1936. RGASPI f. 17, op. 114, d. 751, ll. 82–114; f. 17, op. 114, d. 763, ll. 79–9ob.

[117] A. Artizov and O. Naumov (eds.), *Vlast' i khudozhestvennaia intelligentsiia* (Moscow: Mezhdunarodnyi fond 'Demokratiia', 1999), p. 769n.

[118] This became a fully fledged Ministry in March 1946.

significance, as it assumed responsibility for monitoring the Committee's film production plans. Stalin continued to 'help' the work of cinema by attending regular screenings in the Kremlin, editing scripts, and adjudicating on the fate of films. The story of the stifling atmosphere of the 1940s and early 1950s for filmmakers has been told before – this '*malokartin'e*', or period of few films, reached its nadir in 1951 when nine films were completed, predominately historical and biographical epics including *Taras Shevchenko* (I. Savchenko), *Belinskii* (G. Kozintsev), *Przheval'skii* (S. Iutkevich), and the Stalin cult film, *Nezabyvaemyi 1919* (M. Chiaureli).[119] Whether or not this was his intention, cinema's supreme patron had succeeded in virtually destroying what he had campaigned for in the mid-1930s: choice for the viewer and entertaining films on contemporary topics. Far from 'seeing himself in films', all that the viewer could now see (with a few exceptions) were a series of 'great men', including, of course, the greatest of them all – Stalin himself.

[119] P. Kenez, *Cinema and Soviet Society*, p. 188.

12   Stalin as producer: the Moscow show trials and the construction of mortal threats

William Chase

Long before the judges entered the courtroom to preside over the August 1936 case of the Trotskyite-Zinovievite Terrorist Centre, show trials had become an established feature of Soviet political life. The trial of the Socialist Revolutionaries, the Shakhty trial, the trial of the Industrial Party, the Menshevik trial, and the Metro-Vickers trial were but the most publicised of this genre of political struggle played out on a judicial stage.[1] But the Moscow show trials of 1936, 1937, and 1938 differed from their predecessors in three significant ways: the political composition of the defendants; the seriousness of the threats that the defendants allegedly posed; and the use of the defendants' confessions, and the trials' verdicts, to justify a conspiratorial explanation of politics and mass repression. For these reasons, these trials stand apart from the other show trials of the Soviet period and they continue to fascinate and perplex. This essay examines these trials to explore how Stalin used them to construct a series of threats, to define who and what constituted the threats, and to mobilise citizens to unmask and crush those threats. In short, it explores what the show trials sought to show.[2]

The Bolsheviks hardly originated the idea of using the judicial system to construct and expose threats to a community. On the contrary, the use of the judicial system for such ends is a longstanding European tradition. Lenin appreciated the power of show trials and was keen to use them against those who threatened the new Soviet state. In a February 1922

---

[1] The 1920s also witnessed agitation trials. For a discussion, see Elisabeth Wood, 'Agitation Trials and Show Trials. One and the Same or Different Animals?', paper presented at the 2002 AAASS Convention, Pittsburgh, Penn., USA.

[2] This is essay is not concerned with issues of guilt or innocence. The review and rehabilitation commissions during the Khrushchev and Gorbachev periods concluded that the accused were innocent of the alleged crimes. No evidence has yet appeared to call their conclusions into question. Nor does the essay address what aspects of the trials Stalin believed to be true.

letter to People's Commissar of Justice Kursky regarding 'strengthening the repression against political enemies of Soviet power and the agents of the bourgeoisie (in particular Mensheviks and Socialist Revolutionaries)', Lenin recommended 'staging a series of model trials' that would administer 'quick and forceful repression' in 'Moscow, Piter [Petrograd], Kharkhov and several other important centres'. He stressed the importance of an '*explanation* of their significance to the popular masses through the courts and the press'. Lenin understood clearly that 'the educational significance of the courts is tremendous'.[3]

Party leaders, as well as Soviet journalists, film-makers, dramatists, and others, were quick to take Lenin's advice. As Julie Cassiday has shown, show trials became a major motif of Soviet film and drama in the 1920s and 1930s. In fact, the show trial film became a genre in and of itself, and films that focused on real or fictional show trials played to large and fascinated audiences. Cassiday's and Lars Lih's studies of the staging, dramatic and melodramatic qualities, and publicising of show trials demonstrate clearly the trials' theatrical aspects and the use of the media to transmit the message.[4] The focus of this essay is different. It focuses on the messages rather than the media.

As the 1928 Shakhty trial and subsequent trials demonstrated, Stalin shared Lenin's views on the powerful didactic qualities of a show trial. He also appreciated that staging a trial rested to a significant degree on the threats and messages such a trial would transmit, and how effectively they could be conveyed. Constructing the appropriate threat and the correct message was no simple task. In 1930, Stalin proposed one way to ensure that what became the 1931 Menshevik trial would convey the correct message:

By the way, how about Messrs. Defendants admitting their mistakes and disgracing themselves politically, while simultaneously acknowledging the strength of

[3] V. I. Lenin, 'O zadachakh Narkomiusta v usloviiakh novoi ekonomicheskoi politiki. Pis'mo D. I. Kurskomu', *Polnoe sobranie sochinenii* (Moscow: Gospolitizdat, 1964), XLIV, pp. 396–400, esp. 396–7. Lenin sent copies of the letter to Molotov (for the members of the Politburo, including Stalin, Tsiurupa, Rykov, and Enukidze).

[4] Julie A. Cassiday, *The Enemy on Trial. Early Soviet Courts on Stage and Screen* (Dekalb: Northern Illinois University Press, 2000); and 'Marble Columns and Jupiter Lights: Theatrical and Cinematic Modeling of Soviet Show Trials in the 1920s', *Slavic and East European Journal* 4 (1998), 640–60. Lars Lih's intriguing study of show trials as melodrama also stresses the importance of film. See Lars T. Lih, 'Melodrama and the Myth of the Soviet Union', in Louise McReynolds and Joan Neuberger (eds.), *Imitations of Life: Two Centuries of Melodrama in Russia* (Durham: University of North Carolina Press, 2002), pp. 178–207; and Lih's longer unpublished essay of the same title. My thanks to Lars for sharing his work with me.

the Soviet government and the correctness of the method of collectivisation? It wouldn't be a bad thing if they did.[5]

'Defendants admitting their mistakes and disgracing themselves politically' became the trademark of the 1936–8 show trials. In fact, it is the confessions, the statements of repentance, and the final pleas to be forgiven by and readmitted into the Soviet community that have transfixed people since the trials. Eyewitnesses, contemporaries, novelists, scholars, students, all have found the confessions and attendant political debasement intriguing, perplexing, confounding.[6] They remain so. Yet the confessions were but a means to an end: the construction and legitimisation of serious threats to the Soviet community that had to be crushed.

Stalin appreciated that staging a successful show trial is a risky affair.[7] A show trial requires the participation, or at least the compliance, of many people (investigators, prosecutors, defence attorneys, judges, witnesses, the press corps, and the defendants) who act out of shared beliefs or under duress, although the latter motive can be most unpredictable. Orchestrating such a complex undertaking is daunting.

Nonetheless, Stalin played an active role in many of the show trials during his rule.[8] Although the precise details of his roles in the 1936, 1937, and 1938 trials still remain somewhat unclear, we know that Stalin played a direct role in ordering investigations, crafting the indictments,

---

[5] An English translation of Stalin's 2 September 1930 letter to Molotov can be found in Lars T. Lih, Oleg V. Naumov, and Oleg V. Khlevniuk (eds.), *Stalin's Letters to Molotov, 1925–1936* (New Haven: Yale University Press, 1995), p. 210.

[6] One of the best known treatments of why the defendants confessed is Arthur Koestler's harrowing novel, *Darkness at Noon*, trans. Daphne Hardy (New York: Macmillan, 1941). Scholarly and polemical works since the trials tend to stress the importance of torture in explaining the confessions. For an interesting example of an eyewitness account that grapples with the issue of confessions, see the report from the US Embassy in Moscow. In particular, see National Archive and Records Administration (NARA), State Department Decimal File, 861.00/11652, Report (Dispatch) No. 2177, 31 December 1936, Enclosure 5, pp. 10–25. My thanks to Oleg Ken for calling this material to my attention.

[7] In 1930 Stalin wrote about the advisability of staging what became the 1931 Menshevik trial and expressed a certain trepidation about the risks involved: 'Are we ready for this? Do we consider it necessary to take this 'case' to trial? Perhaps it will be difficult to dispense with a trial.' Lih et al. (eds.), *Stalin's Letters to Molotov*, p. 210.

[8] For a discussion of Stalin's role in the 1928 Shakhty trial, see Kendall Bailes, *Technology and Society under Lenin and Stalin: Origins of the Soviet Intelligentsia, 1917–1941* (Princeton: Princeton University Press, 1978); Hiroaki Kuromiya, *Stalin's Industrial Revolution. Politics and Workers, 1928–1932* (Cambridge: Cambridge University Press, 1988). For a discussion of same in the Metro-Vickers Trials, see Gordon W. Morrell, *Britain Confronts the Stalin Revolution: Anglo-Soviet Relations and the Metro-Vickers Crisis* (Waterloo: Wilfrid Laurier University Press, 1995). For a discussion of a postwar trial, see Joshua Rubenstein and Vladimir P. Naumov (eds.), *Stalin's Secret Pogrom. The Postwar Inquisition of the Jewish Anti-Fascist Committee* (New Haven: Yale University Press, 2001).

selecting the defendants, prescribing sentences, and influencing how to package and transmit the 'lessons' of these three (and other) trials. It was Stalin who, in early 1936, ordered re-opening the investigation into Kirov's murder and appointed Ezhov to oversee that investigation, which resulted in the August 1936 trial.[9] In March 1936, he approved 'transferring the cases of Trotskyists whose guilt in terrorist activities has been established ... to the Military Collegium of the Supreme Court' and sentencing them to be shot.[10] Yezhov wrote and Stalin edited the 29 July 1936 Central Committee secret letter 'Concerning the Terroristic Activity of the Troskyite-Zinovievist Counter-revolutionary Bloc', which announced the August 1936 trial, and detailed the allegations and 'the facts' proving the defendants' guilt.[11] Stalin played a similar role in the trial itself by 'rewording the indictment, selecting the final slate of defendants, and prescribing the sentences',[12] and in managing and recommending media coverage of the trial.[13] He was equally as involved in preparing and directing the January 1937 trial of the Anti-Soviet Trotskyist Centre.[14]

Stalin's role in the buildup to the trials was not always straightforward. On occasion, he acted to slow the organisation of a show trial. Such was the case at the December 1936 Central Committee Plenum, when he alone proposed 'to consider the matter of Bukharin and Rykov unfinished' and defer it to the next plenum.[15] At the February–March 1937

---

[9] *Izvestiia TsK KPSS* 8 (1989), 85–92; *Voprosii istorii* 10 (1994), 21–6; J. Arch Getty and Oleg V. Naumov, *The Road to Terror. Stalin and the Self-Destruction of the Bolsheviks, 1932–1939* (New Haven: Yale University Press, 1999), pp. 247–8.

[10] Yagoda proposed this in his 25 March 1936 letter to Stalin. Stalin then sought Vyshinsky's legal opinion, which is contained in his 31 March 1936 letter to Stalin. An English translation of that letter can be found in Getty and Naumov, *The Road to Terror*, p. 249. The English translation found in the above text comes from their translation. For a summary of Yagoda's letter and a reproduction of Vyshinsky's letter, see *Izvestiia TsK KPSS* 9 (1989), 35.

[11] An English translation of the letter can be found in Getty and Naumov, *The Road to Terror*, pp. 250–5.

[12] *Ibid.*, p. 256. Getty and Naumov are careful to note that Stalin played these roles with Yagoda and Vyshinsky, who had 'assembled the scenario'.

[13] Stalin appears to have played a role in getting Rakovsky, Radek, and Pyatakov (all defendants in future trials) to write and publish articles in *Izvestiia* denouncing the defendants of the August trial and calling for the 'supreme penalty'. The articles appeared in the 21 August 1936 issue of *Izvestiia*. For Stalin's calling for the articles to be reprinted abroad, see document 763 in Oleg V. Khlevniuk, R. W. Davies, L. P. Kosheleva, E. A. Rees, and L. A. Rogovaia (eds.), *Stalin i Kaganovich. Perepiska, 1931–36gg.* (Moscow: Rosspen, 2001), pp. 642–3. See also, William J. Chase, *Enemies Within the Gates? The Comintern and the Stalinist Repression, 1934–1939* (New Haven: Yale University Press, 2001), pp. 150–1.

[14] *Izvestiia TsK KPSS* 9 (1989), 39–43, esp. p. 42. That trial is also referred to as the trial of the 'Parallel Anti-Soviet Trotskyist Centre'.

[15] As quoted in Getty and Naumov, *The Road to Terror*, p. 324. For a fuller discussion of this issue, see pp. 322–30.

Central Committee Plenum, he alone proposed transferring that same matter to the NKVD.[16] Such delays appear to have been the exception. In fact, the practice of staging confrontations, in the presence of some or all of the Politburo's members, between people under interrogation and comrades whom they denounced, served to hone the indictments and to affect the casting of the central show trials.[17] So too did Stalin's ordering of the arrest and torture of individuals to provide evidence in ongoing investigations. In August 1936, for example, Stalin wrote to Kaganovich that Glebova, Kamenev's wife, 'must be brought to Moscow and subjected to a series of meticulous interrogations. She might reveal a lot of interesting things'.[18]

Stalin's advocacy of show trials was not confined to those in Moscow. He actively promoted such trials in the provinces and, at times, recommended the types of defendants and the sentences.[19] For example, in August 1937, he recommended organising 'public show trials of enemies of the people' in the provinces and ordered Party officials to 'broadly publicise the course of the trials in the public press' because 'collective farmers are not being mobilised to struggle with wrecking and its perpetuators'.[20] Trials in the provinces involved witnesses from the local population, which gave them a clear sense of legitimacy and of *carnival* that served to vent social tensions.[21] The Moscow trials served a very different purpose. They created tensions and insecurity by exposing mortal threats to the community.

Constructing a serious and credible threat so as to fan and direct society's fears is the purpose of a show trial. A successful trial provides a mobilisational narrative for society. Hence, identifying the threats transmitted to the audience is essential to understanding the trials. Stalin was

---

[16] *Ibid.*, p. 413.

[17] For materials on the confrontations between Radek and Pyatakov and Radek and Bukharin, see *Istochnik* 1 (2001).

[18] See Khlevniuk et al., *Stalin i Kaganovich. Perepiska*, pp. 642–3.

[19] On the trials in the provinces and Stalin's role, see: Sheila Fitzpatrick, 'How the Mice Buried the Cat: Scenes from the Great Purges of 1937 in the Russian Provinces', *The Russian Review* 3 (1993), 299–332; Roberta Manning, 'Massovaia operatsiia protiv kulakov i prestupnykh elementov: apogei Velikoi Chistki na Smolenshchina', in E. Kodin (ed.), *Stalinizm v rossiiskoi provintsii. Smolenskie arkhivnye dokumenty v prochtenii zarubezhnykh i rossiiskikh istorikov* (Smolensk: SGPU, 1999), pp. 230–54, and 'The Mass Operation against "Kulaks and Criminals": The Apogee of the Great Purges in Smolenshchina', paper delivered at the 2002 AAASS Convention. My thanks to Roberta for sharing this unpublished essay with me. For orders from Stalin regarding organising trials and prescribing verdicts, see: *Izvestiia*, 10 June 1992; Getty and Naumov, *The Road to Tevvor* pp. 454–62.

[20] As quoted in Manning, 'The Mass Operation against "Kulaks and Criminals" ', 18.

[21] On this point, see Fitzpatrick, 'How the Mice Buried the Cat'.

keenly aware of the power of propaganda to a successful show trial. He played an active role in directing, and in some case controlling, the presentation and transmission of the threat. Sometimes his intervention took the form of editing or ordering the revision of declarations about certain threats.[22] Sometimes it took the form of critiquing and making concrete suggestions about the form and content of a piece of propaganda. For example, following the January 1937 trial, the Comintern Executive Committee (ECCI), after much discussion, issued the resolution 'On carrying out the campaign against Trotskyism', which was meant to provide the fraternal parties with the correct line on the trials. Stalin was very critical of the Comintern Central Executive Committee's efforts, but not its political line: 'The resolution is nonsense. All of you there in the Comintern are playing right into the enemy's hands. There is no point in making a resolution; resolutions are binding. A letter to the parties would be better'.[23] Sometimes his interventions took the form of recommending that officials publicise the executions of convicted enemies in the local press.[24] At other times, he urged Party leaders to mobilise social groups in support of an outcome that had already been decided upon. Such was the case in June 1937, when Stalin sent the following telegram to Central Committee members and regional Party officials: 'In connection with the upcoming trial ... of Tukhachevsky, Yakir, Uborevich and the others, the Central Committee suggests that you organise meetings of workers ... peasants ... and soldiers to pass resolutions calling for the application of the supreme penalty'.[25] Perhaps most egregiously, Stalin ordered the local press to conduct a vigorous campaign against show trial defendants who had not yet been identified or arrested, and in support of the inevitable death penalty.[26]

Stalin played an active and direct role in the formulation and execution of show trials. But it bears repeating that the Moscow show trials, like all show trials, were complex undertakings that depended upon a large cast of devoted or compliant characters to be successful. Trials were not

---

[22] Such was the case, for example, involving the Central Committee of the Polish Communist Party's draft declarations declaring former Politburo member Jerzy Sochacki a provocateur, Chase, *Enemies within the Gates?*, pp. 119–20. Stalin also read the Comintern Executive Committee's resolution to dissolve the Polish Communist Party. *Ibid.*, pp. 286–9.

[23] *Ibid.*, pp. 201–5. That he had no problem with the ECCI resolution's political interpretation but quibbled with the form in which it appeared illustrates both Stalin's efforts to manage how the show trials' lessons were portrayed and the fact that many Party leaders had internalised the 'lessons' to be learned from the trials.

[24] This in relation to the defendants in the Andreevo *raion* 'wreckers' trial on 27 August 1937. *Izvestiia*, 10 June 1992, p. 7.

[25] *Ibid.* [26] *Ibid.*

created from whole cloth. Between a person's arrest and a trial, there were depositions, interrogations, confrontations with accusers or witnesses, confessions, the compilation of evidence and dossiers, and the various administrative and judicial preparations for the trials.[27] These were essential to the success of a trial and to conveying its legitimacy to the citizenry. Many Soviet leaders and citizens shared Stalin's views on the perceived dangers that threatened the USSR. Their beliefs enabled them to play active and reliable roles in organising or publicising the trials. Their public and private actions served to legitimise, fuel, and deepen political and societal fears.[28] Because the trials were the result of many people's efforts, finding a single label to define Stalin's precise role in the trials is difficult. He was, in varying degrees, an initiator, a director, an author, a publicist, an editor. In his public statements and those at closed meetings, he helped to construct the threats that provided the *raison d'être* of the trials. Given that he performed these roles and others, it is most appropriate to view Stalin as a producer.

The publication of trial transcripts in other languages conveys succinctly the importance that Stalin attached to publicising the lessons of these trials and the threats that they revealed.[29] The format of the published 'transcripts' changed over time. The publication for the August 1936 trial was not a transcript but rather a 'report of court proceedings' that included lengthy quotations from the court transcript. Transcripts were published for the January 1937 and March 1938 trials. Why the format changed is unclear. Nonetheless, these documents provide a consistent body of evidence that allow one to chart the ways in which the nature of the threat evolved over the course of the three trials. The ensuing discussion uses those texts to examine the evolving nature of the threats that the trials revealed.

---

[27] For an example of a portion of the processes and paperwork that preceded the August 1936 trial, see the materials in the Volkogonov Collection, Container 4, Papka 38, pp. 1–275, in the Manuscript Division of the Library of Congress, Washington, DC. My thanks to Oleg Ken for alerting me to these materials.

[28] For examples of shared beliefs, see Getty and Naumov, *The Road to Terror*; Chase, *Enemies within the Gates?*; Lewis Siegelbaum and Andrei K. Sokolov, *Stalinism as a Way of Life: A Narrative in Documents* (New Haven: Yale University Press, 2000).

[29] The transcripts as well as the many pamphlets written on aspects of the trials played an important role in transmitting the lessons of the trials to the outside world. See, for example, the ECCI directive 'On carrying out a campaign of enlightenment in connection with the trial of the "Bloc of Rights and Trotskyites"' that details in which languages the trial's transcripts were to be published, in full or in abridged form, and which comrades were to write 'pamphlets on the trial'. Rossiiskii gosudarstvennyi arkhiv sotsial'no-politicheskoi istorii (henceforth RGASPI) f. 495, op. 18, d. 1238, ll. 29–33; see also, Chase, *Enemies within the Gates?*, pp. 295–8.

Sixteen defendants appeared in the dock when the case of the Trotskyite-Zinovievite Terrorist Centre[30] opened on 19 August 1936. Among them were leading Zinovievites (Zinoviev, Kamenev, Yevdokimov, and Bakayev),[31] leading Trotskyites (I. N. Smirnov, Ter-Vaganyan, and Mrachkovsky), loyal adherents to one of those factions (Dreitzer, Holtzman, Reingold, and Pickel), and five foreigners who had been members of the German Communist Party (KPG) (Olberg, Berman-Yurin, David, M. Lurye, and N. Lurye). All five had been oppositionists and lived in the USSR at the time of their arrest. Several of the defendants had been previously convicted and came to the court from their cells. The key defendant – Trotsky – was not in the dock, but rather in exile in Norway.

As in all three of the Moscow trials, the defendants were of two types. There were the lead defendants. They were well-known people with very public histories of opposition, histories that were re-written to construct a threat. These defendants had repeatedly opposed, and been expelled from, the Party. Their longstanding history served to underscore the importance of conspiracy and made the charge that they had long been engaged in hostile conspiratorial activities credible. As defeated politicians who held no powerful position, they made very convenient defendants for a show trial. The other type of defendants were the 'direct agents', the co-conspirators who carried out the sinister plans. In each trial, their composition differed so as to give credibility to the alleged threat. Dreitzer, Holtzman, Reingold, Pickel, Olberg, Berman-Yurin, David, M. Lurye, and N. Lurye played this role in the 1936 trial. The charges were quite straightforward:

At the end of 1932 the Trotskyite and Zinovievite groups united and formed a united centre ... The principal condition for the union of these counter-revolutionary groups was their common recognition of individual terrorism against the leaders of the C.P.S.U. and the Soviet government ... [A]cting on direct instructions from *L. Trotsky* ... the united centre organised special terrorist groups, which prepared a number of practical measures for the assassination of Comrades *Stalin, Voroshilov, Kaganovich, Kirov, Orjonikidze, Zhdanov, Kossior, Postyshev* and others. One of these terrorist groups ... carried out the foul murder of Comrade S. M. Kirov on December 1, 1934.[32]

---

[30] All references will be to: People's Commissariat of Justice of the USSR, *Report of the Court Proceedings: The Case of the Trotskyite-Zinovievite Terrorist Centre*. (Moscow: People's Commissariat of Justice of the USSR, 1936). For consistency and ease of reference, this essay uses the official English-language translations of the three show trials.

[31] They had all been convicted in January 1935 for being the ideological and political leaders of the so-called Moscow Centre that bore 'moral and political responsibility' for Kirov's murder. They had been imprisoned since their conviction, as had Smirnov who had been previously arrested.

[32] *The Case of the Trotskyite-Zinovievite Terrorist Centre*, p. 11. Emphasis in the original.

Equally straightforward was the alleged motive: 'the only motive for organising the Troskyite-Zinovievite bloc was their striving to seize power at all costs'.[33] In short, the defendants were terrorists with no coherent political platform whose only reason for conspiring to assassinate the country's leaders was to gain personal power.

Given that Stalin helped to craft the indictment and list of defendants, it seems odd that he orchestrated a trial for political 'has beens' who lacked a coherent political platform. No less perplexing is the fact that Stalin was on vacation in Sochi during the trials. Being in Sochi created real and political distance between him and the trial. His being there also underscores the extent to which the success of the trials themselves depended upon others. Stalin did, nonetheless, receive regular summaries of the trial, usually from Yezhov and Kaganovich.[34]

While the defendants confessed to and were convicted of treason and terrorism, the trial's purpose was to highlight the threats that such people – unrepentant oppositionists turned enemy agents and terrorists – posed to Soviet society and to the Party. The explanatory power of the trial was quite limited. It revealed who had orchestrated 'the foul murder of comrade Kirov' and why, and announced that plans to murder Stalin and other leaders had been thwarted. In one sense, then, the trial provided closure. It might seem that having arrested and convicted the conspirators, the danger had passed. But the trial served two other purposes. On the one hand, it made clear that some former Trotskyists and Zinovievites were not simply unrepentant oppositionists, but had, in fact, become criminals who served foreign masters.[35] It also exposed an even more serious threat: double-dealers.

Double-dealers were especially dangerous. Such people said one thing and did another. Their word could not be trusted. Many of the defendants had been expelled from the Party, confessed to and repented for their errors, and sought forgiveness and readmission to the Party on one or more occasions. The Party had forgiven them. It had readmitted them into its ranks. But these double-dealers had betrayed the Party, betrayed their comrades, betrayed the country. Because they served foreign masters and enemies of the USSR, double-dealers posed a great danger to the nation. At Trotsky's instigation, they had formed conspiratorial networks for the purpose of murdering the nation's leaders while remaining trusted

---

[33] *Ibid.*, p. 12.

[34] For examples, see documents 744, 745, 752, 755 in Khlevniuk et al. (eds.), *Stalin i Kaganovich. Perepiska*, pp. 630–8.

[35] One month after the trial, the Politburo redefined Trotskyism in an even more dramatic manner. See below for its 28 September 1936 resolution announced on 'the Trotskyite-Zinovievite scoundrels'.

members of the Party. Some of the defendants had met personally with Trotsky or his son, Sedov. Some, like M. Lurye, confessed to working with Gestapo agents and to having received orders from disgraced KPG oppositionists.[36] The trial served to unmask these double-dealers and to warn the Party and society of the dangers such 'traitors' posed.

The trial conveyed two other important lessons. The first was that the alleged anti-Soviet conspiracies were quite complex and international in scope. Zinoviev, Kamenev, and Smirnov constituted the command staffs of two interlocking terrorist Centres: a Moscow Centre and a Leningrad Centre. Precisely because the Centres' leaders were in prison, Trotsky and his Gestapo allies needed direct agents and hence ran parallel organisations. It was the lesser-known defendants with oppositional pasts in the VKP(b) or the KPG (Berman-Yurin, David, Olberg, N. Lurye, M. Lurye) who served as the direct agents. Hence, the trial announced that former oppositionists and people with foreign ties, be they émigrés, refugees, visitors, or illegal aliens, posed a potential danger. Party committees responded by reviewing their membership files and compiling lists of former oppositionists and people with allegedly suspicious pasts or associations.[37] The defendants' confessions and convictions jolted Party organisations into scrutinising more closely their members, especially those who were foreign-born or who had been oppositionists. They exerted an even greater pressure on the commissions charged with verifying those members of fraternal parties who were living in the USSR.[38]

The second lesson was that the anti-Soviet conspiracy was, in fact, much wider than originally announced. During the course of the trial, the defendants named several prominent Party and state leaders, and military officers (Putna and Primakov). Vyshinsky ended the case for the prosecution by announcing that his office would investigate Tomsky, Rykov, Bukharin, Uglanov, Radek, Pyatakov, Serebryakov, and Sokolnikov.[39]

---

[36] *The Case of the Trotskyite-Zinovievite Terrorist Centre*, p. 75. The KPG oppositionists mentioned were Ruth Fischer and Arkady Maslow. For Fischer's views on her and Maslow's political activities, see Ruth Fischer, *Stalin and German Communism. A Study in the Origins of the State Party* (Cambridge, Mass.: Harvard University Press, 1948).

[37] For examples, see: the ECCI Cadres Department memorandum 'On Trotskyists and other hostile elements in the émigré community of the German CP', RGASPI f. 495, op.74, d. 124, ll. 11–31 (portions of which appear in Chase, *Enemies within the Gates?*, pp. 163–74); the ECCI organisation's 'List of VKP(b) members formerly in other parties, having Trotskyist and Rightist tendencies, as well as [those] having received party reprimands', RGASPI f. 546, op. 1, d. 376, ll. 30–6 (portions of which appear in Chase, *Enemies within the Gates?*, p. 178–84). Both documents are dated 4 September 1936.

[38] For a discussion of selected verification commissions' responses to the 1936 trial, see Chase, *Enemies within the Gates?*, pp. 187–90.

[39] *The Case of the Trotskyite-Zinovievite Terrorist Centre*, pp. 115–16. Of these, Radek, Pyatakov, Serebryakov, and Sokolnikov were defendants in the January 1937 trial.

The possibility that a wider conspiracy existed and that leading Party, state, and military officials might be members portended a more serious threat and future trials.

The role of the audience during the 1936 trial was quite simple. Its primary role was to bear witness to the defendants' perfidy and betrayal, a role made easier by the extensive newspaper and media coverage that the trial received. Such treacherous behaviour demanded that citizens be vigilant and learn how to detect and unmask double-dealers. Although Party committees, factory committees, and other organisations passed resolutions calling for the death penalty for the defendants, Party leaders, not the public, were the intended victims. But executing the defendants in response to the demands of a community betrayed served to include the audience and to demonstrate that double-dealers, terrorists, and traitors would be shown no mercy.

The very circumscribed role for the public suggests that the real audience for the August 1936 trial was the Party membership, especially the nomenklatura. All of the defendants were former Party members with oppositional pasts. Although it had been officially defeated in 1927–8, Trotskyism appeared in the 1936 trial as an active Party opposition, not as a rival party. The number of Trotskyists in the Soviet Communist Party was quite small. Stalin announced in February 1937 that there were only 'about 12,000 party members who sympathised with Trotsky. Here you see the total forces of the Trotskyist gentlemen'.[40] Why then did Stalin use the 1936 trial to sound the tocsin for a vigilance campaign against Trotskyists?

The answer lies less in what distinguished Trotskyism from Stalinism than in what they had in common. Adherents of both claimed to be the true heirs to the Leninist Party line, both spoke the language of Bolshevism and employed Bolshevik tactics, and both viewed reform socialists with a contempt comparable to that reserved for imperialists, the bourgeoisie, reactionaries, and fascists. It was, in fact, these shared attributes that made Trotsky and Trotskyism so menacing and feared among Stalinists. Trotsky could legitimately claim to offer a Leninist alternative to the USSR and Stalin. Trotsky had the international revolutionary credentials to use Bolshevik rhetoric and Leninist logic to attack the USSR's Stalinist policies. Precisely because he did so, Trotsky and his followers posed a threat far greater than their numbers suggest. As all Bolsheviks knew from the experience of 1917, numbers did not dictate who would win the hearts and minds of the revolutionary proletariat.

---

[40] As quoted in J. Arch Getty, *Origins of the Great Purges: The Soviet Communist Party Reconsidered, 1933–1938* (Cambridge: Cambridge University Press, 1985), p. 140.

Making Trotskyists so serious a threat without providing a precise political definition of what Trotskyism constituted in August 1936 suggests that their political 'crime' lay in having opposed the party line. In December 1936, Stalin was unequivocal about his distrust of former oppositionists: 'The word of a former oppositionist cannot be trusted'.[41] One of the trials' purposes was to explain why they could not be trusted. Toward that end, the trials sought to criminalise Trotskyist thought and link anyone associated with Trotsky to foreign threats to the USSR. As a result of the trial, the campaign against Trotskyism began to fuel and meld with a growing xenophobia, as a September 1936 resolution indicates: 'The Trotskyist-Zinovievite scoundrels ... must therefore now be considered foreign agents, spies, subversives, and wreckers representing the fascist bourgeoisie of Europe.'[42]

The Party nomenklatura responded appropriately by issuing calls for vigilance and a thorough review of Party membership rolls. Doing so was in their political interests. Had the alleged conspirators succeeded in murdering Stalin and his lieutenants, it was the members of the nomenklatura whose lives would have been most directly affected.

During the five months between the first two Moscow show trials, several significant events changed the nature of the threat that the January 1937 trial was to reveal. Some of these events were within Stalin's control. It was at the urging of Stalin and Zhdanov that Yezhov was appointed to head the NKVD. In December 1936, Yezhov reported to the Central Committee plenum 'on the counter-revolutionary activities of Trotskyists and rightist organisations and of future defendants Pyatakov, Sokolnikov, and Serebriakov in particular'.[43] On 16 December, Stalin discussed Sokolnikov's confessions with his closest lieutenants.[44] He helped to arrange face-to-face confrontations between future defendants.[45] He had distributed defendants' confessions to some comrades, apparently so as to prepare them for the political campaign that surrounded the trial.[46]

---

[41] Stalin made this comment at the 4 December 1936 meeting of the Central Committee plenum. Georgi Dimitrov recorded it in his diary. See the entry for 4 December 1936, Ivo Banac (ed.), *The Diary of Georgi Dimitrov, 1933–1949* (New Haven: Yale University Press, 2003), p. 38. Underlining in the original.

[42] RGASPI f. 17, op. 3, d. 981, l. 58, as cited in Getty and Naumov, *Road to Terror*, p. 273. See also *Izvestiia TsK KPSS* 5 (1989), 72.

[43] See the entry for 4 December 1936, Banac (ed.), *Diary of Georgi Dimitrov*, p. 38.

[44] See the entry for 16 December 1936, *Ibid.*, pp. 42–3. This entry records Dimitrov's attending a meeting in the Kremlin with the 'Five' – Stalin, Molotov, Kaganovich, Voroshilov, Ordzhonikidze.

[45] *Istochnik* 1 (2001).

[46] *Diary of Georgi Dimitrov*, entry for 11 January 1937. In this entry, Dimitrov records that he received copies of Radek's and Ustinov's confessions, as well as materials relating to Bukharin's confrontation with one of the defendants, apparently Sokolnikov.

While Stalin controlled aspects of the January 1937 trial, there were other realities that structured the trial and confessions that he could not control: the formation of the Anti-Comintern Pact in the autumn of 1936, the transformation of the Spanish Civil War into an international battle between fascist and anti-fascist forces, the USSR's military commitment to the Spanish Republic, the Kemerovo mine disaster (and a spate of other industrial accidents), the deepening of the USSR's economic downturn, and the onset of epidemics within the country's livestock herds. These events no doubt affected Stalin's view of the threats that the USSR faced and the nature of the threat that the January 1937 trial would reveal.

The January 1937 trial of the Anti-Soviet Trotskyite Centre differed from the first show trial in several significant ways, and the threats revealed by the trial changed accordingly. Whereas some of the lead defendants in the 1936 trial had been in prison for more than a year before the announcement of their trial, the defendants in the January trial still held prominent positions while Zinoviev and company were in the dock. Many were Party members until the time of their arrest. There were no foreigners among the defendants.[47] Nor were the defendants the powerless and defeated remnants of former oppositions. Although some had supported an opposition in the 1920s, they had since admitted their errors. From then until the 1936 trial, these defendants had been trusted comrades, who had been responsible for administering key sectors of the economy. Some were among the country's most powerful economic officials: Pyatakov was the deputy People's Commissar of Heavy Industry, Livshits was the People's Commissar of Railroads. The appearance of such powerful men in the dock sent the message that some high-ranking officials posed a serious threat to the economy.

The defendants in the August 1936 trial had been convicted for their roles in a clandestine terrorist organisation, the goal of which was to seize personal power. Those in the dock in January 1937 had allegedly engaged in far more sinister conspiracies. Although some were charged with 'the preparation of terrorist acts', specifically plans to assassinate Stalin and Molotov, the charge of terrorism paled in comparison to their alleged acts of espionage, diversion and wrecking. Pyatakov, Radek, Sokolnikov,

---

[47] Why there were no foreigners among the defendants given the prominence of the charge of espionage is unclear. Perhaps the presence of foreigners in the dock ran diplomatic risks. This might explain why Vyshinsky went to great pains to repeatedly remind the defendants in the 1937 and 1938 trials not to mention the name of representatives of foreign governments. There were two foreign-born defendants, Hrasche and Arnold. Both had renounced their homelands and taken Soviet citizenship, so they posed no chance of diplomatic problems.

Livshitz, and Serebryakov were the leaders of a so-called parallel centre, which had been a reserve centre 'formed on the direct instructions of *L. D. Trotsky* for [sic] the eventuality of the criminal activities of the Trotskyite-Zinovievite bloc being exposed'.[48] 'The main task which the parallel centre set for itself was the overthrow of the Soviet government with the object of changing the social and state system in the USSR'.[49] Specifically, the defendants were charged with seeking the restoration of capitalism, the dissolution of the collective and state farm systems, the leasing of Soviet enterprises to foreign capitalists, the undoing of all progressive wage and labour policies, and the granting of territorial concessions to the Germans and the Japanese. These defendants did not simply seek personal power, they had a coherent platform. Under Trotsky's direction, they sought to overthrow Soviet socialism, to restore capitalism, and to partially dismember the USSR.

According to their confessions, the defendants, and Trotsky, realised that the only way to achieve their goal was 'as a result of the defeat of the USSR in war'. Hence they had to weaken the economy before the war, to 'hasten the clash between the USSR and Germany', and to adopt 'a defeatist attitude in this war'.[50] Unlike the Trotskyite-Zinovievite bloc that had links to the Gestapo, the leaders of the parallel centre, acting on orders from and in concert with Trotsky, were direct agents of German fascism and Japanese imperialism.[51]

The division of labour among the lead conspirators was relatively straightforward. Those who held key economic positions within the national government (Pyatakov, Serebryakov, and Livshitz) used them to weaken the Soviet economy, while Sokolnikov and Radek used their positions to meet and conspire with the 'representatives of certain foreign states'.[52] The other defendants played a role similar to that of the secondary defendants in the August 1936 trials, acting as the direct agents of the chief conspirators and of foreign powers. These 'agents of the German and Japanese intelligence services' carried on espionage, 'wrecking and diversive acts in socialist enterprises and on the railways, particularly in enterprises of importance for the defense of the country'.[53] The accused had ordered the explosion in the Kemerovo mine disaster, the wrecking of troop trains, the sabotage of chemical enterprises, and the planning of 'bacteriological' contamination of troop trains, as well as the transmission

---

[48] People's Commissariat of Justice of the USSR, *Report of the Court Proceedings in the Case of the Anti-Soviet Trotskyite Centre* (Moscow: People's Commissariat of Justice of the USSR, 1937), p. 5.
[49] *Ibid.*   [50] *Ibid.*, pp. 9–10.   [51] *Ibid.*, p. 10.   [52] *Ibid.*, p. 18.   [53] *Ibid.*

of important production and construction information to the Germans and Japanese.

In the 1936 trial, there had been only one victim – Kirov – and the audience had been consigned to the role of indignant observers who demanded 'justice'. The defendants in the January 1937 trial had confessed to much more murderous actions that constituted a much greater threat to the audience itself. They confessed to engaging in wrecking and other activities that had resulted in the deaths or injury of scores of working people and service men. In this trial, the audience, either as Soviet citizens whose motherland was in danger, or as victims of the 'enemies" wrecking, or as hardworking people whose standard of living suffered because of the defendants' sinister actions, had become the collective victim. As Vyshinsky's final words to the court made clear, he was vividly aware of the role that the audience played in this trial:

I am not the only accuser! Comrade Judges, I feel that by my side here stand the victims of the crimes and of these criminals: on crutches, maimed, half alive, and perhaps legless, like Comrade Nagovitsina, the switch-girl at Chusovskaia Station, who ... lost both her legs in averting a train disaster organised by these people! I do not stand here alone! I feel that by my side here stand the murdered and maimed victims of these frightful crimes ... I do not stand here alone! The victims may be in their graves, but I feel that they are standing here beside me, pointing at the dock, at you, the accused, with their mutilated arms ... I am not the only accuser! I am joined in my accusation by the whole of the people![54]

Party members constituted a special group within the audience. Pyatakov, Radek, Serebryakov, and others had been prominent Party members at the time of their arrest. Their appearance in the dock sent the message that defeated oppositionists were not the only ones to pose a threat: Party leaders themselves could do so. Vigilance took on a new form as Stalin called on the 'little people', the Party rank-and-file, workers and collective farmers, to unmask enemies regardless of their rank. And the 'little people' responded, in many cases by denouncing their superiors in public or in private. More so than the 1936 and 1938 trials, the 1937 trial provided a rationale and opportunity for popular participation in the repression. Stalin's use of the trial to scapegoat economic officials for the problems afflicting the economy and to legitimise popular criticisms of powerful Party members suggests how important the selection of the charges and defendants was to the show trials' (and Stalin's) success.

---

[54] *Ibid.*, p. 516.

The January trial underscored even more dramatically than the 1936 trial the danger posed by double-dealers. These defendants had held powerful positions in the economy up to the moment of their arrest. They confessed to having used their positions to undermine the socialist economy. By so doing, they had betrayed the trust of the Party and the nation. Their double-dealing was the theme to which Vyshinsky returned repeatedly. Consider the image of the double-dealer that he conjured in but a single paragraph in his concluding speech for the prosecution:

> The Trotskyites went underground, they donned the mask of repentance and pretended that they had disarmed. Obeying the instructions of Trotsky, Pyatakov, and the other leaders of this gang of criminals, pursuing a policy of duplicity, camouflaging themselves, they again penetrated into the Party ... even managed to creep into responsible positions of state ... [where they plied] their old Trotskyite, anti-Soviet wares in their secret apartments, together with arms, codes, passwords, connections and cadres.[55]

Vyshinsky continually underscored the defendants' duplicity. He asserted that he himself did not know if defendant Rataichak 'is a German or a Polish spy, but that he is a spy there cannot be any doubt'. He stressed Arnold had no fewer than five aliases,[56] and that Hrasche had 'at least' three citizenships. He claimed that Pyatakov

> has persistently and skillfully camouflaged himself, has always been an old enemy of Leninism, an old enemy of our Party ... 1915, 1916, 1917, 1918, 1919, 1921, 1923, 1926, and 1927 – for more than a decade Pyatakov constantly defended the Trotskyist position, waged an open struggle against Lenin, against the general line of the Party.[57]

One of the major purposes of the show trials was to underscore the danger and to unmask double-dealers. Vyshinsky repeatedly crowed about the success of the trial in achieving this goal: '[The accused] have been caught red-handed. The mask has been torn from their faces once and for all. They stand exposed as enemies of the people ... agents of foreign intelligence services'.[58] But as in the 1936 trial, the unmasking of the alleged double-dealers in the January 1937 trial offered little comfort that all 'enemies' had been unmasked and brought to justice. On the contrary, new names arose during the trial and investigations into allegations against comrades, like Bukharin and Rykov, ensued. The

---

[55] *Ibid.*, p. 464.
[56] Arnold's defence counsel offered little insight into who the mysterious Arnold was: 'who is Arnold ... whom did he serve?' his defence counsel asked. 'This question arouses doubts even in me, his Counsel for Defence ... The nationality of Arnold is likewise unknown.' *Ibid.*, p. 525.
[57] *Ibid.*, pp. 475–6.   [58] *Ibid.*, p. 479.

conspirators in the January 1937 trial may have been unmasked, they may have confessed, but the conspiracy had not yet been uprooted.

The explanatory power of the January 1937 trial was substantial. It provided an explanation for the economic problems and hardships that the country and its citizens faced. Its purpose was to convey that the economic policies of the leadership and state laws and regulations (indeed, the socialist system itself) were fundamentally correct. Had the system not been sound, the conspirators would not have lacked a social base of support, would not have had to engage in wrecking to engender popular discontent, and would not have had to conspire with hostile foreign powers to weaken the system. The trial also made clear that Stalin and his lieutenants would leave no stone unturned in their struggle to root out enemy agents and double-dealers. But they could not do it alone. 'Real Bolsheviks' and good Soviet citizens had to participate in unmasking these enemies by being vigilant and exposing double-dealers and suspicious activities. In this way, the January 1937 trial significantly transformed the roles of the audience, which henceforth was cast in the roles of victim and avenger.

The events of the fourteen months between the January 1937 trial and the March 1938 trial of the Anti-Soviet 'Bloc of Rights and Trotskyites' contributed to a significant widening and deepening of the alleged conspiracies against the USSR. The arrest of many of the country's military officers, Party leaders, and key economic personnel, as well as the unleashing by the Politburo of the so-called kulak and national operations and the setting of quotas to be arrested and executed, exemplify the extent to which a conspiratorial explanation of reality had transformed the country. By the time that Bukharin, Rykov, Yagoda, and the other eighteen defendants stepped into the dock in March 1938, the nature of the threat that the trial sought to reveal had changed into something profoundly different from its predecessors.

The indictment alleged that the twenty-one defendants had, 'on instructions of the intelligence services of foreign states hostile to the Soviet Union, formed a conspiratorial group named the "bloc of Rights and Trotskyites" '. This bloc, which constituted 'varieties of one and the same phenomenon',[59] had allegedly 'united within its ranks underground anti-Soviet groups of Trotskyites, Rights, Zinovievites, Mensheviks, Socialist Revolutionaries, and bourgeois nationalists of the Ukraine, Azerbaijan, Georgia, Armenia, Byelorussia, and the Central Asiatic

---

[59] People's Commissariat of Justice of the USSR, *Report of the Court Proceedings in the Case of the Anti-Soviet 'Bloc of Rights and Trotskyites'* (Moscow: People's Commissariat of Justice of the USSR, 1938), p. 639.

Republics'.[60] The purpose of the trial was to prove that 'there is a world conspiracy of reaction and fascism directed against the Land of Socialism'.[61] It was a 'world conspiracy' played out on a world stage: 'The "Bloc of Rights and Trotskyites" ... is only an advance detachment of international fascism ... with whose aid fascism is operating in various countries, primarily in Spain and China ... [It is] the very same as the Fifth column, the POUM, the KuKluxKlan'.[62] The trial presented the Trotskyists as totally unprincipled enemies of Soviet power. 'Trotskyist' had become an elastic shorthand term for all of the perceived enemies of the USSR.

It was a vast conspiracy indeed, a conspiracy that united parties and groups that represented very different ideologies and had fought each other for many years. Creating a conspiracy of former rivals and enemies served to highlight Trotsky's and the defendants' political bankruptcy. Each of the men in the dock had been carefully chosen to personify one or more of the charges. The allegation of a conspiracy of former rivals united only by a common enemy speaks volumes about the Manichean and conspiratorial worldviews of its architects. By claiming that an omnipresent conspiracy threatened the country, the trial revealed the extent to which Stalin and the leadership understood and framed politics as conspiratorial behavior.[63]

By March 1938, there was ample reason for Soviet leaders to fear war. Japanese aggression in the Soviet Far East and in China, the Spanish fascists' victories over the army of the Spanish Republic and the International Brigades, Germany's increasingly menacing policies and its occupation of Austria, and the anaemic reaction of Western powers to these events and the failure of the Soviet efforts to achieve collective security provided sufficient cause for concern in Moscow. Yet such realities differ immensely from a world conspiracy.

The foreign intelligence services for which the accused worked had also changed. The 1936 trial had 'proven' that the accused had become agents

---

[60] *Ibid.*, p. 5.

[61] Such was the formulation in the Comintern's March 1938 directive 'On carrying out a campaign of enlightenment in connection with the trial of the "Bloc of Rights and Trotskyites"', RGASPI f. 495, op. 18, d. 1238, l. 29. The directive is reproduced in Chase, *Enemies within the Gates?*, pp. 295–8. Emphasis in the original.

[62] *The Case of the Anti-Soviet 'Bloc of Rights and Trotskyites'*, p. 629. In February 1937, the journal *Communist International* asserted that 'the struggle against Trotskyism is a component part of the struggle for a Republican Spain'. *Communist International* (February 1937), 108.

[63] On the importance of viewing politics as conspiracy, see Gabor T. Rittersporn, 'The Omnipresent Conspiracy: On Soviet Imagery of Politics and Social Relations in the 1930s', in J. Arch Getty and Roberta T. Manning (eds.), *Stalinist Terror: New Perspectives* (New York: Cambridge University Press, 1993), pp. 99–115.

of Trotsky who had links to the Gestapo. The 1937 trial had 'proven' that the defendants had engaged in anti-Soviet activities for the German and Japanese intelligence services. The 1938 trial 'proved' that the defendants had served many masters for many years. According to the indictment, Krestinsky had been a German spy since 1921, Rosengoltz had been a German spy since 1923 and a British spy since 1926, Rakovsky had been a British spy since 1924 and a Japanese spy since 1934, Sharangovich had been a Polish spy since 1921, and Grinko had been a Polish and German spy since 1932. One of the reasons for their espionage was that foreign governments paid a 'subsidy for counter-revolutionary Trotskyite work'.[64] Germany, Japan, Poland, and England were presented as the most active foreign enemies of Soviet power.[65] Why Stalin allowed the defendants to testify to such long service as foreign agents is unclear as it raised questions about how they went undetected for so long.[66]

Like those in the 1937 trial, these 'spies' and agents of hostile governments had a political platform. They, too, sought the overthrow of the socialist system and the restoration of capitalism. But unlike the earlier defendants, these men sought the large-scale 'dismemberment 'of the USSR. Germany was to get Ukraine, Poland was to get Belorussia, England was to get the Central Asian republics, Japan was to get the Maritime Region, and so on. They conspired to destroy socialism and to destroy the Soviet nation.

That these men had hidden their espionage for so many years high-lighted the dangers posed by double-dealers. All of the defendants con-fessed to having been longstanding double-dealers. For example, Vyshinsky went to great lengths to expose Bukharin's longstanding oppos-ition to the Party, opposition that dated to his role in the attempted overthrow of the Soviet government and the attempted assassination of Lenin in 1918. Yagoda, too, had long been a double-dealer: 'All my life I wore a mask. I posed as an irreconcilable Bolshevik. Actually, I never was a Bolshevik in the real sense'.[67] In his summation, Vyshinsky stressed

[64] *The Case of the Anti-Soviet 'Bloc of Rights and Trotskyites'*, p. 9.

[65] According to V. Khaustov, 'Deiatel'nost' organov gosudarstvennoi bezopastnosti NKVD SSSR (1934–1941gg.)', Ph.D. diss., Akademiia FSB RF (1997), pp. 315–18, 265,039 of the 1,575,269 people arrested in 1937–8 were charged with being spies for foreign governments. This does not mean that the accused were foreign born. But this figure probably underestimates the proportion of foreigners arrested because many foreigners who were arrested were charged with other crimes.

[66] Many members of the Central Committee of the Polish Communist Party also confessed to having engaged in anti-Soviet activities for a long time, in some cases dating back to 1917. Why such a confession was essential is unclear. For a discussion of this, see Chase, *Enemies within the Gates?*, pp. 266–73. Dimitrov's notes on the 'confessions' of these Poles can be found in RGASPI f. 495, op. 74, d. 411, ll. 1–62.

[67] *The Case of the Anti-Soviet 'Bloc of Rights and Trotskyites'*, p. 691.

the threat that double-dealers posed and highlighted the 'really tremendous historic significance' of the trial:

> The trial sums up the results of the struggle against the Soviet state and Party of Lenin-Stalin waged by people who … spent the whole of their lives behind masks … who … served not the revolution and the proletariat, but the counter-revolution and the bourgeoisie, who deceived the Party and the Soviet government in order the more conveniently to do their black work of treachery …
>
> By means of deception, hypocrisy, and double-dealing these detestable criminals succeeded in postponing the hour of their exposure until very recently. But this hour has arrived, and the criminals stand exposed, exposed completely and to the end.[68]

One is tempted to read into Vyshinsky's comments a foreshadowing of closure. Whether or not that was the case, the 1938 trial differed from the first two in another notable way. Whereas the first two trials had portended the unmasking of conspiracies for which people would subsequently be arrested, the 1938 trial reflected the types of charges that had driven the mass repression since June 1937. These charges reflected and encapsulated Stalin's and the NKVD's fears of enemy conspiracies and their belief that conspirators had penetrated important sectors of Soviet society.

The trial provided explanations for the mass arrests that had engulfed the country since mid-1937. Military battles with the Japanese in the Far East, Germany's increasingly aggressive foreign policy, especially in Spain and Austria (the Anschluss occurred during the 1938 trial), and Britain's active role in opposing intervention in Spain no doubt contributed to the inclusion of these countries in the trial. The fear that Red Army officers had conspired with hostile powers deepened the anxieties about alleged spies conspiring to weaken the country's military might. Indeed, these fears were both cause and effect of the so-called national operations. Beginning in August 1937, the Politburo authorised the NKVD to begin the national operations, which resulted in the wholesale arrest of people based exclusively on their nationality.[69] The Polish operation was the most virulent

---

[68] *Ibid.*, p. 637.

[69] On the Polish operation, see 'Ot pol'skoi komissii obshchestva "Memorial"', in A. E. Gurianov (ed.), *Repressii protiv poliakov i pol'skikh grazhdan* (Moscow: Zvenia, 1997); V. N. Khaustov, 'Iz predystorii massovykh repressii protiv Pol'iakov. Seredina 1930–xgg.', in *ibid.*, pp. 10–21; and N. V. Petrov and A. B. Roginskii, '"Pol'skaia operatsiia", NKVD 1937–1938gg.', in *ibid.*, pp. 22–43. On the German operation, see I. L. Shcherbakov (ed.), *Nakazannyi narod: po materialam konferentsii 'Repressii protiv rossiiskikh nemtsev v Sovetskom Soiuze v kontekste sovetskoi natsionalnoi politiki'* (Moscow: Zvenia, 1999), especially the essays by V. Khaustov, 'Repressii protiv sovetskikh nemtsev do nachala massovoi operatsii 1937g.', pp. 75–83, and N. Okhotin and A. Roginskii, 'Iz istorii "nemetskoi operatsii" NKVD 1937–1938gg.', pp. 35–75. On the Finnish and

and destructive of these.[70] Stalin had long been suspicious of the Polish Party and Yezhov believed that the Polish Party was a 'major supplier of spies', some of whom had penetrated the NKVD itself.[71] These beliefs no doubt account for the inclusion of espionage for Poland among the charges. The forcible relocation and arrest of people from the borderlands throughout the decade needed to be explained. The allegation that leaders from some border regions (e.g., Ikramov, Khodjayev, Sharangovich) conspired to dismember the USSR provided this explanation.[72]

The 1938 trial offered explanations for other problems as well. For example, Grinko confessed to using his position in the Commissariat of Finance 'to dislocate the economy and thus rouse among the population discontent ... over taxes ... bad savings banks service [sic], delays in paying wages, etc'.[73] Zelensky confessed to widespread wrecking within Tsentrosoiuz, while Rozengoltz did the same in the area of foreign trade. The government's economic policies were sound. It was the hostile actions of wreckers such as these that created problems.

How had these 'sworn enemies of Soviet power', this 'rabid and desperate gang of felonious criminals', managed to operate undetected for so long?[74] The answer to this question provided an overarching explanation for many of the hostile activities exposed by the trials. Yagoda proved to be 'one of the biggest plotters, one of the foremost enemies of Soviet power, one of the most brazen traitors ... [It] was Yagoda himself, who instead of directing our glorious intelligence service to promote the interests of the Soviet people ... tried to turn it against our people ... Yagoda was exposed'.[75] Yagoda also confessed to having organised Kirov's murder ('Kirov was assassinated by the direct decision of the "Bloc of Rights and Trotskyites"')[76] and to planning 'the murder of Comrade N. I. Yezhov by means of a poison specially prepared for the purpose'.[77] Only Yagoda's removal as head of the NKVD ended these terrorist activities.

Finnic operations, see Michael Gelb, '"Karelian Fever": The Finnish Immigrant Community during Stalin's Purges', *Europe-Asia Studies* 6 (1993), 1091–116; Michael Gelb, 'The Western Finnic Minorities and the Origins of the Stalinist Nationalities Deportation', *Nationalities Papers* 2 (1996), 237–68; and Michael Gelb, 'An Early Soviet Ethnic Deportation: The Far-Eastern Koreans', *The Russian Review* 3 (1995), 389–412. See also Terry Martin, 'The Origins of Soviet Ethnic Cleansing', *The Journal of Modern History* 70 (December 1998), 813–61.

[70] The spring 1937 confessions by members of the Polish Central Committee that they had conspired against the USSR (since 1917 in some cases) helped to fuel the Polish operation. On this, see RGASPI f. 495, op. 74, d. 411, ll. 1–62 (portions of which appear in Chase, *Enemies within the Gates?*, pp. 266–73).

[71] On this, see: Chase, *Enemies within the Gates?*, pp. 103, 107, 122–5, 235; Getty and Naumov, *Road to Terror*, pp. 560–3.

[72] For a discussion, see Martin, 'Soviet Ethnic Cleansing', pp. 813–61.

[73] *The Case of the Anti-Soviet 'Bloc of Rights and Trotskyites'*, p. 18.   [74] *Ibid.*, p. 638.

[75] *Ibid.*, p. 693.   [76] *Ibid.*, p. 678.   [77] *Ibid.*, p. 28.

The audience for the 1938 trial also grew dramatically. As in 1936 and 1937, the nation was the audience. In both trials, 'the whole people' demanded justice. In the 1937 and 1938 trials, the Soviet people had been victims of the defendants' villainous activities and 'dark deeds'. The accused had betrayed the nation, they had sabotaged 'our national economy'. 'The entire people see what these monsters are'. And as in the previous trials, Vyshinsky cast the audience as participating in demanding justice: 'Our whole people, from young to old, is awaiting and demanding one thing: the traitors and spies who were selling our country to the enemy must be shot like dirty dogs'.[78]

Precisely because the defendants were the agents of international fascism, there was also a larger international audience. Vyshinsky stated it directly so that the international press corps at the trial could hear it: 'The exposure of the "bloc" ... is of enormous importance not only for our Socialist revolution, but also for the whole international proletariat ... for the cause of peace throughout the world ... for the whole of human culture ... That is why this trial is being followed with bated breath by the working people throughout the world'.[79] On the battlefields in Spain, China, and the Far East, the international audience also became a victim. In his closing remarks, he reminded the judges that 'our people and all honest people throughout the world are waiting for your just verdict'.[80]

The 1938 trial provided one final explanation much more explicitly than had the two earlier trials: Stalin was the people's defender and hope. In the first two trials, Stalin's name appeared infrequently and usually as a potential victim. In 1938, Vyshinsky cast him in a different role. Vyshinsky's final words to the court convey this new role and Stalin's relationship to the audience very clearly:

Time will pass. The graves of these hateful traitors will grow over with weeds and thistles, they will be covered with the eternal contempt of honest Soviet citizens, of the entire Soviet people. But over us, over our happy country, the sun will shine with its luminous rays as bright and as joyous as before. Over the road cleared of the last scum and filth of the past, we, our people, with our beloved leader and teacher, the great Stalin, at our head, will march as before onwards and onwards, towards Communism![81]

The three Moscow show trials defined what Stalin and his lieutenants perceived to be the major threats to Soviet society. In some respects, the threats seem to have remained unchanged. The defendants were internal manifestations and the direct agents of the external threats to society.

---

[78] *Ibid.*, pp. 696–7.   [79] *Ibid.*, p. 629.   [80] *Ibid.*, p. 697.   [81] *Ibid.*, p. 697.

Many had been former oppositionists. All were double-dealers. But over the course of the trials, the threats changed markedly. In 1936, the major threats were terrorists, the 'murderers' of Kirov and those who planned to assassinate the country's leaders for the purpose of seizing personal power. In 1937, the primary threat came from wreckers, spies, and saboteurs in the service of Trotsky, Germany, and Japan, who sought to weaken the Soviet economy on the eve of a war. By 1938, the defendants were the vanguard for a 'world conspiracy' against the USSR. They were spies, wreckers, and saboteurs who sought to overthrow Soviet socialism, restore capitalism, and dismember the USSR for their foreign masters: Trotsky, Germany, Japan, Poland, and Britain. With each trial, the dimensions of the threat to the USSR posed by capitalist encirclement and their double-dealing agents escalated.

Show trials exist to show the community who or what threatens it and how to recognise and unmask an enemy. Their purpose is to teach the citizenry about real or perceived dangers, and to direct the people's anger. The Moscow show trials of 1936, 1937, and 1938 did just that. In so doing, they also provide insights into how Stalin understood and constructed threats, and into his conspiratorial understanding of politics in the late 1930s. As the producer of the trials, he pushed the idea of politics as conspiracy to the centre stage. Not only did the trials define the nature and dimensions of the threat facing the USSR, they also provided a mobilisational narrative that showed citizens on what and whom to focus their vigilance. Precisely because the gravest threat emanated from carefully crafted conspiracies of double-dealers, that is from threats that were not easy to identify, the mobilisational narrative actually empowered local actors, be they citizens or local NKVD officials, to ferret out these enemy agents from their midst. Stalin, therefore, used his power to define the threats, but left it to local officials and the 'little people' to identify precisely who posed a threat. Once identified, local NKVD officials used 'a series of meticulous interrogations' to obtain confessions, which 'proved' that the threats were real. In this way, the show trials of 1936–8 played a crucial role in defining, and circumscribing, political attitudes and behaviours in the late 1930s.

13 Stalin as symbol: a case study of the personality cult and its construction

David Brandenberger

In 1956, N. S. Khrushchev denounced Stalin's cult of personality as a psychosis having little connection to Soviet ideology as a whole. Arguing that the cult 'took on such monstrous proportions because Stalin himself supported the glorification of his own person, using all available methods,' Khrushchev illustrated his contention with reference to Stalin's official *Short Biography*.[1] Few since have questioned this characterisation of the cult, in part because of the difficulty of reconciling the promotion of a tsar-like figure with the egalitarian ideals of Soviet socialism.

Although the cult of personality certainly owed something to Stalin's affinity for self-aggrandisement, modern social science literature suggests that it was designed to perform an entirely different ideological function. Personality cults promoting charismatic leadership are typically found in developing societies where ruling cliques aspire to cultivate a sense of popular legitimacy.[2] Scholars since Max Weber have observed that charismatic leadership plays a particularly crucial role in societies that are either poorly integrated or lack regularised administrative institutions. In such situations, loyalty to an inspiring leader can induce even the most fragmented polities to acknowledge the authority of the central state despite the absence of a greater sense of patriotism, community, or rule

Research for this chapter was supported by the International Research and Exchanges Board (IREX), with funds provided by the National Endowment for the Humanities and the United States Department of State, which administers the Russian, Eurasian, and East European Research Program (Title VIII). It has benefited from comments by Katia Dianina, Loren Graham, A. M. Dubrovskii, Adam Ulam, and participants in the 2003 conference of the Study Group on the Russian Revolution 'Stalin: Power, Policy, and Political Values.'
[1] '"O kul'te lichnosti i ego posledstviiakh": Doklad Pervogo sekretaria TsK KPSS tov. Khrushcheva N. S. XX s"ezdu Kommunisticheskoi partii Sovetskogo Soiuza,' *Izvestiia TsK KPSS* 3 (1989), 157. Despite the influential nature of Khrushchev's analysis, it is doubtful that he actually subscribed to such a view. P. N. Pospelov, his ghost-writer, certainly understood the cult's function, having been one of its chief architects.
[2] See Immanuel Wallerstein, *Africa – The Politics of Independence: An Interpretation of Modern African History* (New York: Vintage Books, 1961), p. 99; Clifford Geertz, *Local Knowledge: Further Essays in Interpretive Anthropology* (New York: Basic Books, 1983), pp. 121–48.

of law.[3] The cult performed precisely such a function in the USSR during the interwar years, serving – in the words of one commentator – as an unifying mechanism at a time when 'most of the components of civil society or of the modern state were missing: a reliable bureaucracy, a unitary consistent notion of citizenship or polity ... or even a sense of psychological inclusion'.[4]

Of course, this view of the personality cult is a distinctly modern one, grounded in social anthropology and cross-cultural analysis. Yet Stalin seems to have had a similar understanding of the cult's role in Soviet society. In the mid-1930s, he commented to M. A. Svanidze that 'the people need a tsar, i.e., someone to revere and in whose name to live and labour'.[5] Shortly thereafter, Stalin elaborated on this point with Leon Feuchtwanger, contending that the cult did not focus personally on him so much as on his role as the personification of socialist state-building in the USSR.[6] This conflation of the cult with broader Soviet propaganda efforts became so routine over time that Stalin eventually assigned his own *Short Biography* a central role in the Party catechism.[7] Such gestures, despite their obvious immodesty, reveal that that the cult was designed to serve as a mechanism for political mobilisation by advancing a larger-than-life hero capable of embodying the power, legitimacy and appeal of the Soviet 'experiment'.

Although a connection has long been posited between the cult and the idea of charismatic leadership,[8] this is the first investigation of its kind to focus tightly on the question of agency within the Stalinist ideological establishment. It links the emergence of the Stalin cult to the party's inability to rally popular support by more orthodox Marxist-Leninist

---

[3] Max Weber, *Economy and Society: An Outline of Interpretive Sociology*, ed. Guenther Roth and Claus Wittich (New York: Bedminster Press, 1968), III, pp. 1111–26.

[4] J. Arch Getty, 'The Politics of Stalinism', in Alec Nove (ed.), *The Stalin Phenomenon* (London: Weidenfeld and Nicolson, 1993), p. 119.

[5] 25 April 1935 diary entry published in Iu. G. Murin and V. N. Denisov (eds.), *Iosif Stalin v ob"iatiiakh sem'i: iz lichnogo arkhiva. Sbornik dokumentov* (Moscow: Rodina, 1993), p. 176.

[6] Lion Feikhtvanger (Leon Feuchtwanger), *Moskva 1937 goda* (Moscow: Khudozhestvennaia literatura, 1937), pp. 64–5.

[7] Rossiiskii gosudarstvennyi arkhiv sotsial'no-politicheskoi istorii (henceforth RGASPI) f. 629, op. 1, d. 54, l. 23.

[8] See Getty, 'The Politics of Stalinism,' p. 119; Moshe Lewin, 'Stalin in the Mirror of the Other', in Ian Kershaw and Moshe Lewin (eds.), *Stalinism and Nazism: Dictatorships in Comparison* (Cambridge: Cambridge University Press, 1997), pp. 107–34; Sarah Davies, *Popular Opinion in Stalin's Russia: Terror, Propaganda, and Dissent* (Cambridge: Cambridge University Press, 1997), pp. 163, 167; Jeffrey Brooks, *Thank You, Comrade Stalin! Soviet Public Culture from Revolution to Cold War* (Princeton: Princeton University Press, 1999), p. 59; Sheila Fitzpatrick, *Everyday Stalinism* (New York: Oxford University Press, 1999), p. 24.

means during the mid-to-late 1920s. In the context of failed grain procurement campaigns, the 1927 war scare and difficulties associated with the
First Five-Year Plan, the cult – much like party's subsequent indulgence in
populism and russocentrism during the so-called Great Retreat – is best
seen as a desperate attempt to mobilise a society that was too poorly
educated to grasp the philosophical tenets of the Party line.[9] Blaming the
ineffectiveness of indoctrinational efforts on the abstraction of early Soviet
propaganda, Party ideologists after 1929 turned to the Stalin cult as a new
way of bolstering popular loyalty to the Party and state.

The construction of Stalin's official biography provides an ideal case
study for appreciating the charismatic dimensions of the cult of personality.
Not only was the *Short Biography* a seminal propaganda text of its day, but
its publication history dovetailed with the rise and fall of the cult itself.
Moreover, Stalin's biographers left behind a detailed paper trail at a time
when Soviet publishing houses' routine destruction of manuscripts and
correspondence swept away most traces of the cult's internal dynamics.[10]
But perhaps most important is the fact that biography as a genre lies very
close to the heart of the personality cult. One of the most ancient forms of
literary composition, its pedigree dates back to early religious hagiography.
In modern times, biography has come to enjoy almost unparalleled popularity within non-fictional literature because of its compelling subjects, its
emphasis on temperament, character and accomplishment, and its tight
narrative focus on a single protagonist. Few other genres, it would seem,
are so suited to the promotion of charismatic authority.[11] Ultimately, the
fact that both Stalin and Khrushchev singled out the *Short Biography* as
epitomising the very essence of the personality cult makes this text an ideal
vehicle for the ensuing investigation.

[9] On this shift from materialism to populism, see David Brandenberger, *National
Bolshevism: Stalinist Mass Culture and the Formation of Modern Russian National Identity,
1931–1956* (Cambridge: Harvard University Press, 2002), chs. 1–3.

[10] Two models pervade the secondary literature on the inner workings of the cult: George
Orwell's depiction of an efficient, totalitarian monolith in *Nineteen Eighty-Four* and
Khrushchev's image of Stalin as the cult's meticulous editor-in-chief in the Secret
Speech. See Roy Medvedev, *Let History Judge: The Origins and Consequences of Stalinism*,
(New York: Columbia University Press, 1989), pp. 817–19; D. A. Volkogonov, *Triumf i
tragediia: Politicheskii portret I. V. Stalina* (Moscow: Novosti, 1989), I, p. 387; Arkady
Belinikov and Max Hayward in M. Dewhirst and R. Farrel (eds.), *The Soviet Censorship*
(Metuchen: Scarecrow Press, 1973), p. 17. This study reveals the Stalin cult to have been
rife with political intrigue, and at least as ad hoc and poorly organised as other major
projects of the era. Stalin's own participation in the cult turns out to have been no more
consistent. While his role is best described as supervisory, such a description fails to capture
the arbitrariness of his involvement.

[11] The arts may rival biography in this regard. See Evgenii Gromov, *Stalin: Vlast' i iskusstvo*
(Moscow: Respublika, 1998); Jan Plamper, 'The Stalin Cult in the Visual Arts,
1929–1953' (Ph.D. diss., University of California at Berkeley, 2001).

Although commentary on Stalin was not uncommon in the USSR in the years following the October 1917 Revolution, it was not until almost a decade later that the compilation of several hundred descriptive profiles of leading Bolsheviks for the *Granat Encyclopedic Dictionary* necessitated the production of a serious biographical statement.[12] I. P. Tovstukha, a secretary of Stalin's closely associated with the Marx-Engels-Lenin Institute (IMEL), drafted the manuscript. The final result, describing Stalin's career through 1924, boasted a narrative which – if almost entirely fictional – was at least quite accessible. It appeared in 1927, both in the encyclopedia, and as a separate fourteen-page brochure, complete with frontispiece, entitled *Joseph Vissarionovich Stalin: A Short Biography*. Published in large, bold type in a modest print run of 50,000, this pamphlet was a relatively unassuming production.[13]

Slightly enlarged and re-edited to cover the 1924–8 period, Tovstukha's biography resurfaced in 1929 during the commemoration of the General Secretary's fiftieth birthday, when it ran in *Pravda* on 21 December as an unsigned 'official' complement to articles by L. M. Kaganovich, K. E. Voroshilov, and others in the paper's jubilee double edition. On the back page, OGIZ, the state publishing house, advertised the original 1927 pamphlet and heralded the imminent publication of a new, more elaborate biography. Aimed at a wide audience, it had been 'designed for every literate worker and peasant' and was to be printed in massive numbers.[14]

Such priorities were indicative of a broader reorientation of Soviet ideological efforts underway during these years. Difficulties with social mobilisation had already compelled Soviet ideologists to search for new ways of rallying popular support in the late 1920s. Fundamentally, their problem was one of educational level, as most Soviet citizens were only functionally literate and few had had more than a few grades of formal schooling. Even among urban residents and Party members, rates were not much higher.[15] This meant that Soviet propaganda's longstanding

---

[12] Until 1926, such sketches of Stalin were brief, e.g. B. Volin (ed.), *12 biografii* (Moscow: Rabochaia Moskva, 1924), pp. 46–51.

[13] I. Tovstukha, 'Stalin', in *Entsiklopedicheskii slovar' Granat* (Moscow: Russkii biografi- cheskii institut Granat, 1927), XLI, sect. 3, pp. 107–10; I. Tovstukha (ed.), *Iosif Vissarionovich Stalin (Kratkaia biografiia)* (Moscow: Gosizdat, 1927). On its develop- ment, see RGASPI f. 558, op. 11, dd. 1277–8; and Robert C. Tucker, *Stalin as a Revolutionary, 1879–1929: A Study in History and Personality* (New York: W. W. Norton, 1973), p. 428.

[14] 'Iosif Vissarionovich Stalin (Biografiia)', *Pravda*, 21 December 1929, p. 4 (excerpted in *Trud* and *Komsomol'skaia pravda*); 'Knigi I. V. Stalina', *Pravda*, 21 December 1929, p. 8.

[15] Moshe Lewin, *The Making of the Soviet System: Essays in the Interwar History of Soviet Russia* (New York: Pantheon Books, 1985), pp. 39–41, 209–40; K. B. Litvak, 'K voprosu o partiinykh perepisiakh i kul'turnom urovne kommunistov v 20-e gody', *Voprosy istorii*

focus on materialism and anonymous social forces was simply too arcane for most to grasp.[16] As early as 1929, M. Gorky and others concerned with mass mobilisation had begun to talk – hesitantly at first – about promoting famous names from the Revolution, Civil War, and ongoing socialist construction as heroes who could personify the official line in more accessible terms.[17] It was this new approach to propaganda that led OGIZ to advertise its forthcoming Stalin biography.

Despite all assurances to the contrary, the biography never saw the light of day. This is rather curious, because Stalin's 1929 jubilee is generally considered to mark the launching of the Stalin cult and Tovstukha's thin brochure was clearly insufficient to play a central role in the new campaign. But aside from the publication of a small, impenetrable article in the *Minor Soviet Encyclopedia*,[18] nothing even vaguely reminiscent of a Stalin biography rolled off the presses during these years.

What can explain this peculiar absence? Although some have attributed the lack of an official biography during the early 1930s to modesty on Stalin's part, this conclusion seems unsatisfactory.[19] By 1934, sixteen and a half million copies of Stalin's various works were in circulation, complemented by increasingly large amounts of hagiography in the party press.[20] Modesty, then, did not prevent the production of a new biographical statement.

A better explanation points to the fact that between the late 1920s and the early 1930s, Soviet ideologists – like many others in society – were caught in the throes of cultural revolution. Confusion reigned. One of the biggest controversies concerned how best to characterise the role of the individual in history. Officially, the materialist tenets of Marxism-Leninism had long stressed the primacy of anonymous social forces as described in *The Communist Manifesto* ('the history of all hitherto existing

---

KPSS 2 (1991), 79–92; John Barber, 'Working Class Culture and Political Culture in the 1930s', in Hans Gunther (ed.), *The Culture of the Stalin Period* (New York: St. Martin's Press, 1990), pp. 3–14.

[16] Witnessing this confusion firsthand, John Scott commented later that 'to give students of a very limited general education "Anti-Duehrung," [sic] "The Dialectics of Nature," or "Materialism and Empiro-Criticism" to read was only to invite blatant superficiality.' See John Scott, *Behind the Urals: An American Engineer in Russia's City of Steel*, ed. Stephen Kotkin (Bloomington: Indiana University Press, 1989), p. 45.

[17] 'Iz perepiski A. M. Gor'kogo', *Izvestiia TsK KPSS* 3 (1989), 183–7; S. V. Zhuravlev, *Fenomen 'Istorii fabrik i zavodov'* (Moscow: IRI RAN, 1997), pp. 4–5, 153–4, 180–1.

[18] M. V. Vol'fson, 'Stalin', in *Malaia sovetskaia entsiklopediia* (Moscow: Sovetskaia entsiklopediia, 1930), VIII, pp. 406–12. The only other biographical statements to be published before the end of the decade consisted of short chapters or sub-chapters in party history textbooks and even more brief entries in the collected works of prominent party leaders.

[19] Medvedev, *Let History Judge*, pp. 817–18.

[20] *XVII s"ezd vsesoiuznoi kommunisticheskoi partii(b) 26 ianvaria–10 fevralia 1934 g. Stenograficheskii otchet* (Moscow: Partizdat, 1934), p. 620.

societies is the history of class struggle'). Yet propaganda constructed according to this principle tended to be too abstract to resonate with the USSR's poorly educated population. Moreover, the official veneration of Lenin since 1924 had followed a very different, individualistic trajectory. After considerable hesitation, Soviet ideologists apparently decided to invest in Stalin-centered propaganda patterned after the Lenin cult in order to augment the inscrutable nature of Marxism-Leninism with the celebration of a tangible, living hero familiar to one and all.[21]

But if Stalin's OGIZ biographers found their assignment challenging from an ideological standpoint, the situation was further complicated in October 1931 with the publication of Stalin's infamous letter to the journal *Proletarskaia revoliutsiia*. Provoked by Party historians' apparent willingness to second-guess Lenin, Stalin assailed the Soviet ideological establishment as a whole, defaming even fanatic loyalists like E. M. Iaroslavskii as 'archival rats'. Declaring Lenin's legacy to be unimpeachable, Stalin ordered ideologists to devote their attention to the heroic deeds of Party leaders rather than to source-study and other academic exercises. While there is some controversy over what precisely precipitated Stalin's intervention, and even what his intentions were, the ramifications of the letter are clear.[22] Encouraged by the machinations of Stalin's inner circle, the letter triggered a witch hunt in the lower ranks of the historical profession that decimated the discipline over the next several years, rendering virtually all existing work on Party history and the Soviet leadership obsolete.[23] Elites understood the *Proletarskaia revoliutsiia* letter to be a 'turning point'. From that time, discussions

---

[21] Although there was little room for individual actors in the classic Marxist understanding of historical materialism, in 1931 Stalin identified a prominent role for decisive leaders from among the people who grasped the possibilities and limitations of their historical contexts. See 'Beseda s nemetskim pisatelem Emilem Liudvigom', *Bol'shevik* 8 (1932), 33; also I. Merzon, 'Kak pokazyvat' istoricheskikh deiatelei v shkol'nom prepodavanii istorii', *Bor'ba klassov* 5 (1935), 53–9; *Istoriia Vsesoiuznoi kommunisticheskoi partii (bol'shevikov): Kratkii kurs* (Moscow: Gospolitizdat, 1938), p. 16. Gorky and A. N. Tolstoi, among others, promoted the new interest in heroes with the support of A. A. Zhdanov. See *Pervyi vsesoiuznyi s"ezd sovetskikh pisatelei, 1934: Stenograficheskii otchet* (Moscow: Khudozhestvennaia literatura, 1934), pp. 8, 17, 417–19, etc.

[22] Compare John Barber, 'Stalin's Letter to the Editors of Proletarskaya Revolyutsiya', *Soviet Studies* 1 (1976), 39–41; and Robert C. Tucker, 'The Rise of Stalin's Personality Cult', *American Historical Review* 2 (1979), 355–8.

[23] Longtime rivalries within the discipline contributed to the firestorm. See George Enteen, 'Marxist Historians during the Cultural Revolution: A Case-Study in Professional Infighting', in S. Fitzpatrick (ed.), *Cultural Revolution in Russia, 1928–1931* (Bloomington: Indiana University Press, 1978), pp. 154–79; Entin (Enteen), 'Intellektual'nye predposylki utverzhdeniia stalinizma v sovetskoi istoriografii', *Voprosy istorii* 5–6 (1995), 149–55; A. N. Artizov, 'Kritika M. N. Pokrovskogo i ego shkoly', *Istoriia SSSR* 1 (1991), 103–6.

concerning the Party and its leaders were no longer to be dispassionate or diverge from the official line.[24]

Although this crisis seems to have stymied OGIZ's Stalin biographers, it had the effect of stimulating the growth of the cult as a whole as members of the Soviet establishment attempted to prove their loyalty in a frenzy of deferential writing.[25] Such panegyrics were reinforced in the next two years by the Party hierarchs' call for a broad reconceptualisation of Party and civic history,[26] as well as their official endorsement of Socialist Realism in literature and the arts.[27] As Stalin somewhat laconically explained during a private critique of Comintern propaganda during these years, orthodox materialism was unpopular on the mass level because 'the people do not like Marxist analysis, big phrases and generalized statements'.[28] Instead, he and other party bosses demanded that propagandists break with the focus on abstract schematicism and anonymous social forces and produce animated narratives, populated by identifiable heroes and villains. Unsurprisingly, the General Secretary and his entourage were to occupy a central position in this new Soviet Olympus – as P. F. Iudin declared in early 1934,

the greatest people of the epoch stand alongside us – we had Lenin and we now have Stalin, Molotov, Kaganovich, and Voroshilov. But people with such intelligence or revolutionary sweep-of-the-hand as our leaders don't yet figure into our artistic literature. It is imperative to represent such people in our literature.[29]

Kaganovich was even more direct, noting that 'the role of Comrade Stalin still awaits its comprehensive and profound evaluation. We not only

---

[24] Nadezhda Mandelshtam, *Vospominaniia* (New York: Izdatel'stvo im. Chekhova, 1970), p. 277.

[25] Although Tucker's conclusion that Stalin geared the whole process toward promoting the personality cult probably overestimates the leader's foresight and ability to control events, the cult did at least haphazardly begin to take shape in the wake of this affair.

[26] See the Central Committee resolution of 17 January 1932 'Ob usilenii Kul'tpropotdela TsK rabotnikami i o perestroike raboty Kul'tpropa v dukhe sistematicheskoi propagandy marksizma-leninizma', in *Spravochnik partiinogo rabotnika* (Moscow: Partizdat, 1934), vyp. 8, p. 288; 'Razvernut' rabotu po izucheniiu istorii partii', *Proletarskaia revoliutsiia* 4 (1934), 9; Central Committee resolution of 15 May 1934 'O prepodavanii grazhdanskoi istorii v shkolakh SSSR', *Pravda*, 16 May 1934, p. 1.

[27] On the rise of the hero in Socialist Realism, see Katerina Clark, *The Soviet Novel: History as Ritual* (Chicago: University of Chicago Press, 1980), pp. 8–10, 34–5, 72, 119, 136–48; Katerina Clark, 'Little Heroes and Big Deeds: Literature Responds to the First Five-Year Plan', in Fitzpatrick (ed.), *Cultural Revolution*, pp. 205–6.

[28] 7 April 1934 entry in Georgi Dimitrov, *Dnevnik (9 Mart 1933–6 Fevuari 1949)* (Sophia: Universitetsko izdatelstvo 'Sv. Kliment Okhridski', 1997), p. 101. The author is grateful to Terry Martin for this reference.

[29] 'Novaia, nevidannaia literatura: vystuplenie tov. P. Iudina', *Literaturnaia gazeta*, 22 January 1934, p. 3.

know of Comrade Stalin's role, but we feel it as well – it is in our heart and in our soul'.[30]

Despite the priority of this agenda, efforts to develop more animated, evocative propaganda did not immediately produce results during the mid-1930s. Although Party ideologists and historians struggled to reframe their Marxist-Leninist analysis in more populist terms, political literature remained dominated by arcane theoretical tracts, poorly anno-tated speeches and crude sloganeering. Chronic indoctrinational pro-blems persisted as a result: when a certain Petrushenko was asked who Stalin was in a study circle in 1935, his answer – 'someone like the tsar used to be' – got him reported all the way to Moscow.[31] Petrushenko's example illustrates why the absence of a Stalin biography was so keenly felt. Such a narrative promised to synthesise the Party's corpus of abstract theory and lofty rhetoric into a coherent, compelling statement on what it meant to be Soviet.[32]

Of course, it was not for lack of trying that such a book failed to appear. Pursued vigorously, the project suffered a stunning series of setbacks. Several accounts exist of S. M. Kirov being dragooned into writing a biography in the early-to-mid 1930s before an assassin's bullet cut short his nascent literary career. Gorky, the most revered of the court littér-ateurs, also considered working on a manuscript before his death in 1936, as did M. A. Bulgakov before dying in 1940.[33] Little came of these efforts, however.

More fruitful biographical projects involved less visible members of the Soviet elite. While still a rising Party boss in Georgia, L. P. Beria engi-neered the establishment of the Tbilisi Stalin Institute in February 1932. Its charter declared that:

along with the collection of all materials pertaining to the revolutionary activity of Comrade Stalin, the institute is also given the task of organising scholarly research to work out issues concerned with Stalin's biography and his role as theoretician

---

[30] 'Ot shest'nadtsatogo k sem'nadtsatomu s"ezdu partii: doklad L. M. Kaganovicha o rabote TsK VKP(b) na Moskovskoi ob"edinennoi IV oblastnoi i III gorodskoi partiinoi konferentsii 17 ianvaria 1934 g.', *Pravda*, 22 January 1934, p. 4.

[31] RGASPI f. 17, op. 120, d. 176, l. 45. For other examples, see Davies, *Popular Opinion*, pp. 168–9.

[32] Robert C. Tucker, *Stalin in Power: The Revolution from Above, 1928–1941* (New York: Norton, 1990), p. 333.

[33] Amy Knight, *Beria: Stalin's First Lieutenant* (Princeton: Princeton University Press, 1993), pp. 57–8; Tucker, *Stalin in Power*, p. 335n. 109; Edvard Radzinskii, *Stalin* (Moscow: Vagrius, 1997), pp. 13–15; *Dnevnik Eleny Bulgakovoi* (Moscow: Knizhnaia palata, 1990), pp. 272–9, 284, 383–4. On Bulgakov's Stalin-centered play *Batum*, see M. A. Bulgakov, *P'esy 1930-kh godov* (St. Petersburg: Iskusstvo-SPb, 1994), pp. 211–56, 498–548.

and organiser of the party, particularly including the study of Stalin's role as organiser of the revolutionary workers' movement in the Transcaucasus.[34]

Tbilisi did not monopolise the research for long, however. Tovstukha joined the fray in 1932, resuming his role as *de facto* official biographer despite serious illness. One of his first moves was to begin shifting relevant documents from Georgia to the Marx-Engels-Lenin Institute in Moscow in order to prepare for the publication of Stalin's collected works.[35] Within a year, however, territoriality became an issue when M. G. Toroshelidze took control of the Tbilisi institute with the intention of producing a Stalin biography of his own. He, in turn, was checked by Beria, who also fancied writing a book on Stalin's exploits in the Transcaucasian revolutionary underground. Beria's rising prestige in the Party gave him a tremendous advantage, allowing him to make short work of his rivals and even publish an article of his own in the Party's flagship, *Bol'shevik*, in mid-1934. In the wake of this coup, he placed his ghost-writer, E. A. Bediia, in command of the Tbilisi institute and instructed him to use the resources at his disposal to expand his Stalin-centred history of the Bolshevik movement in the Transcaucasus.[36]

Tbilisi was not the only scene of intrigue. In Moscow, Iaroslavskii began gathering material for a book about Stalin through official and unofficial channels, apparently believing that such a project would restore his good name within the Soviet ideological establishment. 'I am working on a book that I am certain will be useful to the entire party as well as to the Transcaucasian comrades,' he wrote to a Georgian Party official in early 1935.[37] Writing to Tovstukha, Iaroslavskii asked for help and advice, speaking of the need to publish 'a fairly detailed, popularised biography'. Tovstukha responded rudely that while there was no doubt about the pressing need for such a book, Iaroslavskii was the wrong man

---

[34] Beria's patronage over the Georgian Stalin cult included support for the collection of oral histories, the creation of a museum, and the erection of a marble pavilion over Stalin's humble childhood home. See S. V. Sukharev, 'Litsedeistvo na poprishche istorii [Beriia – apologet kul'ta lichnosti Stalina]', *Voprosy istorii KPSS* 3 (1990), 105–6.

[35] Willi Munzenberg, a German communist, had urged Tovstukha to return to the project in 1931, asking him to have IMEL publish a 'communist-written' biography in order to refute exposés being published in Germany by renegades like Boris Bazhanov, Stalin's former secretary. See RGASPI f. 155, op. 1, d. 85, ll. 1, 3. For the vast materials Tovstukha assembled, see f. 71, op. 10, dd. 192–218, 364–73.

[36] L. P. Beria, 'Bol'sheviki Zakavkaz'ia v bor'be za sotsializm', *Bol'shevik* 11 (1934), 24–37. Beria was not the only biographer to undermine his rival. Both Toroshelidze and Iaroslavskii eagerly attacked their competitors as well. See Sukharev, 'Litsedeistvo', pp. 105–7, 110–11, 116.

[37] RGASPI f. 89, op. 8, d. 1001, ll. 7. See also l. 5 and more generally, dd. 1001–14.

for the job. 'It will not turn out as a *biography* of Stalin – it will just be another history of the party and Stalin's role therein'. 'A detailed biography of Stalin', averred Tovstukha, 'one exceptionally vivid and rich in facts', would take years to complete. Denying that he was writing a Stalin biography of his own, Tovstukha flatly refused Iaroslavskii's request for assistance.[38]

Insulted by Tovstukha's tone, Iaroslavskii refused to be discouraged. Instead, he wrote back, threatening that he had allies in the Politburo and that he would proceed with his planned biography with or without Tovstukha's assistance.[39] Unbeknownst to Iaroslavskii, however, it was actually Tovstukha who enjoyed favour in the Party hierarchy,[40] and he found Iaroslavskii's demands presumptuous and threatening. Determined to check-mate his rival, Tovstukha wrote to V. V. Adoratskii, the then director of IMEL, that 'if Iaroslavskii moves toward what I am working on … please steer him away decisively … In particular, he must not get any hint of the translations of [Stalin's] articles from Georgian'.[41]

Stymied by this stonewalling, Iaroslavskii attempted during the following months to convince his patrons in the Politburo to overrule Tovstukha and Adoratskii. In August 1935, he finally appealed directly to Stalin himself:

C[omrade] Stalin! Sergo [Ordzhonikidze] called me today … and said that he had talked to you about my planned book *Stalin*. Only you can remove the exceptional obstacles that he told you about – it is imperative that either you or Comrade Poskrebyshev order IMEL or the Archive of the October Revolution to allow me to use *all* the available materials and documents. Otherwise, they will not permit me to make use of them.

Stalin's response, scrawled across Iaroslavskii's letter, was as decisive as it was duplicitous. 'I am against the idea of a biography about me,' he wrote. 'Maksim Gorky had a plan like yours, and he also asked me, but I have backed away from this issue. I don't think the time has come for a Stalin biography.'[42] Not one written by Iaroslavskii, in any case.

---

[38] RGASPI f. 155, op. 1, d. 88, l. 1; f. 89, op. 8, d. 1001, ll. 23–4; f. 155, op. 1, d. 90, ll. 1–1ob.

[39] RGASPI f. 155, op. 1, d. 88, l. 2.

[40] In early 1935, Tovstukha confidentially relayed to V. V. Adoratskii that '[A. I.] Stetskii recently proposed that I write a biography of Stalin. This is thus the *fourth* such offer I have received in the past year, suggesting that the issue is already fully mature.' See RGASPI f. 155, op. 1, d. 70, l. 28. Stetskii had apparently discussed the matter with Stalin a day after his fifty-fifth birthday. See 'Posetiteli kremlevskogo kabineta I. V. Stalina', *Istoricheskii arkhiv* 3 (1995), 149.

[41] RGASPI f. 155, op. 1, d. 70, ll. 33–4ob.

[42] RGASPI f. 558, op. 1, d. 5089, l. 1 (the draft is at f. 89, op. 8, d. 1020, l. 1). Volkogonov misquotes the letter and errs with its citation in *Triumf i tragediia*, I, pp. 338–9.

Ironically, despite all of Iaroslavskii's and Tovstukha's efforts, it was ultimately Beria who succeeded in publishing the first major biographical statement on Stalin. After delivering an address on Stalin's early revolutionary career in Tbilisi in July 1935, Beria promptly produced a book-size manuscript on the subject entitled *On the Question of the History of Bolshevik Organizations in the Transcaucasus*.[43] Clever and resourceful, the Georgian party boss' ghost-writers had produced a narrative that charted Stalin's past and established a firm chronology for his professional activities through the prism of Transcaucasian party history. Moreover, by focusing on the Transcaucasus and relying on the testimony of hand-picked local Party veterans, the book's authors were able to skirt later, more controversial episodes in the General Secretary's career that were confounding his other potential biographers. Published in *Pravda* and then promptly in a massive hardcover edition, Beria's book won the immediate endorsement of the Central Committee.[44] Organisations were instructed to have their 'activists, propagandists and party members study Comrade Beria's presentation ... which has provided new material of the richest kind on the role of Comrade Stalin as our party's leader and theoretician ... Comrade Beria's presentation is to be used in future courses as mandatory reading material'.[45]

The presence of a detailed account of Stalin's early career and repeated calls from the Central Committee for additional new materials[46] heightened the need for a more comprehensive biography at a time when other projects were faltering. Tovstukha succumbed to illness and died. Toroshelidze's grumbling about Beria's book (or rumours to that effect) precipitated his arrest.[47] Iaroslavskii was drafted to help compile what was to be the Party's central ideological text, the *History of the All-Union Communist Party (Bolsheviks): Short Course*.[48] Ultimately, a full biography would not appear until 1936, and even then, from a rather unexpected

---

[43] Sukharev, 'Litsedeistvo', pp. 112–13.

[44] See *Pravda*, 29 July to 5 August, 1935, and L. P. Beria, *K voprosu ob istorii bol'shevistskikh organizatsii v Zakavkaz'e* (Moscow: Partizdat, 1935). On its development, see RGASPI f. 558, op. 11, dd. 704–5; op. 4, d. 662, l. 428.

[45] *Zaria Vostoka*, 2 September 1935, cited in Sukharev, 'Litsedeistvo', pp. 115–16. On its use as a biography, see A. G. Solov'ev, 'Tetradi krasnogo professora (1912–1941gg.)', in *Neizvestnaia Rossiia – XX vek* (Moscow: Istoricheskoe nasledie, 1993), IV, p. 189.

[46] Central Committee resolution of 14 June 1935 'O propagandistskoi rabote v blizhaishee vremia', detailed in N. Rubinshtein, 'Nedostatki v prepodavanii istorii VKP(b)', *Bol'shevik* 8 (1936), 32–42.

[47] Sukharev, 'Litsedeistvo', p. 106.

[48] Iaroslavskii was recruited to work with P. N. Pospelov and V. G. Knorin (although Knorin was purged in summer 1937). See RGASPI f. 17, op. 120, d. 383, l.1.

source. Roy Medvedev explains that after repeated failures among Stalin's potential Soviet biographers,

the search spread to distinguished Western authors. In early 1936 a biography of Stalin by the prominent French writer Henri Barbusse was published as a serial in the large-circulation periodical *Roman-gazeta*. Barbusse received all the material he needed for this book directly from the party's Central Committee. However, within a year the book was removed from all the libraries because it referred to dozens of Stalin's 'comrades-in-arms' who had been arrested soon after the book appeared.[49]

The effect of the Great Terror on this and similar projects is difficult to overestimate. As Medvedev and others have observed, the unpredictable nature of the purges within the Soviet elite made it virtually impossible to describe the General Secretary's Party career in print without risking accidental mention of enemies of the people.

To a certain extent, the Barbusse debacle was eclipsed by the continuing success of Beria's book and other new Stalin-centred histories of the Civil War and the Red Army by Gorky and Voroshilov, respectively.[50] The publication of the long-awaited *Short Course* in 1938 also helped the situation. The fact that these institutional histories were appearing at a time when few other propaganda texts made it past the state censor should not be particularly surprising, of course. Unlike traditional biographies, institutional histories did not have to detail Stalin's personal relationship with the Party and military elite. Instead, they focused on Stalin and Soviet leadership in general terms and survived the Great Terror by avoiding mention of the rank-and-file by name whenever possible.

Such volumes were, however, only a temporary solution to the problem. Not only did they make for difficult reading, but, with the exception of the *Short Course*, they proved to be too narrow and bloodless to offer an overall sense of the era. In fact, this literature actually had the effect of stimulating new calls for a major Stalin biography.[51] But if there was little doubt about the priority of releasing a comprehensive biography, the task of writing it remained something akin to Russian roulette. The greatest

---

[49] Medvedev, *Let History Judge*, pp. 817–18; Anri Barbius (Barbusse), *Stalin: Chelovek, cherez kotorogo raskryvaetsia novyi mir* (Moscow: Khudozhestvennaia literatura, 1936). On the text's development, see RGASPI f. 558, op. 11, dd. 699–700; more generally, see Tucker, *Stalin in Power*, pp. 335–6. On efforts to recruit Feuchtwanger and André Gide, see A. Kemp-Welch, *Stalin and the Literary Intelligentsia* (Basingstoke: Macmillan, 1991), p. 228.

[50] *Istoriia grazhdanskoi voiny v SSSR*, I, *Podgotovka Velikoi Proletarskoi revoliutsii* (Moscow: Istoriia grazhdanskoi voiny, 1935, 1938); K. E. Voroshilov, *Stalin i Krasnaia Armiia* (Moscow: Partizdat, 1936).

[51] RGASPI f. 17, op. 120, d. 307, l. 269.

threat stemmed from the Terror, as each wave of arrests immediately transformed everything even mentioning its victims from prescribed literature into proscribed contraband.[52] But excessive veneration could also create problems for prospective biographers. In 1938, for instance, Stalin sharply rebuked Detizdat, the Children's Publishing House, for a book demonstrating a clearly 'Socialist-Revolutionary tone':

I am decisively opposed to the publication of *Stories of Stalin's Childhood*.

The little book is filled with a mass of factual errors, distortions, exaggerations and undeserved praise. The author has been misled by fairy tale enthusiasts, liars (perhaps 'honest' liars) and sycophants. A pity for the author, but facts are facts.

But that is not most important. Most important is that the book has a tendency to inculcate in the consciousness of Soviet children (and people in general) a cult of personalities, great leaders [*vozhdei*] and infallible heroes. That is dangerous and harmful. The theory of the 'heroes' and the 'mob' is not a Bolshevik theory but an SR one. *The SRs say* that 'Heroes make a people, transform a mob into a people.' 'The people make their heroes,' *say the Bolsheviks*. This little book will assist the SRs. Every such book will contribute to the SRs and *will harm* our general Bolshevik cause.

I advise you to burn the book.

I. Stalin.

16/II 1938.[53]

Stalin's rejection of this paradigm must have caused his potential biographers to despair. Of course, Stalin was technically correct: the Party line on historic individuals had stated quite clearly since 1932 that leaders emerge from among the people, though Soviet mass culture had rarely followed this directive and routinely characterised Stalin as playing a paternalistic role in relation to Soviet society. Such an erratic attitude

---

[52] Glavlit censored manuscripts and withdrew books according to a constantly changing list of prohibited names, themes, and events. See A. V. Blium, *Sovetskaia tsenzura v epokhu total'nogo terrora, 1929–1953* (St. Petersburg: Akademicheskii proekt, 2000).

[53] RGASPI f. 558, op. 1, d. 3218, ll. 1–4, published in P. N. Pospelov, 'Piat'desiat' let Kommunisticheskoi partii Sovetskogo Soiuza', *Voprosy istorii* 11 (1953), 21. See also Tsentr khraneniia dokumentov molodezhnykh organizatsii (henceforth TsKhDMO), f. 1, op. 23, d. 1304, ll. 57–8; d. 1251, l. 126. Although Stalin clearly understood the logic behind the personality cult, he also objected to its excesses. In 1933, he wrote to the Society of Old Bolsheviks to protest the launch of several projects devoted to his career: 'I am against them as such undertakings will lead to a strengthening of the "cult of personalities", something which is dangerous and incompatible with the spirit of our Party.' Two years later, he took a dislike to a picture of himself leading the famous 1902 Batum demonstration in a draft textbook on Party history by Iaroslavskii, Knorin, and Pospelov, scribbling into the margin: " ? there was no such thing." He struck out similar passages in an early draft of A. V. Shestakov's 1937 *Short Course on the History of the USSR*. See RGASPI f. 558, op. 1, d. 1572, quoted in Sukharev, 'Litsedeistvo', p. 104; RGASPI f. 558, op. 3, d. 74, l. 81; d. 374, ll. 115–16, 139, 175. See also Gromov, *Stalin: Vlast' i iskusstvo*, pp. 143–4.

toward the literary dimensions of the personality cult ultimately limited biographical material in the mid-to-late 1930s to institutional histories like the *Short Course* and books by Beria, Gorky, and Voroshilov.[54]

Things changed with the end of the Great Terror in 1939. Iaroslavskii, at the height of his career following the successful release of the *Short Course*, eagerly returned to the idea of writing a Stalin biography. Although much of the Stalin material that he had attempted to interpolate into the *Short Course* had been cut during the final stages of the book's editing,[55] now the *Minor Soviet Encyclopedia* and other publications were urgently requesting new biographical articles to mark the leader's sixtieth jubilee late that December. Aspiring to fill a specific void in the existing Party literature, Iaroslavskii wrote to A. A. Zhdanov that 'the need for a biography is colossal, especially in the newly liberated regions of Poland, the army, the schools and the collective farms.' Favourable initial reviews of Iaroslavskii's biography manuscript faded, however, as his editors expressed concern over its bulk and density. With the deadline nearing that fall, they demanded that Iaroslavskii make the piece more accessible. A stalemate ensued when his revisions proved unsatisfactory.[56] Frustrated, Iaroslavskii appealed to Stalin two months later for permission to publish his manuscript separately as a short book, stressing the importance of getting a biography into circulation and assuring his erstwhile patron that it had been written in a 'simple style accessible to the masses.'[57]

Although the book, *On Comrade Stalin*, did ultimately appear in print in late 1939,[58] Iaroslavskii's triumph was short-lived, insofar as his biography was immediately upstaged by another project bursting onto the scene at the same time. Unbeknownst to Iaroslavskii, M. D. Mitin, P. N. Pospelov, G. F. Aleksandrov, and I. I. Mints had been working in parallel on another biographical statement at IMEL with the help of the Central Committee directorate of propaganda and agitation.[59] Completed just weeks before

---

[54] See Iu. Polevoi, 'Chto chitat' o zhizni i deiatel'nosti tovarishcha Stalina', in *K shestidesiatiletiiu so dnia rozhdeniia Iosifa Vissarionovicha Stalina (V pomoshch' agitatoram)* (Ulan Ude: n.p., 1939), pp. 36–67. Exceptions include *Stalin i Khashim (1901–1902 gody)* (Sukhumi: n.p., 1934); *Rasskazy starykh rabochikh Zakavkaz'ia o velikom Staline* (Moscow: Partizdat, 1937); *Batumskaia demonstratsiia 1902 goda* (Moscow: Partizdat, 1937).

[55] [M. V. Zelenov,] 'I. V. Stalin v rabote nad "Kratkim kursom istorii VKP(b)"', *Voprosy istorii* 11 (2002), 6.

[56] RGASPI f. 89, op. 8, dd. 996, 1017–18; d. 1016, l. 1. On Iaroslavskii's correspondence with the encyclopedia, see d. 1017, ll. 14–19.

[57] RGASPI f. 89, op. 8, d. 1020, ll. 2–3. The book's drafts are at d. 995.

[58] E. Iaroslavskii, *O tovarishche Staline* (Moscow: Gospolitizdat, 1939). Print-runs never exceeded 200,000.

[59] The 1939 text was written by M. S. Pozner, P. S. Cheremnykh, M. S. Volin, and V. D. Mochalov and edited by Mitin, Aleksandrov, Pospelov, and Mints. See RGASPI f. 629,

Stalin's jubilee, the proofs were hurriedly circulated for review within the Party hierarchy.[60] When a copy was sent to Iaroslavskii, the latter realized that he had again been outflanked and wrote back bitterly:

I am saddened that IMEL has taken such a wrongful position in regard to me, that *only at the last moment, 9 days* before Comrade Stalin's 60th birthday, I receive an invitation to make some comments – all the more because long ago I wrote to you personally and said that I have been working in this area and could take part in the compilation of a biography. This isn't [just] a personal insult, as I look upon the writing of Stalin's biography as *a serious Party affair.*

After making a number of recommendations, Iaroslavskii begged Mitin to go over the text 'again and again ... as it is going to the masses. The masses must sense in every line a deep love for Comrade Stalin'.[61] While Iaroslavskii was scribbling away, another copy landed on Stalin's desk, as was typical for the pre-war years with manuscripts of this importance. Equally typical, Stalin returned it to IMEL unread, a note jotted on the cover page stating bluntly: 'no time to look at it'.[62]

Gambling on its acceptability, IMEL advanced the biography into production, to be published a day before Stalin's birthday in *Pravda*, *Bol'shevik* and *Partiinoe stroitel'stvo* under the title 'Iosif Vissarionovich Stalin: A Short Biography'. Attributed anonymously to IMEL, the piece was a bloodless institutional history of Stalin's Party career based on a plagiarisation of Tovstukha's 1927 prototype and the materials that the latter had collected before his death. Released as a hardcover in the last week of 1939 and printed throughout 1940, the book scrupulously reproduced the *Pravda* text. Comprised of eighty-eight pages of dense type with ten chapters, forty-eight footnotes, and a new frontispiece, it appeared in a run of more than 1.2 million copies.[63] Even more telling of

op. 1, d. 55, l. 52; R. Koniushaia, 'Iz vospominanii ob izdanii sochinenii I. V. Stalina i ego kratkoi biografii', *Edinstvo*, 19 January 1995, p. 3. Ironically, Iaroslavskii has traditionally been given credit for writing the *Short Biography* with Mitin and Pospelov. See A. Antonov-Ovseyenko, *The Time of Stalin: Portrait of a Tyranny* (New York: Harper and Row, 1981), pp. 198, 201, 233. Several other unpublished manuscripts languish in the former Party archives: RGASPI f. 71, op. 10, d. 257, ll. 9–161; f. 558, op. 11, dd. 1497–8, 1500–3.

[60] Copies of the IMEL draft from early December 1939 are stored at RGASPI under f. 71, op. 10, d. 258, ll. 1–43, 46–122, 123–211; f. 558, op. 11, d. 1279.

[61] RGASPI f. 89, op. 8, d. 1022, ll. 1–2; f. 71, op. 10, d. 258, ll. 42, 44.

[62] RGASPI f. 558, op. 1, d. 3226, l. 1. Stalin is often described as a meticulous editor. Although he did occasionally live up to this reputation (e.g., with the 1938 *Short Course*), his library is full of books in which the corrections fade after the first few pages, testifying to a lack of time or patience (or both). See, for example, op. 3, dd. 74, 350, 374, and 381.

[63] 'Iosif Vissarionovich Stalin (Kratkaia biografiia)', *Pravda*, 20 December 1939, pp. 2–6; also in *Bol'shevik* 23–24 (1939), 12–56; and *Partiinoe stroitel'stvo* 23–4 (1939), 7–41; 'Kratkaia biografiia tovarishcha I. V. Stalina', *Pravda*, 26 December 1939, p. 4; *Iosif Vissarionovich Stalin (Kratkaia biografiia)* (Moscow: Gospolitizdat, 1939).

the prominence of the IMEL biography is that it, and not Iaroslavskii's piece, eventually appeared in the *Minor Soviet Encyclopedia*. Recommended reading lists for the study of the *Short Course* were also reissued in order to include references to the *Short Biography*.[64] Supplying a much needed component of the Party catechism, this text effectively ended the search for an official Stalin biography.

While Iaroslavskii's piece was probably the better of the two in literary terms, *On Comrade Stalin* was too complicated and detailed to remain current in the shifting geopolitical context of the early 1940s.[65] The *Short Biography*, by contrast, skirted controversial issues with remarkable dexterity and remained in print. Half-a-million copies rolled off the presses between 1942 and 1944, with another 500,000 following in 1945 – significant numbers under wartime conditions.[66] And although the *Short Biography* must have made peculiar wartime reading, insofar as it made no mention of the ongoing hostilities with Nazi Germany, it enjoyed a prominent place in Soviet society. D. A. Volkogonov recalls being presented with a copy in school in 1943 as a reward for good grades.[67]

Although Party propaganda and agitation waned amid the exigencies of war, it returned to the fore after 1945. In particular, efforts were made to balance the russocentrism of the wartime period with other sorts of sloganeering – an impulse that quickly returned the cult to centre stage.[68] As a part of this campaign, IMEL launched its long-planned

---

[64] 'Iosif Vissarionovich Stalin (Kratkaia biografiia)', in *Malaia sovetskaia entsiklopediia* (Moscow: Sovetskaia entsiklopediia, 1940), X, pp. 319–92; P. Pospelov and G. Aleksandrov (eds.), *Ukazatel' osnovnykh pervoistochnikov v pomoshch' izuchaiushchim 'Kratkii kurs istorii VKP(b)'* (Moscow: Gospolitizdat, 1940), pp. 25, 50, 61. The only other biographical statement published in 1939 was printed in A. V. Shestakov (ed.), *Istoriko-revoliutsionnyi kalendar'* (Moscow: OGIZ, 1939), pp. 631–49, reprinted in *K shestidesiatiletiiu so dnia rozhdeniia Iosifa Vissarionovicha Stalina*, pp. 1–35.

[65] Before a second edition could be released, Iaroslavskii had to adjust passages on Japan, the Molotov–Ribbentrop Pact, and the Polish campaign and add new commentary on Finland and the concept of Soviet patriotism. See pp. 138, 145, and 113 of the draft at RGASPI f. 89, op. 8, d. 995, l. 29, d. 1015.

[66] The number of pages differed, but the text was identical – see *Iosif Vissarionovich Stalin (Kratkaia biografiia)* (Moscow (printed in Kuibyshev): Gospolitizdat, 1942); *Iosif Vissarionovich Stalin (Kratkaia biografiia)* (Moscow: Gospolitizdat, 1944, 1945). It was reprinted in abbreviated form as 'I. V. Stalin (Kratkaia biografiia)', *Sputnik agitatora* 44 (1944); and *I. V. Stalin (Kratkaia biografiia)* (Moscow: n.p., 1945). See RGASPI f. 71, op. 10, d. 268, ll. 10–16, 26, 29–31. The official biography was also published in fifteen union and foreign languages. See f. 17, op. 125, d. 355, l. 18.

[67] D. A. Volkogonov, *Sem' vozhdei: galereia liderov SSSR* (Moscow: Novosti, 1996), I, p. 258.

[68] The extent to which Party ideology returned to an orthodox line oriented around Marxism-Leninism and party-mindedness should not be exaggerated. As before the war, postwar ideologists attempted to enhance the persuasive appeal of the official line with populist imagery drawn from the Russian national past, the war, and the Stalin cult.

publication of Stalin's collected works and decided to update the biography as well. As Stalin's sixty-seventh birthday approached in 1946, a second edition of the IMEL biography was prepared, boasting two new chapters and a rewritten conclusion.[69] Stalin, however, refused to authorise the manuscript's publication, poring over its proofs for several weeks before calling Pospelov on the day after his birthday to complain about its shortcomings. Stalin concluded this conversation by summoning the entire editorial brigade to the Kremlin for a collective dressing-down. 'There's some idiocy in the biography draft,' he noted. 'And it is [Agitprop chief] Aleksandrov who is responsible for this idiocy'.[70]

The next day, 23 December 1946, Pospelov, Aleksandrov, and eight other leading ideologists assembled in Stalin's office.[71] According to Pospelov's handwritten notes, the session began with Stalin explaining that his biography was to play an introductory role in Soviet indoctrinational efforts. After all, 'the toiling masses and simple people cannot begin the study of Marxism-Leninism with Lenin's and Stalin's writings. They should start with the biography. The biography is a very serious issue – it has enormous meaning for the Marxist enlightenment of the simple people.'[72]

Digressing, Stalin turned to the subject of Lenin's biography. Attacking several books by the now deceased Iaroslavskii and P. M. Kerzhentsev that had long enjoyed canonical status, Stalin declared them to have lapsed into obsolescence. When Aleksandrov interjected that IMEL had developed a short Lenin biography to match their work on Stalin, the General Secretary responded curtly that 'we need a detailed biography – not a short one'. Asserting that such books were 'a proven way of helping the simple people begin their study of Marx[ism]', he then commanded Agitprop to 'prepare a good, responsible biography of Lenin'.[73]

Compare R. G. Pikhoia, *Sovetskii soiuz: Istoriia vlasti, 1945–1991* (Moscow: RAGS pri Prezidente RF, 1998), p. 62; Timothy Dunmore, *Soviet Politics, 1945–53* (New York: St. Martin's Press, 1984), p. 130; William McCagg, *Stalin Embattled, 1943–1948* (Detroit: Wayne State University Press, 1978), pp. 98–117, 249–54; with Brandenberger, *National Bolshevism*, chs. 11–14; Brooks, *Thank You, Comrade Stalin*, ch. 8.

[69] V. S. Kruzhkov, the director of IMEL, informed A. N. Poskrebyshev of the biography's completion in November 1946. The text had been reworked by S. B. Sutotskii, M. R. Galaktionov, and G. A. Obichkin, and re-edited by Aleksandrov, P. N. Fedoseev, and Kruzhkov. See RGASPI f. 629, op. 1, d. 55, l. 52.

[70] RGASPI f. 629, op. 1, d. 54, l. 22.

[71] Present were Pospelov, Aleksandrov, A. A. Kuznetsov, N. S. Patolichev, Fedoseev, M. T. Iovchuk, Mitin, Kruzhkov, Galaktionov, and Mochalov, as well as Poskrebyshev. See 'Posetiteli kremlevskogo kabineta I. V. Stalina', *Istoricheskii arkhiv* 4 (1996), 130. Stalin's harsh treatment of Aleksandrov foreshadowed his denunciation of Aleksandrov's *History of Western European Philosophy* during the second half of the meeting. See Ethan Pollock, 'The Politics of Knowledge: Party Ideology and Soviet Science, 1945–1953' (Ph.D. diss., University of California at Berkeley, 2000), pp. 44–6.

[72] RGASPI f. 629, op. 1, d. 54, l. 23.   [73] *Ibid.*, ll. 23–4.

Having already hinted at his dissatisfaction with IMEL's work on his own biography, Stalin attacked the manuscript head-on. His chief complaint was that the biography was 'SRish,' echoing objections that he had raised before the war about *Stories of Stalin's Childhood*. By 'SRish', he apparently meant that too much of the book focused solely on his accomplishments as leader without connecting his feats to those of the Party and society as a whole. A number of the biography's subsections were particularly weak in this regard, ranging from the historical origins of the Russian revolutionary movement to commentary concerning collectivisation, industrialisation, state-building, and 'the victory of communism in one country'.[74]

Irritated with the obsequiousness of the manuscipt, he sneered that it 'attributes to Stalin many teachings, up to 10 teachings'. Similar shortcomings marred the treatment of historical events in the narrative. On the subject of the Transcaucasian underground, for example, he demanded that the authors 'add more leading figures in Baku. It's as if [Stalin] arrived and did everything on his own. There were many people and they ought to have been listed. There were both Russians and Muslims. These people should have been included.'[75] Skipping ahead, he noted that 'you don't make any mention of people like Dzerzhinskii, Frunze and Kuibyshev after Lenin's death. There should be a discussion of those who took up Lenin's banner.'[76] A more diverse cast of characters was to be added to the chapter on the war as well, specifically those who 'gathered around the Supr[eme] Command'.[77] He also noted as an afterthought

---

[74] *Ibid.*, l. 24; Koniushaia, 'Iz vospominanii', p. 3.

[75] RGASPI f. 629, op. 1, d. 54, l. 25. The following names were subsequently added to the text: I. T. Fioletov, V. F. Saratovets (Efimov), I. P. Vatsek, I. V. Bokov, I. V. Malygin, P. A. Dzhaparidze, Khanlar (*sic*, Kh. Safaraliev), Memedov (*sic*, M. Mamedliarov), M. A. Azizbekov, and Kiazi-Mamed (*sic*, K. Mamedov). See G. F. Aleksandrov, M. R. Galaktionov, V. S. Kruzhkov, M. B. Mitin, V. D. Mochalov, and P. N. Pospelov (eds.), *Iosif Vissarionovich Stalin: Kratkaia biografiia*, 2nd edn., corrected and enlarged (Moscow: Gospolitizdat, 1947), p. 46.

[76] RGASPI f. 629, op. 1, d. 54, l. 25; Koniushaia, 'Iz vospominanii', p. 3. Fifteen names were subsequently added to the text: V. M. Molotov, M. I. Kalinin, K. E. Voroshilov, V. V. Kuibyshev, M. V. Frunze, F. E. Dzerzhinskii, L. M. Kaganovich, G. K. Ordzhonikidze, S. M. Kirov, E. M. Iaroslavskii, A. I. Mikoian, A. A. Andreev, N. M. Shvernik, A. A. Zhdanov, and M. F. Shkiriatov. See *Iosif Vissarionovich Stalin: Kratkaia biografiia*, p. 105.

[77] RGASPI f. 629, op. 1, d. 54, l. 26. Twenty-eight new names were promptly added to the text: N. A. Bulganin, V. V. Vasilevskii, I. S. Konev, L. A. Govorov, G. K. Zhukov, Vatutin (*sic*, L. S. Vaturin), I. D. Cherniakhovskii, A. I. Antonov, V. D. Sokolovskii, K. A. Meretskov, K. K. Rokossovskii, R. Ia. Malinovskii, N. N. Voronov, F. I. Tolbukhin, N. D. Iakovlev, M. S. Malinin, K. N. Galitskii, S. G. Trofimenko, A. V. Gorbatov, S. M. Shtemenko, V. V. Kurasov, S. I. Vershinin, A. E. Golovanov, Ia. N. Fedorenko, P. S. Rybalko, A. Bogdanov, M. E. Katukov, and D. D. Leliushenko. See *Iosif Vissarionovich Stalin: Kratkaia biografiia*, p. 220.

that 'something should have been added about the role of women'.[78] These suggestions reflected Stalin's belief that his *Short Biography* was to function as a beginners' course in Soviet social studies and that expanding the book's pantheon of heroes would not only strengthen readers' familiarity with the Soviet elite, but ultimately make the text more accessible and persuasive as well.

These directives and Stalin's extensive line-editing of the biography's proofs probably caused the IMEL brigade considerable anxiety in the days and weeks that followed.[79] Aleksandrov was particularly hard-pressed. Not only had he been repeatedly criticised during the Kremlin meeting, but as head of Agitprop, he had been tasked with the preparation of a Central Committee resolution that would accompany the *Short Biography*'s imminent release. Presented to the Orgburo only on 3 February 1947, this draft resolution went on at considerable length about how the uninitiated would henceforth be introduced to Party history and Marxism-Leninism through the lives of the Party leaders. To this end, Aleksandrov proposed that the new *Short Biography* be heralded by a massive barrage of articles in the press that would encourage the study of Lenin's and Stalin's biographies throughout Soviet educational institutions.[80] Aleksandrov's inclusion of Lenin's biography here was somewhat optimistic, as such a volume would not be ready for release until the early 1950s.[81] A month later, the Orgburo granted the proposal its tentative approval, assigning the final editing of the resolution to Aleksandrov, Zhdanov, and M. F. Shkiriatov.[82] Stripped of much of Aleksandrov's grandiloquence and detail, the resolution ultimately couched the campaign in surprisingly straightforward rhetoric:

For many workers and peasants, the study of Lenin's and Stalin's writings is a difficult and inaccessible affair. The study of V. I. Lenin's and I. V. Stalin's biographies will provide them with serious help. The biographies, which illuminate the lives and professional activities of the leaders of the Bolshevik party in a simple and

---

[78] RGASPI f. 629, op. 1, d. 54, l. 26; Koniushaia, 'Iz vospominanii', p. 3. Women subsequently received substantial coverage. See *Iosif Vissarionovich Stalin: Kratkaia biografiia*, pp. 120–5.

[79] Koniushaia, 'Iz vospominanii', p. 3. Stalin's manuscript copy, a 1939 *Short Biography* with editorial insertions glued into the margins, is stored at RGASPI f. 558, op. 11, dd. 1281–3; Pospelov's copy is at f. 629, op. 1, d. 55, ll. 2–49. See V. A. Belianov, "I. V. Stalin sam o sebe: redaktsionnaia pravka sobstvennoi biografii," *Izvestiia TsK KPSS* 9 (1990), 113–29.

[80] RGASPI f. 17, op. 125, d. 503, ll. 18–19.

[81] On the stalling of a new Lenin biography, see RGASPI f. 17, op. 132, d. 105, ll. 138–41; Rossiiskii gosudarstvennyi arkhiv noveishei istorii (henceforth RGANI) f. 5, op. 30, d. 51, l. 126; d. 7, ll. 122–6; d. 90, ll. 59–62, 110–12.

[82] RGASPI f. 17, op. 117, d. 697, l. 1. For the draft resolutions, see f. 17, op. 117, dd. 697, 708; f. 17, op. 125, d. 503.

accessible form, will help the toilers to prepare for the study of V. I. Lenin's and I. V. Stalin's writings and will thus serve as a stimulating means of promoting the study of [Marxist-Leninist] theory and provide the key to its fundamental principles.

Ordering all provincial, regional, and republican Party organisations to publicise the biography and facilitate its study, the resolution also instructed non-Russian organisations to translate it quickly into their respective languages.[83] A million copies were ordered in Russian alone.[84]

Within weeks, the *Short Biography*'s second edition emerged amid great fanfare as a handsome, 244-page simulated leather volume designed to accompany Stalin's collected works. Illustrated with thirteen pictures, it also boasted a heavily retouched reprint of the frontispiece that had graced Tovstukha's original 1927 biography.[85] Accompanying press coverage described the central role that the biography was to play in indoctrinational efforts without mentioning the Party's lack of faith in its population.[86] Between 1947 and 1948, the *Short Biography* was issued in a massive printing of over 3.25 million copies. Further unacknowledged refinements were made to a run of 1.5 million in celebration of Stalin's seventieth birthday in 1949, with four million more coming off the presses before the leader's death in 1953. Estimates of the total print-run of the *Short Biography* go as high as eighteen million volumes, making it one of the most widely published books in the world at mid-century.[87] As V. A. Belianov concludes:

the multimillion-copy print-runs of this book can be explained by the fact that it was mandatory for pupils' and students' studies in all educational institutions, as well as those studying in the Party and Komsomol education systems and even in the numerous preparatory and refresher training courses for personnel. In other words, I. V. Stalin's biography became something of a 'catechism' for society. Its study formed a framework for understanding the history and structure of society, as well as its laws, values and operative principles. In this it essentially complemented the

---

[83] RGASPI f. 17, op. 116, d. 300, l. 2.   [84] RGASPI f. 17, op. 117, d. 708, l. 73.

[85] *Iosif Vissarionovich Stalin: Kratkaia biografiia*, reprinted in *Bol'shaia sovetskaia entsiklope-diia* (Moscow: Sovetskaia entsiklopediia, 1947), III, pp. 535–622. A third edition was planned after Stalin's death in 1953 that would have increased the party's visibility – see RGANI f. 5, op. 30, d. 7, ll. 49–50; also RGASPI f. 558, op. 11, dd. 1284–6.

[86] E. Gorodetskii, 'Vtoroe izdanie biografii tovarishcha I. V. Stalina', *Kul'tura i zhizn'*, 31 January 1947, p. 3; E. Burdzhalov, 'Vtoroe izdanie biografii I. V. Stalina', *Partiinaia zhizn'* 2 (1947), 15–31.

[87] Print-run estimates are based on a survey of weekly editions of *Knizhnaia letopis'* between 1939 and 1954. The *Short Course* was the most widely published book in Russian in 1949 with slightly fewer than forty million copies in print; Stalin's *Problems of Leninism* and *On the Great Patriotic War of the Soviet Union* followed with roughly seventeen million each. Although the *Short Biography* ranked fourth in 1949, its large print-runs in the early 1950s may have catapulted it into second place. T. Zelenov, 'Bibliografiia', *Bol'shevik* 23 (1949), 89–90. See also Volkogonov, *Sem' vozhdei*, I, p. 174.

1938 *Short Course* by means of its account and evaluation of the prewar period, the course and results of the Great Patriotic War, and the first postwar years.[88]

In such a discussion of Stalin's cult of personality, it is of course important not to conflate the construction of the cult with its popular reception,[89] insofar as it is surprisingly difficult to gauge the extent to which the *Short Biography* actually catalysed support for the regime on the mass level. Anecdotal evidence indicates that although the IMEL brigade succeeded in framing Party history and ideology within a fairly conventional biographical context, Soviet citizens tended to read the book rather selectively. Contrary to official expectations, familiarity with Stalin's revolutionary career did not automatically translate into a broader appreciation of the philosophical tenets of Marxism-Leninism, nor did it necessarily give rise to a strong patriotic affinity for the Soviet cause. Instead, when Soviets talked about Stalin's service to the Party and state, they expressed themselves in formulaic, clichéd terms that hint at a rather equivocal pattern of popular reception.[90]

There are several possible explanations for this ambivalence. Despite its populist agenda, the biography was written in remarkably ponderous, stultifying prose. This shortcoming was compounded, in turn, by the dogmatism and rote learning that marred political education efforts in Party study circles.[91] But popular ambivalence *vis-à-vis* the cult may have also stemmed from the inability of Stalin's biographers to emplot their narrative as a Socialist Realist *Bildungsroman* – something which inhibited the book's potential to intrigue and inspire.[92] Unable to diverge from Stalin's traditional depiction as an infallible, unwavering, iconic representative of Soviet power, Party ideologists failed to take advantage of the biographical genre in order to characterise the General Secretary in more accessible, 'literary' terms. Even Bulgakov's famous attempt to cast Stalin as a romantic hero in his 1939 play *Batum* was met with a stinging rebuke from the Party authorities.[93] As Tovstukha had predicted years earlier, this state of affairs ultimately doomed the *Short Biography* to be little more

---

[88] Belianov, 'I. V. Stalin sam o sebe', p. 113.
[89] On the distinction, see Michel de Certeau, *The Practices of Everyday Life*, trans. Steven F. Randall (Berkeley: University of California Press, 1984), pp. xii–xiii and ch. 3; Brandenberger, *National Bolshevism*, ch. 6.
[90] See, for instance, Tsentral'nyi arkhiv obshchestvennykh dvizhenii Moskvy (henceforth TsAODM) f. 4, op. 39, d. 165, l. 4; d. 196, ll. 7–37; Davies, *Popular Opinion*, pp. 167–82.
[91] See TsAODM f. 3, op. 81, d. 225, l. 64; f. 4, op. 39, d. 196, ll. 3–5; d. 201, ll. 70–93.
[92] See Clark, *The Soviet Novel*, pp. 14–15, 57. For a similar interpretation of the cult's aesthetic limitations, see Plamper, 'The Stalin Cult in the Visual Arts', p. 11.
[93] 17 August 1939 diary entry published in *Dnevnik Eleny Bulgakovoi*, p. 279.

than a Party history textbook, a fate that clarifies its poor reception on the popular level all too well.

But if this may call for a broader reevaluation of the resonance that the cult of personality elicited within Soviet society, it does not alter the fact that between 1929 and 1953 the Party hierarchy invested heavily in the Stalin cult in general, and in his official biography in particular. This case study has demonstrated that the cult was much more of a populist effort than it was an exercise in self-aggrandisement. Stalin and his lieutenants clearly viewed the promotion of charismatic leadership as a way of bolstering the authority and legitimacy of the Soviet system. A reaction to Party ideologists' frustration with more orthodox Marxist-Leninist propaganda during the 1920s, the Stalin cult was intended to celebrate an individual who would symbolise the Soviet experiment in familiar, personal terms. Regardless of the cult's actual reception on the mass level, the timing and nature of its emergence indicate that it was genuinely expected to win the hearts and minds of the Soviet populace.

14 Stalin as the coryphaeus of science: ideology and knowledge in the post-war years

Ethan Pollock

In late December 1946 Joseph Stalin convened a meeting of high-level Communist Party personnel at his office in the Kremlin. The opening salvos of the Cold War had already been launched. Disagreements about the political future of Germany, disputes over the presence of Soviet troops in Iran, and conflicts over proposals to control atomic weapons had all contributed to growing tensions between the USA and USSR. Inside the Soviet Union, the devastating effects of the Second World War were painfully obvious: cities remained bombed out and unreconstructed; famine had laid waste to the countryside, with millions dying of starvation and many millions more malnourished.[1] All this makes the agenda for the Kremlin meeting surprising: Stalin wanted to discuss a book on the history of Western European philosophy.

It is certainly rare for the leader of a powerful country to take the time amidst international and domestic crises to discuss something so decidedly academic as a philosophy book. But for Stalin, no subject was beyond politics. Or, to put it another way, Marxism-Leninism did not merely define a political system or an economic interpretation of history, it constituted an all-encompassing worldview. Stalin's attention to scholarship was remarkable during his last years, when the Soviet press added the 'coryphaeus of science' to his growing list of epithets.[2] As the

The Harriman Institute at Columbia University provided the time and financial support to write this article. I would like to thank Sarah Davies and James Harris for the opportunity to present my ideas to the Study Group on the Russian Revolution and Stephen Bittner and David Engerman for reading and commenting on earlier versions of this work.

[1] Elena Zubkova, *Russia After the War: Hopes, Illusions, and Disappointments, 1945–1957* (New York: M. E. Sharpe, 1998), pp. 40–50; Donald Filtzer, *Soviet Workers and Late Stalinism: Labour and the Restoration of the Stalinist System after World War II* (Cambridge: Cambridge University Press, 2002), pp. 41–76; and Vladislav Zubok and Constantine Pleshakov, *Inside the Kremlin's Cold War: From Stalin to Khrushchev* (Cambridge, Mass.: Harvard University Press, 1996), pp. 36–78.

[2] We might think of 'coryphaeus of science' as the intellectual counterpart to Stalin's cultural, social, and political identities as outlined in Alfred J. Rieber, 'Stalin, Man of

coryphaeus, or choirmaster, he actively marked scientific reports, influenced scholarly debates, and even wrote two long essays of his own. His interest in the mutually reinforcing relationship between scholarship and Party doctrine went beyond such traditional Marxist strongholds as philosophy and political economy. He also became embroiled in disputes about biology, physics, linguistics, and physiology. In short, he and the party formulated an opinion on everything from the 'free will of electrons' and the control of nature to the origins of languages and nationalities and the shaping of the human mind.

How can we explain Stalin's involvement in science during this period? Some historians dismiss Stalin's scholarly forays as the ultimate ravings of a dying megalomaniac.[3] Others interpret his essays and behind-the-scenes manoeuvres as one piece of a broader campaign to keep the intelligentsia in line after a period of relative ideological freedom during the Second World War.[4] And for still others, Stalin's interventions in science masked hidden agendas, such as fanning political conflicts among his lieutenants or escalating tensions between the USSR and the West in the Cold War.[5] None of these interpretations, however, explain why Stalin so persistently monitored and participated in scientific debates. As both an editor and an author, Stalin displayed deep concern about the content of scholarly work and its overall implications for Marxism-Leninism. Indeed, instead of revealing ulterior motives behind Stalin's actions, top secret documents are saturated with the same Marxist-Leninist language, categories, and frames for understanding the world that appeared in the public discourse. The USSR, in other words, did not keep two sets of books, at least on ideological questions.[6]

the Borderlands', *The American Historical Review* 106 (2001), 1651–91. The phrase was invoked in 1939 when Stalin became a member of the Soviet Academy of Sciences, but it did not come into widespread use until after the war. See Alexei Kojevnikov, 'President of Stalin's Academy: The Mask and Responsibility of Sergei Vavilov', *ISIS* 87 (1996), 18–50.

[3] See, for instance, Adam B. Ulam, *Stalin: The Man and His Era* (New York: Viking, 1973), pp. 729–31.

[4] Alexander Vucinich, *Empire of Knowledge: The Academy of Sciences of the USSR (1917–1970)* (Berkeley: University of California Press, 1984) and V. D Esakov and E. C. Levina, *Delo KR: sudy chesti v ideologii i praktike poslevoennogo stalinizma* (Moscow: Institut Rossiiskoi Istorii RAN, 2001).

[5] Werner G. Hahn, *Postwar Soviet Politics: The Fall of Zhdanov and the Defeat of Moderation, 1946–53* (Ithaca: Cornell University Press, 1982) and Nikolai Krementsov, *Stalinist Science* (Princeton: Princeton University Press, 1997).

[6] Recent scholarship has also emphasised the influence of ideology, in combination with other factors, on Soviet foreign policy during the Cold War. See Zubok and Pleshakov, *Inside*, pp. 1–8, Nigel Gould-Davies, 'Rethinking the Role of Ideology in International Politics During the Cold War', *Journal of Cold War Studies* 1 (1999), 90–109, and Melvyn P. Leffler, 'The Cold War: What Do "We Now Know"?', *American Historical Review* 104 (1999), 501–24.

Stalin organised and monitored scientific discussions for reasons that went beyond vanity or instrumentalist politics. He recognised that in some respects the legitimacy of the system relied on the coherence of its ideology. In theory, Marxism-Leninism was scientific, and science was supposed to flourish if it was based on dialectical materialist principles. Science and Soviet Marxism led to the same discoveries about the nature of things and, together, progressed steadily to absolute truths. On the surface, scientific discussions always resulted in declarations of harmony between ideology and science. Behind the scenes, however, Stalin and his subordinates recognised that the Soviet Union faced a formidable ideological crisis. Stalin's efforts as the 'coryphaeus of science' constituted an attempt to deal with that crisis.[7]

Stalin's decision to call people to his office in 1946 to voice criticism of the book on the history of philosophy was anything but exceptional. In 1947 he organised a broad discussion of the book and carefully edited the keynote address. In 1948 he worked closely with Trofim Lysenko to outlaw the studying of Mendelian genetics in the USSR. In the first half of 1949 he cancelled a major conference on 'physical idealism' and 'cosmopolitanism' in physics and in the second half of the same year he looked into questions of physiology in preparation for a union-wide conference in that field. In 1950 he met three times with political economists to discuss the details of their draft of a textbook, while also editing and writing a series of articles on linguistics. Clearly, Stalin liked carrying the coryphaeus' baton. This paper describes Stalin's participation as an editor and author in two fields: linguistics and political economy. Both cases show him engaged with the substance of academic disputes, concerned about the broader implications of the relationship between ideology and science, and cognisant of the ideological crisis. Together they also reveal how Stalin's participation deepened the problems in these fields, instead of opening them to the sort of exchanges which he claimed to be essential for reinvigorating Marxism-Leninism.

In the late 1940s, linguists, like scholars in other disciplines, pushed for an ideologically coherent understanding of their field. Debates in philosophy and biology and the campaign to weed out so-called cosmopolitan influences in Soviet culture established what the Party demanded of Soviet scientists, including linguists. Soviet science was politically engaged and based on Marxist-Leninist principles. The Cold War divided science and scientists as well as nations and economic systems.

---

[7] For a more thorough development of this argument see Ethan Pollock, 'The Politics of Knowledge: Party Ideology and Soviet Science, 1945–1953', Ph.D. diss., University of California, Berkeley, (2000).

Soviet science was patriotic and homegrown; it challenged idealist, Western science along ideological, practical, and political 'fronts'.

By the spring of 1950, linguists working under the supervision of the Academy of Sciences and Central Committee had attacked Western linguistic schools, removed Soviet linguists sympathetic to Western scholarship from positions of power, and trumpeted the supremacy of Soviet, Marxist linguistics. Perhaps most importantly, they placed the work and legacy of N. Ia. Marr – who united Marxism and linguistics in the 1920s – at the centre of the discipline.[8] Marr, like Ivan Michurin for biology and Ivan Pavlov for physiology, served as such a convenient focus for Party propaganda that publicly attacking him or his adherents was futile. Writing in the 1920s, Marr had emphasised class as the dominant criteria for understanding language development. As a more essentialist view of nationality gained strength in the 1930s, however, even Marr's followers revised and at times abandoned various aspects of his work.[9] But with the Academy and Party declaring Marr an exemplary scholar along the lines of Michurin and Pavlov, linguists were reluctant to mention any revisions of his ideas. Indeed, if empty proclamations of Soviet superiority in linguistics were all that mattered, it is hard to imagine serious challenges to Marr's position in the pantheon of Soviet scientists during Stalin's time.

Some linguists, however, recognised that Marr's work was dangerously out of step with the needs of the USSR in the post-war period. In late December 1949, Arnold Chikobava, a Georgian linguist and consistent target of the Marrists, convinced the First Secretary of the Georgian Central Committee, Kandid Charkviani, to send a letter to Stalin about the problems in the discipline and in particular the dominance of Marr's disciples.[10] Stalin's marginalia suggest he read the letter carefully and agreed with Charkviani's enumeration of Marr's errors.

The letter pointed out that if all languages were class-based, as Marr claimed, it became impossible to explain the use of language during primitive communism, when classes had yet to form. Marr also suggested

---

[8] Rossiiskii gosudarstvennyi arkhiv sotsial'no-politicheskoi istorii (henceforth RGASPI) f. 17, op. 132, d. 336, ll. 11–13; Archive of the Russian Academy of Sciences (ARAN) f. 2, op. 1–50, d. 12, ll. 1–2.

[9] For a description of the shift in nationality policy in the 1930s, see Terry Martin, 'Modernization or Neo-Traditionalism? Ascribed Nationality and Soviet Primordialism', in Sheila Fitzpatrick (ed.), *Stalinism: New Directions* (London: Routledge, 2000), pp. 348–67. On the contradictions of Marr's popularity in the late 1940s, see Yuri Slezkine, 'N. Ia. Marr and the National Origins of Soviet Ethnogenetics', *Slavic Review* 55 (1996), 826–62.

[10] Arn.Chikobava, 'Kogda i kak eto bylo', *Ezhegodnik iberiisko-kavkazskogo iazykoznaniia* 12 (1985), 9–14.

that languages went through stages of development along the lines of modes of production. Contemporary languages represented various points along this uni-directional progression towards an advanced stage, which according to Marr had already been reached by Semitic and modern European languages. Charkviani pointed out that this challenged the particular linguistic and ethnic development of individual national cultures. Further, Marr posited that all languages could be traced back to four fundamental sounds. Charkviani countered that Marr had presented no credible evidence in defence of this idea. Marr argued that the main goal of Soviet linguists was to work towards a single, world language; Charkviani cited a quotation from Stalin supporting the notion that nations and national languages would persist in the first stage of the worldwide dictatorship of the proletariat. In the name of bringing about a world culture, Marr supported the imposition of Latin alphabets throughout the Caucasus. Charkviani saw this as an insult to the ancient languages of the region. In sum, Charkviani argued that Marr was a rootless 'cosmopolitan'. What appeared revolutionary and Marxist in the 1920s, now foolishly disregarded the importance of national traditions and interests.[11]

Charkviani included a series of Chikobava's articles along with his letter. Though Stalin was in the midst of discussing the timing of the invasion of South Korea with Kim Il Sung, he still made time to study the two Georgians' concerns about the state of Soviet linguistics.[12] In early April, Chikobava accompanied Charkviani on a trip to Moscow expecting to discuss their complaints 'with the Party secretaries'. Instead, Stalin summoned them to his dacha in Kuntsevo. At the meeting, Chikobava informed Stalin that two Armenian linguists had been wrongly removed from their administrative positions as a result of the pro-Marrist crusade. Stalin immediately called the Secretary of the Armenian Central Committee, A. G. Arutiunov. Stalin's end of the conversation went as follows: 'You have fired professors Acharian and Kapantsian? ... Why? ... There were no other reasons? ... Comrade Arutiunov, you have acted wrongly'. At which point Stalin hung up the phone. Within days Kapantsian and Acharian reclaimed their former positions in the Armenian Academy of Sciences and Erevan University.[13]

---

[11] Stalin's copy of the letter is in RGASPI f. 558, op. 11, d. 1250, ll. 2–14.

[12] Kim Il Sung spent most of April 1950 in Moscow. See Evgueni Bajanov, 'Assessing the Politics of the Korean War, 1949–1951', *Cold War International History Project Bulletin* 6–7 (1995–6), 87.

[13] Chikobava, 'Kogda', pp. 9–14. Roy Medvedev relays the conversation slightly differently, without citing his sources. According to him Stalin asked: 'And who are these people?' Arutiunov responded: 'They are scientists, Academicians.' Stalin retorted: 'And

During the meeting at the dacha, Stalin spoke with Chikobava at length, listening carefully as the linguist related his critical stance on Marr and Marrism. Towards the end of the meeting, Stalin asked Chikobava to write an article for *Pravda* on the subject. Knowing that the pro-Marr campaign in the press ran counter to his views, Chikobava asked, 'Will the paper publish it?' Stalin responded, 'You write it and we'll see. If it works, we'll print it'.[14] A week later, Chikobava sent to Stalin a draft of the article, in which he systematically developed the criticisms Charkviani had outlined in his letter. Stalin edited it line by line, at times eliminating or adding words, sentences, or paragraphs. Most significantly, he excised one of his own quotations and emphasised in his comments that languages were national in character, not class-based. On 2 May, Chikobava sent Stalin another draft. Again, they met to discuss Stalin's editorial comments.[15]

On 6 May, Stalin approved Chikobava's final draft, whereupon he sent it with a note to the rest of the members of the Politburo asking that the article be published as part of a 'free discussion' of the situation in Soviet linguistics. In his note, Stalin criticised the Marrists' monopoly of the field, noted that Marr's work contained errors, and expressed his hope that the discussion could help put linguistics back on a correct course. He suggested that *Pravda* dedicate a number of pages each week to the discussion.[16] On 9 May 1950, Chikobava's article 'On Certain Problems in Soviet Linguistics' appeared on a three-page spread in *Pravda*, whose editors introduced the article echoing Stalin's concerns and calling for an 'open discussion in *Pravda* ... to overcome stagnation in the development of Soviet linguistics'.[17]

I thought they must be accountants since they were so easily removed from one place and placed in another. You rushed things, Comrade Arutiunov, you rushed things.' See Roy Medvedev, 'Stalin i iazykoznanie', *Vestnik Rossiiskoi Akademii Nauk* 67 (1997), 1037.

[14] Chikobava, 'Kogda', pp. 9–14; Slezkine, 'N. Ia. Marr', pp. 857. Chikobava's account is neither supported, nor explicitly contradicted by the record of visitors to Stalin's office published in 'Posetiteli kremlevskogo kabineta I.V. Stalina – zhurnal (tetrady) zapisi lits, priniatykh pervym gensekom, 1924–1953gg.', *Istoricheskii arkhiv* 1 (1997), 11. Since Chikobava says he met with Stalin at his dacha, the Kremlin office records cannot corroborate that the meeting took place. However, it is clear that Charkviani met with Stalin on the night of 12 April at the Kremlin, thus confirming Chikobava's claim that his patron was in Moscow on official business at the time.

[15] RGASPI f. 558, op. 11, d. 1251 contains three drafts of the article with Stalin's corrections on ll. 122–63, 62–121, and 3–61.

[16] *Ibid.*, ll. 1–3.

[17] For this and subsequent articles in *Pravda* on linguistics I will cite both the issue of *Pravda* and the page in Ernest J. Simmons (ed.), *The Soviet Linguistics Controversy* (New York: King's Crown Press, 1951) which contains excellent English translations by John V. Murra, Robert M. Hankin, and Fred Holling. I occasionally make minor alterations to their translations for clarity and readability. Simmons; *The Soviet Linguistics Controversy*, p. 9 and *Pravda*, 9 May 1950, p. 3.

Chikobava challenged Marr's assertion that 'There is no common national language but there is a class language.' Such a theory simply could not explain the use of a single language in a single country through many economic stages of development. In Marr's place, Chikobava proposed that 'A Marxist-Leninist history of language must be built on rigorously checked and accurately established facts.' Marr could not successfully challenge Western idealist theories of language, since he never fully understood Marxism-Leninism. 'If ever criticism and self-criticism were needed, it is just in this area [of general linguistics].' Establishing a Soviet linguistics based on Marxism required critical analysis of Marr's theory and the reorientation of work in the field.[18]

Some readers assumed that Chikobava's article opening the discussion was equivalent to Lysenko's speech to biologists in 1948 in that it set out to establish the new orthodoxy. Others were less sure. The historian Roy Medvedev recalled that one of his friends at Leningrad University thought 'Chikobava was a brave man to attack Marr's science.'[19] One of Marr's leading supporters evidently believed that the discussion had been organised in order to expose Marr's enemies and then remove them.[20] Indeed, *Pravda* gave no indication of where the Party stood on the discussion. The following Tuesday, Meshchaninov, Marr's leading disciple, offered a rebuttal to Chikobava's argument. Over the course of the next month and a half, *Pravda* published articles attacking Marr, defending Marr, and straddling both camps. Each Tuesday, readers witnessed an academic battle with no clear victors.

Joseph Stalin's article 'On Marxism in Linguistics', published on 20 June as part of the linguistics discussion, completely altered the field. It is no exaggeration to say that the article also brought about a major shift in Soviet efforts to understand the relationship between Party ideology and knowledge. Stalin's participation became a central reference point for all subsequent discussions of science during his lifetime. Yet the implications of Stalin's articles for other fields were never entirely clear, leaving as much confusion as clarity in their wake.

Stalin began his article with an explanation for his participation. He claimed that a group of young comrades had asked his opinion about the linguistics discussion and he reasoned that his knowledge of Marxism gave him the authority to speak on the subject. As he put it, 'I am not a linguist ... but as to Marxism in linguistics, as well as in other social

---

[18] Simmons, *The Soviet Linguistics Controversy*, pp. 9–19 and *Pravda*, 9 May 1950, pp. 3–5.
[19] Medvedev, 'Stalin', p. 1037.   [20] RGASPI f. 17, op. 132, d. 337, l. 164.

sciences, this is a subject with which I have a direct connection.'[21] His somewhat self-deprecating tone was matched by an understated presentation. Like the other articles in the discussion, Stalin's contribution appeared on pages three and four, with little fanfare, and with 'J. Stalin' printed simply at the bottom of the last section.

Stalin organised the article around a series of questions, presumably from 'young comrades', and his responses. The first question was: 'Is it true that language is a superstructure over the base?' The super-structural nature of language had been one of the few points of agreement in the discussion and it had been the one aspect of Marr's theory that even his critics accepted as true. Stalin's response broke new ground: 'No, it is not true.' Language was neither part of the economic base nor the political or cultural superstructure. Since 'the Russian language remained basically the same' under feudalism, capitalism, and socialism, he reasoned that language served all classes and all societies, regardless of economic systems.

Stalin then responded to a question about the class nature of language and the claim that all languages are class based. He dismissed the notion of 'language of the bourgeoisie' and 'language of the proletariat' which had been used to replace the concept of national languages with one of class languages. Dialects and jargons associated with certain classes existed, but this did not mean that languages on the whole were class based.

Stalin pushed the discussion in a new direction by calling attention to the state of Soviet linguistics in general and what could be done to help the discipline advance in the future. He praised the *Pravda* discussion, seeing great benefit in its exposure of a 'regime in the centre and in the republics ... not typical of science and men of science'. Stalin likened the Marrist's monopoly of the field to the policies of Arakcheev, a Minister associated with the harsh measures of Alexander I's reign. The discussion, Stalin emphasised, was useful precisely because it helped to crush this Arakcheev regime in science. In a sentence that signaled a potential policy change for scientists in all fields, Stalin stated: 'It is universally recognised that no science can develop and flourish without battles of opinions and without open criticism.'[22]

---

[21] Quotations from Stalin's article are taken from *Pravda*, 20 June 1950, pp. 3–4 and Simmons, *The Soviet Linguistics Controversy*, pp. 70–6. Original versions of his article are in RGASPI f. 558, op. 1, d. 5301.

[22] This statement even became a springboard for criticising Trofim Lysenko, who between 1948 and 1950 was beyond reproach. An Agitprop report to the Central Committee Secretariat strongly rebuked Lysenko for not allowing the 'battle of opinions' necessary for scientific progress. See, for instance, RGASPI f. 17, op. 119, d. 1036, l. 70.

Subsequent articles printed as part of the discussion in *Pravda*, and indeed articles in a variety of other publications, praised Stalin's insights and leadership. Historians, philosophers, physiologists, biologists, economists, and archeologists, as well as a full range of non-scholars, wrote letters to *Pravda*, *Kul'tura i zhizn'*, the Central Committee, and to Stalin personally. Stalin had not delivered a major theoretical statement in years, which only increased the significance given to his article. The press praised it as a 'triumph for Soviet science' and 'a new and important stage in the development of science'.[23]

The article also elicited a series of moves by the Central Committee to reorganise Soviet linguistics. Administrative changes reflected a renewed emphasis on the importance of national languages, especially Russian. A Russian-language specialist took charge of the new linguistics institute of the Academy of Sciences. A specialist in Russian and Church Slavonic became the assistant director of the institute, an expert in the history of Russian became editor of the major journal in the field, and a scholar of nineteenth-century Russian syntax became a scientific secretary of the Presidium of the Academy of Sciences. Agitprop also brought in a Russian-language expert to help it sort out disputes in the field.[24] This national emphasis, as opposed to Marr's transnational linguistic theory, fit with the patriotic fervor of the era.[25]

But other issues raised by Stalin's articles could not be addressed so easily or directly. Letters flooded *Pravda* and the Central Committee asking for clarifications of the implications of what Stalin had written. A select few even earned responses from Stalin, which were published in *Pravda* on 2 August 1950. One letter, written to Stalin by a student from Murmansk, sought to understand what appeared to be a fundamental contradiction in the work of the coryphaeus: Stalin's article suggested that the hybridisation of languages could never form a new language. But in his speech before the Sixteenth Party Congress in 1930 Stalin had stated that under Communism languages fuse into one common language.[26]

---

[23] *Pravda*, 4 July 1950, pp. 3–4.

[24] RGASPI f. 17, op. 118, d. 969, ll. 36–7; d. 970, ll. 232–50, and RGASPI f. 17, op. 3, d. 1083, ll. 25–6.

[25] Stalin did not necessarily see a contradiction between the emphasis on Russian language and patriotism and his understanding of Marxism more generally. See Erik van Ree's chapter in this volume.

[26] *Pravda*, 2 August 1950, p. 2 and Simmons, *The Soviet Linguistics Controversy*, p. 97. Others did not hesitate to challenge Stalin directly. One teacher wrote to Stalin: 'You write that no science can develop without freedom of criticism and the open struggle of opinions. I am sure that you will allow criticism of your own work. Allow me to expound my view.' RGASPI f. 17, op. 132, d. 336, l. 150.

Stalin defended the apparent contradiction by declaring that the letter writer had made the erroneous assumption that 'conclusions or formulas of Marxism, derived as a result of studying one of the periods of historical development, are correct for all periods of development.' As an example, Stalin noted that Marx and Engels analysed nineteenth-century capitalism and determined that the socialist revolution could not be victorious in one country, a conclusion that became a central principle of Marxism. But Lenin, seeing the existence of monopoly capitalism and its weakness, concluded that the socialist revolution 'might very well be fully victorious in one country'. Stalin explained that both conclusions, in a sense, were correct because they applied to two different periods of economic development. Only 'Talmudists' – the anti-cosmopolitan campaign could not have been far from his mind – would insist on the universal application of laws derived from the analysis of a single system. This defence left open the question of which aspects of Marxism were subject to similar reinterpretations. What in Marxism remained sacred? Stalin suggested that Marxism should not become dogmatic, and his articles on linguistics seemed to lead the way. He concluded by outlining a vibrant Marxism, suggesting that the post-war ideological struggles were indeed about advancing ideology, rather than simply imbibing it:

Marxism, as a science, cannot stand still; it develops and perfects itself. In the course of its development Marxism cannot help but be enriched by new experience, by new knowledge; consequently, its individual formulas and conclusions must change with the passing of time, must be replaced by new formulas and conclusions corresponding to new historical tasks. Marxism does not recognise immutable conclusions and formulas obligatory for all epochs and periods. Marxism is the enemy of all kinds of dogmatism.[27]

The letters responding to Stalin's articles attest to the fact that some Soviet citizens heeded his call to examine both the relationship between language and ideology and where Soviet Marxism had become dogmatic.

Many of the letters posed questions about the implication of Stalin's work for linguistics, nationality, and science. Even after Stalin's follow-up article, Agitprop identified areas of confusion that required further explication either by Stalin, philosophers, linguists, or natural scientists. One group of letters asked fundamental questions about language theory: What constitutes the form of language and what is its content? How can the dialectical method be applied to the study of language and to what extent is the comparative-historical method compatible with dialectical materialism? Is there any use for an international language, like

---

[27] *Pravda*, 2 August 1950, p. 2 and Simmons, *The Soviet Linguistics Controversy*, p. 97.

Esperanto? Is it advisable to create words derived from one or another national language, or should the Russian name-label be used? If the liquidation of capitalism is delayed and communist society is built while the USSR is still surrounded by capitalist countries, will nationalities and languages persist in the USSR or will they solidify into one nation and one common language, even before the victory of socialism in the whole world? Agitprop leaders recognised that the linguistics discussion had far from settled disputes about language in the USSR. It remained unclear who could answer the questions besides Stalin himself.[28]

Other letters ventured beyond linguistics, seeking to understand the implications of Stalin's work for science in general. Was science part of the superstructure or did it have an independence from base and superstructure similar to that of language? If so, what was the relationship between dialectical materialism and science? What was the meaning of party-mindedness (*partiinost'*) in science? Did the formula of class-based science mean that some truths, discovered by science, are class-based truths?[29]

Neither Agitprop nor the academy seemed anxious to answer the questions. In fact, the failure to respond to the issues raised in the wake of Stalin's articles potentially paralysed more than just linguistics. In 1951, the editor of the *Great Soviet Encyclopedia* expressed his frustration to Malenkov in diplomatic terms:

Stalin's brilliant work *Marxism and Questions of Linguistics* gives a deeply scientific treatment of the understanding of the base and superstructure in society, revealing its details and destroying the previous vulgar scheme which placed all spiritual phenomena in the superstructure, and all material ones in the base. In connection with this a question has been discussed for a number of months: what about science? On this question a number of different opinions have been expressed and they often contradict one another. Whatever answer that might be placed in the *Great Soviet Encyclopedia* will meet with strong protests from one or another side. An answer to the question must be given in the entries for 'Natural science', 'Science', 'Superstructure', 'Social science', etc. We cannot claim in the encyclopedia that the question is being debated, or remains subject to discussion, especially because Comrade Stalin laid out the path for answering it. How should we proceed? How should the question be answered and by whom? Who will determine that the answer is correct and how?[30]

The memo to Malenkov summed up the difficulty of making concrete decisions based on Stalin's articles and highlighted significant tensions in formulating post-war Soviet ideology more generally. Not only were the

[28] RGASPI f. 17, op. 132, d. 338, ll. 245–7.   [29] *Ibid.*, ll. 247–9.
[30] RGASPI f. 17, op. 133, d. 4, ll. 60–1.

answers up for debate, the fact that Stalin had broadcast his views made such a debate awkward at best. There was no accepted method of continuing discussion after the time for official discussion had concluded. Stalin's decisive role only deepened the quagmire.

When Stalin read Charkviani's letter and drafts of early articles, he identified a serious problem in Soviet linguistics. The Academy of Sciences and the Central Committee had fully endorsed Marr as the champion of Marxist linguistics on the assumption that he represented the field's best example of an ideologically engaged scholar. But with the help of Chikobava and Charkviani, Stalin recognised that Marr's internationalist and economic-based theories were out of step with the postwar emphasis on heritage and national tradition.

Stalin blamed the linguists' failure to adapt to broader shifts in Soviet ideology on a monopoly in the field. When he called for science to evolve through criticism and the free exchange of opinions, he did so with the presumption that scientific truth would mesh with Marxist-Leninist ideology. But the ultimate, and in the end only, authoritative interpreter of the ideology was Stalin himself. No amount of scientific debate could produce a truth more powerful than the ones declared by Stalin. Thus his statements on linguistics became both the starting points for further research and the only safe endpoints linguists could reach in their conclusions. Instead of encouraging open discussion, his articles had the opposite effect, prescribing the number of legitimate topics in the field. Concentrating scholarly authority and Party authority in one body – the 'coryphaeus of science' – did not solve the tension between scientific and political truth. Instead, it amplified the irony of Stalin's dictating answers in the name of the free exchange of opinions.

Stalin confronted a similar paradox when he addressed the ideological crisis confronting political economists, in particular their Sisyphean attempts to write a definitive textbook on their subject. Stalin hoped the book would provide a stunning critique of capitalism and a powerful description of communism as Marx's kingdom of freedom. In short, the book would be a 'New Testament' of Marxism-Leninism. As Stalin put it in a private meeting with the book's authors: 'The textbook is intended for millions of people. It will not only be read and studied here but all over the world as well. It will be read by Americans and Chinese and it will be studied in all countries ... it will be a model for everyone.'[31]

Stalin's interest was no passing fancy: he was directly involved in the content of the political economy textbook for his last sixteen years. He

[31] RGASPI f. 17, op. 133, d. 41, ll. 8–17.

originally commissioned the book in 1937 as a 'Short Course on Political Economy', presumably to serve as a companion volume to the *History of the All-Union Communist Party (Bolsheviks): Short Course*. After he read and closely edited a number of drafts and met with the authors, a final version appeared ready for publication in 1941, when the German invasion stopped the book's progress.[32] The Second World War and its aftermath brought changes to world affairs that required changes in the book's content. Would the crisis of capitalism lead to another war? Were there separate paths to socialism? The project was further hampered by inconsistent political stewardship: Andrei Zhdanov, who Stalin put in charge of the project, died in 1948. And Nikolai Voznesenskii, the other Politburo member overseeing the textbook's progress, was arrested and shot.[33] In 1950, Stalin once again stepped in. Around the same time he was coordinating the linguistics discussion, he met with the authors of the political economy textbook three times in his Kremlin office. (To get a sense of perspective, Stalin only met with Igor Kurchatov – the scientific director of the atomic project – twice during the entire period from 1945 to 1953.[34]) In his conversations with economists, Stalin emphasised the book's importance to Soviet ideology. In order to win the struggle for the hearts and minds of people around the world, the book had to be objective and scientific. Yet this was not simply a matter of culling the right quotes from Marx and Lenin. In 1941 Stalin had warned the authors, 'If you search for everything in Marx, you'll get off track … In the USSR you have a laboratory … and you think Marx should know more than you about socialism.' Yet in 1950 he complained that the authors 'showed a complete misunderstanding of Marx'.[35] Economists in all fields were caught in a bind: they had to adhere to the classics of Marxism-Leninism, yet Stalin insisted that they produce innovative work.

The authors also had a weakness for pat phrases. In one meeting Stalin admonished them: 'It is not advisable to use bizarre propaganda and popularising language; it will seem like some grandfather telling fairy tales.' Instead, Stalin sought to 'influence people's intelligence'. His

---

[32] ARAN f. 1705, op. 1, d. 166, ll. 14–26 and L. A. Openkin, 'I. V. Stalin: poslednii prognoz budushchego', *Voprosy istorii KPSS* 7 (1991), 113–28.

[33] For recent documents on the 'Leningrad Affair' and Voznesenskii's arrest, see O. V. Khlevniuk et al. (eds.), *Politbiuro TsK VKP (b) i Sovet Ministrov SSSR 1945–1953* (Moscow: Rosspen, 2002), pp. 274–311.

[34] See 'Posetiteli', *Istoricheskii arkhiv* 6 (1994); 2–6 (1995); 2–6 (1996); 1 (1997); 4 (1998). The meetings with economists took place on 22 April, 24 April, and 30 May 1950.

[35] ARAN f. 1705, op. 1, d. 166, ll. 14–26; RGASPI f. 17, op. 133, d. 41, ll. 18–25. For a complete translation of minutes from the three meetings in the spring of 1950, plus one in 1941 and another in 1952, see Ethan Pollock, 'Conversations with Stalin on Questions of Political Economy', *Cold War International History Project Working Paper Series* 33 (2001).

goal was to present a scientific explanation of the history of economic development, not propaganda. He feared that the authors were reluctant to disagree with one another and that there were 'no arguments over theoretical questions'. The results clearly frustrated the leader: 'Soviet power has been around for 33 years and we don't have a book on political economy. Everyone is waiting.'[36]

A little over a year after the three meetings at the Kremlin, the wait appeared to be over. In November 1951, the Politburo summoned over 250 economists and party leaders to the Central Committee to discuss the latest draft of the book. Georgii Malenkov, Stalin's second-in-command in the Party and government, presided, with other high-ranking Central Committee members in attendance. The meeting was supposed to have lasted less than a week. Instead, it went on every day for a full month, with dozens and dozens mounting the podium. None of the speakers was entirely satisfied with the draft. As the meeting dragged on, it seemed possible that Stalin himself would give the closing remarks. As it was, the participants were in an awkward and potentially dangerous position. They knew Stalin had helped edit the textbook and had offered his critical comments to the authors. But most of them did not know the content of those comments.[37]

Malenkov concluded that the draft was unacceptable. He reported to Stalin that the book contained, 'a series of theoretical errors in the interpretation of key problems of political economy, mistakes of factual and statistical material, imprecise formulations of an editorial nature and a number of questionable or weakly argued sentences.'[38] Stalin's efforts over thirteen years had not helped scholars pin down an official version of political economy. But he pushed on. In early 1952 he read through the minutes of the meeting and wrote fifty pages of notes in response. At one o'clock in the morning, perhaps flush with the excitement of what he had written, Stalin telephoned one of the authors of the textbook. According to the author's hastily written notes, they decided to distribute Stalin's remarks to all the meeting's participants and to invite a select few to discuss them with Stalin personally at the Kremlin.[39]

This meeting took place on 15 February 1952. The members of the Politburo and eighteen economists attended. The economists immediately asked Stalin if they could publish his notes. They hoped that doing so would provide cover for any future criticism of their work. But Stalin

[36] RGASPI f. 17, op. 133, d. 41, ll. 8–25.
[37] The conference is covered in detail in chapter six of Pollock, 'The Politics of Knowledge', pp. 378–479.
[38] RGASPI f. 83, op. 1, d. 8, ll. 19–77.   [39] ARAN f. 1705, op. 1, d. 166, ll. 55–6.

held firm, pointing out, 'Publishing my remarks in the press is not advisable ... and is not in your interest. People will understand that everything in the textbook was determined in advance by Stalin. I'm worried about the authority of the textbook.'[40] Even as he was dictating details for the textbook behind the scenes, he seems to have recognised that there were advantages to not letting his role be known publicly. In principle, science emerged from discussions and debates, not from Stalin's dictates.

This concern about the authority of scholars was a central theme in his remarks, which, despite this initial reluctance, he published as part of the long pamphlet *Economic Problems of Socialism in the USSR*. Stalin emphasised that economic laws, like the laws of the hard sciences, were beyond human ability to create or destroy. It was up to scientists, and in this case political economists, to uncover those laws, not to invent them.[41] Since the First Five-Year Plan, Soviet economists had argued that the Party dictated economic laws. Now Stalin suggested that economic laws were 'objective'.

But Stalin's proclamations did not increase productivity any more than his earlier interventions. As it turned out, economists had a much easier time producing work once Stalin was dead. The political economy textbook finally came out in 1954, but it was hardly a 'New Testament' of socialism. Unlike other textbooks in other subjects, it did not receive a stamp of approval from the Central Committee. In very un-Soviet fashion, it even contained an introductory note asking readers to offer criticisms and suggestions for future editions.

Stalin's forays into linguistics and political economy, as well as his involvement in other scientific discussions during the period, reveal a pattern of interest in the relationship between ideology and knowledge. In 1948 when Lysenko wrote that 'any science is class-oriented', Stalin crossed it out adding in the margins, 'HA-HA-HA!!! And what about Mathematics? And what about Darwinism?'[42] In physics, Stalin sided with those who sought to separate Western ideas from their philosophical implications.[43] His essays on linguistics challenged traditional Marxist-Leninist definitions of ideology by suggesting that there were areas of thought that were independent of the economic base or political superstructure. His interventions in political economy also rejected the notion

---

[40] *Ibid.*; RGASPI f. 17, op. 133, d. 215, ll. 2–13; RGASPI f. 588, op. 11, d. 1267, ll. 4–17.

[41] I. V. Stalin, *Ekonomicheskie problemy sotsializma v SSSR* (Moscow: Gospolitizdat, 1952).

[42] Kiril Rossianov, 'Editing Nature: Joseph Stalin and the "New" Soviet Biology', *ISIS* 84 (1993), 728–45.

[43] David Holloway, *Stalin and the Bomb* (New Haven: Yale University Press, 1994), pp. 210–12.

of class-based truths and suggested that scientific laws were objective and universal.[44] Indeed, the seeds of science's rising prestige in the post-Stalin decades were planted during the twilight of Stalin's reign.

Acknowledging a distinction between scientific truth and doctrinal truth, however, potentially eroded the authority of Soviet Marxism. So, the Party and scholars undertook persistent efforts to show that new ideas about nature, language, atomic structure, and domestic and foreign economic developments went hand in hand with Soviet ideology. They understood that a failure to do so could weaken the foundations of the system.[45] Still, memos circulating in the party apparatus reveal a strong undercurrent of confusion, despite the fanfare. Key ideological questions remained unanswered in linguistics, philosophy, biology, physics, and political economy – the very subjects the Party had addressed most concretely.

What then do we make of Stalin as the 'coryphaeus of science'? He did not venture into scientific laboratories, monitor specific experiments, or solve equations. He was the choirmaster of science, but he could not always read the score.[46] Today, no one would be the least interested in the content of his essays and remarks had he not also been one of the most powerful and destructive men of the twentieth century. Still, Stalin's personal involvement in each of these discussions reveals a side of the aging dictator that supplements what we have long known about him from the extensive memoir literature. He was not simply a reclusive old man. The evidence suggests that he was more concerned about ideology and science than was previously known. Regardless of the intellectual merit of what Stalin had to say about linguistics, political economy, or any other subject, the mere fact that he consistently spent time on scientific disputes suggests that he recognised their significance. He may even have understood that his participation exacerbated the very problems he was trying to solve. Historians can never fully understand the motives of a historical subject, and it is unlikely that any material will surface that will reveal what Stalin 'really thought' about his essays on linguistics and

---

[44] The archives give more credibility to the significance of this trend, which David Joravsky remarked on in *Russian Psychology* (Oxford: Oxford University Press, 1989).

[45] If we accept David Priestland's characterisation of Marxist ideology as consisting of a tension between a rational or technical side and a romantic and activist side, then during Stalin's last years the chief concern shifted towards the former. See David Priestland's chapter in this volume.

[46] On this point I am paraphrasing the physicist Peter Kapitsa's criticism of Lavrentii Beria's administrative control of the Soviet atomic project. As Kapitsa explained to Stalin in 1945, 'Comrade Beria's basic weakness is that the conductor ought not only to wave the baton, but also to understand the score.' P. L. Kapitsa, *Pis'ma o nauke, 1930–1980* (Moscow: Moskovskii rabochii, 1989), p. 243.

political economy. But it is clear that careful and critical analysis of Stalin's participation in scholarly discussions broadens our understanding of him personally and of the role of ideology in the Soviet political system.

In many respects, Stalin's stint as a philosopher king constituted a faint echo of earlier political leaders' desires to be taken seriously as thinkers. From Alexander the Great to the 'enlightened despots' of the eighteenth century, heads of state have sought to justify their place atop the political landscape by situating their rule within a broader intellectual context. It should come as no surprise that a self-defined Marxist-Leninist should also insist on the unity of his political system and the scientific ethos of his age. Having said that, Stalin's use of the full force of the state and Party apparatus to enforce his notions of truth was unprecedented.

Rober Tucker has described Stalin's 1924 book *Foundations of Leninism* as an effective means for Stalin to 'prove himself a Bolshevik leader of large theoretical horizons'. In the struggle for succession, the book helped Stalin shore up his weak credentials as a Marxist-Leninist thinker, while outlining a version of Leninism that was both in line with his doctrinaire notions of ideology and accessible to the new, young, less intellectual Party cadres who would help him secure power.[47] His post-war essays share some of the same features, only instead of struggling for power, his new concern became the health of the Soviet system. In this context, science – and there is no doubt he saw his own writings as scientific – could help invigorate an ideology that had become calcified by years of intellectual dogmatism.

It bears emphasis that Stalin was not alone in recognising the relationship between scientific progress and political legitimacy. Americans such as Vannevar Bush, James B. Conant, and Robert K. Merton had a similar faith in the righteousness of their system when they argued that Western democracy and science mutually reinforced one another.[48] In 1950, Conant essentially presented the mirror image of the Soviet argument: 'Scholarly inquiry and the American tradition go hand in hand. Specifically, science and the assumptions behind our politics are compatible; in the Soviet Union by contrast, the tradition of science is diametrically opposed to the official philosophy of the realm.'[49] In the middle of

[47] Robert Tucker, *Stalin as Revolutionary, 1879–1929: A Study in History and Personality* (New York: W. W. Norton, 1973), p. 319.

[48] David A. Hollinger, 'The Defense of Democracy and Robert K. Merton's Formulation of the Scientific Ethos', *Knowledge and Society* 4 (1983), 1–15, and Jessica Wang, 'Merton's shadow: Perspectives on Science and Democracy since 1940', *Historical Studies in the Physical and Biological Sciences* 30 (1999), 279–306.

[49] Quoted in Peter Novick, *That Noble Dream: The 'Objectivity Question' and the American Historical Profession* (Cambridge: Cambridge University Press, 1988), pp. 296–7.

the twentieth century, Americans and Soviets alike sought to distill universal principles about knowledge and power from the particular time and place in which they lived. In this sense, Stalin's efforts as the coryphaeus of science do more than reveal the peculiarities of the ideological crisis in post-war Stalinism. The Soviet campaign to show Marxism-Leninism and scientific advancement as part of the same coherent worldview also represents an extreme variation – but a variation none the less – on the broader story of the relationship between politics and science in the modern world.

Index